LEEKE'S LEGACY

DAVID PATERSON

LEEKE'S LEGACY

A HISTORY OF KING EDWARD VI SCHOOL NUNEATON

Matador
5 Weir Road
Kibworth Beauchamp
Leicester LE8 0LQ, UK
Tel: (+44) 116 279 2299
Fax: (+44) 116 279 2277
Email: books@troubador.co.uk
Web: www.troubador.co.uk/matador

ISBN 978 1848767 461

British Library Cataloguing in Publication Data.
A catalogue record for this book is available from the British Library.

Typeset in 10.5pt Adobe Garamond Pro by Troubador Publishing Ltd, Leicester, UK
Printed and bound in Great Britain by TJ International Ltd, Padstow, Cornwall

Matador is an imprint of Troubador Publishing Ltd

For my King Edward History colleagues over many years –
personal as well as professional friends.

CONTENTS

Foreword

The current King Edward VI Sixth Form College, which has evolved over half a millenium from the original Foundation, currently has over 1000 students and 100 staff. It is an interesting fact that at the time of the Foundation the whole population of Nuneaton was only about 800. Its growth and success reflects that of the town.

At the time of writing the current college is under threat from a number of sources. If one thing is clear from this history 'twas ever thus'. These threats may be from more benign influences than drunken school masters, students armed with muskets, religious persecution, or Nazi bombs. Nevertheless, the Foundation's future remains an uncertain one in 2011 due to the political flux we are currently experiencing.

The Foundation has metamorphised into a variety of shapes and sizes in the last 500 years, but its focus remains clear: to educate the young people of Nuneaton, raise their aspirations and help them to lead fulfilled lives.

This history of the Foundation, charted with such meticulous, scholarly integrity by David Paterson, is undoubtedly a fascinating one. This is not just for those who are, or have been associated with it, but also for anyone who has an interest in the local and national history which has shaped the institutions representing the Foundation over this long period.

The history you are about to read is characterized by David's deep knowledge of his subject and an affection for the institution. It is full of historical insight and a mine of fascinating anecdotes which reads as a chronicle of the King Edward Foundation set against a tapestry of English social history spanning more than five centuries.

The Foundation has always adapted to survive. It is fiercely independent, with, as David puts it, "a long tradition of suspicion of outside interference." I am sure those of us who care about the institution; staff, governors and students past and present (along with this History) will seek to ensure John Leeke's legacy continues for a few more centuries to come.

David Butcher: Assistant Principal, King Edward VI College Nuneaton

Acknowledgments

I am very grateful to the following:

For help with historical research:
Warwick County Record Office have happily endured my many requests for documents, answered my enquiries and even shared my frustration with the Data Protection Act. **Lesley Caine and Rosalind Green** have been especially supportive, not least in preparing the latest King Edward archive in a suitably catalogued form for my researches. Thanks also to the **Nuneaton Library staff** and particularly **Jane Sutton and Margaret Wilson** who assisted me, especially towards the end of my researches when the local studies section of the Library was *re-organised*. The staff at the **National Archives in Kew** were similarly helpful. **The Librarian at King Edward's, Kerry York** kindly allowed me very long term loans of the two previous books on the subject as well as suggesting helpful literature.

For specific assistance:
I must thank **Trevor Osgerby** for grappling heroically with the obscure medieval Latin of the Wills of the two John Leekes. **Dr. Steven Gunn** helpfully shared his insights with me regarding mortmain licences at the end of the reign of Henry VII and also suggested some valuable further reading. A chance meeting with **Tom Arkell** in Warwick Record Office led him to most generously giving me a transcript of the 1665 *Tumult in Nuneaton*. I exchanged useful information with **Chris Holland** who supplied me excellent material about boys killed in the 1914-18 conflict. The Churchwardens at Witherley willingly allowed me inside the church to take Isaac Whyley's picture. **Sally-Anne Veasey** generously gave me access to Ted Veasey's wonderful photo collection while **Michael Cawthorne** very thoughtfully sent me several old pictures from his family's archive. **Bob Gibson** also kindly put himself out to find an early frontispiece of Robert Burton's *Anatomy of Melancholy*. I also had a helpful discussion with **Professor Kathryn Hughes** on Thomas Docker, Robert Evans and Isaac Evans regarding the nature of the school around 1830.

For memories of King Edward's and Nuneaton:
Though oral evidence is just one source among many and only applies for 80 out of the

435 years, it has been very enlightening to talk to **Trevor Carpenter, Tony Collett, the late Dick Fincher, Don Jacques, Beryl Kerby, Sheila Humberstone, James Sambrook and Jacqui Simkins** who have all given generously of their time and shared their memories with me: one or two have also looked over a section of the book. Their insights and memories have doubtless enhanced the account but any remaining imperfections are mine alone. Beryl and Don also made me feel very welcome at the **Coton Heritage centre** where we discussed sources and photographs on several occasions.

Thanks also to **Dr. Esther Maughan**, Principal of King Edward VI College, for permission to publish photographs from the Edwardian Magazines and from previous histories. Also to Old Edwardian **David Butcher**, formerly Head of English and now Assistant Principal at King Edward's, for kindly writing the Foreward. David has been a member of staff for over 25 years. His family's association with the Foundation goes back half a century as his father, Ted, was Head of English at the Grammar school and eventually Deputy Head of the College.

I am grateful to **Troubador** publishing and especially Terry Compton for their ever-helpful presence and support.
Above all I thank my family for their interest, help and support –to my sons **Keith and Colin,** the latter taking some of the photographs, reading proofs and assisting with photographic technology. My wife, **Marie**, also gave much assistance with the photography and came on numerous occasions with me to the Record Office, helping with research and giving me the benefit of her expertise with census material. She has also lived with my researches for two and a half years so perhaps it is not surprising that after reading through a provisional chapter yet again she came up with the title of the book. So it is to her – as with so many authors – that I owe my greatest thanks.

David Paterson May 2011

For permission to publish photos:
Warwick County Record office (page) 15, 23, 27, 37, 46, 48, 84, 78, 156, 179, 197, 211, 218, 219, 222, 228, 232, 254
King Edward VI College 127, 159, 171, 190, 199, 203, 205, 210, 213, 217, 235, 237, 242, 245, 246, 257, 259
Coton Heritage Centre 183, 184, 185,194
Ted Veasey Collection 129, 151, 161
National Archives 3, 75, 133

Roy Page, Headmaster High Wycombe Royal Grammar School 260
Michael Cawthorne 173,178
Bob Gibson 40
Ian Jones, Centre plate
Churchwardens at St Mary's Witherley 88
Walter Brelstaff Archive 92

A note on words and spellings in the text

Quotations are presented in *italics*

John Leeke. Original documents vary in the spelling of this surname. A number of older ones spell the name Leke with one E in the middle but enough use the two Es to justify the use of the modern spelling of the name. Crucially his important Will of 1508 does so.

Pounds Shillings and Pence. As all but the last few months of this history is under the old £sd currency I have kept to the values of money as originally stated. 20 shillings = one pound and 12 pence = one shilling. e.g. 7/4d = Seven shillings and fourpence. 7/- = Seven shillings and no pence. Where marks are mentioned early in Chapter One I have converted them to them to their value in modern currency.

Newdigate Newdegate. The original spelling of the name had an 'i' in the centre. After Francis Parker inherited the Newdigate estate in 1806 he changed his name to Francis Newdigate Newdegate. The change of vowel applied to the middle of the surname. Hence the 19th and 20th Century references to Newdegate use the middle e.

Dating. Before 1753 the New Year did not begin until Lady Day 25th March. It then reverted to 1st January. I have kept to modern dating, that is any event occurring in January or February of whatever date, I have treated it as being in the New Year.

Introduction

This history of the King Edward VI educational foundation in Nuneaton covers almost 435 years of its history from the foundation of the first school in Nuneaton around 1540 (pre-dating the Edwardian foundation) to the introduction of the Sixth Form College in 1974 and the formal end of usage of the term, Grammar School. It has not been written to mark a particular anniversary, neither is it intended to be an uncritical celebration of the successes of King Edward's over past years: the history of the school is a chequered one and this will consider *warts and all*, appropriately most apparent in the 17th Century. Rather, it has been written because the story is a complex and interesting one which simply needs to be told in more depth than hitherto. The archive is rich and fascinating and one that enlightens and informs us about many aspects of this country's educational past from Chantry schools through Tudor endowments, a myriad of legal disputes and Civil War conflict. There are Masters of every hue and description, ability, age and overall approach. There is also the varying role of the Governors, the Church and the State as well as the buildings and re-buildings, and the social background of the pupils. Perennial educational issues surface frequently, the predominance of boys' education over girls', the growth of games and extra-curricular activity, the changing curriculum and the development of the modern teaching profession being just a few.

In order to be fully appreciated, many aspects of Nuneaton's history need to be seen in the context not only of the town's story as a whole, but also in regional and national history. Nowhere is this truer than with King Edward VI School. On many occasions developments appearing to be purely town based have been discovered to have a wider context. Nonetheless the Grammar School's history does throw up some interesting angles on educational development which have a fresh and distinctive local flavour. With a rich archive it has been possible to spread the story evenly over the centuries. This does, however, mean more difficult decisions about selection of modern material as accrued evidence of the past becomes thicker. I can only apologise if someone's distinctive memory of the school is not here: there is so much else that could have been written about. For those who feel that this or that distinguished old boy is not mentioned I draw your attention to Headmaster Samuel Waters' comment in Chapter Nine.

I owe a great debt to Dr. Edward Noel Nason whose history of the school was published in 1936. It involved remarkably painstaking work in the archives and the precious transcription of some documents now illegible in their original form. Without his efforts the current volume would lack much. But it is now nearly 80 years since he began his researches. While the story was updated by Reed Brett in 1952 for the Quartercentenary of the foundation he used much of Nason's original text. Moreover 1974 is a better stopping place then 1952. In addition, there is the advantage of internet research and census information simply not accessible to earlier generations: we need a 21st Century perspective on the Foundation's history. That said, the internet age of instantly available information and immediate opinion has not overtaken the need for traditional historical research through original documents in order to gain a full and measured picture of historical development. Neither has it removed the need for a balanced perspective on educational – or any other – history.

All writers are affected by the times in which they live and this book has been prepared against the background of a challenge to the importance of history as a school subject and a utilitarian approach to education where any value has to be seen to be measured, often crudely; with modern pressures it is more difficult for teachers to see their profession as a vocation involving more than classroom activity. If any bias shows through I hope it is a belief in the value of a liberal education, not solely a vocational one. Stopping at 1974, the formal end of the Grammar School, gives a chance for that measured historical perspective (and also a later historian) as well as avoiding my own involvement in King Edward VI College. I hope that Old Boys, all local people and anyone interested in the history of education and of the town will finds things to reflect on.

CHAPTER ONE

Insecure Foundations 1492-1559

'Ordinary people can be observed playing an active role
in the drama of Reformation'
(Ethan Shagan, *Popular Politics and the Reformation*)

Although King Edward VI Grammar School, Nuneaton, was, strictly speaking, founded in 1552, its origins go back further. That the first school in the town was founded at all, and then managed to negotiate its infancy, was revealing. Its tender years coincided with a time of upheaval in the country's dynastic, political and religious arrangements. Creation and survival were partly due to the foresight of some of Nuneaton's inhabitants. In addition fortune smiled: what began as a modest educational venture soon attracted the Royal patronage which secured its future.

1. The Land for the School's Endowment

The story begins with land transferences in the 15th Century and involves two men named John Leeke, father and son, and others, including Richard Astell. In 1472 John Leeke (probably senior), later described as coming from Erdebury, (Arbury)[1] was among four people granted lands in Chilvers Coton by Richard Werell[2]: in 1476 with Richard Cocks, vicar, and Richard Astell, one of the Leekes acquired tenement property in *le Bondynd* from John Baker of *Nuneton*.[3]

The Leekes were prosperous and loyal landowners with wide-ranging property. In 1489 when Henry VII levied subsidies (taxes) of 1/15th and 1/10th *for the speedy and necessary defence of the realm*, a John Leeke was one of the gentlemen in Warwick chosen to collect the tax.[4] Leeke senior died in 1492, the year of the conveyance of his land in the churchyard and burial at his request in the Chapel of St Mary at *Erdebury*. His Will indicates property not only in the Warwickshire and Leicestershire area but also in Northamptonshire, Shropshire and London. [5]

In the same year, probably as a result of his father's death, John Leeke junior, as well as

William Milwarde and others had conveyed to them a *messuage* (a dwelling including other buildings and land nearby) in Nuneaton in *le churchyarde* by William Bywarcke, gentleman of *Noneton*, Belman [6] (probably a town crier). Nothing else is known about this building apart from its approximate location situated *between the highway and the millpond*, but it was probably the lands on which the first Nuneaton school stood. What is clear is that John Leeke Junior and Richard Astell's land dealings were to set up the circumstances that produced the first school in Nuneaton.

In 1502 Leeke junior also acquired property in Fillongley and Shustoke granted by Thomas Dawe and witnessed by Richard Astell.[7] In 1505, three years before their deaths, both in 1508, Leeke and Astell had also acquired (with Richard Wightman) 100 acres of the *Hydes* the area just on the Warwickshire side of Watling Street conveyed by John Brome.[8] The Leeke wealth was substantial: however, of the two families the Astells retained the stronger connections with Nuneaton, Richard and brother William holding burgage properties in the Market place adjacent to Chantry land, several tenements and closes *from the King's Highway to the River Anker*. By contrast the Leeke family held only three tenements and the messuage that would be the first site of the school. [9] Leeke's land at the Hydes was sold off by 1514.[10] Both the Astell and Everard families were generous in their Wills towards local religious institutions[11] yet it is John Leeke's more modest legacy which eventually made the foundation of a school financially possible.

2. The Start of Leeke's Chantry

John Leeke junior – like other well-off men of his day – left some of his property to establish a Chantry, setting up an endowment for a priest to pray for the souls of the departed, particularly the founder's family. Lands to the annual value of 4 marks (£3. 66) were left *to maintain a chaplain in the parish church of Nuneaton for ever* to pray for his parents and *those to whom my Father was in any way bound in satisfaction.*[12]

It was standard practice in the Roman Catholic Church to pray for the souls of the dead who entered purgatory[13] and prayers for whom might assist their subsequent passage to heaven and lessen their time in purgatorial agony. The word Chantry from the Latin *cantaria* meant the priest was singing (chanting) the mass. A separate Chantry priest would officiate at this mass since, according to canon law, priests could not celebrate this sacrament more than once a day. Though the word chantry strictly referred to the

The Start of Leeke's legacy: John Leeke's Will of 1508.

endowment it became associated with a building. In order to say the masses there would be either a separate building /chapel or –as in the case of Leeke – an extension to an existing part of the Church. Priests responsible for a Chantry were, from the late 14th Century, frequently also linked to educational duties.[14] However, unlike some, Leeke's bequest did not include any educational provisions.[15] His bequest was relatively small because he diversified his giving:

8 marks (£7.32) for the repair of the Arbury Chapel where his father was probably buried.
4 marks (£3. 66) for the Chapel of St Mary at Nuneaton, now known as the Leeke chapel.
£2 to St Mary's Arbury.

There were bequests elsewhere, such as for *an Altar at St Edmundsbury.* [16]

Leeke's decision to set up a Chantry was probably made when nearing death himself. In 1507 a licence in mortmain[17] was obtained to the value of 10 marks in the honour of the Blessed Virgin Mary. In June 1508 his Will was drawn up shortly before his death. The Chantry would be set up to employ a chaplain to pray for his parents and – shortly – himself and his wife Agnes. Obits (Anniversary prayers) were also to be done yearly at Nuneaton and Erdebury (Arbury Priory).[18] To this end the original Lady Chapel on the south side of St Nicolas Church in Nuneaton was altered, a pair of new windows inserted and the roof raised. This was now the Leeke Chapel, as it is still called, where the Chantry priest would pray for the souls of the Leeke family. If a *Cantarist* (as the Chantry priest was known) died or resigned, another would be appointed.

3. Leeke's Will and the Origins of the first School in Nuneaton

The town school's distinctive story was based on a significant clause in Leeke's will. The Chantry prayers were to be offered *if they can be enjoyed without interruption by the King. Otherwise* [said Leeke] *I will they be sold and distributed to the poor in works of charity.*[19]

The exterior of the Leeke Chapel showing the new pair of windows inserted at a higher level when the roof was raised for the Chantry.

This suggested that if Chantries were ever abolished, the endowment could be re-directed. An educational establishment might be seen as a fit and proper purpose for such re-direction and, very broadly speaking, a valid interpretation of the relevant clause in Leeke's Will providing the education was offered without charge.[20] This is indeed what happened later. The Chantry continued for over 30 years but was then shut down by the local inhabitants and the endowment used to finance a *free* school in Nuneaton, the first in the town (see below).

Although the final Will was drawn up within weeks of his death, Leeke had probably written an earlier draft before he had obtained the licence in mortmain. These licences were notoriously difficult to obtain at the end of Henry VII's reign[21] and so Leeke, uncertain of a successful application, probably inserted his additional clause to cover himself should the licence be refused, ensuring some good was done with his money. This seems the most likely explanation for the final form of the Will. Fortunately for him the licence was granted. The wording, designed to facilitate alternative action in the event of a possible refusal, simply remained (for further detail and other theories see Appendix One).

4. Was there a Chantry School in Nuneaton?

With the licence in mortmain granted, Leeke's Chantry was set up. For the moment there was no sign of any school though it is possible there was one run by the Chantry priest. Decrees of the province of Canterbury in 1530 ordered parish priests to *pray, preach or instruct boys in the alphabet, reading, song or grammar.* [22] Later in the decade Bishop Lee of Lichfield and Coventry reminded parish clergy of their teaching function and that the Lord's Prayer, Hail Mary, Creed and Ten Commandments should all be learnt, though this would not necessarily involve general literacy. There is evidence that as a result of the upheavals of the early 1530s more Chantry priests were taking on the task of teaching children,[23] so a Nuneaton priest may have taught reading and song. This could have been a man who – for a time at least – doubled as the Leeke chantry priest; investigations into late medieval Chantries show many of their priests did teach.[24] While only a quarter of the Chantry schools closed showed a song school attached, a lot more were probably not recorded, as they were thought of little significance.[25] Nuneaton possessed a fine parish church of St. Nicolas, only recently completed,[26] and there might have been a call to educate boys to sing in its choir. However, it must be stressed there is no hard evidence for this speculation.

The fortunes of educational development in Nuneaton between 1530 and 1560 were

The Nuneaton Parish Church of St. Nicolas: a close if not always harmonious relationship with the school.

intimately connected with national events, with the development of the English Reformation and the consequent abolition of Chantries such as Leeke's. To understand what happened in Nuneaton – a place with around 800 inhabitants in the mid 16th Century[27] – we need to examine the national picture. Henry VIII had been a defender of the Roman Catholic faith against the Lutheran ideas that spread through Germany in the 1520s, later known as the Protestant Reformation. However, by the start of the 1530s, faced with a Pope denying him the divorce he craved, Henry initiated through Parliament a break from Rome and by the end of the decade had dissolved the Monasteries. Nuneaton Priory was one of the later ones to surrender in September 1539[28] and the lands eventually passed to Sir Marmaduke Constable, a member of a Yorkshire family with no previous connection to north Warwickshire.

As Reformation thinking developed, local men of property in Nuneaton sensed both the need and the opportunity to start a school. Increasing emphasis on Bible reading for all in the vernacular (mother tongue) was a major driving force in the desire for a literate population; better off merchants were now bequeathing an endowment for a new school rather than leaving their money for a Chantry.[29] However, Nuneaton lacked this kind of wealth and so, given the lack of positive evidence for a Chantry school, any kind of educational establishment is unlikely before 1540.

5. The Foundation of the first School in Nuneaton

After this date, however, with monastic dissolution and talk of Chantry abolition, the local worthies of Nuneaton used the Leeke chantry money exclusively for educational purposes. This met the growing need for literacy and reduced the dangers of confiscation of the Chantry income, the motives being both positive and precautionary. The endowment of the Chantry was small[30] and could only be used to pay a priest or lay (non-ordained) schoolmaster for the teaching and not the prayers. With the local Monastic foundations plundered and the possibility of a similar fate for the Chantries, those administering the Nuneaton Leeke Chantry decided to interpret Leeke's wording of his Will liberally. In anticipatory mood they invoked Leeke's clause about diverting the money if Chantries could not continue. The Nuneaton Chantry was closed and a Free School set up on the limited proceeds of the endowment. Leeke's legacy was destined to be an educational one. The forethought of a few of Nuneaton's inhabitants, a virtue in which some of their successors were sadly lacking in educational matters, proved by a narrow margin to be a match for the rapacity of Henry VIII and his successor Edward VI.

Leeke's Will asserted that only after closure by the King would his other clause concerning aiding the poor come into operation; so for the Chantry to close legally, the agreement of Leeke's heirs was required. Permission could have been withheld on grounds of belief – that the family thought the prayers efficacious and would shorten Leeke's time in purgatory – or on sentimental grounds of local connection to Nuneaton. But there was increasing criticism of purgatory as a valid theological concept, and the Leeke's family connections with Nuneaton were very limited.[31] Therefore it is not surprising that the heirs gave their consent.

Though its approximate location was adjacent to the church of St Nicolas, little is known about the school founded when the Chantry closed, probably in 1540-41 (see below and Appendix One). The Chantry priest may have remained in a purely teaching capacity acting as a curate at St Nicolas to supplement his income but there is no record of this. The state of the building remains unknown and who taught in it uncertain. A Chantry priest William Molisdayll is mentioned in Thomas Wele's (vicar of Nuneaton)

The Leeke Chapel in St. Nicolas, 2010.

Will of 1519 and an unnamed Chantry priest in John Everard's Will of 1525.[32] He may have been the schoolmaster, paid by Leeke's legacy, if a modest song school was set up while the Chantry was still running. Otherwise he was pensioned off, an expensive option. So unless the Chantry priest conveniently died at the right time, and thus triggered the idea of conversion from Chantry to School, it is likely that Molisdayll – or more probably his successor – was the first teacher.

With the Reformation and the use of the vernacular there was no need to teach young boys Latin in order to sing in the language. So if Nuneaton school was to survive with a similar curriculum as a Grammar School, that is a school teaching Latin Grammar, it would be for the purpose of learning the language for slightly different purposes, that is humanistic reasons, studying Latin for its own sake, imbibing its noble and civilising ideas and its fine literature, and also for its numerous contemporary vocational applications. These two broad justifications for a Grammar School education continue to rub up against each other for the rest of the School's History.

6. The Chantries are Dissolved, will Nuneaton's first School Survive?

The decision to end Leeke's Chantry at the start of the 1540s, and establish a school on the proceeds, had been timely. By 1545, with war expenses still high, Henry VIII's attention had moved on from Monastic riches to Chantry wealth and Parliament passed a Chantries Act, transferring their assets into the hands of the King. Ostensibly the change was effected on the grounds that some chantries had been dissolved (like Nuneaton) by local wealthy men who had dismissed the priest – on grounds of discipline or theology – and (unlike Nuneaton) taken the income for themselves. There was certainly evidence for this. [33] However, in reality financial advantage was another powerful motive for the Act. Sales from property such as Nuneaton Priory helped finance wars with France in the early 1540s. The sale of Chantries raised over £500,000[34] which, though only 25% of that acquired from the sale of Monastic lands, was still a substantial amount.

Although Henry VIII had not quite dissolved the Chantries, their days seemed numbered. Chantry priests were urged to *exercise themselves in teaching youth to read and write and bring them up in good manners and other virtuous exercises.*[35]After the succession of Edward VI in 1547, Chantries were subjected to more radical attack. Belief in the purgatory that made Chantries desirable was now seen as a *vain opinion* as parliament pronounced in November 1547. Chantries were merely *perpetuating blindness and ignorance* [36] [and a] *superstition… brought into the minds and estimation of men by reason of their ignorance of their very true and perfect salvation through the death of Jesus Christ*[37]. The attack was no longer on the abuse of Chantry money – it assaulted the whole theological concept on which Chantries rested. In 1548 a new Act set up the mechanism for their dissolution.

Even Chantries which had been dissolved and where a school had been set up, such as Nuneaton, were not necessarily safe. The Government of Protector Somerset[38] was out to get its hands on all the money it could. On Easter Day 1548 all Chantries and all *intercessory institutions*[39] became the possession of the Crown.[40] In the short run education really suffered. It was acknowledged that many chantries had schools attached and it was claimed that they would be converted *to good and godly uses, as to the erecting of Grammar Schools to the education of youth.* The preamble to the Act talked vaguely about the fact that the King and his Council would *alter* and *convert* the Chantries.[41] However, many schools associated with Chantries were closed and though a good number were re-founded, it was sometimes after a crucial delay. Because its citizens had already taken action earlier, changes in Nuneaton are an interesting variant on the main theme.

7. When was Nuneaton's first School Founded?

The two previous publications on the history of the school stated that Nuneaton's first school was founded in 1542.[42] However, we cannot be sure; it probably began a year or two earlier. When they came to Nuneaton the local County Commissioners reported

Statue of King Edward VI outside the school. 'Royal dignity combined with vulnerability through the sculptor's choice of facial expression and gesture' (George Thomas Noszlopy Public Sculpture of Warwickshire, 2003).

to Special Commissioners Mildmay and Kelway[43] that the prayers for the souls of Leeke's family, *hathe allwayes bene accomplished accordinglye, vntill nowe, abowte syxe years paste, yt was concluded amongst the parochians theare … that the revenues … shollde be convertyd to the maytenaunce of a Schoole Master theare, the which for that yt hathe not bene convertyed to the use of a Chauntrye within these syxe yeres I take it to be oute of the compass of the statute, and therefore I have omitted the certificat thereof.*[44]

Because of this crucial little judgement Nuneaton's school was saved. On the basis of this information the Commissioners did not issue their confiscation certificate, leaving the Nuneaton funds alone. *Aboute syxe yeres paste* has been interpreted as *six years ago* and the foundation of Nuneaton's first school therefore given as 1542. However, it seems likely that *about* was used in the old English sense of *more than* and 1540 (or possibly 1541) is a more likely date. (See Appendix One)

8. Nuneaton's Grammar School Survives

It was fortunate that Nuneaton's Chantry wealth was modest as it was less likely to be targeted prematurely by the Crown or local bodies. Back in the 1530s some Chantries were dissolved, but only by act of Parliament, such as in the city of York in 1536. However, by the 1540s such procedures were increasingly deemed unnecessary. *The financial needs of the living* were placed *above the spiritual needs of the dead.* [45] Even a small sized Chantry like Nuneaton's was not a complete guarantee of safety. The fact that the Leeke Chantry income brought in less than £5 in annual value saved the day. Up to this figure would go on a pension for any surviving Chantry priest[46] but as in Nuneaton's case he does not appear to have survived, the town's claim that the Chantry had been shut for some time was accepted.

Another reason for Nuneaton school's survival was its proper use of the endowment for educational purposes. The Chantry Commissioners were not only satisfied that a school had existed in Nuneaton for some time but also believed it to be functioning correctly. The money formerly used for the maintenance of a Chantry was being rightly directed. If the Chantry had already been completely replaced by a school for some years, Nuneaton was not unique. Admittedly some Chantry appointments continued to be made in the diocese of Lichfield and Coventry as late as August 1548 .[47] However, there were other instances where in the years prior to this the Chantry land was granted to (or bought by) the local inhabitants.[48] This was especially true if a vacancy occurred on the death of a Chantry priest, thus eliminating the problem of pensions. This idea of supplementing small chantry endowments seen as inadequate for a proper school[49] was to benefit Nuneaton a little later.

Nuneaton's inhabitants acted properly,[50] but in many other cases Chantry lands were confiscated by rapacious laymen plundering the church's wealth. This suggests the government might have been justified in taking action – until one sees that they acted from identical motives, being more interested in the wealth of the endowments than the use to which the money was to be put. Still, Nuneaton is an interesting case as the inhabitants were clearly intending to put the money to good use. The endowment was very small, four marks (£2. 66p), to support a priest/teacher who would find it harder to supplement his income now Chantries had gone. However, his income may have been supplemented. In 1551 an inventory of church goods authorised by the King revealed in Nuneaton's case that ornaments including copes, vestments and crosses had been sold to pay for *sutes for a free schole there which is now established by our said sovereigne*.[51] The wording suggested the Commissioners had not arrived before May 1552 and the start of the King Edward Foundation but the sale was certainly earlier. It would have been an attempt to raise money for a larger endowment with which to fund the school before the Royal approval of increased funds in May 1552.

Again, Nuneaton was not unusual in selling church goods to help finance their school. Other towns did likewise, trying to act before they were confiscated.[52] However, in Nuneaton the money was spent on education and other social ends rather than private gain. *Reparation for highways* was also mentioned in Nuneaton's case as was *alteration of* ...[the] *church*. These actions may have been pragmatic but the result was that, in many places like Nuneaton, Reformation ideas were hastened. There was a conscious or unconscious *complicity* with the principles of the Reformation whatever the actual religious beliefs of the inhabitants.[53]

In Nuneaton the people responsible for transferring the income from Chantry to school are unknown. However, they may have been among those selected as Governors for the King Edward foundation in 1552 (see below page 15). After 1539 the dominant landowner was Sir Marmaduke Constable who, as we have seen, had been granted the local Priory lands; this was despite the fact that his father had risen up against Henry VIII in 1536 in the Pilgrimage of Grace,[54] a rebellion which had, ironically, protested against Monastic dissolution. In the survey of Constable's Nuneaton lands in 1543 the Leeke Chantry money is recorded as worth 6/8d.[55]

Even if we are uncertain as to the identity of those who set up a school, we can be sure that acting when they did ensured its survival at a time when many schools were lost. If the school at Nuneaton had not commenced some years before 1548 and Leeke's endowment had continued to be used for prayers for dead souls, the income would have certainly been seized. So any future endowment for education would have to have been diverted from other sources rather than confirmed (and increased) from existing ones, a much less likely occurrence. Nuneaton had a population estimated at about 800 in 1543 according to Veasey's calculations based on the Constable rent roll.[56] The town may have found itself ignored and the school closed through lack of funds. It would have required someone influential and wealthy to push for a financially aided re-foundation. Apart from the new landowner Constable, whose connection with the area had only just begun, there was no other major source of wealth in Nuneaton, a place of very modest pretensions.

9. The Start of the King Edward Endowment

The funds derived from the Leeke Chantry were limited: they still only amounted to the original four marks (£2 13s 4d). This modest figure was not unusual for a small Chantry; many of them were valued at producing a yearly income of under £5.[57] While it might have been adequate for a celibate priest who could supplement his income elsewhere, more was needed to attract a schoolmaster of high calibre. The sale of Church valuables by 1551, alluded to above, would have helped a little but extra resources were urgently required. By 1552 the school had successfully petitioned for an increase in the endowment. It was re-named – if not re-founded. A Royal Charter was obtained from King Edward VI on 11th May and more generous endowments obtained to augment Leeke's money. Many other towns, having lost all their previous endowments on the dissolution of the Chantries, were unsuccessful when they petitioned for a similar grant but Nuneaton was more fortunate. This is likely to have been because of the influence of the Duke of Suffolk who lived at nearby Astley and was, temporarily, influential in Government at the crucial time (See Appendix One Section D).

By 1552 the worst of the financial crisis which had triggered the confiscation of Chantry wealth was over and new foundations could now be afforded. Nuneaton's enhanced income came from Coventry; three closes of land from the dissolved Coventry Guilds of Holy Trinity and Corpus Christi were added to the existing endowment (Moorfields, Chortleys Boltons and Pennyfields and a croft).[58] This provided an adequate sum[59] with the endowment now calculated at £10 15/ 8d, sufficient to maintain a master on an annual salary of £10.[60] The Coventry property was to increase its value considerably over time and in the late 19th Century was sold for an excellent price for urban development, thus enhancing the school's financial position and enabling the construction of the new school building in 1880 (See Chapter Eight).

The letters patent of King Edward VI, translated from the Latin in the early 18th Century, make it clear that the endowment was *for the erection and establishment of a Grammar School for the teaching and instruction for boys and youths.* It was to be called *The free Grammar School of King Edward VI …* [for education] *in grammar to endure for all times* and the school was to have one Master. The Governors were to be *men of discretion and probity* and twelve were appointed *for life* and a Corporate Body set up to *select and name another fit person* to fill any vacancy. They had *full power and authority* to *name and appoint a tutor of the said school as often as the said school be void of a tutor.* His salary would be *out of the rents and revenues of the land and tenements* a phrase later found legally imprecise. Unusually for a foundation which just applied to a single school, and no other form of charity, it set the £10 Master's salary as a fixed fee. This later gave rise to the question whether the master's salary should be raised as the revenues increased. Another important issue was the interpretation of *Grammar* school. The letters patent announced that the Governors were to *find and maintain a tutor sufficiently learned in Latin* [to] *teach freely the boys resorting thither.*[61] This legal obligation to teach Latin was of great long-term significance for Nuneaton and many other similar schools.

10. The First Governors

The Governing body was to consist of twelve men chaired by Sir Marmaduke Constable who had acquired the lands of Nuneaton's dissolved priory in 1540 (see above) and therefore become the principal landowner in a small town not noted for local landed gentry. It was expected that this social class would patronise and encourage educational developments. Of the other Governors, described as yeoman, all are noted as landholders in the Constable Survey though on a modest scale. One of the most *marked features* of the period after 1550 in the Midlands was *the rise of the substantial yeoman farmer.*[62] Many of the Governors fitted into this category. They may have included those responsible for the decision to end the Chantry and divert the funds to start a school, but this lacks proof.

The Governors' wealth and social status varied. At least seven owned some land.[63]

Names of the First Governors in the translation of the school's letters patent of King Edward VI (Undated –early 18th Century).

The Original Governors

Name: Sir Marmaduke Constable
Occupation: Landowner
Place of Residence / Land: Hoarstone Grange Lord of the Manor. Had lost the family estates in the East Riding of Yorkshire.
Comment: Chairman of the Governors.

Name: Richard Vyncent
Occupation: Yeoman
Place of Residence / Land: Hoarstone Grange 14 Virgates,[64] about 420 acres.
Comment: Held jointly with brother Robert.

Name: Edward Povey
Occupation: Yeoman

Place of Residence / Land: Messuage with three cottages in St Nicolas Street, two and a half virgates, about 75 acres, and three other properties including a copyhold.
Comment: The three cottages were near the school.

Name: Ralph Thomson
Occupation: Yeoman
Place of Residence / Land: Copyholder[65]of *The Hollowside* with freeholds in Abbey End and Market Place and three rods and two poles *in the fields of Etone.*

Name: John Rotherham
Occupation: Yeoman
Place of Residence / Land: Freeholder leasing tenements and messuages in Church End Abbey End and the Market Place.
Comment: Sir Marmaduke aside, Rotherham was probably the wealthiest of the Governors; his daughter married William Willoughby who was to leave money for the school in 1587.

Name: William Worshipp
Occupation: Yeoman
Place of Residence / Land: Two messuages, in Bake House Lane and Abbey End as well as a copyhold and three orchards.

Name: Alexander Smythe
Occupation: Shopkeeper
Place of Residence / Land: Market Place
Comment: Brother William, Baker

Name: Richard Ratclyff
Occupation: Landlord
Place of Residence / Land: Crown Pub. Rented three Chambers above the Manor Court Hall near his hostelry.[66]
Comment: He also occupied pasture land known as *the heath* and *Hurdman's Groove.*

Name: John Oughton
Occupation: Draper

Place of Residence / Land: Blackwaterfeeld a croft and catmeadwe. [67]
Comment: Marmaduke Constable had leased Oughton the property though he had reserved the right to dig for the *stone colles* already known about in the area.

Name: William Asseburn
Occupation: Tenant at Will
Place of Residence / Land: Cottage in Church End.

Name: Roger Mantel
Occupation: Tanner
Place of Residence / Land: Cottage in Church End.
Comment: The odour of tanners (they continually smelt of their trade) would have diminished his social status.

Within a year of the granting of the Charter (original now lost) Edward VI had died and, after the nine days reign of Lady Jane Grey, the Roman Catholic Queen Mary ascended the throne. Previous historians Nason, Reed Brett and Leach, suggested the application to have the Charter confirmed under Mary eighteen months later followed the disgraced Duke of Northumberland's *great interest in the neighbourhood*.[68] Again, it seems more likely to have been through the Duke of Suffolk. Suffolk had been one of the Councillors to proclaim Lady Jane Queen. He was involved in a plot at the start of 1554 to remove Queen Mary – Wyatt's Rebellion. When it was clear this too had failed, Suffolk was found hiding in an oak tree on his Astley lands, arrested, executed and his local property forfeited. But by that time the Charter had been safely confirmed.

The reasons behind this early renewal of the Charter remain mysterious. If the area, as a hotbed of Protestant activity, needed Catholic re-education, would not a school be just the thing to achieve this? Mary's Parliaments, though sympathetic to her efforts to re-establish Roman Catholicism, would not countenance any reverse of the sale of Chantry lands, for many schools had by this time been established by use of endowments. The targets for change were Protestant teachers not Protestant schools, as individual teachers were seen as important agents of the state in the propagation of the official religion. In 1554 Mary ordered her Bishops to remove *suspect schoolmasters*. [69]

Queen Mary's Charter for King Edward VI School, 1553

So in applying for a Charter renewal from Queen Mary, the Governors were probably being over-cautious. Leach (with his unrivalled knowledge of these matters) was mystified as to the reason and pointed out that re-issuing Charters was very rare. He suggested that the lateness of the Charter in the reign might account for the need to have it renewed; but that of King Edward VI School at Stratford was issued later, only a few weeks before the King's death in 1553[70]and was not renewed. One possible explanation is that there had there been some misinformation supplied at the time of the Chantry Commissioners visit back in 1549. Since the pre-existence of a school was a significant factor in the granting of the original Charter, the application for its confirmation may have been prudent if incorrect information had previously been supplied. The Governors' cautionary action continued as further confirmations were obtained in June 1559 – from Queen Elizabeth eight months after she came to the throne – and in 1604. (see Chapters two and three) In any event the future of the school was now secure.

CHAPTER TWO

Latin For All? The Elizabethan School 1559-1595

The most … easy is to teach [in] a school, and for that he shall have a falconer's wages, ten pound per annum…so long as he can please his patrons.
Robert Burton (Old Edwardian) *The Anatomy of Melancholy 1621*

King Edward's had a difficult start; illiterate or insolvent Governors; a rapidly changing Master; a relatively small, poor population and uncertain religious direction. But within forty years, aided by national, political and religious stability, it had prospered, not only from increased endowments but also in the quality of scholars it was turning out and its plans for a new building.

1. The Building: What Was It Like?

The first Nuneaton school building lasted up to 1595, but our knowledge of it is patchy. Unlike some small schools of the period it was, though close to the church, physically distinct. There are accounts for its repair with frequent references to the *schole house*. Possibly in the Churchyard, it was more likely the *messuage* that John Leeke had bequeathed in 1508 since details of this transaction were found in the Governors' papers.[1] *Between the highway and the millpond* suggests it was between the highway to Coventry (just south of the market place) and the mill pools.[2] This makes the position near to the church, but, unlike the subsequent building, not too close. The style of building and materials used were probably local and there were no architects as such. *Groups of townspeople and merchants now entered the field of school building.*[3]

The school would have been timber framed, built by local craftsmen using traditional techniques. In the 1560s financial records for King Edward's show money spent on wattle and daubing.[4] This very old method of construction was used in the Tudor period for cladding a timber framed structure. The wattles were

19

set in holes bored into a horizontal timber above and the stakes were then woven with twigs and fitted into a groove in the corresponding timber below before being daubed with clay. Furniture was limited. A raised dais with a special Master's chair at one end of the school room was the standard design so that he could see all that was going on. The boys would sit on forms, a word that persisted even after buildings were transformed. Desks were only supplied in larger and better equipped schools. Contemporary opinion was *when they have to write let them use their knees for a table.*[5]

Within a few years in Nuneaton (and many other new Grammar Schools) there were older boys as well as younger ones; so an assistant master – an Usher – was appointed. A building would cope with this in one of two ways. The Usher's more modest seat could be placed at the opposite end of the room to the Master, or the large single schoolroom sub-divided. As early as 1567 the school accounts show an Usher being appointed in Nuneaton.[6] At this stage, it may have been decided not to have one large room but divide the premises. The expenses for alterations or repair in 1566 confirm the modest nature of the building: *Two loads of clay* [at three shillings each] *for mending school house* [and] *6/- and for 5d watlying and daubying* is recorded in the accounts.[7] This could have been, as it suggests, merely for repair. However, the timing, shortly before the appointment of the first Usher, indicates a possible division of rooms. Paradoxically, a small room would be more likely to be divided, since one room became very noisy as pupil numbers grew. However, the school may not have been growing quickly enough to justify a division. In the years immediately after 1552 the numbers, while varying from year to year, were not likely to have exceeded 40 and may have been lower. The limited population of Nuneaton, under 1,000,[8] the nature of the buildings and the low social status of the large

---

THE REPAIRS OF 1584

- lyme, keyes, lockes, windows, tymber, tyles, rodds, neales, bricks, joysts, bords to make the study door
- 3 Horseloads of lime
- 8 foot piece of timber (8d)
- Two keys and locks: possibly a spare pair or it may indicate a room division.
- Whyting window repair (1/8d)
- 500 tiles (5/4d)
- Nails and steppings
- A syll for the study
- Two ledges and joysts
- A bench for school house
- Clay sand and lime
- 17 foot of glass supplied by John Fawcett
- Sand, tiles and lime alone cost over two pounds.
- This work took up 41 and a half days labour costing £1 13/4d.   (Source – Transcripts)

majority of its inhabitants would have ensured a modest size. Nevertheless, in the late 16th Century, the growing prosperity and confidence of the yeoman class led them to allow their children to attend school for a while rather than earning a wage. So, expansion of pupil numbers may help to explain the re-building of 1595. (see below)

There was further repair of the old building before 1595. In 1570 £1 8/7d was *paid to Mr. Donne*. Substantial work in 1572 cost well over £8. In 1577 repairs amounted to £4 6/5d and the feeling that the building was bursting at the seams is confirmed by the figures for 1584.[9] In this year the total spent was £25 – costs suggesting an extension – and implying that the small building was not coping with a modest increase in the numbers attending, even possibly falling apart under the strain. There was a long list of materials (see side bar).

The Master's premises were improved with a bill *for his study*.[10] This was possibly to emphasise his position above the Usher. The Elizabethan age was one where social status was increasingly important and where households were often being separated into master and servants' quarters.[11] It is not surprising that a new purpose built school was constructed in the 1590s. The building may have been decaying despite the efforts at repair.[12] An increased demand for places could have been the cause of the change for not only was Nuneaton's population increasing but, more significantly, the demand for education was growing generally and other schools were developing in the area to meet it. For instance, in 1567 Rugby school was founded as a result of the will of former inhabitant Lawrence Sheriff. For nearly 200 years it remained a very similar school to King Edward's, indirectly influencing its fortunes.[13]

2. Finance: The School And The Governors Become Wealthy

The Governors could afford both the repairs and, later, consider plans for building a new school. Their endowment lands were doing well and the school's capital grew, making both school and Governors rich. The property was let short term at fixed rents and these were reviewed frequently. In Elizabethan times yeoman farmers were getting excellent prices so land values, despite fluctuations, generally rose substantially. This meant a *fine* (not our modern meaning but more of an additional charge) could be levied, often a substantial sum of money, recognizing the increase in the value of the land before the lease renewal. This large fine would meet little objection if land rentals had been kept low. Wood sales from the Coventry properties owned by Governors, such as Chiltern's Lees £54 in 1570 [14] brought in additional revenue over a number of years and there were also some additional bequests (see below). However, although evidence is patchy, the fines were the principal reason for the increase in revenue. Rents were steadily collected and added to the coffers bringing around £12-15 a year either side of 1570 but increasing to a steady £18-£19 annually ten years later.[15] The overall result was a rapid increase in capital or stock as the governors termed it.

The Rapid Growth Of The Endowment[16]

Date	Value of the Stock
1563	£19 7/-
1567	£21 10/-
1568	£23 4/-
1569	£27
1573	£37 3/8d
1574	£44
1577	£77
1582	£81

The finances were aided by further bequests. The affluent merchant or manufacturer now frequently left money for education as their ancestors had done for Chantries. From 1550-1620 (apart from a recession in the 1590s) money from merchant based and landed wealth flowed into Grammar Schools for a variety of motives, religious and altruistic, but also to aid the supply of literate apprentices, for book keeping, cartography and surveying or merely for self-promotion. While Nuneaton was not part of a wealthy or populous area, it benefited from the generosity of local well off gentlemen. In 1563 John Wheatley's charity authorised Coventry Corporation to donate (in addition to his charitable giving in Coventry) ten shillings a year for the benefit of 24 poor householders.[17] Six Warwickshire towns, including Nuneaton, were involved. King Edward's Governors became responsible for this distribution in addition to running the financial affairs of the school. Records, extant from 1571 to 1585, show four different poor men benefited each year. Some may have been related to the Governors: John Ratclyff was one of the first to receive a distribution.[18] These funds were used for charitable purposes generally and not for the school but they added to the funds available to the Governors.

Another school benefactor was one Mr. Fyndern, who could have been William Fyndern the last *receiver* (administrator and collector of rents) of Nuneaton Priory, but more probably Robert Fyndern, whose heirs owned two cottages and a tenement in Abbey End occupied by Governor John Oughton *on which four cottages were formally situated.*[19] He left a bequest for the Usher and Fyndern's widow regularly passed over £2 a year to the school, starting in 1573.[20] The last prior of Arbury, Thomas Dagle, bequeathed £9 *for the free grammar school in Nuneaton* in 1568 and this appears regularly in the 16th century accounts (once as *Mr. Daggett's* in 1572), producing a modest but regular sum of between five and eight shillings annually.[21] William Willoughby's link with Nuneaton by marriage was to benefit the school with another bequest. By his will dated 3 Oct. 1587 he gave 10/- to the governors of the Grammar School for *books for poor scholars.* [22]

Queen Elizabeth's Charter for King Edward VI School, 1559

Two governors were appointed bailiffs to administer the endowment, being responsible for collecting the rental and then looking after the capital. Each year one bailiff would stand down, the newest continuing, so that there was continuity but also a sharing of the responsibility and workload.[23] Some of the money went on schoolhouse repairs as we have seen but there was little increase in the Master's annual salary for the time being: it remained initially at £10 and later only rose by a small amount,[24] a point causing major difficulty later.

Capital was accumulating more rapidly than the development of a better banking system. Most Governors were granted *parcels* of money to look after and invest as they saw fit. The temptation to spend at least some of it was great, especially for the bailiffs. In 1562 Richard Chaplyn and Edward Povey owed over £16, evenly divided. Povey agreed to take over the whole debt (he had owed £8 18/-) and so free Chaplyn from further obligation. In 1569, finding themselves with increasing profits, the Governors distributed nine parcels of £9 to fellow Governors.[25] Richard Willoughby, Robert Lee[26] and Richard Vynsent all signed as well as the illiterate John Suffolk the elder, Robert Vynsent, John Bayliss and William Wright. In 1586 the money had accumulated to such an extent that meetings were held to discuss the re-allocation of the Stock and legal advice was taken, costing – with the attendant meetings – the substantial sum of £10 13/-8d. This included *opinions from one learned in the law at Lichfield.* [27]

As a result of these deliberations bonds were now issued not only to the Governors but to a much wider range of people in the community. So in 1586 the people of the town were invited to share in the largesse. £2 each was given to 44 different inhabitants.[28] If there were difficulties with repayments, Bailiffs made it clear they would take legal action, though not always immediately. In November 1595, when money was urgently required to pay for a new building, Robert Vynsent senior was ordered to pay the £6 he owed by Jan 1st or he would be sued.[29] A similar request for £4 was made to Marmaduke Lee though the outcome remains unknown as the financial records end here.[30] With their new found wealth the Governors decided they could afford to enjoy themselves, organising meetings with food and drink at the expense of the King Edward Foundation, the start of a long tradition. Earlier records on this are rare though 1/6d was spent on *bread and drink* in 1566/7.[31]

But it is in the 1580s with rapidly accumulating funds that considerable expenses are recorded for this purpose. This may be simply because of a change in the way the financial accounts were compiled, for from Nov 1583 they were written by a different person. Capital was accumulating and could be – literally at times – sloshed around. Two pence for drink at the Crown was hardly surprising (this was Governor Richard Ratclyff's pub) but wine – much more expensive at 1/3d – now appears on the expenses sheet. [32] Expenditure multiplied at a much quicker rate than the Master's salary.[33]

GOVERNORS' EXPENSES INCREASE

1584	Dinners	7/-
1585	Wine	6/8d + ale consumed at the Crown and the Boar
1585	Refreshments*	2/-
1586	Repairs and meetings	£10 13/8d
1586	Pots of ale	8d

* At a meeting for choosing the new master at Lewis Forde's house (probably the brief Mastership of Mr. Yates).   Source: Transcripts pp57-8, 66-68.

However, obtaining bequest and rent money was not always straightforward as the list below illustrates.

PROBLEMS WITH DEFAULTERS/ADDITIONAL EXPENSES

- 1563. Governors chased a bequest of £5 from Thomas Thomson unpaid by executors which was not fully paid until 1573 (Source: Transcripts (T) pp7 and 26)
- 1568. £6 was paid to Mr Magre of Coventry for the rendering of Wheatley's lands (T17)
- 1570. £1 of rent written off – owed by Mistress Fisher (T19)
- 1576. Richard Over defaulted and Governors gave John Rotheram plenary powers to sue him and transfer the lease to himself. A new lease was issued for 21 years paying five shillings annually. (T32-3)
- 1582. After the death of Richard Vynsent, Ambrose Vynsent was now obligated to pay the £20 the deceased had taken. (T50)

---

3. Governors: What Were They Like?

Of Marmaduke Constable as Chairman of the Governors we hear little but what we do is unexpected. The Constable family had not been uninterested in education, Sir Marmaduke's eponymous uncle endowing four scholarships at St John's College Cambridge in 1522.[34] With Sir Marmaduke acquiring many of the Nuneaton Priory lands, one might have expected beneficence to King Edward's given he was by far the largest landowner in the Nuneaton area. However, in the years before his death in May or June 1560, Constable was borrowing money from the school capital. In 1563 bailiff

Robert Chaplyn received 20/- *in part of such debt as Mr. Constable did owe unto the said school.* This was from Sir Marmaduke's widow since later in the year £3 of the £10 still owed by Sir Marmaduke had yet to be repaid by her.[35] He had expended his fortune in legal fees trying to recover some of his Yorkshire lands, lost when his father rebelled against Henry VIII. His heart was really in the Yorkshire family property but it remained literally in Nuneaton since he was buried in an impressive tomb in the town's parish church of St. Nicolas.[36]

Sir Marmaduke Constable's tomb in St. Nicolas Church

Constable's lands were sold both before and after his death. Sir Marmaduke's son Robert eventually succeeded in winning back the family patrimony but for Nuneaton a benign interest in the school from local landed gentry was generally lacking.[37] Even after the Newdigates came to Arbury in 1586 they showed more concern with their home parish, neighbouring Chilvers Coton. So, after Constable, the existing Governors of largely yeoman background had to take the financial initiative. In their ambition to turn schoolboys into literate men, they exceeded their own personal achievements: many were illiterate. Seven out of twelve governors could not write their name to a Resolution[38] of 1563: in 1569 Lewis Forde, Richard Ratclyff, John Suffolk, Robert Vynsent, John Bayley and William Wright all had to make their mark with Richard Willoughby, Robert Lee and Richard Vynsent being able to sign.[39] Things had not changed twenty years later. In

1583 when the Governors had to sign for the parcels of stock they had received, six out of nine had to make their mark; clearly business was possible without being literate.[40]

There were still Governors making marks rather than signatures as late as 1595.[41] Those educated back in the 1540s and 1550s were now of an age to assume responsibilities of Governorship. Perhaps very few attended the school in the early days or they had forgotten the art of writing or only learned to read and sing. Possibly the successful ones had moved away from the area. Nuneaton was not unique for illiteracy was still rife in rural areas. [42] One reason for their continuing inability to write may have been the slow changes in Governor personnel. The post offered them prestige and a chance to hold parcels of money, so they remained Governors. With no patron such as a member of the Leeke family to please and no guild or corporation involved in the endowment, Governors were free to fill vacancies from among their own relatives, friends and social equals.

Marks of Illiterate school governors in accounts of the school bailiffs, 1563

There was, admittedly, a higher turnover in the first few years before the money making aspects of a Governorship were fully apparent. When the account records first appear at the end of the 1550s new Governor names are on the list: by January 1562 (our dating) eight governors are recorded as conducting business, but four of them had not been Governors ten years earlier. Povey, Rotherham and Willoughby did remain and of the others we can conclude that Richard Ratclyff was absent on this occasion since his name soon re-appears. The new Governors are: Robert Vyncent who has joined his brother Richard, Lewis Forde, William Chapleyn and Richard Holmes.[43]Forde was a tenant at will and had a granary on burgage land recorded back on the Constable rent rolls of 1543. He also occupied a pasture called *Stocking* near the *stocking ford* as well as a meadow worth nine shillings.[44] Holmes was the stepson of Ralph Thomson. He was involved in a legal dispute with him from 1556-1558 over non-payment *of price of closes in Nuneaton and detention of a lease of the same and of other closes there.*[45]

There were inevitably changes in Governors after the death of Marmaduke Constable in 1560, though evidence for a specific replacement as Chairman is lacking. But despite these early alterations, many remained in post a long time. Evidence of long-serving Governors includes:

Lewis Forde	1562-1585
Edward Povey	1552-1567 (or later)
Richard Radclyff	1569 (or earlier)-1595
John Rotherham	1552-1577 (at least)
John Suffolk Junior	Served from 1586 (or earlier) to past 1595
John Suffolk senior	1569 (or earlier) - 1586 (at least) [46]
Richard Vynsent	1552-1582
Robert Vyncent	1562-1595 (at least)
Richard Willoughby	1563-1595 (at least)
William Wright	1569-1586 (at least) He was recorded as a

freeholder in 1543 with two cottages and a messuage in Abbey End

Governors did not always get on: in the Court of Chancery records for 1551-3 when the negotiations were underway for a Charter from Edward VI, John Rotheram had been in dispute with Edward Povey (and Richard Vyncent) about under-leasing of tithes in the town.[47] In 1570 two Governors fell out over property, so that John Oughton was ordered to *sett his house upright that it do not annoye his neighbour Richard Vynsent before mydsomer in pain of ten shillings*[48] the dispute here being lean-to buildings encroaching on to the highway. One wonders how well they co-operated on the Governing body.

4. The Pupils

The King Edward Nuneaton school statutes were not published until 1609 but would have reflected earlier routines. They ordained a start time of six in summer and seven in winter, a reminder of how, over 400 years ago, the routine of the day was based on natural light and no summer time. The later start in winter was to save on candles. The hour to depart was not defined but would likely be five or six in the evening, again depending on the light. These hours seem very long. However, the midday break was substantial: it would be from 11 until 1 o'clock though this would be *sooner at his* [the Master's] *pleasure*,[49] most likely in the winter so there could be an earlier finish in the light. Given the size of Nuneaton many could walk home for refreshment in the middle of the day and the two hour break also gave the Master a good rest. Otherwise, all must have flagged towards the end of the day. Educational philosophy was very different to today. In the 16th Century children were merely seen as young adults not requiring special treatment.[50] Moreover, the educational emphasis was not on the development of the individual but on the need to acquire a considerable body of learning in a limited amount of time. Schools were run to fulfil the needs of the community rather then the individual student.

There were four quarters of study based on the religious calendar. Christmas, Easter and Pentecost would all have *holydays* in both religious and non-working senses. The Christmas break would involve the period from around the 15th – 17th December until just after Epiphany, January 6th. An Easter break would be shorter from Maundy Thursday until a week after Easter Day which was *The ancient custom of all Grammar Schools of England.*[51] No mention is made of a summer holiday but many Saints days meant time off. There are no admission registers before the mid-19th Century. However, since Nuneaton Grammar school took younger boys (petties) from the late 1560s boys would have entered the school comparatively early, at about eight years old. Some might only remain two or three years but others stayed. They would study the more advanced Latin until 14, the age when seven-year Apprenticeships typically began, or even as late as 16, possibly studying Greek as well as Latin, after which a few of these older pupils might enter Oxford and Cambridge as did the Burton brothers (see below). When Greek was studied, the most likely book after 1597 was Camden's *Grammar*, published that year and soon widely used.

5. A Free School?

There has been some debate of the meaning of the phrase Free Grammar School. Dr. Edward Noel Nason, writing in the 1930s, was influenced by what he saw as the threat to the independence of King Edward's from state control. He argued that *libera* never had any financial significance in Latin and it meant free from monastic control which, he argued, had been the norm. He asserted that *free* continued to mean free in the sense of independence from Church in medieval times or the state in the 19th and 20th Centuries. By contrast, A.F.Leach argued that in original early charters *free* was sometimes coupled with the lack of need to pay and that when schools did expect payment –because for instance the endowment was small – the word free was generally omitted. This seems the most plausible interpretation and that there was no charge as such to attend the school. [52]

The endowment took care of the Master's salary and the expenses of construction and maintenance of the building. With no house for the Master in Nuneaton there was no opportunity for boarders to supplement his income. In many schools there was a one-off entry fee of up to one shilling, sometimes restricted to boys from outside the area, but in Nuneaton these expenses do not appear in the accounts. Any heating and lighting costs would be met by parents' payments. In some schools they even supplied the birches for the Master to give their boys a thrashing. The boys may have done their own sweeping to keep themselves warm. Most schools did not have latrines until the 17th Century. [53]

Parents might give the Master a gift: *In some grammar schools… it is lamentable to see what bribery is used… that poor men's children are commonly shut out and the richer sort received, apothecaries, lawyers and scriveners, Yeomen, substantial husbandmen, merchants, tradesmen and artisans.* [54] This may have applied to Nuneaton. The school statutes of 1609 emphasised that *the schoolmaster lovinglie shall receive all manner of scholars and teach them freelie to his best power notwithstanding he maie accept and take that which is freelie offered in gratitude.* [55] This last phrase negates the suggestions of complete social equality implied at the beginning of the statute, suggesting the wealthy could buy additional favours and the Master accept them without fear of illegality. If the Schoolmaster could supplement his income in this way he was less likely to pester Governors for a higher salary. This statute was doubtless influenced by the dispute that had just started at that time with Schoolmaster Richard Inge. (see Chapter Three) However, this practice of accepting perquisites was well established and was an Elizabethan custom.

6. Who Attended?

Nuneaton's education was only for boys though there was a school for girls at nearby Polesworth in the 16th Century, one of the very few in the country giving them more than a very elementary education.[56] In Nuneaton's case there was no legal reason why females should not have been included. The wording of Leeke's will only referred to benefits to the *poor*, But Founders were rarely explicit in using a phrase such as boys and girls and so the social conventions of the time normally resulted in the exclusion of girls by default.[57]

As it was free, one might expect boys of the poorer classes to attend the boys' Grammar School. The Nuneaton accounts of 1608 record items purchased for the *poor scholars*.[58] However, this phrase needs to be treated with care. It most likely means poor compared with the riches of the landed gentry, many of whom did not send their children to any sort of school but had them educated at home by a tutor. In Nuneaton where wealthy landed gentry were rare, *poor* would have included those of modest wealth who might attend the school as well as unskilled labourers' sons who would go straight to employment. Parents would frequently want their children out working and earning as soon as possible. At best, the poorest classes, if they did attend at all, would remain as petties for the Usher to instill some basic literacy. However, there were increasing employment opportunities for a widening social group including a growing need for trained lawyers to implement legal and trading regulations. Many trades were now looking for a *more effective schooling than that obtainable from parish clerk or chantry priest*. [59] Nuneaton yeoman would see increasing opportunities for their properly educated children in medicine, law and the church.

7. The Curriculum: The Predominance Of Latin: Central Direction

The emphasis was on a classical education ever since medieval times when *every cathedral* [is] *to provide a schoolmaster to teach clerks and poor scholars free of charge.* [60] Latin still remained vital for careers in the church and the law, medicine, diplomacy and government work. Court records, careers in the military, architecture, and music would all use the language. There were official letters to write, records and accounts to administer, deeds and instruments to engross (to make a finished copy of a legal document), foreign business to transact. Clerks, notaries and land agents all needed Latin. Until 1660 it was used for official state correspondence by secretaries. Latin was also seen as vital for a rounded education, studying the classical world's philosophy, eloquence and logic. This approach still influenced the significant educational developments in the changing and expanding Grammar Schools of the late 19th Century and helps to account for the retention of Latin after its vocational use had been reduced.

In Nuneaton Latin would have been taught in similar ways to everywhere else. William Lily's *Latin Grammar* of 1540 would probably have been used because the book was authorised by the King to be used in grammar schools to the exclusion of all others. The King himself justified his imposition of Lily's Grammar in the Royal Preamble to the first edition of 1540. (See side bar) Henry VIII's *one absolute and uniform sort of learning* was confirmed in an act of filial piety (though sisterly rivalry) by Queen Elizabeth in 1559. *Every schoolmaster and teacher shall teach the Grammar set forth by King Henry VIII of noble memory and continued in the name of Edward VI and none other.* [62] 10,000 copies of Lily's grammar were produced, a very large print run by the standards of the time and enough to supply all grammar schools with several copies. The new King Edward VI Grammar school in Nuneaton would take advantage of technical advances in printing including stronger iron screws replacing wooden ones. By 1570, ink was no longer spotting all the areas of the paper and the type looked a good deal more regular.

8. The Role Of The Church

Religious instruction was a central part of Nuneaton Grammar School's teaching. As well as studying the pre-Christian classical world, there was active concern with imparting Christian religious belief. The Elizabethans saw no contradiction here: it was important to read the Bible's contents in the vernacular (native language) and for an educated minority to consult it in the original tongues.[63]

Henry VIII explains his imposition of Lily's Latin Grammar [61]

As his majesty purposeth to establish his people in one consent and harmony of pure and true religion; so his tender goodness toward the youth and childhood of his realm, intended to have it brought under one absolute and uniform sort of learning. For his Majesty, considering the great encumbrance and confusion of the young and tender wits by reason of the diversity of grammar rules and teachings, for heretofore every master had his grammar and every school divers teachings, and changing of masters and schools did many times utterly dull and undo good wits.

In Nuneaton the Governors appointed the Master – and Usher – of the Grammar School but the church was also influential. Schoolmasters of Grammar Schools were frequently in priests' orders. Since priests were now expected to be knowledgeable and articulate enough to preach sermons it was assumed they had the necessary qualities for a Grammar School teacher. According to the letters patent for the school *the said governors had to have the advice of the Bishop of Coventry and Lichfield*[64] when drawing up the working statutes of the school. So a knowledge of Latin (and sometimes Greek and even Hebrew) as well as a sound grounding in the Reformed Christian faith, were the general educational aims of the *The Free Grammar School of Nuneaton*. Classical learning would be *permeated with piety*.[65]

But unlike the King's instructions on Lily's Grammar, effective church control of schools varied from diocese to diocese. From 1559 every schoolmaster appointed had to conform to the Church of England by subscribing to the Act of [religious] Uniformity before being licensed by the Bishop. Neither the Bishop of Lichfield and Coventry nor his Archdeacon of Coventry observed the formalities. In Nuneaton no Statutes for the Master and his pupils was drawn up in this period as the Bishop would need to approve them.[66] Schoolmasters – and Governors – accepted church control. Although its intrusion might not always be welcome the church could guarantee to put down unauthorised schools and unlicensed teachers – potential competitors.[67]

In the Nuneaton School Statutes, finally produced in 1609, it was decreed that *praier* was to be used at the beginning and end of each day. Despite the vagueness in the Statutes on other religious points, this custom would have been observed since 1540. In addition, when the parish church was adjacent as in Nuneaton, it would also be easy for the whole school to attend the Sunday service at St. Nicolas, which was large enough to take all the boys. This was not an opportunity for relaxation or inattention for on the Monday pupils were asked to repeat the content of a sermon they had heard the day before. In addition, the Bible would be read and all pupils would learn the Lord's Prayer, the Creed and a simple Catechism (question and answer document containing an outline of the faith). Scholars would be expected to have a Primer (service book for the laity) and in Nuneaton this was supplied free for the poor children. It was universally used in schools until the mid 17th Century. In a more secular age it is easy to forget the former centrality of religion to the educational experience.

9. School Life

Boys would have to bring some of their own equipment, not only pen, paper and ruler but also plummet and pen-knife.[68] In Nuneaton, the absence of accounts for these items in the 20 years of financial records from the mid 1560s to the mid 1580s means they were paid for by the scholars. While some schools possessed a *Fireplace and chimney in the middle of one of the sides of the schoolroom* [69] this was not universal. Pupils would bring their own candles and, possibly wood fuel. King Edward records are silent on these items and there may have been no fire at all. Boys were expected to attend regularly and, according to the statutes, Nuneaton's parents had to promise that *they shall continually resorte, tymes of their private sickness only excepted, or in tyme of mortal plague or other tymes of recreation herafter lymetted.* The boys had to *come to school ornately and cleanly in such apparel as they have.*[70]

> **THE FIRST TEACHER AT KING EDWARD'S?**
>
> Henry Grene appears as Sir Henry a courtesy title used for clergy, though dropping out of use by the end of the C16th. It was used for a non-graduate member of the church, confirming the likelihood that the early Masters were probably not graduates and therefore their abilities in Latin unknown. The record is on the torn first page of the school accounts and the evidence is literally patchy. Grene is the first teacher we know about but clearly he had predecessors.

Corporal punishment was normal[71] and the Master might wish to *beat out* original sin. Nobody would have questioned this – the only debate would have concerned its severity and frequency. In an Elizabethan school it was normal to have: *a birch* [up to two feet long] *and ferula, a flat piece of wood like a ruler widened at the inflicting end into a circular shape.* [72] Damage could be lasting. If the implement was pierced with a hole it would cause blisters. Birches were about two feet long on average – there might be a whipping post, a permanent reminder of possible punishment.

The Nuneaton school site was cramped from the first and Nuneaton churchyard was inappropriate for play. Football was seen as rough and dangerous and often banned. There was nowhere for the boys to let off steam. The everyday nature of living would be seen as providing sufficient exercise. If any were encouraged it would be shooting or wrestling. Pastimes such as dice or bowling were disliked more for their associations with drinking than for any intrinsic shortcomings. The Master was given some discretion in the Nuneaton statutes to allow the children *tymes of plaie for the schollars* according to his *wisdom.* He was to grant the boys time to: *as he shall perceive needful and according to their diligent deserte.* [73]

10. The Masters

In Elizabethan times living accommodation for the schoolmaster was rare. Only from the start of the 17th Century – soon after the new Nuneaton school building of 1595 was constructed – did founders of new schools make frequent references for an endowment to provide for the Schoolmaster's accommodation. The Nuneaton Statutes refer tantalizingly to the *mansion* of the Master but this was merely the school in which he is to teach and there is no evidence he lived there. The unsatisfactory nature of arrangements for their living conditions at this time played a part in the high turnover of Masters in Nuneaton.

Rather than academic qualifications, school statutes referred to the personal qualities required of a Schoolmaster, often idealistically. King Edward's statutes refer in detail to his appointment, admittance, stipend, disciplining if necessary and action if he died in office. Many qualities were required: patience, diligence, the ability to encourage pupils when appropriate, to be *sober discreet honest and virtuous*. Academically, he must be *learned in humanitie and poetry*.[74]

We have no knowledge of any teachers in the eleven – twelve years before the King Edward foundation. After 1552 the person appointed by the Governors was sometimes known to them as in the case of Nicholas Cleyton, later to become vicar of Nuneaton. (see below) A graduate of Oxford or Cambridge would be ideal for the Master though unnecessary for the Usher. The income, varying in the 16th Century between £10 and £14, remained fixed in an era when there was a substantial price rise and might be reduced to pay an Assistant. The growing wealth of the investments and the static nature of the Master's salary was the cause of later friction.

Young clergymen would normally apply, since ordination to the priesthood could not be completed until the age of 24; with many graduating around the age of twenty a teaching job might provide a useful stopgap. But the prospects of a more substantial living in the Church resulted in a rapid turnover of Masters. Owing to the great religious uncertainties created by the Reformation struggles there was a fall off in candidates for the priesthood in the twenty years prior to 1558. So, a substantial parochial living for a capable candidate would be readily available in the 1570s and 1580s. This means we can no longer assume, as earlier writers about Nuneaton Grammar school did, that all the early Masters were ordained and M.A.s of Oxford or

Cambridge. They worked in isolation for moderate reward, and had no specific training.[75] Their abilities would vary. After 1558 eight Masters were appointed in five years, effectively having temporary contracts. Henry Grene, probably the Reverend Henry Grene[76] (see side bar) is the first mentioned but, given the rapid turnover, he is most unlikely to have been the first in post.

Grene (paid in 1558) was followed by men named Ellyot, Walton and Sadler, all by 1560 and therefore only staying a few months. Their names are remembered because for the last 40 years of the Grammar School (1935-74) the names of these first four known teachers of King Edward VI School were designated as the names for the four School Houses (See Chapter Ten). In the early 1560s, hiring of a Master seems to have taken place almost on an annual basis with Mr Harmon in 1560, Mr. Leven 1561, Mr Walker 1562 and Mr Betts (hired at Coventry) 1563[77] (See Appendix Twelve for the full list) .

No code of Regulations was drawn up by the Governors. Contracts were initially rudimentary but in 1563 Nicholas Cleyton undertook to serve for 20 marks a year (a mark was 13/4d or two thirds of a pound) just under £13 a year. In Cleyton's case the increase above £10 may have been decided upon because both sides agreed on three months notice.[78] This raising of the salary is significant. By this action the Governors acknowledged that £10 was not seen as enough in a period of inflation; the profits from their lands and additional bequests were such they could afford to pay the Master more.

Two years after his appointment Cleyton became vicar of Nuneaton and probably served out his time at the school since an interregnum of three months is recorded for the living of St Nicolas Church at that time.[79] He did not hold both positions at once, though clergy in similar circumstances sometimes did combine two posts like this, (see Chapters Five and Six) especially if the school was adjacent to the church. The living of St. Nicolas was a lucrative one – at this stage the vicar was pocketing around £25 a year[80] at least twice the schoolmaster's salary. At least one previous vicar had done some teaching when there was a vacancy.[81] If this tactic was employed more in the early years of the school the boys might have been lucky enough to have been taught by Robert Whittinton (vicar 1521-53) in the days of the pre Edward VI School in the 1540s or Nicholas Cartwright (vicar 1553-58) in the early days after the Royal Foundation.[82] Whittinton was a leading educationalist of his day and Cartwright a distinguished

Oxford Scholar. However, these two men were almost certainly non-resident vicars and so their appearance in the school to teach is disappointingly unlikely though not impossible. Sadly, at this stage, people of their intellectual quality rarely took a schoolmaster's post in a small town Grammar School. However, Whittinton's views on education may have influenced the Latin teaching in the school in Nuneaton through his text book.[83]

Only a limited proportion of clergy were considered sufficiently well educated to be licensed to preach and many lacked degrees. So, standards in Nuneaton were probably low. The attempt to gain some permanence with Cleyton seemed to be working until he made the lucrative move to St. Nicolas. After him the name of the Master receiving

School accounts of 1576 showing the paying off of a schoolmaster 'not thought sufficient'

the salary is not always given in the accounts though we know a Mr Bowley was followed by a Mr. Bonner in the later part of the decade.[84] But for most of the 1570s the records are silent on names. Some received more than the official salary of £10 [85] and the following year's accounts record the discharge of a schoolmaster *not thought sufficient.*[86]

The rapid change of Masters must have been unsettling and makes it unlikely official formalities were followed. Lichfield and Coventry Diocesan records do not show the licensing of schoolmasters until the next Bishop, William Overton, in 1579. He did enforce the subscription of thirty five schoolmasters in his last years in the diocese, 1597-1609 and a few before then. So, for instance, we know that Mr. Burton was in place as Master by 1579[87] even though his name does not appear in the school accounts until 1582. In 1584 Bishop Overton had come to realise the very variable standard of qualification, competence and religious orthodoxy of the Schoolmasters in his Diocese. This would certainly be true of Nuneaton. The Bishop launched a campaign of improvement, undertaking a large-scale factual survey, the *liber cleri* (list of clergy but including many schoolmasters). As a result he withdrew all existing schoolmaster licenses after finding *obstinate untowardness in religion in divers young gentlemen* [which] *doth argue a manifold and most intolerable corruption in ...schoolmasters.*[88]

Mr. Burton's tenure of office, if it had lasted from 1579-1584, came to an end soon after the *liber cleri* though we cannot be sure of any link. He was replaced by Mr. Yates. His tenure, however, was as brief as many of his predecessors and by 1586 Mr. Heath was in post.[89] He may have stayed until 1594/5 and if so taught the Burton brothers (see below).[90]After a brief return to a £10 salary in the late 1570s, the strong financial position of the investments led to an increase in 1581 to £13 6/8d (fractionally over 20 marks)[91] but it was still not keeping pace with the growing profits from the investments.

11. The Usher

As the country moved towards political and religious stability in the late 1560s a wider social range of parents began to become interested in formal education for their children; so the numbers of petties taught by Ushers – or assistant Masters – increased. Nuneaton was a typical if quite early example of this trend, common by the 1570s . [92] Pay was small and variable. Relatives of the Governors seem to have been employed.[93] When the Usher's salary increased the Master's was reduced. This would reflect a change in the balance of ages of boys in the school with an increase in the number of petties leaving the Master fewer boys to teach. Ushers, like Masters, were not always named in the early financial records. Robert Chaplyn was Usher from 1567- 1581(For a list of Ushers and their pay see Appendix Twelve).

Contemporaries could be scathing about the standard of instruction; in 1597 Francis Clement in *The Petty School* refers to the ignorance of the Ushers in a bold generalisation as *Altogether rude and utterly ignorant.*[94] Looking back, Foster Watson referred to *ABC schoolmasters* as *men of the slightest qualification.*[95] In Nuneaton, if Ushers were relatives of Governors, some of whom were illiterate, the teaching standard is questionable, though it is clear from the books acquired and a few personnel that others received a much higher level of classical education. Edward Launder recorded in 1610 that he had been an Usher some time before in the days of schoolmaster Mr. Cranford, probably between Heath in the late 1580s and the appointment of Inge in 1594. He asserts that since their time *I do not see that your schole hath greatelie profited eyther with grammarians or pettits.*[96] As well as showing us the variable intake of the school, this distinguished between the two types of scholars. Not all petties went on to become grammarians.

12 Willoughby And The Burtons

Some of the boys who attended Nuneaton aspired to a high level of achievement in the Classics with the church, the law and medicine seen as possible occupational avenues. Since the Governors themselves were mainly of yeoman stock one might wonder how many would aspire this high in an age which, after the upheavals of the Reformation, re-emphasised one's social position in life as largely fixed. However, some social climbing could still be done. Moreover, we have evidence that a proper classical education was indeed to be had. The earliest example we have for Nuneaton is Gilbert Willoughby, admitted as Pensioner to Gonville and Caius College in 1578: his Nuneaton teacher is recorded as Mr. Downs, coming to the end of his stay as Master of King Edward's. Gilbert's father, William, is referred to as *residing in Nuneaton* though his family came from Normanton, Nottinghamshire. [97] He had married Anne Rotherham, daughter of the King Edward's Governor John Rotherham.[98]

However, Nuneaton Grammar School's most distinguished scholars from the 16th Century were brothers William and Robert Burton. William, born in 1575 probably attended the school in the period 1584-1591. His family, modest country gentry, came from Lindley Lodge on Watling Street by the Leicester/Warwick border, within walking distance of the Grammar School for a fit and enthusiastic boy. Graduating from Brasenose College Oxford in June 1594 William was admitted to the Inner Temple and later called to the bar though he spent much of his time as a writer. His most noted publication was *A Description of Leicestershire* (1622). Considering his prowess in the classics the school must have given him a good start in this field. He wrote an unpublished Latin comedy, *De amoribus Perinthii et Tyanthes*, in 1596 and the following year, with Thomas Creede, published a translation from the Greek of his *The History of*

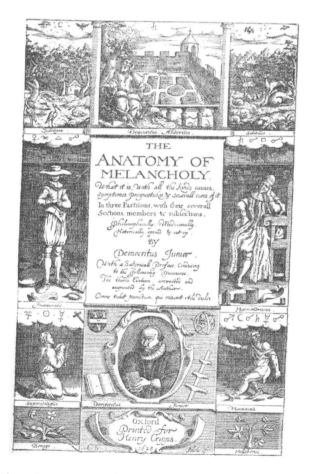

An Old Edwardian masterwork: Robert Burton's Anatomy of Melancholy: the Frontispiece of the edition of 1628

Cleitophon and Leucippe. This means Nuneaton Grammar almost certainly taught Greek. The Oxford entry in the *Dictionary of National Biography* cites Burton as *the pivotal figure in a circle of antiquaries operating in the midlands from the 1590s to the 1650s.*[99]and that his main interest in his younger days was classical scholarship; Nuneaton had clearly inspired him; his teacher was probably Mr Heath. Burton's uncle Robert (or Richard) Burton had taught him Latin even before he went to King Edward's at the age of nine.[100]He thus avoided the petties and got straight on to more advanced study. [101]

William's brother Robert Burton became even better known. This was for his book *Anatomy of Melancholy* (1621) a tour de force of the analysis of melancholy written with an extremely wide range of literary knowledge. It became a book much used in Grammar Schools probably including Nuneaton. Whether King Edward's can all take the credit, however is questionable. Robert also attended Bishop Vesey's school at Sutton Coldfield as well though the order is not clear and why he moved from one to the other is also unknown. The mystery continues: born in 1577, and so at school a little later than his brother, he matriculated early, at Brasenose, in 1593 when he was just 16; but then there is a gap in his life because he graduated from a different College, Christ Church, as late as 1602. One theory is that he was unwell and suffered from the melancholia he was to write about so memorably in the 1620s.[102] If as seems plausible he followed his brother and attended Nuneaton before Sutton Coldfield, the question is why he moved schools. It could have been ill health or dislike of the school. It may have been overcrowded with pupils as his attendance was at the time immediately before the new building. If he encountered an inadequate schoolmaster this might explain his departure. However, he may have attended Sutton Coldfield first and it was this school that that he disliked. Some of his money was left to King Edward's but not to Bishop Veasey's. We cannot be sure; but he does comment on his school experiences in the *Anatomy* when analyzing the causes of Melancholy. He argues that *children are made to think no slavery in the world (as once I did myself) like to that of a Grammar Scholar* (My emphasis). Burton's point might just be general rather than personal because his subject is melancholy. However, he goes on to argue that teachers can also cause problems to scholars by being too lax but does not relate *this* to himself: it seems likely he was indeed unhappy in at least one of his schools.[103]

It seems unlikely that Burton's famous near contemporary, the Hartshill poet Michael Drayton (1563-1631), attended school in Nuneaton. Coming from a humble background he entered service at the latest by 1580 and one dedication in his writings says he was beholden to *the happy and generous family of the Gooderes* for *the most part of my education*.[104] However with only 1,000 in population, and entry at this stage often confined to the parish, (thus normally excluding Chilvers Coton), few other boys in Nuneaton were likely to come from the social background which saw a classical education as both useful and desirable. Many of the Grammar schools were far from teaching just classics even if their statutes said so. In the country grammar schools writing might be taught by an itinerant scrivener though in Nuneaton the Usher performed this task. To get on in the world and be a school governor, though illiterate, was possible in the past but not for much longer. The Grammar School at Nuneaton managed to have a more flexible curriculum. While keeping broadly to the general pattern for Grammar Schools it adapted to local circumstances. Unless the Master positively wanted fewer pupils those who applied were generally accepted. Providing the aptitude was there, an education was waiting. By 1590 numbers had increased and were such that the Governors made a major decision; to erect a new schoolroom.

CHAPTER THREE

Disputes and Development: the Grammar School in the early 17th Century 1595-1642

Governors… share the improvements among themselves, take all above the salary for lawful prize, and leave the Master to the bare old allowance notwithstanding the vast increase in the old rents.
Marchamont Nedham *A Discourse concerning schools and School-masters 1663.*

Bitter legal disputes, usually between Governors and Masters, mar the story of Nuneaton's Grammar School's history. These were at their most acute and long-running near the start of the 1600s when a decade of legal frenzy thrust educational development into the background. However, as occurred on numerous occasions, King Edward's recovered and had re-built its reputation by mid-century when it then faced a different challenge – the Civil War.

1. The Building Of The New School 1595

By the 1590s it was clear that the governors' investments were continuing to do well and Willoughby and the Burton brothers' successes indicated some degree of academic progress. Ambitions rose and there was now sufficient capital to purchase ground for a new building. This was on the north side of the Churchyard close to the original building but nearer St Nicolas Church. This is the site that, incorporating re-building 100 years later, the Old Grammar School still occupies. The building was rough-cast and took four to five years to erect.

Nicholas Linney undertook the responsibilities of construction. The first entry in the accounts in 1595 is *to Mr. Linney in earnest for building the school* and there are further payments to him in 1596. He supplied the materials and was paid £40 for his work.[1] Architects' names rarely appear before the 1620s[2] and Linney was described as a master carpenter. But surviving evidence stresses his importance to the project. When restorative work was done on the Old Grammar School after the Second World War, roof beams from the 1595-9 building were uncovered and the date 1596 with some initials is prominent. These include NL for Nicolas Linney suggesting his efforts were acknowledged. School Bailiffs Robert Hill and John Suffolk (either senior or junior) also have their initials as do two other men, Edward Povey and Seymour Roger Mantil: these two were original Governors from 1552, probably the only two still alive. The total cost of the construction was £119 4/11d. Expenses included buying twelve trees (£6) hiring horses (for 2/6d a day) and food for the workmen.[3]

The Governors should have been able to afford the expense incurred without difficulty because of the success of their investments. However, having loaned money to the

Tudor School beam of 1596: the building was constructed at that time on the same site as the current Old Grammar School. NL is Nicholas Linney the Carpenter (C) but effectively the architect. EP and SM stand for Edward Povey and Seymour Mantil two old Governors.

1596 Building. The Bailffs (B) noted are Robert Hill (RH) and John Suffolk (JS)

townsfolk, they now needed to re-acquire it to pay for the new construction. In a special meeting at Richard Forde's house six of the Governors pressed for the return of the borrowed capital.[4] But money also needed to be returned from some of the forty four who had borrowed it a decade earlier. Bailiffs were to be *able on demand…to gather up all persons as do owe or have any goods of the school in their hands and do refuse to pay the same to the said bailiffs being lawfully issued they will sue.*

Governor literacy had improved; five Governors signed this order: Alexander Turner, Robert Hall, John Suffolk, Richard Forde and Richard Willoughby and one made his mark Richard Suffolk. They regained enough capital to go ahead with constructing the new building. [5] Though larger and more substantial than the previous one, it was still of limited size and took the traditional form of a one-room schoolhouse.

2. Books Used At Nuneaton

The first period of this new building coincided with a time when fewer school financial and building records survived. However, in the case of books used, the reverse is the case. In 1570 and 1572 records show 3/8d and 6/9d being spent. [6] After that the accounts are silent on this point until evidence of specific volumes in 1608 with an addendum to a book of accounts for an earlier, Elizabethan, period. (see Appendix Two)[7]

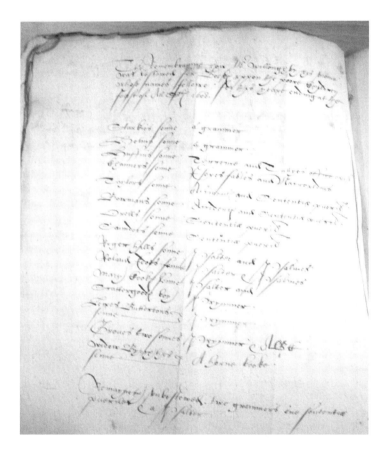

The first named school books: 1608

Most of these books were fairly elementary. Hornbooks and Primers for instance were for a study of alphabet and spelling. However, *Aesop's Fables* was used in the second and possibly third years of school. Like much of this early material this had the advantage of not only aiding learning in the linguistic sense but also adding a dimension of moral training from the nature of the stories. No less an authority than Martin Luther felt that next to the Bible, Aesop was one of the best books to study for the young child.[8] Shakespeare refers to at least seven of *Aesop's Fables* including some not mentioned in the only existing English translation at this time and he also attended a Warwickshire Grammar school in the late 16th Century. Based on this evidence of Nuneaton's books, Leach, though admitting there may be other volumes, looks down on the low standard (to him) of the Nuneaton's school classics; hornbooks, he asserted, were virtually never found in Grammar schools.[9] If this was true in the mid 16th Century things soon changed as Ushers increasingly taught petties in many schools in the last quarter of the century.

3. Confirmation Of The Charter 1604. The School Statutes 1609

After the death of Elizabeth I in 1603 the new Monarch James I introduced a tightening up of the regulations concerning schoolmaster subscription a year later. Revised canons meant that Masters now had to subscribe to the 39 Articles of Religion and the Prayer Book as clergy had always done.[10] This was about twelve months before the Gunpowder Plot. The attempt at maintaining central control of what was taught – as well as the belief of those who taught it – was also emphasized. These regulations hardly amounted to a revolutionary change yet King Edward Governors thought it necessary to obtain another confirmation of the Charter, having also done this with James' predecessors Elizabeth and Mary (see above).

Three and a half centuries later the *Edwardian* School Magazine of 1959, in reporting the tracking down of the numerous Charters, wondered why there had been so many. Was it legal uncertainty about Leeke's wishes? After all he had said nothing about a school, merely mentioning the poor; or was it, suggested the Editors, (only half in jest?) a chance for Governors to take an expenses paid trip to the capital? Governors might, in view of impending events, have been advised to seek to revise the Charter first and tighten up the wording regarding the Master's salary.

Nuneaton's Governors had still not got around to developing written statutes. The words of the letters patent of 1553 told them (with the advice of the Bishop see p14-15 above) to devise *wholesome statutes and ordinances in writing touching the order of the Government and direction of the tutor and scholars of the said school to be inviolably observed for ever.* [11] But only now under the pressure of a dispute with a Master, Richard Inge, (see below) were they so devised in 1609. Their initial draft was subsequently revised by the Bishop who used his rights of amendment under the original Letters Patent of 1553. But what the Governors wished to include is revealing.

There was a section which the Bishop amended on *What things appertaineth to an apt and meet schoolmaster*. This is peppered with traditional phrases and a couple of Latin tags to sound as learned as possible. Phrases such as *We have known in our tyme some masters that have done as much good sleeping as waking* had probably been lifted from other sources and clearly relate to difficult experiences the Governors had encountered with a Master or two. The desire for a Master to be *well mannered sober discreet honest virtuous and diligent* is typical of the statutes of the time in laying out the qualities of their ideal teacher. The Governors were keen to emphasize in the Statutes that: *the nomination of the said school-master shall appertain for evermore to the Governors' of the said school and to their successors* and that if the position be vacant they *shall immediately, with as much convenient speed as they can, provide one sufficiently learned and apt to teach grammar* though they had to acknowledge that this was an appointment *to be allowed by the Bishop*. Another section influenced by the Governors experiences was entitled *Correction of the Master for his negligence* whereby a Master would have three warnings as to his conduct. He would then be dismissed if there were further offences.[12]

Late arrival (1): Copies of the orders for the Free school of Nuneaton 1609, over 50 years after they were supposed to have been written

Yet the statutes had come too late as a major dispute was already underway. King Edward's was hit by bitter legal disputes to the detriment of the Grammar School in general and to several generations of schoolboys in particular.

4. Legal Disputes – A. The General Position

The more complex society that developed in the 16th and 17th Centuries with a great increase in market activity was much concerned with *prices, profits and bargains*. Honesty and reliability suffered in the more complex economic and financial world that was developing. Governors in schools like Nuneaton at the start of the 17th Century were the first generation to deal with financial matters on a scale frequently unknown to their predecessors. Trust of others became harder to guarantee and – for it to work – the sanction of the ultimate back up by the law was needed. With the growing capital of their endowments Nuneaton Grammar School Governors now had the financial means to resort to legal action. Later generations developed greater expertise in dealing with accounts, and increased caution when it came to legal niceties, with more preliminary consultation of lawyers. Institutions developed which could arbitrate in matters of difficulty and issue directives. But in the 17th and early 18th Centuries Governors were confronted by increasingly complex financial affairs and solutions were slow and expensive.[13]

Difficult relations between Governors and Master in Nuneaton were common and exacerbated by the awkward relationship endowed Grammar Schools had produced. On the one hand the Master frequently had virtual freehold and could be quite cavalier in insisting on his rights, literally so in the case of Royalist William Trevis after the Stuart Restoration of 1660 (See Chapter Four). On the other, a well-qualified Master could find himself *reduced to the status of a pupil in the matter of the school income* or as it was put in contemporary terms in the 1670s: *the onely man in the Parish judg'd proper from whom the value of his estate be conceal'd*.[14] Some schools were prepared to use endowment money to pay off unsuitable teachers[15] but this did not happen in Nuneaton – unless a clandestine offer was refused. Others, such as King Edward VI Chelmsford, had a similar long running legal dispute with a Master, who was appointed in the same year as Nuneaton Head Richard Inge.[16]

At this time, Governors' knowledge of education appeared frequently confined to the one school – they lacked points of comparison. Sometimes they feared to reform because of the threat of legal action but this did not apply to Nuneaton. In some other foundations where the administration was entrusted to an Oxbridge College something might be done; but in Nuneaton's case twelve townsmen acting on their own produced little save a cabal of mutual interest.[17] The endowment income lined the pockets of the Governors more than the Schoolmaster. As a near contemporary remarked at a slightly later time *lay men (ignorant fellows)… receive the rewards of the Master's industry.* [18]

The quality of early teachers at King Edward's is uncertain but the quick turnover and short term yearly contract hardly inspired confidence. Governors might have hoped for better quality teachers by 1600. Education had become more widespread, clergy – increasingly the main teachers in grammar schools – were more often graduates. This reflected a surge in numbers at Oxford and Cambridge by the turn of the century. More schoolmasters –some clergy and some not – were setting out on a career path of teaching rather than merely seeing it as a temporary expedient for a young newly ordained man before a good ecclesiastical living could be found. Schools could reasonably hope for the greater stability that could be gained by an increasingly experienced permanent teacher. However, in Nuneaton's case the relative longevity of its first 17th Century teacher did not lead to the desired stability.

5. Legal Disputes – B. The Case Of Richard Inge 1595-1614

The School Governors' dispute originated with the local church of St. Nicolas as well as with the Schoolmaster, Richard Inge. As a result of the new school building of 1595-9, which encroached on to Church property, William Gurie, the vicar of St. Nicolas, received £5.00 compensation for his *hurt.*[19] This began an up and down relationship between the School and the Church which ebbed and flowed well into the 20th Century.

When Gurie's successor as vicar was appointed (by the Crown) in 1604, the Governors lobbied successfully for a local man, locally educated, William Butterton.[20] They anticipated that this would lead to good relations between School and Church but they were mistaken. Vicar and Schoolmaster would now unite against Governors.

Schoolmaster Inge had been appointed in 1595.[21] The school had grown to about 50 pupils when he arrived, leading to the construction of the new building. Numbers, though, had declined by 1610 and the Governors became discontented with Inge's performance. In their charge against him they complained that *about last September 12 months* (1609) he had been *very negligent in his duties* that there was *daily complaint* from the parents as to the lack of education of their children.[22] The Schoolmaster/ Governors disputation that followed was all the more bitter because the Governors were incensed by the attitude of their protégé, vicar Butterton. He took the side of the schoolmaster and asserted his own right of possession of part of the land on which the new school had been built. More than this he claimed right of entry and control of the school property.

The Governors had warned Inge concerning his behaviour – the shortcomings of which were never made very specific – and reduced his annual salary from over £13 to £10 until he mended his ways and agreed to remove Butterton's influence from the schoolhouse.[23] However, following Butterton's lead, Inge fought back with a legal action of his own (see side bar and Appendix 2).

The legal position was complex: on Inge's refusal to accept the reduced salary, the Governors now implemented their threat that if the Schoolmaster *did not mend his manners he should depart hence.*[24] Inge was dismissed, probably in late 1610, and the school building re-possessed by the Governors. They appointed a new Schoolmaster, Richard Farmer, but Inge now took legal action to regain his position, sparking off ten years of legal wrangling. The argument had widened. It was no longer merely regarding salary, but of the rights of occupation concerning the building. It was not clear who now held the position of Master, legally, Inge or Farmer the new teacher.

> **Governors' disputes with Richard Inge and Anthony Reay.**
>
> 1610 Inge sacked
> 1611 Farmer appointed new Master
> 1611 Inge and Nuneaton vicar Butterton take legal action against the Governors regarding the occupation of the Schoolhouse and the Master's salary
> They appeal to the Commission of Charitable Uses and then to the Court of Common Pleas but are defeated on both occasions
> 1611 Legal inhibitions against both Inge and Farmer teaching in the school
> 1612-1614 Inge makes further unsuccessful attempts to regain his position
> 1613 Farmer leaves to take up a position in Daventry
> 1614 Anthony Reay appointed Master
> 1617-8 Reay and townsman Richard Chamberlain sue Governors for the right to a greater share for the Master of the endowment income
> 1619 The Lord Chancellor rules in favour of Chamberlain and Reay. The Master's salary and position are secure

It seems likely that Inge and Butterton attempted to re-enter the school since Governors now spent money on a night watchman apparently to prevent Inge's re-entry. One wonders what the boys made of it all. The town was becoming seriously divided over the question. Inge's replacement Richard Farmer was the innocent party in all these disputes and had been regarded as a valuable acquisition. Graduating from Pembroke College Cambridge around 1597 he was elected *tanquam socius* in 1601.[25] This was a special honorary fellowship unique to Pembroke and suggests he was highly thought of. He was typical of those intended eventually for ordained parochial life but who started out as a schoolmaster. Unsurprisingly he decided to leave Nuneaton, taking a living at Charwelton in Northamptonshire in 1613. [26]

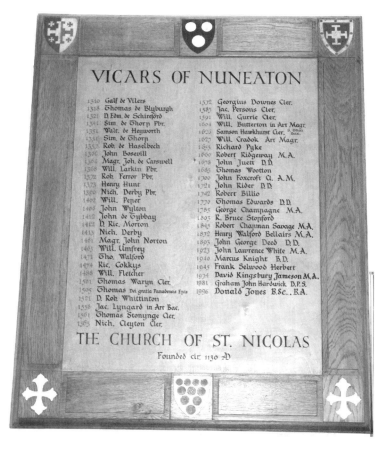

Vicar's Board: St. Nicolas Church. Cleyton, Butterton, Pyke, Savage, Bellairs and Deed all played a significant role in the history of King Edward's

After much quarrel and expense (see Appendix 3) the Governors were successful in removing Inge from his post. But despite this victory vicar Butterton had not forgiven or forgotten. The relationship between the vicar and his supporters in the town, and the Governors and their backers, was still dire. Accusations of misuse of school funds continued and took a new turn in July 1615 leading to further law suits.[27]Butterton had behaved in a high-handed manner. He and his supporters were accused of a conspiracy to *deprive the Governors of their possession of the school-house*. [28] The dispute with the vicar became even more intense. Butterton had seemed indifferent to an unseemly scuffle in the Church when two of his supporters physically attacked the two school Governors, John Suffolk and John Stratford, who had been most active in the controversy. At the time of the attack Stratford was holding one of the Grammar School account books.[29] While Stratford managed to hold on to the book its contents had already been noted by the anti-Governor party and its secrets were shortly to be revealed. (See Appendix Three)

The Governors had an extremely low opinion of the vicar and his claims upon school land. So it is hardly surprising that they demanded *punishment* of Butterton and his allies who, they claimed, should appear before the Star Chamber and explain themselves. But while the Governors got their documents back it was without anyone being punished: Butterton remained vicar until 1624.

6. Legal Disputes – C. The Case Of Anthony Reay

In 1615 the Governors appointed a new young teacher Anthony Reay. But the opportunity for a fresh start was soon thrown away and for this the Governors must bear a share of the blame. Within a year or two they had lost the support of their new teacher. Enemies of the Governors such as Richard Chamberlain had shown little liking for Reay when he had arrived. Chamberlain sent his own children elsewhere to school and initially saw Reay as a creature of the Governors, yet soon afterwards Chamberlain backed Reay in yet more legal disputes.

The opponents of the Governors had a clear advantage, having acquired knowledge of the school accounts from the locked chest. The Governors were sitting on plenty of capital but only a small proportion was being ploughed back into the school. By agreeing to pay new Master Reay £20 a year (as well as £8 a year to any Usher appointed)[30] they implicitly both acknowledged the inadequacy of the previous salary and their ability to pay more – even after expensive legal actions. But Governors were also expressing their desire to avoid a repetition of the problems that had plagued them under Inge.

However, the Governors – cautious after the disasters of the Inge period – were only prepared to employ Reay a year at a time and so they faced further legal action. The Governors later claimed in their legal assertions that within a couple of years of Reay arriving they were as unhappy with his performance as they had previously been with his predecessor Inge. They accused him of *ill behaviour* being *negligent in his place* frequently arriving late and keeping the Usher and pupils waiting. He was also seen guilty of *suffering his schollars to follow their passtimes rather than their books* and indulging in cock-fighting (sometimes involving the pupils) at *undewe times.* It was claimed that the number of pupils attending the school had declined from 60 to 20 though some of this may well have been as a result of the previous legal difficulties.[31] It was suggested by the Governors– for the first recorded time in the school's history but not the last – that the Usher was a better teacher than the Master. The Governors' version of events suggests that Reay –not performing well and fearful of summary dismissal because of his annual contract – decided to look for support among the Governors' enemies, of which there were still plenty. So Nuneaton townsman Richard Chamberlain now took Reay's side and supplied him with the two ingredients required for success – detailed knowledge about the school's financial position and sound legal advice to make the most of this. (See Appendix 3)

This time the Governors were comprehensively defeated. Costs were awarded to the plaintiffs – Chamberlain and Reay – but not to the defendants – the Governors. The Court had been unimpressed by the evidence given which had criticised Reay's competency as a teacher. Samuel Muston, a pupil, asserted that cock fighting took place three times a week in the school for about one month until the Governors had ordered it to cease. Perhaps the Court felt Muston had been put up to it. This was not the last time that public accusations of impropriety against a Master would be made, and then dismissed. A much greater set of protests by pupils and parents against a Schoolmaster 50 years later (see Chapter Four) was equally unsuccessful. The Court concluded that the case had been *A very necessary suit commenced against [the Governors] for very good grounds* [sic] *for the benefit of the said school.* Some Governors were now in danger of losing their position and the social standing that went with it. The Court ruled that *unfit governors* would be *examined* and *removed* if necessary. The verdict used strong language for a legal judgement. *Divers of the said Governors are personally of small credit and ill behaviour and unfitting to be Governors.*[32]

Cheek by jowl (1) : the Old Grammar School and St Nicolas Church. Their proximity led to land ownership disputes

To add further insult to the financial injury already suffered, the Court ruled that as Reay had not received any wages for a year, the Governors should pay him £20 *forthwith*. Also, Richard Chamberlain, Reay's supporter and financial backer, should be paid an extra £5 by the Governors in compensation for the *delay* the Governors had caused by the long prepararation of their case. The Governors had presented an extremely long defence of their conduct – running to forty pages. Their lengthy explanations included defending themselves against Reay's charge that at one point the Governors had locked him inside the school. Governors claimed the school bailiffs had removed the lock and key in order to make copies but that Reay had remained in the school *of his own free will.*[33]

In addition the judgment ruled that only *grammatical students* attend the school, that is all must study Latin. This would have been welcomed by Schoolmaster Reay. It made an Usher less likely and, if one had been appointed, the money would have been taken out of the Schoolmaster's salary. Later in the18th Century Masters such as the three Liptrotts (see Chapter Five) took the same line, preferring to interpret the grammatical clauses strictly, keeping the School small and the salary all to themselves. Alternatively, a Master might choose an easier life with a smaller salary, the bulk of the boys being taught by an Usher – who would probably be overworked and underpaid. This was the option favoured by Master Hugh Hughes at the start of the 19th Century; but he had other forms of income. (See Chapter Six)

Apart from details of these legal cases, the Grammar School records are not as good for the early 17th Century as for earlier periods. So it is largely unclear how far the Governors were replaced, or reformed their financial practices. There is one tantalizingly brief reference, undated, (possibly 1617) recording that Richard Williams and Mason Lee were lawfully prevented/demoted from being Governors.[34]. But later in the century (see Chapter Four) the endowment income appeared very healthy, so perhaps the advice of the Court had been taken to heart. There was deep irony in the Governors' position at the time of these disputes and they do not come out of them well. They had exposed their own dubious financial activities and ensured the Master a security of tenure that would make an inadequate teacher almost impossible to remove in the future. With his victory Reay had confirmed security of tenure for the Schoolmaster, a fact for which a few subsequent ones would be grateful. He stayed until the end of 1623.

7. After Reay: Perkins And Packwood

Reay was replaced by Zachary Perkins in Jan.1624.[35]He had been a sizar[36] at Christ's College Cambridge graduating in 1617 and being ordained in 1624 but we have no other evidence for his Mastership and he only lasted 18 months. There are three possible reasons for this: the Governors found him unsatisfactory, he was a stop-gap, or it may be that, despite his youth, he died in September 1625. Perkins was appointed curate at Astley, a small village just outside Nuneaton, unlikely to have had a curate as well as a vicar. The following year a vicar was appointed at Astley and the reason for the appointment was given as *death* in Sept. 1625. This may have been Perkins but the name of the person who died was, unusually, omitted. It was either Perkins or the previous vicar. Since he no longer remained schoolmaster it seems either Perkins died or, more likely, was merely filling in for a sick incumbent.[37]

After the protracted legal wranglings and the brief Perkins interlude, the school seems to have settled down again under Josiah Packwood of nearby Fillongley, Master for nearly fifteen years from 1625 to 1639. Though there is no evidence of him going to King Edward's as a boy, he went to Magdalen Hall Oxford in May 1617 aged 15.[38] He had graduated by 1621, was ordained in 1622, and in August 1625 was installed as the Nuneaton Master. His stay of fifteen years might suggest he was an an early example of the more professional teacher rather than an instance of a clergyman setting out his stall by beginning with a schoolmaster's post. [39] However, in 1637 he became curate of Fillongley whilst still Master at King Edward's until at least 1639[40] and was installed as vicar in 1641 though by this time he had left the Grammar School.

Packwood may have eventually decided that he could not combine the two posts or perhaps the Governors did not wish him to. We lack original sources for this period so cannot be sure. But, if Packwood did want a parish, there are reasons why it might have taken him so long. Firstly, unlike the other developing professions of medicine and law, there was no shortage of well qualified clergy in the early 17th Century with the healthy numbers that had been going up to Oxford and Cambridge. As well as the minimum age limit of 24 for ordination, curates often had to wait some time for an incumbency and so would take to teaching in the meantime.[41] As a strong Puritan, moreover, Packwood may have suffered from lack of personal connections; the High Church party of William Laud (Archbishop of Canterbury 1633-45) became increasingly powerful in the late 1620s and early1630s. So a combination of radical views and tight competition may have accounted for his non-preferment. By 1637, however, when Packwood obtained his position at Fillongley, the religious and political tide was turning. Researches for Warwickshire and Worcestershire schoolmasters show that just over half the clergy teaching at endowed Grammar Schools in the 17th century were what were termed *temporary professionals,* not holding a living simultaneously but neither being a schoolmaster for the whole of their career.

It is not clear if Packwood taught small numbers with a view to sending them to Oxford and Cambridge or if he had a larger group of pupils requiring an Usher. If the former then – given Packwood's background – Oxford may have been more likely but only two boys from Nuneaton are recorded as matriculating there in his time as Master and neither of them is referred to as being at school in Nuneaton. [42] The King Edward's boys were most likely sons of prosperous merchants and master craftsmen with a few poorer boys. The desire to give one's children a good education was starting to spread into the more middling social ranks.[43]

During this period the approach to teaching in a Grammar school like Nuneaton is unlikely to have changed a great deal since Elizabethan times. The early 17th century is seen as a golden period for Grammar schools with the development of a more professional approach to teaching, a concern to capture local talent and an ever-expanding entry list to Oxbridge. Teachers such as John Brinsley from Ashby de la Zouch Grammar School with his influential book *Ludus Literatus or the Grammar School* (1612) reluctantly accepted the necessity to take on pupils whose greatest attributes may have lain elsewhere than in learning Latin declensions. Unfortunately these pupils do not leave the kind of historical record that success at Oxbridge ensures. So we know little about the ordinary pupil and even their overall numbers must be estimated. Different methods of teaching Latin evolved slowly. Brinsley still advocated speaking as much as possible in Latin rather than English in the classroom but he modified the way basic grammar was taught by advocating translations of Latin words and phrases into English by *taking them in the grammatical order normal in English and then re-translating into Latin.*[44] In Nuneaton Packwood was only 15 miles from Brinsley in Ashby and shared his Puritan convictions; he is likely to have followed Brinsley's approach to education. This involved teaching the Church catechism and assuring attendance at church, maintaining the tradition of asking pupils on Monday morning about the contents of the sermon they had heard on the Sunday. If they were wise they had not only attended but taken the appropriate notes. The broad aims of the school were still two-fold: to teach a knowledge and understanding of the Classical world and impart Christian instruction.

Packwood's Puritan views were demonstrated when ousting a more Royalist vicar (Richard Pretty) from Hampton in Arden in 1647 but later being ejected himself on the Restoration in 1660 when Pretty got his revenge by re-taking the post. Packwood died in his native Fillongley in 1666.[45] He had clearly performed a dual role of teacher of boys and – in his sermons on a Sunday – a teacher of the laity where he was a lively preacher. He made quite an impression on Sir Richard Newdigate. Between 1625 and 1631 Sir Richard attended numerous Puritan services in Warwickshire and Leicestershire making assiduous notes in a manner of which a diligent schoolboy would have been proud. Despite their Royalist vicar William Cradock, Nuneaton was the venue for many Puritan lectures in the 1630s, led by Richard Vines, incumbent at nearby Weddington and Caldecote, described as an English Luther. Packwood's views would have been close to Vines. In a sermon of 1631 Sir Richard Newdigate noted that Packwood was keen to educate his congregation. He *Enjoined his audience to eschew the services of folk healers, since their remedies were based on superstition and ultimately inspired by Satan.* Indeed his Puritanical preaching made numerous references to *The Devil and all his works* such as *Wee seeke not to the Devil but to God for help.* But how his general religious views and approach informed his teaching we cannot be certain. His approach was certainly one where he wished to educate. Thus he preached that *God will not have the Devill to be his agent.* [46]

Clearly the Governors chose a very different man to replace Packwood and one wonders whether he had grown too militant for their taste. In any event his replacement William Barford, appointed in January 1640, was a strong Royalist. He came to Nuneaton at a time when his principles would soon suffer severe attack in the ensuing Civil War. His family hailed from Woodloes, Warwick. A plebian at All Souls he was born in 1614 or 1615 matriculating in 1634 aged 19. [47] Barford's appointment appears to have run smoothly; but little else did in the next 50 years of the school's history.

CHAPTER FOUR

The Terrible Trevis: The School in the later 17th Century 1642-1695

Who for false quantities was whipt at school but t'other day and breaking grammar-rule

John Dryden's translation of Perseus, *Satires* 1693

King Edward's suffered the difficulties and uncertainties suffered by many Grammar Schools in the mid-century disruption of Civil War. However, by 1660 the position looked promising. A healthy endowment, a small but not inadequate building and a well qualified Royalist Master welcoming the Restoration of King Charles II. But that Master, William Trevis, was to squander his opportunity. The situation became so bad that even the very existence of the school was in doubt.

1. Civil War Disruption

From the time William Barford became the Nuneaton Schoolmaster at the very start of 1640 life became difficult for supporters of King Charles I. The Civil War began in 1642 and royalist clergymen, schoolmasters and university fellows in areas controlled by the Parliamentarians now ran the risk of ejection for their political views. Moreover, lack of religious conformity was linked with political disaffiliation. Schoolmasters were less vulnerable than those in parochial posts but the position was still worrying for them. Barford was regarded as a distinguished Schoolmaster[1] though there is little record of pupils attending Oxford and Cambridge in his time. The Stratford family, later to become wealthy through coal mining, had recently acquired land in the Nuneaton area[2] and sent Edward Stratford in 1615 to Brasenose College, Oxford: he in turn sent his son John to Pembroke College, Cambridge in 1647[3] but there is no reference to a school attended. As before, the probability is that they were privately educated.

However, the Civil War and its aftermath would have upset the customary routines of the gentry and hence the arrival of pupil Sir Willoughby Aston from Cheshire around

1649. Nuneaton was chosen because the boy's mother, Anne, had just inherited the Nuneaton Priory lands from her father Sir Henry Willoughby.[4] So, young Willoughby is likely to have stayed with relatives in Nuneaton since there is no evidence of boarders at King Edward's. Royalist teacher Barford was seen as suitable and he was successful with Aston who entered St John's Cambridge in 1656. Intended for a legal career, Aston entered the Middle Temple in 1659 at just 19.[5] The precariousness of life encouraged pupils to get their qualifications as quickly as possible.[6]

2. The Master Is Worried About His Position

Aston's leaving the school to go to Cambridge in 1656 coincides with Barford leaving his post. Barford's Royalist views and his willingness to teach children of openly Royalist families such as Aston made him feel vulnerable, especially in an area that saw fighting at Coventry, a Parliament town and, even nearer, Caldecote. W. A. L. Vincent, an authority on education in this period, argued that: *Most of the schools weathered the storms of the Civil War, and in spite of difficulties, disorganisations and distractions, the educational life of the country was not impaired*.[7] This may have been wise after the event. The uncertainties of the time were great and there are exceptions to his assertion: Vincent himself points out action taken by the Parliamentarians. For instance, as early as October 1643 the Committee for plundered Ministers were given *power to inquire after malignant schoolmasters*. On 12th December 1643 an Ordinance was passed against *all scandalous malignant and ill-affected ...schoolmasters,*[8] and County Committees in areas controlled by parliament set about applying this. The addition of *ill-affected* suggested an attack on those Masters who were competent but had the wrong political views.

A few Masters were removed by Parliamentarians[9] and Barford was worried for himself and his wife in case his source of income was to dry up. In practice the distractions of war put removing Royalist schoolmasters low on the scale of priorities, especially if they were able. Nevertheless, Royalists at Oxford and Cambridge *were* more affected. One William Trevis, Fellow of Trinity College, Cambridge was ejected from his post in 1643.[10] We shall meet him in Nuneaton as Barford's successor, shortly. Even after the execution of the King in 1649, *Royalists who were good schoolmasters seem at least in some cases, to have been allowed to carry on their work so long as they did not act openly against the parliament*.[11]

For the time being Barford remained and the economic concerns of some schools at this

Trinity College Cambridge, original academic home of Nuneaton Master William Trevis

time do not appear to have affected Nuneaton.[12] (See Appendix 5) Pressure on Barford mounted after 1653 when Oliver Cromwell removed the Rump Parliament in April and set up his Protectorate the following December. More attention was now paid to schools. In August 1654 *An Ordinance for ejecting Scandalous, Ignorant and insufficient Ministers and Schoolmasters* was issued. While the emphasis was generally on poor behaviour, this included *popish opinions* a vague term that could easily be applied to non-Puritan Anglicans as well as to Roman Catholics.[13] Commissioners were appointed for each county including staunch Parliamentarian William Purefoy of Caldecote barely two miles from Nuneaton. They had powers of ejection and sequestration; indeed they were known as the Ejectors.[14]

The strong Puritan emphasis on education made it unlikely that schools would be shut like the chantry schools of the previous century had been. There was some criticism of parrot fashion learning and an excessive dominance of Latin. However, good masters, if Royalist, would survive if they kept their head down and no one else coveted the post who was politically more suitable. Nevertheless, openly Royalist teachers might be vulnerable not least because many of their fellow Monarchists ejected from the Universities were now looking to teach instead.[15] Pressure on men such as Barford now reached a peak. The 5th clause of an Order in Council, (issued on 21st September 1655 and re-enforcing the ordinance of 1654 above) proclaimed that *none… are to keep their…schoolmasters or… ejected… fellows of colleges nor have their children taught by such*[16] In practice, however, some of these *ejected … fellows* were allowed to teach in a school, as happened in Nuneaton, often to the institution's advantage (though not in the case of Nuneaton). Good school teachers were precious commodities and real ability pragmatically outweighed a known Royalist or Puritan bias. Barford, though, was concerned not just about the possibility of losing his specific and relatively well paid post in Nuneaton but losing the chance to teach altogether. The 6th clause of the Order in Council warned that *none who have been … ejected from any benefice college or school for delinquency or scandal, are after Nov 1st 1655 to keep any school … on pain of three months imprisonment with banishment for a third offence.*[17] The appointment of Richard Pyke,[18] a known Cromwellian supporter, to the living of St. Nicolas, Nuneaton, in 1655 can hardly have lessened local tension: so all this pressure resulted in a remarkable arrangement between Barford and the man ejected from Trinity College back in 1643, William Trevis.

3. The Barford/Trevis Agreement

Under the agreement implemented in February 1656 Trevis would take over the Mastership of the School from Barford. He would pay Barford £10 a year out of his salary for life and Barford's widow as well if she outlived her husband.[19] This arrangement was honoured for ten years at least.[20] There were advantages: on the surface the worried Barford would feel he had a secure if small income and it is possible he could supplement his £10 by continuing to teach in one of the small private schools that ex Royalists were setting up at this time. For his part Trevis had obtained a worthwhile well-paid post (even minus the £10); regaining his fellowship looked most unlikely.

The question of Barford and his wife's guaranteed pension was not a minor one. In October 1649 the Commons ordered all graduates to subscribe to the Engagement acknowledging *the Commonwealth of England as the same is now established without a*

King or House of Lords. There were no pensions for non-subscribers.[21] Moreover, Barford might even be barred from teaching private pupils.

However, the agreement poses a number of questions. If Royalist Barford felt vulnerable during the Protectorate, Trevis had surely more cause to worry. If Barford kept his head down and proved competent he might well survive. Trevis was a marked Royalist on account of his expulsion from Cambridge. Moreover, ability to keep a tactful silence was hardly a quality he would become noted for. So Trevis could well be removed and if he was what would happen to Barford's £10 a year? It is surprising that the agreement worked and lasted, for it was risky in the extreme. Its survival was good fortune.

Until 1660 Trevis *did* manage to keep his head down and then the Restoration of the Monarchy in 1660 – which could hardly have been predicted in 1656 – greatly reduced the danger of his dismissal, though thanks to Trevis' behaviour, not entirely. The unusual nature of the Barford/Trevis arrangement was to cause untold legal difficulty in the years to come. The irregular nature of Trevis' appointment made him vulnerable to attack when he stepped out of line a few years after the Restoration (see below). This emphasises the riskiness of the agreement between the two men. Trevis' period of office proved to be a long one. It lasted nearly 40 years from early in 1656 almost to his death in 1695. This was a dark period in the history of the school and confirms the feeling that the fate of individual schools at this time (and in many other periods) depended more than any other single factor on the personal qualities of the Master.

4. The Start Of The Trouble

Difficulties began within a couple of years of the Restoration of the Monarchy in 1660. Though we have no reason to doubt his ability in Latin, still the principal academic requirement for a Master, Trevis drank too much; this affected both the quality of the education he was able to give his scholars and could at times threaten their physical well-being. Trevis treated his pupils brutally, even by the standards of the 17th Century and this continued for many years.

The first sign to the outside world that things were amiss came in 1662 when the scholars rioted in protest against the Master's behaviour. This was not an uncommon event in England at this time. Strict discipline in many Grammar Schools frequently led to direct and active protest by the boys. There was also a tradition in many schools that one day in the year the Master should be locked out of his school and the building taken over temporarily by the boys. It was known as *shutting out, barring out* or *exclusion*. There was a *Time-honoured custom of exclusion or when the Master was denied admission until he had conceded the boys' demands for extra play days before Christmas.*[22]

Vicar Denounces Schoolmaster

Pyke denounced Trevis in style. On Market Day, Saturday 9th December, just a week after the disturbance, Luke Mortimer the clerk rang the bell a little before noon and announced : O Yee O Yee O yee: Bee it knowne to the towne and Countrye, that, My Master Mr. Richard Pyke Minister of the town and parish of Nunn-Eaton doth from his soule, hate abhor abominate and detest whatsoever Mr. Trevis falsely and untruly alleadged and declared against him yesterday adding this is not the fiurst lye that Mr. Trevis hath told. (Tumult in Nuneaton)

During the siege local custom often required the boys to do their exercises and hang them out of the windows for the Master to collect. However, sometimes this popular (among the boys) event lasted rather longer than was intended and gave rise to difficulty, especially if the Master was disliked for any reason. The post-Restoration period of the 1660s heralded a revival of the custom. Antagonism towards the Master was how the trouble in Nuneaton started. Trevis was more than a little unpopular. Ralph Wright, a parent and governor, encouraged this first protest but it did not last and was successfully controlled by Trevis.[23]

5. The Violence Escalates

However, three years later in November 1665 opposition was more serious and organised: pupils were egged on by their elders. On Tuesday 28th November William Gamble and Edward Lea helped the boys to barricade themselves in the school denying Trevis admittance. Powder, shot and firearms had been supplied from School Governor Gervase Buswell's shop. The protestors did not stop at a threat for the following day (Wednesday) they shot at Trevis when, in his own words, *repairing to the school* [I] *was by the discharge of Pistolls and guns denied entrance.* Nor was this an isolated use of ammunition since Trevis asserted that they *frequently night and day* [were] *shooting off pistols and guns.* When ammunition had been used up *they dispatched to Hinckley for fresh supplies.*

The Church was involved in the protest. Parish clerk Luke Mortimer encouraged the boys not to surrender to Mr. Trevis' allegedly gentle persuasion to attempt to end the siege. He warned the scholars that Trevis had *bundles of birch to punish them with.* Trevis denied this. According to Trevis' testimony, Mortimer was acting *by his Master's* [vicar Richard Pyke's] *order and appointment.* The vicarage, adjacent to the school, was well placed to give both moral support and physical sustenance to the boys. Pyke's son and Luke Mortimer visited the boys, who wished an end to the occupation, and persuaded them *not to submitt on any terms.*

Trevis later claimed that at least eleven men were involved in the *Enterprize* against him. Pyke accused Trevis of falsely claiming that he, Pyke had *formented* the trouble. Trevis denied this and asserted in his deposition that it was Mr Piggott, a gunsmith, who had made the claim concerning Pyke's involvement and would do so on oath if required. [24]

After two days of pupil occupation of the school, matters escalated on the Thursday. William Smythe and Ralph Wright, nephew of parent and Governor Ralph Wright (see above), went armed into the school and encouraged the boys to take pot shots at Trevis' *dwelling house.* According to Trevis they *shut off their guns and pistols against my dwelling (at midnight)* [and] *broke my window in several places.* In the fracas Ralph Wright junior was shot in the finger *which shott if it had bin received in some other part of his bodie might have proved mortall.*[25] It is not clear if this injury was inflicted by mistake or if Trevis had returned fire.

6. Newdigate Intervenes

There was little support for the beleaguered Trevis in the town. Desperately, he appealed to Arbury Hall for help and Sir Richard Newdigate, Serjeant at Law, intervened on the Friday. As he arrived he met Trevis and *reproved* the Master for *not giving him more timely notice.* He got Trevis to agree that the pupils would not be punished providing the siege was ended and the protest not repeated. But as Sir Richard arrived at the school to impart this information to the schoolboys he was made all too aware of the violent atmosphere, being *most gratefully requited by the discharge of a pistol in his face.* This frightening incident brought the protestors up short and soon after they fled out of a back window and over the vicarage garden. The school was in chaos: *heer lying bread beef and turnip, there spoons, hear an old blanket in one place a sword,*[26] further evidence that the boys had been supplied by townsfolk. Sir Richard consulted with local magistrate William Purefoy of Caldecote. Purefoy's parliamentarianism would have made him anti-Trevis but being responsible for local law and order he had to warn the rioters of the dangerous consequences if they persisted in their protests. Several were bound over until the next assizes. Vicar Pyke later offered surety for Buswell, one of a number of protestors bound over to keep the peace. Buswell may well have supplied the boys but evidence suggests they also received assistance from his wife Mary who later confessed to *sending in provisions and a blankett.*[27] Trevis had been shut out of his school four days running; it hardly improved his temper. Many Nuneaton inhabitants, however, were relatively unconcerned about the damage to the school and more enraged about Trevis' alleged brutalities which had caused the protest in the first place. These were regarded as severe even in a more violent age and incensed governors and parents who determined on legal action. A law suit was brought against Trevis and this leaves us evidence that illustrates how Trevis behaved.

Check by jowl (2) The vicarage (left) was close enough to be able to supply the revolting schoolboys with food and blankets for their sit in

7. The Governors Take Action

As may have happened before, and was certainly to happen again, the number of school Governors had declined by the 1660s as those who died or moved had not been replaced. At the time of the troubles there were only six left. Six more were appointed on December 12th, soon after the affray and none supported the Schoolmaster.[28] By 1666 the Governors clearly felt that Trevis was ruining the school and, not surprisingly, pupil numbers were dropping off drastically. Bailiffs Job Muston and Samuel Joliffe decided, with the agreement of all the Governors, to withhold a small amount of Trevis' sixth month salary in March 1666. If Trevis did not accept the reduction, said the Governors, he *should not receive any* [salary] *until he would give an arquittance* [sic, aquittance, meaning absolute discharge of debt] *for the whole half year's rent. [29]* Trevis claimed he was duly officiating in the school and had the approval of the Bishop.[30] He refused to accept the reduction and demanded the whole £33. The Governors refused anything and a legal case was now inevitable. In 1667 the Bishop of Lichfield and Coventry, John Hacket, and Mr. Justice Tyrrell of the Court of Assize in Warwick,[31] were to rule both on the Schoolmaster's salary and whether Trevis was legally in place according to the Statutes. The case had become an attempt to remove Trevis reminiscent of the earlier action against Inge and Reay.

8. The Sworn Depositions

Evidence against Trevis was strong, with sworn statements by many people all testifying to his violence on the boys. Many parents complained about the treatment of their sons. But sometimes it was the boys themselves (a few years older by 1667) who were the ones to testify. Clearly the abuse had gone on for some time. This did not merely leave a temporary soreness and the lasting damage was as much mental as physical. The excessive drinking was corroborated by a number of witnesses. His violent behaviour was not confined to the students as some testified to his drunken aggression towards others.

That so many were prepared to testify against Trevis was significant. Though not unknown it was comparatively rare for so many parents to complain at once. This was not only because the general outlook of the 17th Century accepted a severe level of punishment. It was also because if charges were found to be deliberately false or merely rejected it would often result in the removal of the child from the school. (For depositions see Appendix 4) Had these depositions been accepted by the Court it is hard to see how Trevis would have escaped unscathed. But they were not (see below).

9. The Case Against Trevis: The Governors' Case

The case began at the end of 1666. The Governors' legal approach focused on two broad assertions: that Trevis was not properly appointed in the first place and that he was not doing his job properly. On the first point it was alleged:

- His appointment had not been approved by the Bishop (there wasn't one at the time as it was in the middle of Cromwell's Protectorate). Neither had his appointment been placed by the *instrument aforesaid as ordained and under the common seal*
- Trevis was never elected by the whole Governing Body: his agreement with Barford was irregular and never fully approved.

The argument regarding Episcopal appointment was always a particularly weak one for the Governors. As even they admitted, the appointment was when *the Bishops were not suffered to exercise their jurisdiction.*[32] The question was had the Bishop allowed him to stay after the Restoration? He had: under the 1662 Act of Uniformity all clergy and most Schoolmasters had to go through a process of re-selection and accept the Royal Supremacy, the 39 articles of the Church of England, Episcopacy (the authority of Bishops) and the condemnation of armed resistance to Kingly authority. Trevis, as a good Royalist who had suffered for just such views earlier in his career, was happy to do this. In 1662 he had subscribed to the new Regulations swearing his support for the restored Charles II.[33] Clearly the Bishop had approved of his appointment if only retrospectively.

As regards their own approval of the appointment, again the Governors were on weak ground. They argued that Barford *was forced to desert the…*[school] *for his loyalty* and that some of the Governors *out of their respect for Mr. Barford recommended the said Mr. Trevis.* But how many had formally approved him? Trevis himself claimed the support of seven Governors – a narrow majority. The fact that Josiah Packwood, the Master before Barford, was only appointed by nine Governors was crucial in the ruling that Trevis was properly appointed.[34]

The Governors' second main theme was that Trevis *hath not done the duty of a schoolmaster.* The Court refused to hear the sworn depositions of parents and ex-pupils yet the Governors still had a strong case. Trevis had clearly broken the statutes of the school. As the Governors put it, *By his negligence the said school has utterly gone to decay whereby the said graunt is almost made void and the revenue misemployed being above £60 per annum.* Trevis' defence focussed on the concept of *officiating* in the school which he claimed he had always done.

The evidence that Trevis had not behaved well was clear. In this area six detailed charges were made against him (see Appendix 4) consisting of three broad criticisms: the school had undergone a decline in numbers and behaviour, he had clearly broken the Statutes of the School in terms of both religious and financial principles, and his personal behaviour fell far short of that expected of a teacher and interfered with his job.[35]

However, these charges did not lead to the downfall of Trevis. When Chancery had referred the case back to the Bishop – who had already sided with the Schoolmaster – it was already clear who was likely to benefit from the final judgement. In the area where the Schoolmaster was most vulnerable the testimonies of the parents and former pupils were ruled inadmissible. So in September 1668 the Court found clearly for Trevis. They asserted that he did *constantly and diligently attend the imployment and will deserve the benefit of that place.* They further argued that Trevis had been properly appointed: He *was well elected schoolmaster of Nuneaton by consent of all the Governors of the said school that were then alive.*[36]

Their statement that Trevis did *constantly and diligently attend the imployment* seems an extraordinary comment and may have been chosen because it relates to the wording of the statutes where *diligence* is a necessary quality for the Master. However, more is revealed by their next sentence, that he was a *very loyal and orthodox person to his Majesty for which in the late evil times he was ejected out of his Fellowship of Trinity College in Cambridge.*[37] The Bishop used precedent arguing that *The plaintiff [Trevis] shall have the benefits of the same order against the said Job Muston and Samuel Joliffe and the rest of the Governors as his predecessors had against the former Governors.* [38]

This was the Bishop's public position. In private he was exasperated with Trevis and complained to Sir Richard Newdigate at the time of the hearing in March 1667. While the Bishop felt the Governors had been *incessantly molestious* he felt the cause of this was that Trevis' *carriage … was verie spitefull and uncharitable. I have advised him to mend it but my advice he heeds not.*[39]

10. Why did Trevis get away with it?
Despite the overwhelming evidence against Trevis, the Governors were never likely to win. The legal judgement favouring Anthony Reay back in 1615 had given the Master

a virtual freehold with regard to his right to the income of the endowment. The Statutes, drafted by the Governors in 1609, had asserted that the Master only held the office *at their pleasure* but this had been amended by the Bishop to *during good behaviour*. This made any removal more difficult. Since the testimonies against Trevis were ruled inadmissible it would be difficult to prove bad behaviour.

Leach and Nason mention the two possible reasons for Trevis' survival: his Royalist outlook and that the more serious charges against him were not believed.[40] Leach inclines to the latter view on the grounds that if the complaints of the townspeople had been believed, Trevis would have been removed. Perhaps the cruelty Trevis showed to the boys, while excessively severe to a later mind, would have been seen then as merely harsh and not sufficiently bad to warrant dismissal. But this goes too far. Certainly there was a belief that the innate sinfulness of young boys needed to be beaten out of them if necessary, and even enlightened educational writers in the late 17th Century such as John Locke warned of the dangers of showing too much *tenderness* to children.[41] However, good Puritan schoolteachers such as Hoole and Brinsley were already clear in their condemnation of excessively harsh discipline.[42] Brinsley argued that while the rod needed to be used on pupils sometimes, teachers must avoid *smiting them upon the head, with hand, rod or ferula.*

> **ILL-TREATMENT CONDEMNED**
>
> 'As for the ferula I wish …that it might be utterly banished out of all schools A good sharp birchen rod and free from knots, for willow wands are insufferable and, but fitter for a bedlam than a school as it will break no bones nor endanger any limbs, so it will be sufficient wherewith to correct those who shall deserve it in the lower forms and for the higher scholars that will not behave as they ought to do, a good switch about the shoulders would….seem fitter than a rod elsewhere'. Charles Hoole 1660.

Contemporary accusations of excessive brutality indicate that late 17th Century society did place limits on the degree of corporal punishment thought acceptable, even if the limits were very different from the 21st Century. [43] Trevis had gone much too far. He was exactly the kind of teacher later condemned outright by writer Richard Steele when he referred to *stupid tyrants* [who] *exercise their cruelty without any manner of distinction of the capacities of the children or the intention of parents on their behalf.*[44] Matters were sufficiently serious nationally for a children's petition to be presented to parliament in 1669. [45]

It is possible the Bishop did not believe the evidence because it was brought together by

Trevis' enemies. As a Royalist Trevis had clearly made many of these, not least vicar Richard Pyke, who Trevis despised for being a time server. Pyke's friends were anxious at least to make Trevis' shortcomings well known. However, the most likely explanation is that Trevis survived because he possessed a trump card: he was a stout-hearted Royalist who had been dismissed from his earlier post. In the 1660s in the immediate aftermath of the Restoration, this counted for a great deal: even serious indiscretions could be excused. In the event, the legal judgement in its praise of Trevis as Schoolmaster ignores all the evidence to the contrary. How could Trevis have been described as *constant* and *diligent* in attendance at the school?

11. The Later days of Trevis: the decline of the school

By the end of the 1660s Trevis' position was legally secure. Newdigate and the Bishop had suggested an Usher to assist Trevis and a Schoolmaster's House, but these suggestions fell on deaf ears. Trevis had no intention of sharing his salary with an Usher and the Governors were also intransigent, not wishing to spend more out of the endowment to help the Master they despised.[46] Serious complaints rumbled on. Trevis' running of the school lasted for a further 25 years but past problems continued if not with the same frequency and severity. Nevertheless there was a serious decline in school numbers and King Edward's passed through the darkest days of its history.

Trevis could now do as he liked. Like previous Masters he had won a legal victory over the Governors and could enjoy the fruits of his revenues[47] and his drinking, bowling and attacks on errant students. His salary increased (see below) but pupil numbers plummeted and by 1680 virtually none remained.[48] For a town estimated to have a little under 2,000 people in 1670 large numbers would not be expected but even so generations of schoolboys missed an opportunity given to those before and after.

The Governors revived the question of their Master and his ability to do the job as efficiently as he was taking the substantial salary. So in 1680 they made a plea to the Master of the Rolls. The original documents are damaged but it is clear that the old ground was re-trod with references to Trevis' irregular appointment to replace Barford and to his negligence and cruelty. This time their efforts were not entirely fruitless. With Trevis now about 60 years old, an Usher was to be appointed at £20 a year. Since the Master now received a very good sum, £80 a year, he could have afforded to pay this £20 out of his own salary just as he had afforded Barford's pension; but he probably didn't want to.[49]

Nuneaton's difficulties differed in degree but not in kind from other local Grammar Schools. It was better off financially. The position of many endowed institutions was tricky in the late 17th Century. Heavy taxation could make collection of rents generally difficult. However, Nuneaton's school investments – though we have fewer details for this period than the late 16th Century – produced good income throughout the Trevis era. While other schools had often struggled to maintain a good Master's salary after the deprivations and even confiscations of the Civil War, this had not been the case in Nuneaton. In a list of 50 Warwickshire Grammar Schools Nuneaton's salary stands joint top with Sutton Coldfield with Rugby a little behind. £80 a year was a substantial salary to be able to pay. Almost 20 other schools in Warwickshire rarely offered more than £20 a year in salary.[50]

However, in other ways, Nuneaton Grammar school in the time of Trevis was at a very low point even by the very uneven standards of English Grammar schools at that time. It is true that mid to late 17th Century decline in Grammar Schools was not uncommon. Yet these difficulties could largely be related to the Civil War and both Ashby and Rugby, schools that had also gone through tricky periods, were soon to recover, as did Nuneaton eventually. Not the least of the problems Trevis bequeathed to his successors was his longevity. He did not take boarders, requiring neither the additional work or income. Scholarly implications[51] that teaching stability was good for schools in this period was often true but not in this case. Some schools lost boys because of the tendency of the social elite to patronise a few fashionable schools or educate their children at home: but Nuneaton had never had a substantial social elite. Trevis must take his full share of the blame for the decline of the school.

The weakness of the school in Nuneaton at the end of the Trevis period, as well as some other local schools such as Atherstone was well known. It played its part in the establishment of a new Grammar School at Appleby Magna, a few miles over the border in Leicestershire. It started in the 1690s and was endowed by Sir John Moore from his East India Trade profits. An early applicant for the post of Master at Appleby referred to the great potential for the school in view of the fact that *We have very few good schools about us: Repton, Atherston (sic) and Nuneaton are insignificant.*[52] This comment was, revealingly, at the end of the Trevis period (See Appendix Five for the state of Grammar Schools at this time).

12. Trevis' Rearguard Action

Trevis, who had legally won the right to collect the rents personally, was determined to continue to collect them. His *beere* could certainly be afforded. Otherwise he was inactive and his obstruction continued almost to the end. He had devised a rearguard action against any attempt to give him an Usher whose payment would come out of his salary: refusing to sign the relevant document right through the 1680s.[53]

Only as late as 14th Feb 1689 do we have notification from the Bishop's secretary writing from Coventry confirming that the Schoolmaster had finally signed the order authorising the appointment of an Usher.[54] The reason for this belated agreement may have been to

> **The First Usher for over 50 years?**
>
> John Holmes' Licence was to teach the 3Rs having no other way to get a livlihood for him, and his family. According to the clergy database (CCEd) the 48 year old Holmes was licensed to the Grammar School as Usher on 2nd October 1693. He had been noted as a teacher in Coton as early as their special census of 1684 and a Schoolmaster by 1692 (Gooder p.62) with a salary possibly paid by Sir Richard Newdigate. Perhaps he was not paid by Sir Richard by 1693. It is just possible that he was setting up a separate petty school and the record is inaccurate. If on balance we accept Holmes was appointed as King Edward's Usher, he did not last long. The Liptrott family (who provided the next three Masters) did not want an assistant. Holmes may have been used as a stopgap between the incapacity of Trevis and the arrival of Liptrott, possibly just teaching the petties though the word accidence suggests Latin. The irony was that Holmes was named in the disturbances of 1667 as one of the townsmen protesting against the behaviour of Trevis.

confirm that as a good Stuart Royalist Trevis was happy to accept the deposition of the Roman Catholic James II in 1688 and his replacement by the Protestant William of Orange. But even after the long-awaited signature there were further delays.

An Usher was still not appointed in 1693 when there was a petition for the licensing of John Holmes. This was in the form of a Testimonial pointing out that *for many years* he had kept a pettie school (in Chilvers Coton) and had been *laborious*, a complimentary word at this time (see side bar). He was recommended in the usual form of words as of *sober life and conversation* and *of good repute*. He had been *good to many poor children*. He was to *write and teach the Accidence* and instruct on the church catechism. The application was supported by 10 people including vicar Thomas

Wootton and school Governor Dudley Ryder.[55] However, when the Governors considered having a new Charter so they could start afresh, and formally dismiss Trevis at last, they discovered that back in 1688 they had inadvertently failed to make the oaths to the new Monarchs William and Mary and so were technically non-jurors[56] and not validly holding office. Trevis had escaped again. The Corporation had to be dissolved and a new Charter applied for. It was ironic that having – unusually – applied for new Charters in 1553, 1559 and 1604 when it was not really necessary, the King Edward Governors had failed to do so the one time it was essential.

Will of William Trevis. Being of perfect memory. Did his conscience trouble him?

Matters were not fully resolved until 1694. Trevis made his Will in February.[57] Having personally collected the increasingly prosperous rents since 1668 he had plenty to give away. But not a penny went to King Edward's: it was Trinity College, Cambridge who was the object of his munificence with a gift of £50 to its library. It had been over 50 years since he had been ejected but his affection for it had clearly not dimmed. Nor had his bitterness at being removed from his post there, which may go some way to explaining his behaviour. His wife had pre-deceased him[58] and there was no evidence of any children (unless he had fallen out with them which seems perfectly possible). So, after personal bequests amounting to (including Trinity) £132, including £12 for his maid, most of the rest of his considerable estate went to his cousin Robert Simpson, a Norfolk clergyman. Thus church and education both benefited from the Trevis largesse but the beneficiaries (unsurprisingly) were not the Grammar School or St. Nicolas Church Nuneaton. The only reference to Nuneaton which over nearly 40 years had provided him with a total income of something like £2,800 was £3 for the poor of the town. His real legacy had been the near death of the school which was rather more successful both before and (no thanks to him) after his time. By 1694 Trevis appeared too old to resist further change. The new Charter was granted on 18th April[59] and it seems likely John Holmes temporarily took over the Master's responsibilities, such as they were. Trevis died the following year: a new Master was appointed and the re-building of the school planned. A new era in its history was about to begin.

Wren's magnificent Library at Trinity College: Trevis' only worthwhile legacy?

CHAPTER FIVE

Recovery and Consolidation: The Liptrott Era, 1695-1780

No imployment more publickly useful, none more toilsome and painful; yet none more sleighted even to reproach; no one less rewarded or regarded. This a great scandal to the Nation, as certainly as great a grievance (if rightly considered) that no one sort of men are greater sufferers in this kind than Schoolmasters.

Marchamont Nedham *A Discourse Concerning Schools and Schoolmasters* (1663)

Under three members of the Liptrott family the school recovered from the depredations of Trevis. Academic success returned though the benefits were at times felt by Leicestershire gentry rather than Nuneaton artisans. Nor was the era of legal wrangling quite at an end. Nevertheless an Apprentice scheme developed and the school fared better than some in the period when many Grammar Schools were at their lowest ebb. It remained focussed on learning Latin.

1. The New Charter

The new Charter of 1694 differed in some respects from the old; Governors' powers were more clearly laid down. They possessed *Full power and authority to nominate and appoint a Master of the School* and *a sub-master…as often as the number of scholars … shall greatly increase.* Governors in case of a vacancy would *elect and nominate another fit person.*

The immediate benefit to the Governors of the new Charter was therefore absolute control of the revenue and the right of appointment of a Master without legal obligation to obtain the Bishop's approval. Statutes were still to be drawn up *with the advice of the Bishop of Coventry and Lichfield* but no new ones appeared. While the Christian nature of the school was not in doubt, direct interference from church authorities became a thing of the past.

Salaries were re-defined: £60 per annum would be paid to the Master but if a sub-master was appointed, the Master's salary would be reduced to £50 to enable a £10 salary to be paid to his assistant. The £10 figure could be increased *at the Governors pleasure* suggesting the healthy position of the endowment. A *sub-master* was not employed for nearly another 100 years but when one eventually appeared, his payment soon increased considerably, using the discretionary clause. Both teachers were to be *sufficiently learned in the Latin language*, wording the Governors would come to regret later when applying this principle to the sub-master.[1]

Late arrival (2): Translation of the Letters Patent of William and Mary 1694. The Governors initially forgot to apply for a renewal of the Charter after the change of regime in 1688

The endowment could clearly afford these payments and ensure that the Master would continue *to freely teach the boys coming thereto*. Further profits were anticipated even after payment for the upkeep of the school. To this end an apprenticeship scheme was set up for the *placing out or promoting poor boys educated*. This had to wait nearly 100 years for its full implementation in 1788 and we have very few written records of Apprentices until the early19th Century.

The Governors appointed under the new Charter were:

- Antony Trotman Esq.
- Daniel Monk Apothecary
- John Monks Silkman
- Dudley Ryder gent.
- Martin Bailey
- Richard Lucas
- Robert Gilbert
- William Parker Silkman
- William Dudley
- Robert Nutt
- William Hepworth Jnr.
- Thomas Joliffe

all inhabitants of the town and parish of Nuneaton.[2] This suggests five men regarded as of substance and seven thought less so because neither their occupation nor status were given. The town still lacked many gentry or a substantial middle class. Trotman was one of the wealthiest figures in the town and the Ryder family, of Nonconformist background, were soon to make their mark in church and law[3] (see side box). However,

---

People linked with the Grammar School

Antony Trotman and John Ryder.
Antony Trotman, Chairman of the Governors, from 1695, had married into the wealthy Stratford family and owned land in Wolvey. He and his wife Abigail have an elaborate memorial in the parish church.

Dudley Ryder, Governor, was a successful haberdasher in Nuneaton. His Father, a Nonconformist Minister, had been ejected from Bedworth in 1663. Dudley's own son, John Ryder, was born c.1695-7 in Nuneaton and it is possible though not likely that he attended Nuneaton Grammar School between about 1703 and 1708 before going to Charterhouse and then Queen's Cambridge in 1712. The increased reputation of King Edward's under James Liptrott was perhaps not yet high enough for the ambitious Ryders.

Thomas Wootton and John Foxcroft
Wootton was vicar of Nuneaton until 1700 when he was replaced by Foxcroft. It seems that Wootton's son remained at King Edward's to finish his education with James Liptrott and Foxcroft's son completed it on arrival in 1700. Both boys went to St John's College Cambridge. Foxcroft was a well-known low churchman, who one, hostile, person thought *perfectly a Dissenter* (Anonymous letter to the Archbishop of Canterbury quoted in Paterson and Rowney p. 19). Given this and the family background, the first Liptrott's views may well have been similar.

---

this generation of Governors faded into the background and for about 50 years the school ran relatively smoothly without legal confrontations. With the death of Trevis in 1695 it was inevitable there would be a new era at King Edward's. But few would have predicted that for the next 93 years the school's Master would bare the same name: Liptrott.

The Old Grammar School of 1696 pictured in 2009. It was originally larger: both wings were damaged in the bombing of 1941 although one of them was not finally demolished until 1954

School Governors at the time of the building of 1696

2. The First Liptrott: The Restoration Of The School's Reputation; The Re-Building Of The School

The Liptrott story begins with James. Born about 1662 he had attended Jesus College Cambridge as a Pensioner and was recorded as Master at Ormskirk, Lancashire, in 1685. On 10th April 1695 he was licensed to Nuneaton Grammar School. A career schoolmaster, he was not ordained. He remained in Nuneaton until his death in 1712 when his son William replaced him and when in turn William died in 1731, James' younger son Thomas who was only about 24 years old, became the third Liptrott heading the school; he stayed 57 years.[4]

Schoolmasters relocating to a completely different area were relatively uncommon at this time. The reason why the first Liptrott, James, came to Nuneaton was probably the poor fixed salary he had previously received.[5] Only *an exceptional school … succeeded in securing an allocation of land*[6] but Nuneaton had done just that and so the Master's salary offered was more than adequate reflecting the rude health of the Nuneaton landed income. Rents from the lands received back in the 16th Century in the Coventry area – from the Guilds – were proving their worth. Fixed rent charges were increased to cover inflation and the temptation for Governors to save and re-invest additional rental income rather than increase an already reasonable Master's salary, was great. The annual endowment value was approaching £100.

The Governors felt optimistic about affording the cost of re-building and when the new Master arrived, a new Grammar school was constructed, completed in 1696 on the same site as the one built 100 years earlier. It served as the school for the next 184 years and, part of it survives as a building today as offices for St Nicolas Parish Church and Community Centre.[7] Simplistically, the design was a large schoolroom from where the Master, still occupying a raised dais, would control and teach the boys of differing ages. Unlike a century earlier we lack the financial records for this building. However, its overall plan, though larger, is unlikely to have been very different from its predecessor, since the overall aim and nature of a Grammar School education had changed little. There was a second storey probably with a study room for the Master. Brick built, the school had a central tower with cupola. The middle part of the building still stands, though war damage in 1941 and then post-war road-building, resulted in both the east and west wings eventually being removed in the 1950s.[8]

The intention of the building's design was business as usual or rather business as it should

Memorial to Antony and Abigail Trotman: St Nicolas Church 1703

have been had Trevis been doing his job properly. The initial desire after the Restoration was to return to traditional values in education and maintain a classical bias in endowed schools. However, by 1700 writers such as John Locke were beginning to question the heavy classical and grammatical emphasis of a Grammar school education.[9] While a knowledge of Latin was still seen as the language of the educated higher classes it was no longer so vocationally useful. The Church and the law still required it, but both these professions were narrowing rather than widening the social background of their recruits. However, the Liptrott family took the traditional view that classics should still dominate the school curriculum since the ultimate destination for the successful boy was Oxford or Cambridge, often followed by a career in the law or the church. The new building would therefore prove adequate for the time being.

There could be only one direction for the school to go after the disastrous Trevis reign – up. No longer was excessive consumption of alcohol a problem except on 8th December 1698 when a local man, William Lovell, became drunk and broke several school windows.

Liptrott reported it to the Constable. [10] The Liptrotts restored the numbers to the school and re-established its reputation as a Grammar school offering the classics and a chance to enter Oxford and Cambridge. Indeed at its peak in the 1740s it became a school regularly sending boys to Emmanuel College, Cambridge and its reputation was, temporarily, high.

An early sign that James Liptrott had improved the quality of the Grammar School came in 1700 when Sir Richard Newdigate sent his son Francis (known as Frank) to the school. It was an unusual event for a Newdigate to appear at King Edward's. After private tutoring, the family had sent most of their male children to Winchester probably because of the contrasting social status of the schools or possibly because of Trevis' incompetency. Frank Newdigate was already 18, having been to Winchester College for two years 1698-1700 and then trying to start law at Gray's Inn; but Sir Richard had already accused Frank of behaving *basely and disobediently to me* and it was apparent that Winchester had been unable to get him up to the required standard for his legal studies. So, he was sent to Liptrott who succeeded where others had failed.[11]

At school Frank Newdigate would have met Henry Wootton and John Foxcroft, both children of successive vicars of Nuneaton. Sending their sons to the local Grammar School was another vote of confidence in Liptrott. Whereas Newdigate was to study law, Wootton and Foxcroft's sons would follow their fathers into the Church. For both these professions the Latin that a Grammar school could provide was still *de rigeur*. While these pupils may not have been typical, James Liptrott was building up the school from the low base left by Trevis.[12]

The Master's salary of £60 a year, the same as in Trevis' time, was still reasonable compared with most others in the 17th Century.[13] With low numbers initially, Liptrott would not have an Usher to assist him, so he could retain the whole salary. All three successive Liptrotts took the common if legalistic view that a Grammar School meant study of Latin Grammar to prepare for university. That Classical studies should dominate to the exclusion of nearly everything else was increasingly regarded as narrow-minded and it was to cause trouble to the third of the Liptrotts, Thomas, in later years.

3. The Second Liptrott: The Building Of A Master's House

James Liptrott died in 1712 and his son William continued his educational work. Born in 1690 he would have moved to Nuneaton as a child but any record of him attending the Grammar School as his father's pupil is lacking. He went to Brasenose College

Oxford in 1707 and then briefly held a post at Bolton Free Grammar School for a few months in 1712. However, on the death of his Father later in that year he came south to take over at King Edward's. This suggests the Governors had been pleased with the progress under James Liptrott and wanted more of the same. Unlike his father, William Liptrott was ordained when he moved and accepted two livings: the first was as curate at Burton Hastings in 1716 and the second as vicar of Wolvey three years later.[14] Thus developed a trend – of which we had a few hints earlier – of holding at least one living and being Master of Nuneaton Grammar, a feat that three subsequent clerical Masters were also to perform.

The reputation of the school grew. In 1715 a Master's House was finally constructed and William Liptrott had probably taken the post in the knowledge that this would be the case. All but the humblest schools were now providing accommodation.[15] To build the house the Governors withdrew £200 of surplus capital and provided the Master with virtually rent-free accommodation. It cost £250.[16] Building it on the opposite side of the Church began a slight shift in the centre of gravity of the school, but still emphasising its close connection with St. Nicolas. It also continued the delicate property relationship between the two institutions. The substantial double-fronted building was designed in the Queen Anne style and consisted of three storeys. It established the social position of the Master in the town as well as making it possible for boarders to be taken in the future.

The Master's House: built 1715 demolished 1879/80

William Liptrott's children included a son, John, who was later to become a curate at St. Nicolas Church.[17] Many of his pupils came from Leicestershire: around 1715 Thomas Cooper son of John Cooper, Rector of Wyfordby, near Melton Mowbray, attended the school and in 1721 he matriculated at St John's College, Cambridge. Like so many others the ultimate aim was a career in the Church: Thomas became a curate and later Rector of Boothby Pagnall, Leicestershire.[18] Clergymen of modest means would see King Edward's as a good place to prepare their sons for the Church or the law. This meant the possibility of boarders now being taken since there was a house for their accommodation. Western Leicestershire was accessible but not Wyfordby from the other side of the county. However, the previous vicar of Wyfordby had been the man who became vicar of Nuneaton, John Foxcroft.[19] It seems likely that Foxcroft had recommended the school to his successor and told him of the success of **his** son. Cooper junior probably stayed at Nuneaton vicarage adjacent to the school while he was attending. Boarders on a larger scale remained for the future. Still, Foxcroft's probable recommendation is significant: King Edward's was gaining a good reputation, not least in Leicestershire.

4. Thomas Liptrott: The Long Reign 1732-1788: Academic Success

The peak of academic achievement for the grammar school was to come with the third Liptrott, Thomas, born around 1707 and youngest son of James. He was the first Liptrott definitely to attend King Edward's Nuneaton as a pupil, going to Emmanuel College Cambridge as a sizar, matriculating in 1724. Graduating in 1728 he was ordained deacon in 1728, priest in 1731 probably at the minimum age of 24, was briefly curate at Nuneaton parish church and appointed Master in February 1732 on the death of older brother William. [20] In the previous year he had become a fellow of Emmanuel and this link was to be of great value to the school. At this time Oxford and Cambridge were going through something of a trough, with numbers of undergraduates declining but attendance remained essential for degrees. And so for Nuneaton Grammar School the first 20 years of Liptrott's Mastership were to be a golden era of high academic achievement.

Joseph and George Cardale were two pupils whose successes overlapped the Masterships of William and Thomas Liptrott. The father of the two Cardales, also Joseph, was vicar of Bulkington when his boys attended King Edward's and then, additionally, became vicar of Hinckley. The Liptrott/Cardale connection remained strong and this may have helped to develop the link with Leicestershire gentry and clergy that the Liptrotts cultivated, with Cardale possibly recommending Liptrott to his gentry colleagues.[21]In the *fertile valleys of the Wreake and the Soar* many freeholders traditionally entered a son for the Church.[22]

Even more significant was the strong Liptrott link with Cambridge. Henry Hubbard was Tutor at Emmanuel in the mid 18th Century and made a fellow of the College in the same year as Liptrott, 1732. There developed a close bond. Between 1733 and 1767 when Hubbard was in post, Emmanuel took 334 undergraduates and 15 of them were from King Edward VI Nuneaton, the fourth highest total in the country. Only three schools did even slightly better.[23] Ten of the fifteen were preparing for the Church. Of the five others, two sons of gentlemen are not given any occupation. One was admitted at the Inner Temple in 1744 and later became High Sheriff of Leicestershire, one died while at Emmanuel and of the last one we know nothing of except he came from London. Apart from the Liptrotts, all others came from various parts of Leicestershire.[24] (see side panel)

The Cambridge Link: Emmanuel College

Clearly the traditional Latin Grammar was being effectively taught by Thomas Liptrott. There are likely to have been some changes from the style used by previous Nuneaton Masters, Packwood, Barford and Trevis in the 17th Century. Most schools now avoided talking entirely in Latin from the start and later on plays were enacted to vary the methods of learning and to gain the interest of the pupils. Composing flowery orations in Latin had gone out of fashion after an assault from John Milton in his *Tractate on Education*.[25] But we lack evidence of the books used in the 18th Century until its end, by which time Liptrott had gone. Greek must have been taught to achieve Oxbridge entry but of this there is no record.

Nuneaton Grammar School provides (mainly) Leicestershire clergy after they all attended Emmanuel College Cambridge.			
	Matric.	Deacon	Priest
William Major Rector of Laughton 1754	1744	1750	1751
William Middleton Rector of Hathem 1765-1800	1744	1749	1750
John Liptrott Curate of Nuneaton 1750-?1779	1746	1750	1752
Thomas Squire Died 1768 no incumbency given	1747	1752	1754
Isaac Liptrott Vicar of Oadby 1771-92	1747	1751	1753
Isaac Whyley Rector of Witherley 1756-1805	1748	1752	1753
John Levett Rector of Willoughby Waterless 1756	1750	1754	1756
John Ledbrooke Curate of Bosworth 1759-1770	1753	1757?	1759
Samuel Chambers Rector of Higham 1765-1788	1755	1760?	1762?
John Liptrott Rector of Offham 1777-1800	1761	1766	1767

The school remained solidly Anglican; with nephew John Liptrott curate at the parish church from 1750 to 1756 and with 18th century vicars generally non-resident, the relationship with St. Nicolas church had become closer and more harmonious, in contrast to the 17th Century and the tense relationships with vicars such as Butterton and Pyke. This co-operation would continue into the 19th Century with Hugh Hughes doubling as curate of St Nicolas and Master of the Grammar School (see below). The building of the galleries in the church in 1768 and 1790 would have enabled a special place for Grammar School children to sit at Sunday Service.[26]

5. Pupils' Social Background

Examining the Oxbridge successes, four fathers of pupils were classed as gentlemen, six were priests including three different members of the Liptrott family.[27] As in all other ages, parents were ambitious for their children and sometimes had quite specific aims. Family influence could rival (or exceed) educational achievement or natural ability. The case of Isaac Whyley is revealing. He was the son of Peter Whyley, a mercer, who while still in Nuneaton in 1735, when Isaac would have been three years old, purchased the mortgage on the advowson (right of presentation to the living) of Witherley parish for just over £281. To afford this kind of money his business had clearly been successful. By 1748 when son Isaac left King Edward's to go to Emmanuel, Cambridge, Whyley senior had moved to Birmingham, so perhaps wealthy businessmen did not stay in Nuneaton but moved to larger places. In any event, his long term investment in Isaac was to come to fruition in 1756. In that year, four after graduation and three after being priested, young Isaac at the tender age of 26 became Rector of Witherley. The financial efforts of his Father combined with the teaching prowess of Thomas Liptrott had set Isaac up for life. He remained Rector of Witherley until his death forty-nine years later in 1805.[28]

Isaac Whyley: Old Edwardian and Rector of Witherley 1756-1805

Whyley was not alone. John Levett, from the village of Willoughby Waterless, Leicestershire attended King Edward's and Emmanuel College being later presented with the living of his own village and to Great Peatling in 1756, remaining at the latter until 1800. By this time his father had died but his mother Elizabeth retained control of the living. Samuel Chambers would become Rector of Higham in 1765 by the same route – his father being both the previous incumbent and patron.[29]

Without formal registers of names – not available until the mid-19th Century – we cannot be sure how typical these boys were of the intake of the Grammar School. *The boys who attended … grammar schools* [generally speaking] *are quite hard to characterise. There are few substantial records on them, and the best that most schools can do in their histories is to record a few worthies who attended … [but] … they distract one from the much larger unspectacular group being taught.*[30] However, in the case of Nuneaton the size of the *larger unspectacular* group remained restricted, with barely forty in the school. Population totals and age distribution suggest that, as with the country as a whole, barely 5% of children in the town between seven and fourteen attended school.[31]

6. Smith's Charity School And Its Links With The Grammar School

If the poorer classes were attending school at all, it was elsewhere. This was due to the development of Nuneaton's second school, Smith's Charity School, built in 1715 soon after the second Liptrott, William, had been drafted in from the north to be Grammar School Master and took up the reins from the deceased James. This new institution would provide a non-classical elementary education merely consisting of the three Rs. By the terms of the will of Richard Smith in 1712, who was based in London but owned property in the parishes of Nuneaton, Hartshill and Ansley, school pupils were to come from the parish of Nuneaton.[32] Situated between the Market Place and Mill Walk it was later joined by a school serving the closely neighbouring parish of Chilvers Coton. This was the Coton Free School, founded in 1745 by Lady Elizabeth Newdigate. Between them the two schools soon expanded and in due course educated something like 270 children by the late 18th Century.[33] The significance of Smith's school for the Grammar School was that it reduced the pressure for the Liptrotts to respond to the growing demand for elementary education.

However, Smith's Charity School deserves a place in the history of the Grammar school for other reasons; the two institutions were linked. Smith's School had seven Trustees to be chosen out of the Trustee Governors of King Edward VI Grammar School *if they shall be willing to accept the said trust … and shall be living in the said town.*[34] The two schools were meant to complement one another.

The close link in terms of Trustee personnel – if not in the curriculum or the social class of those attending – was eventually to be of later significance for King Edward's. 180 years after Smith's was founded its endowment was combined with that of the Grammar School making further expansion financially viable. (see below, Chapter Nine and Appendix Six.)

Smith's school was intended for *poor* children. At its widest this could embrace all those who could not afford to pay for University entrance (the vast majority).[35] But it is doubtful whether it included all the *middling* sort between potential Oxbridge students and those who could only afford to go to school for a year or so before going out to work to supplement the family income. Despite their considerable numbers it seems that few of the Smith's schoolchildren ever moved on to the Grammar School. In the 1750s – the first decade for which fuller records exist at Smith's – ten to fifteen children entered that school each year. Some only stayed a year or two and at most five. Starting at about seven years they had usually left by eleven.[36] This was the time when Liptrott was still recruiting from Leicestershire gentry and when few families of this kind of social status resided in the parish of Nuneaton. Moreover the local enclosure of fields from the 1730s onwards meant small freeholders and tenant farmers who might have patronised King Edward's were less well off and demanded that their children started work early. In the 1750s there was rioting over the price of corn, a sure sign of economic difficulty and there was much social tension in the town.[37]

7. What Kind Of Scholar Should Attend The Grammar School?

From the 1730s onwards Thomas Liptrott wanted to retain the Grammar School as a traditional centre for the study of the classics. In order to achieve this he needed to expand his catchment area by recruiting from Leicestershire. Richard S. Tompson concisely expressed the problem in his writings as *Classics or Charity.*[38] He suggested that apart from converting to a fee making institution (probably with boarders) – which would go against the legally expressed wishes of the founder and any charter – the main alternative for Latin bound Grammar Schools in small places such as Nuneaton was to change to non-classical subjects, also subject to legal difficulties. The way round the problem would be to charge for other subjects while retaining the free classical teaching. This would be legal, but in the past many of the families who would want this sort of education were unable or unwilling to pay. Offering free instruction in Latin to the better off while the poorer classes paid for their education probably even struck contemporaries as odd; but this could be the case since the income from many schools' endowments was insufficiently large to offer everything free. In Nuneaton, however, with a healthy endowment and a growing population[39] the Governors decided to add free non-classical subjects thus altering the original charity. In Liptrott's time there is no evidence that anyone challenged the change. In practice *What determined a school's status* [in the late 18th century] *was not what was legal but what its prospective parents would tolerate.* [40] (See Appendix Eight)

By the mid 18th Century Nuneaton Governors argued that there was a middle class market for a non-classical education. They could attract a group consisting of smaller manufacturers and better off artisans; these were placed socially below the Leicestershire gentry but above the working class of labouring families that dominated the intake of Smith's. The Governors were concerned with how the school should develop and the desirability of attracting a wider clientele at a time when many other Governing bodies showed little sign of adapting to social change; even progressive Ashby Grammar School was guilty of excessive caution.[41] Liptrott, though, was uninterested in a less academic intake for two possible reasons: he preferred the classical high flyers or doubted the strength of the middling social group in Nuneaton. While the first seems more likely it is true that the growing desire for elementary education for children of the middling sort was less apparent in Nuneaton than in some other places.

The town itself was experiencing social change. On this point the comments of Lord Mansfield at the time of his Legal Judgement concerning the Grammar School in 1756 (see below for details of the case) are quite revealing. Nuneaton was losing its agricultural and small trade emphasis. This was partly triggered by the enclosure of land from the 1730s onwards. As Mansfield put it with the detached but clearly informed knowledge of the interested outsider: *Since the Enclosure of the Open Fields in 1731 the mass of the inhabitants are manufacturers of tanning, ribbons and hosiery in which their children are employed.* This often meant they wanted their children to start working in the trade as early as possible especially if the family was poor. These were precisely the kind of children meant to attend Smith's charity and they certainly did not receive sufficient education to have any chance of moving on to the Grammar School. Child labour meant very young children or as Mansfield again expressed the point of view of the small-scale employers in the ribbon trade: *They cannot afford to give wages to sons of a more advanced age.*[42] Where was the growing middle class here? The aim of Smith's Charity school was apparent but the Grammar School's function appeared less clear cut; *Charity schools were training poor children for a specific status in society and for specific occupations while endowed schools were struggling to reconcile their roles as providers of basic literacy and of a higher education in a classical tradition.*[43]

A Charity School of the 18th Century

The question persisted as to how far Grammar Schools should offer advanced education outside the classics. Liptrott was reluctant to do so but Governors disagreed and were keen to change the nature of the school. This brought about another legal squabble between Master and Governors, though less fully documented than those in earlier times. Governors (sometimes now referred to as Trustees) had control over any amendment of the school statutes, control of admissions and rules on curriculum. In contrast, the Master's security of tenure seemed absolute, barring serious misdemeanours. So Liptrott's insistence on his own interpretation of the way the school should be run was likely to lead to difficulties.

8. Another Salary Dispute

Despite the success of the school in the 1740s, the bad old days of legal action and Governor/Master quarrels were not over. Ironically, disputes arose over the amount of Thomas Liptrott's salary because of the school's success. In 1747 Liptrott's payment had remained unchanged since the days of his elder brother and father at £60 per annum.[44] The salary had been relatively high compared with other Endowed Grammar Schools in Trevis' time but was now merely average, although the school's investments continued to do well. In the same year £8 was paid to one William Smith to set up *a boy of John Buswick's* for an apprenticeship.[45] It was these sorts of payments to Apprentices, some of which he thought unwise, that made Liptrott feel he could take some of the extra endowment money for an increased salary in view of his narrow-ranging but clear success.[46]

Liptrott's temper over the question of salary may not have been improved by the Governors' profligate expenses claims. In 1769 the pre Christmas claim made on Dec. 21 included dinner with Liquor costing £1 19/4d and Servants £3 6/4d.[47] This is likely to have covered a good deal of the year but was still a substantial sum. In 1771 Robert Beard charged Governors as follows:[48]

Date	Food	Drink
April 1771	1/-	8/8d
July 1771		4/-
Oct. 1771	4/-	10/2d

The first inkling of further legal disputes between Master and Governors comes from 1744. Liptrott – with support from townsmen – commenced a suit against the Governors (and the Bishop) for failing to increase his salary. Doubtless aware of the successful legal precedents in the 17th Century he asked for surpluses rumoured to be as large as £600 to be *applied for the benefit of the Master* as well as *in repair of School House, the Master's House and in placing out poor boys taught in school* which is where all the surplus had been applied in the past. Within a few months the Governors had lodged a cross bill *praying* against the Master.[49]

The Lord Chancellor, Earl Hardwicke, eventually heard the case on the 4th March 1747. He found in favour of the Governors, ruling that revenues were clearly determined by the Charter of William and Mary at £60 a year (or £50 a year with Usher) whatever the profits of the endowment. Any surplus money would go to repairs or in payment of the ground rent to the church of 12/9d per annum.[50] Improving the Master's House fell into the same category as improving the school. Having been bitten by Trevis and, earlier, Reay and Inge, the Governors had got what they wanted by their tactic back in 1694 of structuring their William and Mary Charter so that it was more carefully weighted in their favour than that of the Master, whose salary was fixed.

9. The Dispute Widens

Liptrott had wished for any investment surplus to be added to his salary. In contrast, once the finances had recovered from the expenses of the construction of the Master's House in 1715, the Governors intended to spend this surplus by developing the apprenticeship scheme established by the Charter of 1694. So the dispute over salary increase was linked to the question already much debated, that is what kind of school should there be in Nuneaton? Liptrott still insisted on a traditional Grammar School and since he had been successful in his tuition his approach was unsurprising. Few teachers in the 18th century were likely to have radical educational views, since, successful products of the old system themselves, they would find adaptation to new subjects difficult. While one could apply this argument to any age it was particularly true of the 18th Century. At that time reforming Masters had to cope with all the implications of radical alteration themselves. There was no pressure to change from the state, who kept out of such matters, and no large staff of other teachers who could be asked to assist with new subjects and bear the brunt of innovation. The system encouraged conservatism. Moreover, fewer people were now leaving endowments to Grammar Schools. Charitable giving for elementary schools for the poor such as Smith's Charity took prominence. The Governors' view was different from Liptrott's. They wished to attract a wider clientele and develop the apprentice side of the establishment, and so differences between Governor and Master did not remain confined to salary.

The idea of Latin being vital for a good education was being challenged more and more widely. Many professions now used the vernacular and the numbers still requiring the language were shrinking. Daniel Defoe remarked that *Reading in English may do for you all you want*. John Locke's view was gaining influence; parental attitudes were narrow-minded if they believed that their children had *scarce an orthodox education unless they learned Lilley's* [sic] *Grammar.* [51]

Latin might still be defended as a good part of a liberal education and an indirect aid to good English but this counted for less in the new utilitarian world of the later 18th and early 19th Century. Some questioned the emphasis on Latin even for a liberal education. There was too much memory work and, if Greek was included, an excessive amount of time could be spent on just these two subjects which were needed to an advanced level only by a handful of boys. As reforming educationalist, scientist and Dissenting Minister Joseph Priestley argued, *it can never be worthwhile to torment a hundred boys while making Latin verses for the sake of perhaps one of them.*[52]

The greater interest in banking, insurance and manufacturing resulted in increased support for a more vocational type of education for their children. *Men were bent over ledger books now more often than Bibles.* But even if Masters were prepared to co-operate with what we would now call curriculum change, the restrictive wording of many Grammar School foundations could throw up legal difficulties with respect to radical changes in the organization and curriculum of the school.

As the 18th Century progressed it became easier to set up a Dissenting Academy (or a non-denominational private school) in opposition to an endowed school. You no longer had to obtain a licence or run the risk of prosecution. But since there was no school of this kind in Nuneaton the Governors were keener than Liptrott to introduce modern subjects, and the supposed legal restrictions had stopped some schools elsewhere from doing just this.[53]

By the 1740s Thomas Liptrott had begun to refuse to accept boys who were only likely to stay a short time and therefore not benefit from his successful academic enterprise. He expected parents to guarantee that when boys were enrolled at the school they would promise to stay a minimum number of years. More legal argument developed as to whether this tactic was legitimate; could the Master insist on terms for accepting boys? Legal discussions began as early as 1744[54] though the final judgement was not delivered until 1756 by Lord Mansfield, the newly appointed Lord Chief Justice.

10. The Mansfield Judgement

The governors wanted Liptrott to do two things, namely take all comers into the school and accept the Apprenticeship system. On these two points Lord Mansfield found clearly for the Governors, further confirming the interpretation of the William and Mary Charter.

The case came down to three questions.

Firstly, did the boys have to stay a set time and attain a *certain degree of grammatical or classical learning*? Mansfield examined Liptrott's attitude: *And on the parents refusing to enter into such engagements* [to stay a stated minimum length of time] *he has refused to teach them.* He found against Liptrott on this point. There was no fixed length of stay or degree of literacy required.

Secondly, had the Governors *a discretionary power of advancing children of poor inhabitants* by giving or loaning a proper sum to begin trade with? (Apprenticeships) Mansfield said yes, again siding with the Governors.

Thirdly, Could the Master be sacked for refusing to take pupils? Here Mansfield found for the Master. The Governors had overreached themselves and could not dismiss him.[55] So Liptrott had to admit boys without insisting on any terms but his actual position was secure. There was a potential deadlock.

Even with a Charter that was phrased in a more favourable way for the Governors they still could not remove a Master with ease. Any chance of removing Liptrott would have to be made on entirely different grounds from the previous attack on Trevis. Neither Liptrott's behaviour nor his competence were in question. It was the Governors who were the innovators, wanting the Grammar School to evolve from a narrowly classics-based system of a traditional variety to one which catered for the ordinary sons of the trades people of the town. Liptrott felt the school could not do both but after Mansfield found generally against him on this point he reluctantly accepted the continuation of the Apprenticeship scheme. However, as he got older academic successes dwindled, at least in terms of Oxford and Cambridge admissions. Perhaps the legal battles caused him to lose heart and the taking of Apprentice children diverted his energies. Accepting an Usher would mean a pay cut for him; whether or not this was the reason for his opposition, no Usher was appointed until Liptrott finished teaching at the school.

11. Apprenticeships

It is unclear whether Liptrott took many Apprentices. Records at this time do not survive and the relevant document was not sealed until 1806.[56] So whether a properly organised Apprentice scheme was implemented before 1788, when Liptrott ceased to be Master, is uncertain: but it is clear that he preferred his classical scholars. The Governors' order concerning Apprenticeships, issued on 13th Feb 1788, tightened up what had become a rather casual and lax system. This is indicated first by the precise registration arrangements which do suggest previous activity: *that every application for money to put out apprentice any boy educated at the Grammar School be in writing signifying the name place of abode and trade of the person to whom such boy is intended to be bound apprentice and be delivered to one of the Receivers of the Revenues of the said society* [in effect one of the Governors] … *on or before the 21st day of December in every year.* There were also the time restrictions: *that in future no boy shall be admitted into the school nor any other be put out an Apprentice but at one of our Annual meetings, St Thomas' day* [July 3rd] *and Old Candlemas* [14th February], *and that no person need apply but in those days of our meeting.*[57]

Thomas Liptrott's rural retreat: St James, Weddington

12. Liptrott's Later Years

Thomas Liptrott, born in Lancashire but coming to Nuneaton as a child, put down roots in the area. He married Elizabeth Adderley, sister of Humphrey Adderley of Weddington Castle. There were no surviving children of the marriage but the Liptrotts inherited Weddington Castle from Adderley in 1753.[58] In 1740 he had acquired the living of Weddington presented to him by his brother-in-law and in 1762 Fenny Drayton (almost adjacent but in the next diocese) confirming the trend to hold livings as well as the Mastership. Thomas Liptrott moved at ease with the local gentry of the day and his nephew John (son of the previous Master, James) continued the link with Leicester gentry by becoming Rector of Broughton Astley.[59] Yet there is no evidence he ever established very warm relations with Nuneaton's town elite despite the fact that the Grammar School must have taken up more of his time than clerical duties in two villages, one very small.

In his legal verdict, Lord Mansfield had indicated that Liptrott could only be removed on the grounds the Governors were seeking if they changed the regulations, that is submitted an application for yet another Charter. There is evidence they made the attempt, though it was not successful. An isolated fragment of evidence exists in a letter from 1763:

Governor Joseph Warden wrote: (probably to Liptrott) *Your letter did not a little surprise me especially your specific promise of no longer [sic] shall come?... Our own intentions are peaceable... Why can't we settle without going into Chancery?...* [torn/illegible] *Saving a great deal of money.*[60] While neither the meaning nor the recipient is totally clear it seems likely that high tension remained between Governor and Master.

By 1764 the Governors wanted new powers *for the more extensive application of their charity estates.*[61] As before, some of the surplus money was being spent on yet more litigation. Things moved slowly as did much English law in the 18th Century. The documents are again incomplete. A Mr. Green (apparently representing the school), had called on a Mr. Dudley (probably a lawyer) employing him to get a new Charter. But Green was now uncertain whether Dudley still had the relevant materials. They seem to have been lost.[62] The confusing business dragged on. *Mr Green has the Charter. We want to have this business immediately settled. Lose no time.*[63] But in the end the attempt appears to have been abandoned and Liptrott continued as Master.

By 1780 Liptrott, now into his seventies, was determined to use the law to hang on to office and teach the Classics. The Governors remained equally insistent on developing the school in wider ways, extend the range of subjects, develop the apprenticeship scheme and employ an Undermaster.[64] The scene was set for another Master/Governor struggle.

CHAPTER SIX

Reform Begins: The School Introduces Modern Subjects, 1780-1846

A headmaster, toothless dim-eyed and deaf, whose erudite indistinctness and inattention were engrossed by them at the rate of three-hundred pounds a-head – a ripe scholar doubtless, when first appointed
George Eliot The Mill on the Floss 1860

This period was a time of economic and political ferment in the country as a whole. Nuneaton, having undergone an increase in population, had developed as a comparatively small town with a ribbon weaving emphasis. The Grammar School – like so many in the country – remained legally tied to the wishes of the Founder both in terms of curriculum and finance though this did not prevent what we would now term curriculum innovation thanks to the efforts of Undermaster Benjamin Rayner. The quality of Masters varied but at times inertia set in. Only in the mid-nineteenth century did the serious process of radical educational change begin.

1. Liptrott: A Messy End

By 1770 and now into his sixties Thomas Liptrott required a curate to help him with his clerical duties in one of his two parishes, Fenny Drayton, and by 1783, even the tiny parish of Weddington where he resided.[1] In the 1780s he sold off his Nuneaton properties, planning for the inevitable time when he would no longer be physically capable of doing the job at the school. In October 1785 Liptrott sold *four houses* (formerly three houses and a shop) *on the west side of Church Street, Nuneaton, and certain rights of way, for £160, to Thomas Bacon of Nuneaton, silkweaver*. Two months later he sold *four dwelling houses on the west side of Church Street, Nuneaton, to William Mitchell of Nuneaton, wheelwright, for £145*.[2]

The days of academic success for his pupils at Emmanuel, Cambridge, were over. Around 1780, old Edwardian Isaac Whyley, still Vicar at Witherley, decided to send his son to Rugby rather than Nuneaton, an indicator of the reversing fortunes of the two schools. Liptrott was finding it difficult if not impossible to do his work but unwilling to quit his post and the salary. The Governors responded; the Charter was brought out and dusted down again. In July 1786 an account with Mr. John Burton for the Charter of William and Mary included carriage of 3/-. Mr Edmonds (of the Examiners Office) was paid a total of £3-5/- for translating a copy and £6 12/6d was spent on translating and porterage.[3] The records are incomplete. The Charter may have been bound for London. A final dispute between the Governors and Liptrott was imminent.

In 1788, with Liptrott over 80, the Governors appointed an Undermaster for the first time in living memory, Thomas Trusswell. This was a prelude to replacing Liptrott with both a Master and an Undermaster (as Ushers were now called). Trusswell had to agree to resign *when thereto required with 6 months notice*.[4] The Governors were moving back to appointments at their *will and pleasure*. This restriction on Trusswell's tenure was influenced by the difficulties the Governors were having with Liptrott who refused to retire formally and thus lose his Master's salary. On the question of the freehold nature of his post, his legal position was strong.

On 12th May 1789 Liptrott left the Master's House quitting his post *without leave* as the Governors put it, moving into Weddington Rectory, but he refused to relinquish his right to the Master's salary. The Governors decided he had effectively resigned and on 16th May 1789 Liptrott received £75, this being his usual salary of £60 to Lady Day (25th March) and then seven weeks until mid May. The Governors refused to pay further salary on the not unreasonable grounds that Liptrott was not in post. However, around Lady Day 1791 Liptrott commenced an action against the Governors for non-payment of his salary for the past two years.[5] Moreover he had either leased or presented (the wording is unclear) the School House to Weddington farmer and grazier John Beet[6] and never again attended the school. Governors took legal advice and to their undoubted dismay were told that *they must pay his full salary as he was Master of the School he was entitled to said right*. This was because *although desertion of the school might be a good ground for the application to remove him from the office of master it would not justify the Governors from stopping his salary*.[7]

The previous legal cases, unwisely undertaken by the Governors, were now coming back to haunt them. They had resulted in clearly stated rights for the Master: he was virtually irremoveable. The outcome of the dispute is uncertain but the Governors apparently decided to accept the advice. We lack evidence that Liptrott continued to be paid or whether farmer Beet stayed in the School House, but for a further three years Undermaster Trusswell coped with teaching single-handed. There is no evidence that any legal case ever found for or against Liptrott – he may have been just too infirm to continue the struggle and no longer claimed the salary which he hardly needed.

Trusswell was a local figure of some importance well before he became Undermaster. Both he and Liptrott had patronised the Nuneaton musician Joseph Key, subscribing to the first publication of Key's music in 1774.[8] Trusswell now had charge of the school though his salary and what he taught is uncertain: a new Master was not appointed until 1794. Trusswell continued as Undermaster until his death in 1801 when he was replaced first by William Green, who died the following year, and then by Benjamin Rayner in 1802.[9]

At the end of his life Liptrott was confined to barracks. At the start of 1797 lawyer George Greenway had to *attend him* to discuss the business of Smith's Charity School of which Liptrott remained as Trustee.[10] Later that year Liptrott, still the incumbent of his two parishes, died in Weddington aged 90.[11] Time had solved the problem with the Governors who now made preparations for the post Liptrott era. It was more than a century since Thomas' father had first taken charge of the school.

Liptrott's long tenure of the post of Master had come to an inglorious end. He may have seemed narrow-minded educationally in focussing on Latin Grammar, recruiting the Leicestershire gentry and apparently ignoring local talent. However, in the long run, this may have contributed to the survival of the Grammar School in Nuneaton. In many small towns a lack of demand, a poor endowment and an indifferent Master had seen some endowed Grammar schools became petty or elementary schools. Latin was now seen as even less relevant for a growing range of occupations though the law and church were still demanding it. Over the country as a whole however, by the end of Liptrott's time the teaching of Latin was proving hard to dislodge. It was still seen as the international language of learning for scholars and necessary for a truly rounded education for gentlemen with any cultural pretensions. The appointment of John Spencer Cobbold in 1794 shows that the Nuneaton Governors did not want to abandon entirely the concept of a traditional Grammar School with Latin as a central subject.

2. Cobbold: A New Master

Son of a clergyman from Suffolk, Cobbold had graduated from Cambridge in 1790 where he had won prizes for his writing at his College, Gonville and Caius.[12] He was then a fellow of the College until 1798, overlapping with his King Edward appointment and only relinquishing the post – as was customary – on his marriage. But he also decided to leave King Edward's soon after his nuptials and hitched his star to his father, becoming his curate at first Wilby and then Woolpit, both in Suffolk, succeeding him as Rector in the latter parish where he remained until his death in 1837. He had taught at the Perse School, Cambridge for a year before coming to Nuneaton and his classical and intellectual credentials could hardly be doubted. In the tradition of the time he was a pluralist non-resident clergyman being vicar of the tiny Suffolk village of Shelland from 1793, the year in which he published an essay on *Immortality*. This was followed in 1798 by another essay this time on *Revelation* (of the general kind rather than the Book in the Bible).[13]

Academic success for the school began to return. William Harrington came from Long Melford, Suffolk and after a time at Linton school Cambridge, attended Nuneaton Grammar.[14] Instead of Leicestershire gentry it seemed momentarily as if the school was starting to provide a classical education for Suffolk gentry. The Cobbold link to Suffolk had brought young Harrington to Nuneaton. He was admitted pensioner at Sidney Sussex, Cambridge, in 1802.

Cobbold's religious views were broadly mainstream of the cool and intellectual Anglican variety, in his writings rejecting the kind of Calvinistic doctrines held by Nuneaton Schoolmaster Josiah Packwood back in the early 17th Century, ideas which were attempting a comeback in some quarters of the Church of England. Thus Cobbold adds to the wide range of outlooks held by King Edward's Masters over the years.[15]

3. Hugh Hughes And The Decline Of Latin: Nuneaton Changes: Boarders Arrive

The high academic standards of the Liptrotts were to remain in rather muted form under Cobbold's successor, Hugh Hughes. Like the Liptrotts, Hughes was an outsider who made Nuneaton his own. Son of Edward Hughes of Llangollen, Denbighshire he was born in 1755 and did not attend Jesus College Oxford until he was 21 in 1776. However, he was already ordained deacon by 1778 while still a student at Oxford and yet to gain his BA.[16] In 1779 at the age of twenty-four he was appointed curate at St.

Nicolas Church, Nuneaton when Thomas Liptrott was still head of the Grammar School. Here Hughes performed the regular church duties for three largely absentee vicars, Thomas Edwards (to 1783) George Champagne and (after 1803) Richard Bruce Stopford.[17]

Hugh and Sarah Hughes memorial tablet: St. Nicolas Church

There is no evidence he was teaching in the Grammar School in Liptrott's final decade; neither does he appear to have been involved in the era of Trusswell or Cobbold. However, in 1799 on the departure of Cobbold, Hughes added the Mastership of the Grammar school to his other portfolios. By this time he had also inherited the family post of Vicar of Hardwick in Northamptonshire, though only in the sense of taking the revenues from this position. Nuneaton had another clerical teacher and a pluralist at that. In the past, young clergy usually became Schoolmasters first and only then sought curacies and subsequently a benefice; but in the case of Hugh Hughes it was the other way around. He later became vicar of nearby Wolvey in 1816,[18] presented to the living by Prebendary Samuel Butler. Hughes' son Thomas Smart Hughes had been an outstanding scholar of Butler's at Shrewsbury School and with Butler holding the control of the living of Wolvey,[19] this may explain his father's appointment. However, Hughes the elder's activities were focused on Nuneaton. He was the first Master to accept regular boarders[20] (on more than an individual or occasional basis) an increasingly common development in Grammar Schools. In small places like Nuneaton, successful Grammar schools were generally those where *The Master had succeeded in attracting boarders, and sometimes paying day pupils in addition to the local boys, who were entitled to claim a free education or education at very low charges.*[21] For Masters with increasing opposition from private schools but little chance of an increase in salary, this proved a popular option.

Hughes would have charged boarders a fee but most other pupils received more of an elementary education free of charge paid by the endowment income. For the commercial and manufacturing classes there was some lingering consideration of the value of a liberal education which taught *mental habits of analysis and discrimination*[22] but the main emphasis was on a vocational one which would equip their sons – and it was still just sons rather than daughters – for the growing opportunities in the commercial and industrial world of the coming century. The population of Nuneaton parish had increased from an estimated 1,867 in 1670 to approximately 2,500 by 1740 and 3,500 by 1801.[23] Ribbon weaving had continued to develop and many would enter this occupation at a young age with only a limited desire, if any, for schooling. Other parents, however, may have harboured wider ambitions for their sons looking for a more extended –though not classical – education, possibly culminating in an apprenticeship.

Hughes agreed to accept the assistance of an Undermaster who would take the larger numbers of *lower school* pupils at the other end of the same schoolroom. He would also take boarders whose presence could add to his income. There were alterations to the Master's House costing £250 to accommodate these pupils.[24] Any profits from their payments for maintenance would go directly to Hughes who received £50 a year as curate of St. Nicolas and another £50 as Master. This figure remained unaltered as late as 1815 with school monies also going to Benjamin Rayner as Undermaster.[25]

4. Financial Relations Between Hughes And Rayner

As soon as he took the post in 1799, Hughes farmed out some of his boarders to the School Undermaster for the more elementary subjects, paying him a guinea for each pupil he took. However, when Rayner arrived in 1802 and continued this arrangement, Hughes failed to pay him his due, holding on to any fees parents paid. In practice Rayner taught most of the pupils including some of the boarders. When Rayner complained, he was in a strong position morally but a weak one legally, since the 1694 Charter had acknowledged a separate annual payment for an Usher – but only £10. However, all sides seemed anxious to settle.

The days of legal challenges were not to be resumed. The Governors sorted it out by paying Undermaster Rayner an additional £10, Hughes retaining all his income.[26] Hughes had defended his position and was not prepared to lose any of his salary as *When he was appointed Latin Master he certainly was informed what he was to receive per annum* and would not see it go to someone teaching something else. But he *does candidly acknowledge* [Mr. Rayner has] *done his duty as far as was in his power.*[27] Hughes use of the phrase *Latin Master* makes clear his interpretation of the role: he is there to teach the classics to whoever requires it but not to run the school or teach the majority of boys. One would hardly classify him as a Headmaster but for the fact he occupied the Master's House and took the Master's salary.

The solution of paying extra money to Rayner indicated the financial health of the endowments; the extra figure could easily be afforded and Rayner did valuable work on a small salary. But the Governors also wished to retain the services of Hughes, and not only for his teaching competence. He knew his Latin and just teaching this to a few boys would guarantee the Grammar School status. Equally significant, however, was his willingness to stay on his limited salary and not request more payment. This was because of his more than adequate income from several other sources namely boarders, several ecclesiastical livings, his near rent free occupation of the Master's House with repairs thrown in, and income from mortgages he had arranged.[28] The result was that even this somewhat avaricious man was content with his Master's annual salary remaining at £50, quite a small figure by 1830.[29]

George Eliot has a portrait of Hughes in *Janet's Repentance* from *Scenes of Clerical Life,* where he appears as *old Mr. Crewe the curate in a Brown Brutus wig preaching inaudible sermons on a Sunday*. This was a fictional description written in 1857 recalling the author's childhood in the late 1820s but – where it can be compared with the historical record –it was an accurate picture of Hughes near the end of his life.[30]

Historian as well as great novelist? George Eliot statue by John Letts, Nuneaton town Centre

5. The Law, The Classics And Educational Reform

Legal complications had made it difficult for Grammar Schools to change their curriculum in the past.[31] Wishes of founders such as John Leeke were seen as legally binding and the principle of *cy pres* had been upheld; that is that the desires of the Founder and the phrasing of the original Charter should be honoured as closely as was practically possible: this often meant a curriculum legally restricted to classics. Any challenges were cumbersome, slow and expensive through the Court of Chancery. Some Governors and Trustees of schools encouraged the development of a partially separate school with a different range of subjects. Many children, who started attending at about 8 years old, would leave after two or three years, though a few, who it was felt showed the necessary aptitude, might then move on into the Upper (Grammar or Latin) School. This is what happened in Nuneaton. Through much of Hughes' period as Master there was little change in Grammar schools elsewhere and Nuneaton's approach was not unusual. The effect of the blocking of legal changes to the curriculum in the case of Leeds Grammar School, (which wished to teach non-classical subjects) adjudicated upon by Lord Chancellor Eldon in 1806 may now be considered by historians to have been exaggerated[32] but it can hardly be seen to have encouraged Grammar School reform.

Yet if classical studies were stagnating, many schools including Nuneaton were introducing new subjects by common consent of pupils, teachers, townsfolk and Governors. Some of this may have been technically illegal but Chancery would not interfere in the absence of complaint. When change did come it was slow. Many of the efforts to effect reform over the country were isolated and disconnected. Here Benjamin Rayner's contribution to the survival of the Grammar School in Nuneaton was highly significant. A completely separate school did not develop but Rayner was in charge of his own larger section of King Edward's.

6. Rayner Saves The Day

More than anyone it was Benjamin Rayner who widened the range of subjects taught in Nuneaton's Grammar School. Rayner was paid in his own right a salary of £45 a year,[33] and not, as before, a pittance out of a substantial Master's salary. This reflected the amount of work he was doing, teaching more boys than Hughes; only propriety kept his salary below that of his Headmaster. He undertook a good deal of the administration of the school, his name appearing on many of the Bills and receipts that have haphazardly survived.[34] Like Liptrott, Rayner's role in keeping the school going was a vital one though for different reasons: he maintained a good standard of elementary education in the town when there was little other opportunity for it, kept numbers up and provided the administration that Hughes was unable or unwilling to do. Rayner's other interests, owning three public houses and land in both Staffordshire and Nuneaton,[35] seem to have been secondary.

The range of books in the school increased and Rayner introduced new subjects. With only a few studying Latin there was a larger number of petties, requiring in some cases a little more than an elementary education in order to gain their apprenticeship. So, the healthy state of the finances allowed some purchases. Accounts for 10th February 1810 show history and geography being taught.[36] Traditionally, these areas had been worked in with classical studies but now they were increasingly taking their place as separate subjects at a more elementary level. Some interest in *natural philosophy* (science) was being shown if only at a simple and theoretical level. Prizes awarded included Richard Turner's *Easy Introduction to the arts and sciences being a short but comprehensive system of useful and polite lessons divided into lessons.* This ran into 16 editions by 1814 and was being used to impart a liberal education: the book quoted approvingly from the Latin writer Ovid: *To have learned the liberal arts thoroughly softens the manners and operates as an excellent corrector of ill nature envy and anger.*

Another prize was Bowditch's *Navigation,* officially named *The New American Practical Navigator.*[37] This book, first published in 1799, was updated and reprinted and after 1802 was referred to by its author/reviser as simply *Bowditch.* An American volume, it introduced students to the foundations of modern maritime navigation, showing how much the school was widening its curriculum and was not tied just to the old classical foundation. The contrast between the traditional Hughes with his Latin and his wig, and pub owner Rayner and his new books was marked. More traditionally, Blair's Grammar was probably Hugh Blair's *Letters on Rhetoric* first published in 1783 often attached in summary form to school grammar books from the 1790s and designed to impart polish and style to written prose. One can conclude that the school was an interesting mixture of the traditional and the contemporary.

While Nuneaton's modern curriculum took place at an elementary level some academies and private schools went further, introducing surveying, hydraulics, optics and architecture. In the 18th Century *the curriculum should not be viewed as stagnant or decadent.*[38] By 1818 120/500 schools were teaching *a variety of subjects,* a further 56 *English* subjects only; some 80 more allowed a choice of curriculum.[39] Nevertheless it is clear that what happened at Nuneaton was not uncommon.[40] A school with two major drawbacks, an ageing Master and an ageing Latin course, might well have disappeared without the efforts of Rayner.

The Hughes /Rayner partnership ran from 1802 to 1830 but Hughes' traditional Latin pupils fell away in his advancing years. Boarder numbers also declined and Nuneaton was afflicted with a common problem in the country's endowed Grammar Schools, Masters going on beyond their years of competence into an inactive old age. This had happened in the case of Thomas Liptrott and also William Trevis, though truth to tell Trevis had been little better in his youth. Hughes continued to pay attention to his clerical duties in a formal sense – he officiated at the vast majority of baptisms, marriages and deaths in St. Nicolas parish for over 50 years from 1779 to 1830. But how much else he did is questionable and the school was run more and more by Rayner.

A national school survey of 1818 shows that in Nuneaton the *Eton Grammar*[41] was used and there were 40-50 students on average on the *Foundation*, plus 10-20 others (boarders). Rayner, termed a *Second Master*, officially teaching only *English and Art*, took 40-50; but Hughes did not take all the rest since he paid Rayner to teach approximately ten boarders, leaving only a handful for himself. George Eliot's superficially fictional observations of around 1828/9 (when Hughes was over 70) that Hughes taught just two or three boys seems plausible.[42]

The Grammar School was close to becoming an elementary school as Rayner efficiently coped single-handed with up to 50 or even 60 boys at a time, taking pupils at around eight to nine years of age who stayed for 3-5 years. Each year some were put out to apprentice though not usually more than one or two out of about ten. But Rayner is another figure in the history of King Edward's who, in a very different way from Liptrott, helped it to survive. His efforts prevented the complete demise of the school which did happen in places of similar size to Nuneaton where the Master was, like Hughes, old and losing interest but where there was no efficient Undermaster such as Rayner. The decline of a school because of the old age, not to say decrepitude, of its Master whose security of tenure made dismissal nigh on impossible was a particularly acute problem at this time in Grammar Schools. [43]

Neither did Governors appear to take any great interest. In 1871 the Nuneaton Chronicle retrospectively asserted of Smith's Charity School that *The affairs of this charity were greatly neglected prior to 1823*. This was probably also true of the Grammar School because of the large Governor overlap. A sum of £19-10/3d received by Governor John Burton in 1815 was *lost by his insolvency* but in a complex case there was *no imputation of negligence* on the part of the other Governors.[44] For legal matters they dealt with the local lawyers Greenaway and Buchanan.[45] The tradition of an Annual Dinner in February continued when a Receiver and Treasurer were elected. Another tradition continued – spending endowment money on food and drink: there was a June meeting and supper every St Thomas' Day (July 3rd). Ledger receipts show good income coming from mortgaging land on eight properties as well as a similar number paying rent. Granting a mortgage at 5% guaranteed a decent rate of interest (providing the mortgagee was solvent) and brought in almost £3,000 a year.[46] In 1835 there were just 10 Governors, as they were not always replaced. In the next ten years with death and moving (living outside Nuneaton disqualified you from being a Governor) the number had declined to five.[47] They continued to meet in one of the two rooms on the upper floor of the Grammar School – the other was reserved for the Master's study.

7. The Apprentice Record

There were 64 Apprentices from the school[48] in the forty-five years of the existence of full records (1806-1851), showing that King Edward's was attempting to perform the double function of preparing classical scholars and giving educational and employment opportunities to a wider social range of boys in the town. Governors had attempted to do this in Liptrott's time but the classical side had won out. Now it was the reverse. In the later days of Hugh Hughes, as classics scholars declined in numbers, the Apprenticeship system was put on a more formal footing and the number of boys from the town itself grew both in absolute numbers and in social range. It gives us a unique picture of boys' names, a clue to their social background in the occupation of their fathers and their hoped for occupation through their apprenticeship.

The background of the boys based on their Father's occupation suggests they came from a mixture of the skilled working class and, to a lesser extent, small businessmen in the lower middle class. There were 26 different occupations but few appear more than once or twice. Seven ribbon weavers were the largest group and predictable in view of the employment balance in the town in the early 19th Century. It was not surprising that these fathers did not want their sons to follow in their footsteps in work that experienced fluctuating fortunes well before the disasters of the Free Trade Treaty with France in 1859. Although compulsory Apprenticeships were not formally abolished until 1814, they had long since ceased in many trades, including ribbon weaving[49] (see Appendix Seven).

The provision of Apprenticeships meant that expressions of dissatisfaction with the moribund state of the Grammar/Classical side of the School in the early nineteenth century were limited. Though there were a growing number of ribbon weavers, they did not generally encourage their children to stay long at school. Smith's Charity School was attending to their needs. Moreover, Rayner's Lower School also gave satisfaction. When Charity Commissioners reported on the school in 1834 they expressed *surprise* that he also kept a pub *but no complaint of inefficiency or neglect of duty has been made.* They also confirmed that in the later (and earlier) days of Hughes *the whole superintendance had been left to him.*[50] [Rayner].In some towns there had been demands for change to the Grammar School curriculum[51] seen as too narrowly based on Classics, but these were often unsuccessful and tended to be in places where there were fewer opportunities at a lower level and the whole school had often become moribund as the Master got older and older.

8. The State Of The School

The parlous state of the Grammar School in Nuneaton by 1830 reflected national trends: a declining interest in an exclusively classical education, an elderly Master lacking the remotest degree of zest, small inadequate buildings, nominal interest from Governors, and a cumbersome external regulation which was inefficient and in any case only examined financial questions from a legal point of view.[52] Nuneaton's Grammar school had not made the progress it might have done. True the town had grown little and in Grammar Schools generally *There was often a mismatch between their location and the likely concentration of pupils.* But some schools flourished. Rugby was little better placed than Nuneaton yet in this period lay the origin of their greatness coming to fruition under Thomas Arnold. Moreover Samuel Butler became Head of Shrewsbury School in 1798 with just 20 boys – 18 of them local. By 1836 when he became Bishop of Lichfield and Coventry he had transformed their reputation into a school of national significance producing a long list of classical scholars including ironically Thomas Smart Hughes, son of Hugh. [53]

The concept of state intervention and expenditure was after the days of Hughes but there was already a hint of things to come. From 1810 Lord Brougham was interested in campaigning to investigate the state of the poor, and in the misuse of charity money he saw a waste of resources that needed to be rectified. Grammar School charity money often went to a few privileged boys who would learn the classics. While Nuneaton was not as restricted as some and offered a free education, money like Leeke's was intended for *the poor of Nuneaton* who frequently left school very early if they went at all. A series of Royal Commissions investigated endowed charities and led to the appointments of Charity Commissioners who, initially holding temporary posts, inquired into the nature of bequests and any improper use of the endowment. It was the first hint of a long term change in thinking that would eventually affect Nuneaton.

St. Nicolas dwarfs the Old Grammar School c. 1830. The Almshouses seen behind the school were demolished in 1862/3

The state of the school just before the death of Hughes can be surmised from a Charity Commissioners Report of 1834. Though both retrospective and indirect, the criticisms of Hughes were clear: *a very great improvement has taken place since the appointment of the present Master.*[54] In 1833 numbers were recorded as 45 boys (Smith's had 46) and though this may have grown a little since 1830 Rayner was still teaching the majority.[55]

On the morning of August 3rd 1830, in the unlikely event he was well enough, the 75 year old Hugh Hughes would have first read in the English newspapers of a bloodless revolution in France ousting the old restored Bourbon Monarchy, an event which further excited the already strong reforming opinion in Britain. Other significant news was coming in that very same morning of the return of reforming M.P.s in the ongoing British General election which would lead to a Whig Government, the Great Parliamentary Reform Act of 1832 and other major reforms in local government, factory legislation, the abolition of slavery in the British empire, poor law changes and the first state grant to schools. It seems fitting that Hughes died that very day, for he surely belonged to the pre-reform era.

9. Preparations For The New Era: School Routines: More Legal Action?

Rayner kept the school running after Hughes' death. Over three months later the Governors met at the Newdegate Arms on 16th November 1830[56] to choose a new Headmaster. The delay was in order to repair and improve the Master's House before a new incumbent arrived. They appointed the Reverend Thomas Docker on similar terms to Hughes, a £50 salary plus the School House at a nominal rent of 5/- per annum. There could be up to 20 boarders though this was clearly at the Master's discretion. The well-established hours of 9-12 and 2-5 continued: in the long lunch break many would go home. Church was still attended on Saints days. The six months notice established for the last Master but two, Thomas Trusswell, also continued. Both Christmas and the summer saw a month's holiday. The common practice in school of having an afternoon off in the week (Thursday) but working Saturday mornings had not changed either.

The Master, still likely to be a clergyman, was allowed to hold a clerical living. The rather general statement in the Charter that *No occupation* [was allowed] *calculated to interfere with his due attention to the duties of the said school* did not preclude taking a Sunday service elsewhere. Docker did not exercise this option but his successor, Bucknill, did (see below). As was increasingly common in Grammar Schools, Docker was appointed to *the Headmastership of the Free Grammar School of Nuneaton* but with payment of a Bond by the newly appointed Master, two approved sureties of £500 *conditioned for the due observance and performance of the terms stipulated and conditions of the said Agreement.* This was the attempt of the Governors to deal with the question of security of tenure and an effective legal freehold for a Master that might (especially with age) prove less than competent.[57]

The Governors had finally learnt that removing inefficient and elderly Masters was expensive and time consuming. They attempted to take legal steps to control the Master still further. Between the death of Hughes and the appointment of Docker they had considered applying for new letters patent to clarify and extend their existing powers. They went as far as consulting a lawyer, Mr. Knight of Lincoln's Inn, about its advisibility. The proposal was to double the Master's salary which had remained at £50 since the Charter of 1695. The Undermaster was not required to be versed in Latin, a regularisation of the existing position. The intention was to develop the way the school had evolved under Hughes and Rayner in the first third of the century but with a greater percentage of Latin scholars than in Hughes' later days. This would guarantee the continuation of the endowment, while a virtually separate English School could then be further developed. Even more significantly Governors wanted legal authority to dismiss the Master. They also requested *To have a controlling power over the surplus revenue,* a stronger statement of their rights. Clarification on whether the Master's House could have money spent on it from the endowment income was another aim, because of the House being *some distance* (in fact only about 200 yards) from the school itself. Mr. Knight recommended applying to the court of Chancery rather than for new letters patent. If the Governors tried to change and sharply re-define the legal position argued Knight, *It might induce them to wish matters had stood as they were.* Perhaps he was well-versed in the Governors' previous forays, largely unwise, into legal minefields.[58]

10. Docker's School 1830-1842

Hughes' replacement, Thomas Robert Docker, a Sizar at Pembroke College Cambridge in 1821, had been born around 1803 in Spalding Lincs., a son of the cloth and curate at Coleshill from 1828-1830.[59] Getting a parish living depended on connection as well as ability and a schoolmaster's post continued to be a stepping stone to it. One advantage was the virtually free Schoolmaster's property and the 1841 Census records Docker just before he left in the *Free Grammar School House* with his wife Elizabeth and daughter of the same name. He had taken over the position at the start of 1831 and stayed till 1842. It is just possible that he was recommended for the school by George Eliot's Father, Robert Evans. [60]

Docker succeeding Hughes could be compared to the first Liptrott (James) succeeding Trevis back in 1695. The new incumbent of the position would look fresh by comparison. What was the school like by 1840 after nearly 10 years of Docker? Benjamin Rayner continued as Undermaster so the Governors' idea of a larger classical section, but also the continuation of elementary pupils, had been achieved. The narrow classical base of the Grammar School was further modified. English, History, Geography, Maths and Writing, were taught in addition to Latin. Undermaster Rayner took the second portion of boys for reading, writing and accounts, ensuring an elementary education for some pupils.[61] While a few children may have come from Smith's Charity or possibly Coton Free School, many started their formal education at the Grammar school. They may have previously been educated at home or attended the numerous private schools there were for very young children.[62] Rent and interests were healthy, producing about £300 a year.[63] Docker, however, apart from any gratuities, received the same money as Hughes had done; £50 a year. Encouraging him to take private pupils would possibly make him more content with the limited salary but this did not last for long. Docker was soon granted a gratuity for increasing the numbers in his first year. He had twenty, all but five or six learning Latin and studying English, History, Geography, Maths, Writing, and Accounts. Boys generally stayed three years.[64]

By the time of the Fletcher Report of 1840, near the end of Docker's Mastership, the numbers in school had increased to 60 with 45 under Docker's control. Whether these were all classics students, however, is questionable. Docker may have taught other subjects but the official line was that 45 was the *assigned number he must receive and instruct in the classics*.[65] A proportion stayed on for Latin but many left, since the average stay was only three years. University ambitions would mean staying for four to five years even if they did not attend until 12 and left at 16 or 17. However, there is no record of Oxbridge entrants in Docker's time, as Greek as well as Latin would be required and may not have been taught,[66] though the Master was allowed to take private scholars for Latin to add to the number.[67]

Nevertheless, Docker strengthened the classical side of the school while developing other subjects such as History and Geography. This combination of new and old helped ensure the future of the Grammar School in the 1870s when endowed Grammar Schools, including Nuneaton, were reformed. Registers are not extant for this period. We do know, however, that Dr. Richard Bird Nason, born 1830 – first in line of the prominent Nuneaton medical family – was educated at the school in Docker's final years.[68]

The school's Christian background and clerical tradition of Head Masters was still apparent. The Church catechism was taught though apparently this was the only formal religious instruction. The Anglican flavour of the school like most other ancient endowed Grammar Schools, remained, since parents were expected to conform to the Church of England.[69] The physical proximity of St. Nicolas Church and –after 1845 – the vicar on the Governing Body – must have added to this atmosphere. However, this did not cause great problems in the town. Back in the 18th Century in Nuneaton, religious Dissent, though not as strong as in some areas, was starting to grow[70] and was well established by 1840. At first Dissenters, increasingly now termed Nonconformists, would still be officially excluded from the Grammar School. But during the 19th

Century, especially after the Test and Corporation Acts were repealed in 1828,[71] religious toleration was evolving into religious equality. Quite often, schools were the institutions where the hackles of religious sensibilities were most strongly raised. However, while new Nuneaton vicar Canon Savage was instrumental in building Church of England schools in Nuneaton in the late 1840s (see below) his attitude to Nonconformists was noticeably irenic and he was popular with them.

The questionnaire answers given to Fletcher in his Report of 1840 (see above) were, unfortunately, vague about the social background of the Grammar School boys merely saying their parents were in *various trades* and no information was volunteered on attendance rates which could be poor and/or intermittent. However, the Report recorded that *Tasks* were given to miscreants and if necessary the cane. They could be dismissed from the school if there was *no improvement* but it is unclear if this was ever implemented.

Without the efforts of Docker and Rayner, who assisted Docker as he had Hughes, Nuneaton Grammar School might have suffered like the one at Chelmsford where King Edward VI School was *on the point of collapse by its tercentenary in 1851... and closed temporarily from 1853 to 1856*. King Edward VI Grammar School, Southampton had only nine boys in 1853 and then closed for six years.[72] Rayner in particular had avoided the school being confined to a limited diet of Classics increasingly *unattractive to Victorian townspeople who wanted their sons educated for entry into business, farm management or a profession*.[73]The Governors can take some credit by refusing to be bound by the apparent straightjacket of the legal statutes and, while wishing Docker to revive the Classical side of the school, let Rayner continue to teach a number of other subjects.

This range of subjects studied lead to a wider range of literature being acquired to widen the horizons of the pupils – a national trend in Grammar schools at this time. It is clear that Docker had transformed the role of the Master back to the leading teacher in the school and played a short but crucial role in ensuring Grammar school status for the town at a time of greater concern and action about the state of the Endowed Schools. Children would start young, often at eight years, especially because of the lack of a National School or other schools in Nuneaton parish before the arrival of Canon Savage in 1845. But Docker only tutored a few private pupils, did not take boarders (who disappeared until the 1870s) and so his lack of income other than his basic £50 a year salary –in sharp contrast to his predecessor Hughes – led to financial difficulties. When he left he was insolvent.[74]

11. Samuel Bucknill: New Master

The achievements of Docker were in danger of being lost by his successor, the Reverend Samuel Bucknill: Bucknill's interpretation of the role of Head was to exclude boarders, take a living or two himself, teach a few classical scholars and continue to employ an Undermaster. The advances of the previous ten years were not maintained: it seemed the days of Hughes might return. Bucknill, born in 1810, was probably only the second Nuneaton born Head (as opposed to Undermaster). His father was a Nuneaton doctor and former School Governor, William Bucknill. Bucknill père, faced with a choice of education for his son between the local Grammar School under an ageing Master (Hugh Hughes) and the rapidly up and coming Rugby school, had chosen the latter, a further reflection of the emerging gulf between two schools that had been so similar in centuries past.[75]

Bucknill's academic credentials seemed more than adequate on paper; he was a pensioner at Trinity, Cambridge in 1829 though it took him five years to obtain a B.A., longer than usual.[76] He is also briefly described by George Eliot in the *Amos Barton* section of *Scenes of Clerical Life* as Mr. Furness a *tall young man with blond hair and whiskers who was plucked at Cambridge entirely owing to his genius*. In the novel he is depicted as publishing poems popular with young ladies and preaching sermons not entirely dissimilar which contained *an exuberance of metaphor and similie entirely original and not in the least borrowed from any resemblance in the things concerned*.[77]

Given the date at which George Eliot sets her work (around 1830 and just after) this would be at a time before the real Bucknill was ordained priest in 1836, though Furness is described as a young curate. But while Eliot's description may be ostensibly fictional her unflattering analysis of his character, as with Hughes, may have been close to reality. Bucknill took the Nuneaton Master's post five years later. In 1844 he also became vicar of the small village of Burton Hastings to the south-east of Nuneaton where he took the Sunday service and the stipend adding the sinecure of the Rectory of Stretton Baskerville, a deserted village to the east of the town nine years later. In 1865 there was a further post, Chaplain of the Nuneaton Union for the poor. This range of income – including £100 a year from his Mastership, produced a comfortable lifestyle for Bucknill, his wife, four children and four servants.[78] He rarely took boarders but there was one exception. In 1861 Nuneaton vicar, Canon Robert Savage, accepted the charge of two South African Xhosa chiefs at the vicarage. Initially, however, they stayed at the Grammar School with Bucknill and leant English before studying more advanced work including Euclidian Mathematics. They attended the school until 1865 when one returned to South Africa and the other, on the verge of doing the same, died of an aneurism at the age of 18.[79] Here the initiative had been taken by the vicar and not the schoolmaster.

One can question whether a town of the size and social composition of Nuneaton could sustain a fair sized Grammar school based on the classics without taking boarders. Bucknill's 31 years at the school was identical to Hugh Hughes and their mutual desire for a quiet life with just a few classical scholars and some clerical (religious) work is striking. However, national and local circumstances were not to give Bucknill the same largely unchallenged hegemony enjoyed by Hughes.

CHAPTER SEVEN

Reform Thwarted: The Mid-Nineteenth Century School 1846-1866

An endowment takes no note of competition. It relies... on formal rules and statutes and expects men without the stimulus of hope and fear... to do their duty when it is directly opposed to their interest.
Robert Lowe: *Middle Class education; endowment or free trade?* (1868)

The role of the endowed Grammar School was increasingly questioned and criticised in the mid 19th Century. A more industrialised and utilitarian society argued for a reform of the educational curriculum; a more liberal society wanted its extension to all social classes. And different social classes there were. Government influence now started to become greater than at any time since the days of the Civil War or possibly even the sixteenth century. At first Nuneaton Grammar School struggled to adapt to this brave new world.

1. National Reform In The Air

By 1840 external pressure for change to Nuneaton Grammar School was imminent. It had its origins just after Hughes' death in 1830 when many of the country's institutions underwent great upheaval. With money needed for other reforms the inefficiencies of educational endowments were heavily criticised. The 1834 Poor Law Commission remarked that *If the funds now destined to the purposes of education, many of which are applied in manner unsuited to the present wants of society, were wisely and economically employed, they would be sufficient to give all the assistance which can be prudently afforded by the state.*[1] In 1840 the *Act for improving the condition and extending the benefits of Grammar Schools*, argued for extending the benefits of Grammar Schools to a wider range of boys. The Preamble refers to Grammar Schools which had *ceased to afford a substantial fulfilment of the intentions of the Founders... [the system] ought to be extended and rendered more generally beneficial. The advantages of such Grammar Schools should be extended to boys other than those to whom by the terms of the Foundation or the existing Statutes the same is now limited.*[2]

As to whether Nuneaton Grammar funds had been *wisely and economically employed,* the school had been more progressive than some, widening its range of subjects by having Rayner as Undermaster for over 40 years. Unlike some Grammar Schools, boys not doing Latin also received a free education. No girls attended and boys only within the narrow confines of Nuneaton parish. Analysis of the Registers after 1846 (see below) shows that the Grammar school continued to provide an education for the better off families in the town (if not always the top of the social elite) in higher proportions than the poor boys of the parish. Some felt this was outside the spirit of the original endowment.

When John Leeke had obtained a licence in Mortmain in 1508, he had overcome the opposition of the Crown which was anxious to avoid the *dead hand* of the legally expressed wishes of the founder preventing them getting their clutches on endowments through taxation. For over 300 years this made reform and adaptation difficult: the school was supposed to remain primarily one for teaching the classics. The form of legal application of the dead hand remained the principle of *cy pres* (see above p.107) now removed by the Act of 1840.

2. The Revised Charter 1846 – Imminent Change?

Change began locally in 1846 when a Revised Charter for the school was issued. Nuneaton's healthy endowment (income £304 per annum) and the relatively low yearly salary of the Master (£50 as opposed to £45 for the Undermaster) resulted in enquiries by Charity Commissioners and correspondence with the school. On 15th April 1846 Edwin Shufflebotham from the Charity Commissioners wrote to Headmaster Bucknill outlining how the Act of 1840 should be applied to King Edward's. However, it may be that the Governors and not the Charity Commissioners had first responded to the new atmosphere that the 1840s presented. This was in the form of a new, resident, reforming vicar in Nuneaton in 1845, Robert Savage. Savage may have initiated this correspondence though concrete evidence is lacking. What is clear is that the Commissioners and Governors agreed on a new scheme of Government for the school.[3]

The Charity Commissioner's points mixed traditional and new ideas. It showed the greatest degree of central concern or central interference, (local views would always differ about which it was) since the early days of the school's foundation in the 16th Century. The classics would be taught by a well-qualified Master to local boys. The age of attendance and hours studied were fixed. New Governors were appointed and their meeting dates fixed. The school was no longer exclusively Anglican. Boarders were allowed if desired. [4]

Financial regulation sounded precise. The maximum salaries for the Master (who also had occupation of School House) and Usher were fixed at £100 and £60 respectively. The Commissioners were anxious for a clear distinction in amounts to reflect what they saw as the different degrees of responsibility and qualifications of the two teachers. This distinction was not maintained either in fact or even in theory (see below). After the revisions of 1846 the relative positions of the Governors and the Master were clarified. Section 5 gave the Governors clear power to dismiss the Master – how they would have liked this earlier – and Section 18 the right to suspend or expel errant pupils. But the education and *general management* (Section16) were in the hands of the Master.[5] The existence of the Charity Commission –put on a permanent basis by an Act of 1853 – did help to clarify matters and opened, however cumbersomely, an alternative channel of communication to the Court of Chancery; it was hoped this would avoid the expensive and long drawn out litigation of the past.

Canon Robert Savage Vicar of Nuneaton 1845-71. He transformed many aspects of the town's life but was less successful in his attempts to reform the Grammar School

With four new Church of England elementary schools organised by Canon Savage all opened by 1850,[6] the Grammar School could cease to be an elementary school with a few classical scholars and once again teach a substantial number of boys to an advanced level. Though no longer hidebound by a narrow exclusively classical curriculum, all would learn some Latin. This was the vision of Savage and a great opportunity for the school, but Bucknill's limited interpretation of his role as Master, thwarted these ideas. After Benjamin Rayner had retired from teaching in 1843[7] more academic assistant Masters could – and sometimes were – appointed. (see below) But they found Bucknill's lack of drive – reminiscent of Hughes nearly 50 years before – frustrating. Grammar School reform was one of the few areas of town or educational life that Canon Savage was unable to affect to the extent he wanted. (see below)

3 The Curriculum: Prize Money And New Subjects

With more ambitious plans for the academic development of the school still under discussion, Savage and others oversaw lesser change. Could the healthy state of the endowment help sons of poorer families to stay on? Up to £10 of endowment money was now used – at the Master's discretion – for the award of prizes and £15 for scholarships,[8] presaging future developments when charges would be made and scholarships awarded for poor families. This was to have long term significance though its immediate impact was limited.

Prizes were awarded from 1849, sixteen altogether,[9] reflecting the widening curriculum. Copies of books were kept in some kind of library. A map of Europe and geography books were purchased but not distributed to the pupils as a whole: boys generally bought their own books.[10] The range of subjects expanded further in the 1850s with drawing and writing and in 1854 – on the recommendation of the Inspector – Natural Philosophy.[11] This was the study of the natural universe and a precursor to modern science with a subsequent division into areas such as chemistry, physics and biology. Scientific equipment and laboratories, however, would have to wait. The curriculum was widening in other ways. In 1853 a French master was appointed for the first time when Monsieur Vaillands was engaged at £40 a year for 12 boys with charges to parents of three guineas per annum.[12] Vaillands failed to completely satisfy the Governors. At the end of 1859[13] they commented on *defects* in his teaching which he was asked to address and he soon left. Assistant Masters now were expected to take on French. In June 1860 fifteen boys were studying French[14] but numbers continued to vary.

4. Bucknill And The Classics

While much of the activity in the school was now at the non-classical level, a traditional classical curriculum was followed by a few. A Report of 1866 noted that the boys Bucknill was teaching were working as follows: one on Caesar and the earlier part of the Greek Delectus and another on Eutropius: two had got some way through the miscellaneous Latin Delectus and two more were just beginning *the sentences*. This was probably the simple Latin Sentences for children the *Sententiae Pueriles* [15] (See Chapter Three and Appendix Two)

Bucknill's classical standard in Greek as well as Latin was seen as good and (in theory) he also taught History and Mathematics; but he lacked the initiative to make the Grammar School either a centre for local classical learning or one which could take the initiative in introducing the sciences. He was content to teach a small number in the Upper School. The distinction in salaries between Master and Undermaster meant that Bucknill also received a considerable pay rise by the new arrangements of 1846, with his increase in salary up to £100 a year.[16] Because he had been appointed six years before the new agreement of 1846, Bucknill was not bound by the new clauses such as the one that would in the future effectively end the Master's freehold. The idea, developed through bitter experience, had been to prevent the decline of a school through an increasingly decrepit teacher who could not afford to retire. Indeed the additional salary implied the need for strong leadership, increased numbers, a wider curriculum and a greater range of opportunities for the students. But in Bucknill's case he obtained the advantage of the increased salary without the loss of security of tenure. Predictably, this had precisely the effects that the reform of the system was designed to avoid. Had Bucknill lived any longer than he did (he died in February 1873) radical change to the school would have been further delayed.

Bucknill was also exempt from the ban of 1846 preventing any Head from holding other paid work such as a church living. Ironically, the preferred candidate for Undermaster in 1856, Reverend J. Coling, was not appointed – he was the first choice for the vacancy – since he refused to give up his clerical post at Stockingford as the Charter obliged him to do. Yet Bucknill, appointed before 1846, could continue to hold all his posts. [17]

In 1861 the Charity Commissioners expressed surprise at the relative proportions of

Master and Undermaster salary wise – £100 and £90 were seen as very close together *compared to the relative proportions at the time of the Charter of 1694*.[18] In response Governor Dr. Richard Bird Nason gave an insight into the relative importance of the lower school. Justifying the closeness of the two salaries he remarked that the lower school had 30 boys and was *always full*. The Upper school had merely ten. The *efficiency* of the school depended *quite as much on him* (the Undermaster).[19] This continued to remained true until Bucknill's death. Moreover later assistants were, unlike their predecessors, expected to teach Latin. As in the days of Hugh Hughes and Benjamin Rayner the Undermaster was doing more for the school than the Headmaster. But after Rayner retired in 1843 there were eight Undermasters in the next 20 years and stability was lost.

5. The Position Of Undermaster

The provision of an adequate Undermaster, now a fixed post in the new scheme (Section 3), caused difficulty. At first the policy was to maintain a Rayner type figure, an assistant who would teach elementary subjects at what almost amounted to a separate school. Mr. Suffolk was appointed in 1843 followed by George Perry in 1846.[20] Perry's pay increased from £60 to £80 per annum while the Head Master's annual salary was reduced to £50 but with the other £50 still being paid as a gratuity which could be altered. While there is no evidence this was not paid in full, these arrangements may have suggested less than total satisfaction with Bucknill. [21]

At the end of Perry's time in 1850 a temporary appointment (Mr. Beckwith) was made. In the long term the Governors planned to develop vicar Robert Savage's idea of an expanded school where all pupils would learn some Latin and the Second Master (wording revealingly used for the first time) would be a Classics graduate.[22] Savage continued to take the initiative. With an unconscious sense of future developments Savage wrote for guidance to the Reverend Henry Walford Bellairs, a prominent Schools Inspector.[23] Bellairs was to replace Savage as vicar of Nuneaton twenty years later and play a crucial role in the more successfully implemented changes in the school in the 1870s and 1880s.

There was no shortage of applicants for the advertised post in 1851 (twenty-six candidates) and in line with the new thinking the non-clerical, non-classically trained, temporary teacher Beckwith had his application for the permanent post turned down and a young clerical graduate Charles Thomas Pizey, from St Catharine's College

Cambridge was appointed.[24] Pizey served his year's diaconate in Nuneaton but soon moved to a curacy (and later a teaching post) in Liverpool. Reform now began with changes gradually made to the Lower School. However, not all Pizey's successors were classically trained. [25] The problem was that Nuneaton *is not likely to be able to supply a much larger number of scholars to the classical school than are now in it... the want of competition can only be supplied by an accession of boarders.*[26] The hope that the new National Schools would produce a flood of applicants in due time for the *Latin School* had proved too optimistic. Many parents did not want their sons to learn Latin. However, with the appointment of the Rev. John Barker Bryant as Second Master in 1856 stability returned. When he arrived there was another attempt to provide lower school Latin and by the end of the following year it was remarked that *The Latin of the Lower Schools is very fair* though the arithmetic was *a little weaker.*[27]

The Conditions for admission were now clearly defined. Boys had to be able to read well, be familiar with the first four rules of Arithmetic and be prepared to learn Latin. Bryant was a maturer Undermaster, already aged 32 when he arrived, and coming with a degree and a range of good testimonials.[28]. But after Bryant, difficulties returned. George Perry was re-appointed but now fell out with Bucknill and was dismissed in 1863.[29] Neither was Mr. Shufflebotham, a cleric from Lancashire, a success. This was confirmed, if implicitly, by the later comments of Charity Commissioner Charles Stanton in 1870 that Shufflebotham's successor had to start from scratch. Shufflebotham, present barely a year, only stayed a month after his resignation – clearly an abrupt departure since when his successor George Eustace was appointed he was not available for three months and so a *substitute* had to be found from March until June.[30]

Eustace was much more successful and was the kind of teacher the Governors were looking for. He took on the bulk of the instruction and was teaching a variety of subjects including French.[31] The Governors really wanted him and this was not merely due to the usual good testimonials. He was well known, having been born and brought up in Nuneaton and attended the Grammar School. His father had been the Independent Minister of the Zion Chapel in Nuneaton but later, inspired by Canon Savage, he became an Anglican priest and moved to an incumbency in Yorkshire. Eustace junior attended the Grammar School in the early 1850s (an example of how the school no longer debarred non-Anglicans) and is described in one Inspector's report as *acquitting himself well* in the Upper (Latin) school. The following year he was a prizewinner. He was appointed to teach in his old school when he was 25 years old

George Eustace: Assistant Master: 1865-1873: Head: 1873-1880. The transformation of the school began under him, before the new building

living in his father's old property in Tuttle Hill. Ordained in 1864 he had previously had some teaching experience in Brighton when a young man of about 20 before taking his degree. [32]

The young Eustace brought some stability again to the Undermaster's role. He began the school with prayers every morning at 9 am before Bucknill managed to arrive at 9.30. Here was another of the new regulations of 1846 (no. 20) *The Master shall be present at all times* that Bucknill felt he could ignore.[33] Eustace was well rewarded for his efforts. In addition to the annual salary of £80 he received a £20 House Allowance, £10 for drawing and £10 for French for which he had 15 boys. These pupils paid Eustace 7/6d a quarter; with two private pupils as well his annual income exceeded £160.[34]

6. Standard Of Education

From 1846 the new Regulations established regular school Inspections. Early reports were approving but unpenetrating. The Lower School was efficiently conducted – *it fully answers the purposes for which it was intended* to give an elementary education to children who had few other outlets up to 1846 when the first of Canon Savage's first four National Schools was constructed. The reports by William Drake from 1849 show a more acute analysis of the state of the school: it was *Generally proficient* [but] *I do not consider the standard of education to be sufficiently high*.[35] Drake argued that the school should try to develop a love of learning for its own sake. Because *No exhibition is attached to the endowment,* Oxford and Cambridge entrants were now non-existent. Moreover, Greek was still essential for Oxbridge entry but taught to fewer and fewer boys.[36]

From their different perspectives both Inspector Drake and parent and Governor Savage desired to develop a more academic, but not purely classical, Grammar School rather than a sharp division between the English and Latin *schools*.[37] In 1849 the lower *English* school at King Edward's was *Scarcely reaching the standard of a good National School. Many boys should be placed in the excellent National Schools.* The building was simply not large enough for the numbers coming in the lower school; *the present numbers are beyond the Second Master's ability fully to do justice to.*[38]

The school was not fulfilling its potential. The Inspector argued that *There is no reason why the Grammar School at Nuneaton should not take a high rank among the schools of the County.* He dismissed the argument *that the education provided is no longer for the poor and therefore not in keeping with the intention of the Founder*[39] by asserting that the National Schools made this kind of provision unnecessary. Since a formal separation of the schools was deemed impractical Drake backed the plan that all should learn at least some Latin, defending the subject from contemporary criticism that it was only appropriate for a limited number of high-flying students and arguing for its value in developing language and thought.[40] With more subjects to teach, however, less time was spent on Latin. Bucknill complained that senior boys knew the language insufficiently though not casting any *imputation* on his assistant Eustace.[41] Latin was a language of sufficient complexity to threaten to dominate school hours.

7. Bucknill: The School Stagnates

With the decline of ribbon weaving Nuneaton itself failed to grow in the 1860s. While many areas of the country were expanding rapidly Nuneaton's population actually went down in that decade from 4,658 to 4,547.[42]This stagnation was

The Nason family in the 1860s – several generations intimately connected with the Grammar School

Dr. Edward Noel Nason: (1861-1943) Popular doctor, school governor, school historian, saviour and interpreter of documents

mirrored in the Grammar School. During the 1850s Bucknill lost any enthusiasm he may have had. Inspectors were critical but he was legally secure.[43] With no pension schemes as yet, he was likely to stay indefinitely. Bucknill's approach to corporal punishment – though not on a par with Trevis – was nonetheless vigorous, a not uncommon feature of this period as Dickens was to testify in Nicholas Nickleby. In 1928 Dr. Edward Noel Nason recalled starting to attend the school around 1870. He was taught by the Undermaster but was aware of Bucknill's reputation. Bucknill was seen as *An expert in testing the veracity of spare the rod and spoil the child*. After he arrived each morning boys were tested in Latin and caned when they failed to answer correctly. Nason recalled, *Woe betide the boy who failed to decline Mensa or boggled over his hic haec hoc.* [44]

Disciplinary matters only occasionally feature in the Governors' minutes. Boys were to be sent home if they arrived without washing or wearing clean clothes.[45] There were complaints about boys playing *over the fence* in the Churchyard.[46] One boy was expelled but this was more a disagreement between Master and parent.[47] School uniform started to develop. Dr. Nason recalled the *grammar bucks* wearing a mortar board to which a tassel was added if they reached the upper school. There were initiation rights, common in schools of the time. A new pupil would run through a crowd holding mortar boards (sometimes with stones in them) and get attacked. Those who arrived with a bad reputation were pushed against a post.[48]

8. Social Composition Of The School

Commonly boys arrived at the age of nine or ten and stayed three years in the English school. Longer stays than this or permission to move into the Latin School was at the Governors' discretion.[49] Prior to 1857 school numbers remained low with yearly entries of single figures. Numbers varied according to the qualities of the Second Master. When John Barker Bryant occupied the post (1857-63) they rose; in those years 72 boys entered the school, with 15 arriving in 1859. Briefly the vision of a larger grammar school bloomed, but only one boy entered in 1865 and two in 1866. Numbers recovered after Second Master Eustace arrived, 17 entering in 1870. [50]

Examining the occupations of the fathers (and one mother of a fatherless boy) of the children in the 25 years of entry between 1847 and 1871, we find a mixed social background. [51]

Selected Occupations of Parents 1847-1871	
Farmers	11
Weavers	8
Clerks	8
Innkeepers	6
Railway Workers	3
Agricultural Labourers	3
Orphan	1

Overall Analysis	
Small Businessmen	21
Skilled Labourers	18
Professional and Manufacturing Middle Class	21

The school did not take the children of the wealthiest landowners or those from the very poorest groups. Within those constraints there was some social mix though the class difference between a skilled labourer and some of the lower middle class families would be small. The middle class were particularly well represented with 32 who could be designated comfortable middle class and 36 lower middle class. The 34 working class were, bar the agricultural labourers, from the skilled end of that social group. Sometimes boys were turned down as insufficiently advanced in learning though some successfully re-applied the following year. However, the slump in the weaving trade around 1860 restricted town growth and may have discouraged staying on at school for those capable of earning money for their family in some way. In a notable contrast to their predecessors, when the Governors met at the height of the slump in 1859 they did not dine, giving the three Guineas saved to the workers' relief fund. [52]

Until the 1870s there was nothing of what later came to be termed extra-curricular activities. Religious difficulties were kept out by the broad approach of Canon Savage. He encouraged Nonconformists to attend the Grammar School and they responded positively despite some degree of Anglican atmosphere; in 1857 one boy was admitted on condition *he learns the catechism.*[53]

9. The Buildings

Pupil numbers, though not exceeding 40, were resulting in cramped conditions and larger premises were warranted. The size of the main room for 40 boys was just 24 foot by 15 foot.[54] Moreover, while Governors had also agreed to pay for repairs to the Master's House, none were carried out for some time. Improvements were superficial[55] and the house's poor state became an issue of controversy in the reforms of the 1870s. The reason for this inaction was because of wider plans. In 1861 a request had been made by the Governors to the Charity Commissioners to obtain approval for the future purchase of a new double property for both Masters[56] and build a new school as well as a new Master's House – an ambitious scheme. This initiative developed because the old school was seen as barely coping with the needs of the pupils. In the lower school were *a few old-fashioned clammy desks fixed to the west wall and a few rows of less antiquated benches across the floor.* In Bucknill's upper school was *a half circle of queer old pew-like desks round the walls from the fireplace on the north to the HM study on the south.* The schools were divided by a folding door which was opened for prayers at the start of the day and through which the Upper school boys had to pass.[57]

In 1860 the field on the other side of Church Street to the school had been acquired; while at this stage little more than ridge and furrow with cattle, it proved a valuable acquisition in the long run when there were sporting developments. However, this had not been the original intention. Not unusually, it was Canon Savage who had taken the initiative. Writing to the Charity Commissioners on 22nd March 1860 he saw in the purchase of this field the first step to building improved premises and summarized the problem: *The present school is too small and incommodious in every way and being in the Churchyard cannot be expanded or altered.*

There was no proper place to assemble; Savage referred to this taking place in the churchyard or even the street, and the privy was inadequate, with the Almshouses in the way. Savage not only analyzed the problem succinctly: he pointed out the problem of a satisfactory solution. *One difficulty in preparing a scheme to submit to the Charity*

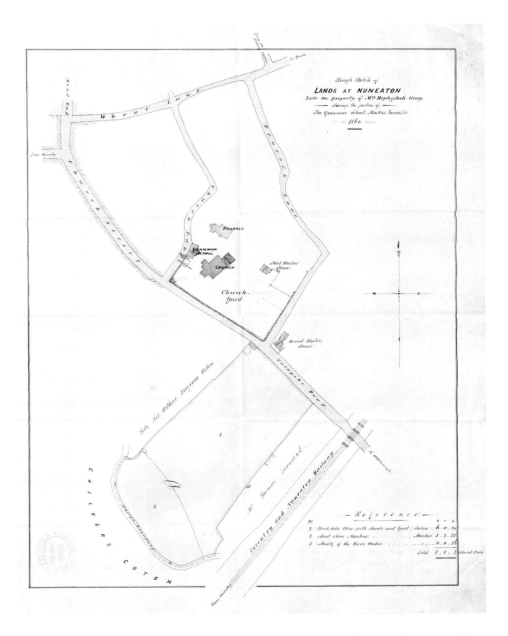

Rough sketch of lands at Nuneaton 1860 showing the field about to be acquired by the school

Commissioners for the improvement of the school has been the lack of a site though the Governors are all practical men. It [the new field] *is the only site on which a school can be built with a playground.*[58]

Savage requested the demolition of the Almshouses: apart from the advantages for the school, it would provide the Church with a little extra ground for an increasingly crowded churchyard. He got his way. In 1862/3 the run down buildings known as the Nuneaton Almshouses (no match for neighbouring Bedworth's) on the north side of the Grammar School were demolished. There were – according to the application at the time to sell or pull them down – no records of who owned the almshouses or what endowment if any they had. They had been allowed to go to rack and ruin. Now for the first time the school could be entered from its nearest road, Church Lane, currently Vicarage Street. Before this the entrance had been from Peacock Lane, later re-named King Edward Road, when the school moved to its new premises. Now this entrance was reserved for the Headmaster from his house of 1715.[59]

However, the bigger vision of a new site for the school was not implemented. While Bucknill lived and coveted his house change was unlikely. By the time he died in 1873 the land was producing useful income for the school[60] and a move to the other side of the Churchyard was seen as a cheaper option. Had the field been used for a new building, the history of the School could have taken a different course. By 1881 the value of the income from the field and the fact it had started to be used for sports mitigated against any major construction on that side. The field soon began its transition into the school sports field. Its tenant, Mr. Batchelor, was given notice that the Grammar School boys were to be given free access to the land, including the *bathing box* at all times.[61]

10. The Investments And The Property

The fact that the purchase of the field could be afforded and ambitious plans made for a new school and Masters' houses was a reflection of the health of the endowment. Income rose steadily to over £340 a year, more than £275 of which was from the seven year land rents mainly from the property at Coventry, over 76 acres[62]. Governors continued to take interest in the landholdings and meetings record occasional business. There were a few problems:[63] in the 1860s Mr. Jeffcoat was a difficult and aggressive neighbour. His encroachments on to school land upset the Governors sufficiently for Messrs Jee and Hands to travel to London to seek the advice of the Charity

Commissioners, reminiscent of trips a century before when Governors lobbied the Court of Chancery. The outcome was similar: the Governors got nowhere, with the Commissioners asserting that *they had very little to do with* the question and advising against legal action as the matter was *a trifling affair.*[64] They suggested a solicitor's letter to Jeffcoat saying Governors would clear out the ditch he had made which was on their property. Jee and Hands acquiesced. It is a shame that previous generations of Governors had not received similar advice to prevent them squandering so much of the endowment income on legal fees.[65]

11. The Governors

In the 1850s and early 1860s death or moving out of the parish removed Governors Bull, Ball, and Robinson senior almost severing their link with the pre-1846 school; of the older Governors only Joseph Taverner remained. Between four and six of the remaining seven Governors attended the meetings held regularly four times a year. These meetings increased in the later 1860s as the Endowed Schools Commission Report (see below) and subsequent investigations raised the level of business.

Canon Savage and Dr. Edward Nason (Dr. Edward Noel Nason's grandfather) played a major role as Governors generally being the ones corresponding with the Charity Commissioners and any others, there being no Governors' Clerk as yet. Farmers were James Hands, Joseph Taverner and Charles Christian Jee. This left only two others, gentleman Thomas Hood, and maltster John Robinson Junior.[66] One might have expected more commercial and manufacturing members (who did come later) but for a time this social group were showing little interest in an institution which functioned either as an elementary school, which they would have regarded as insufficient, or as a classics tuition institution, seen as too narrow. For instance, Thomas Townsend of Attleborough Hall (who moved from Coventry in the 1850s) played a key role in developing the cotton spinning trade in Nuneaton and helping the town pull out of the economic recession that occurred with the ribbon weaving crisis of 1859. Yet his sons Thomas and Charles (born 1855 and 1858) were sent to Leamington to a private school in Beauchamp Terrace.[67] The next generation of industrialists however, were to show considerable interest in the school and – sometimes – sent their sons to it. (See Chapter Nine)

With the deaths of Nason (1869) Hands (1870) and Savage (1871) the number of Governors dwindled to dangerously low proportions, especially in view of the fact that important decisions about the school's future were shortly to be made. Eventually Mr. Dewes, solicitor, was commissioned to write with a list of eight residents to fill the positions selected by the serving Trustees.[68] These gentlemen accepted the offer but within a year or two of their appointment the Endowed Schools Commission wished to replace co-opted Governors with elected Ratepayer Governors and other representative figures. This was to cause a good deal of friction in the next few years.

12. Change In The Offing

So there was only limited change in the nature of Nuneaton Free Grammar school during these years and opportunities missed to change the school in radical new ways. Yet in this period public schools transformed education for the upper classes not only at traditional institutions like Eton, Harrow, Westminster and Winchester but also endowed grammar schools like Rugby and Shrewsbury. These institutions had shown a dramatic improvement over the last 50 to 60 years as had a string of new boarding schools. They both made use of the desire for their kind of education – with the very wealthy upper middle class parents as well as landed gentry – and the means to provide it, railways. There were also private schools varying in quality and social intake. All this meant that many old endowed Grammar Schools, unless they had undergone a dramatic transformation like Rugby, tended to languish. Schools Inspector Frederick Temple had a low opinion of most endowed Grammar Schools asserting that *If 500 were abolished tomorrow not the slightest ill effect would be produced on the education of the country.* [69]

The need to measure the achievement of schools and keep sleepy endowment based schools like Nuneaton up to the mark resulted in a strong move to organise a national system of examinations. The Oxford and Cambridge local examinations boards (essentially the origin of much of our modern examination system) were set up in 1857 and 1858. Their exams fulfilled the contemporary need for a greater degree of precise measurement of educational achievement. However, Nuneaton would only take advantage of this after Bucknill's time. It was later in the century before examinations in Grammar Schools became commonplace.

The relatively limited change in the Grammar school system before the 1880s stood out in stark contrast to educational ferment in other areas. Nuneaton was typical of the country as a whole with the sound progress of the National Schools set up by Robert Savage in the late 1840s, but with a relative stagnation of the Grammar School. In their frank analytical way the Victorians acknowledged the need for different types of schooling with different teaching methods, approaches, buildings, staff, philosophy, vision, curriculum and length of stay for the different social classes in the country. Educational reform was imminent in Nuneaton.

CHAPTER EIGHT

Reform Achieved: The Transformation of the School 1865-1881

*The Victorians invented the concept of education as we now understand it,
even if we believe ourselves to be more egalitarian than they; it is from them
that we derive our … assumption that learning should be formalised …
education institutionalised, the imparting of knowledge the duty of society and
the state to every citizen.*
A.N. Wilson *The Victorians* (2003)

King Edward's was in urgent need of reform by the 1860s: a Master increasingly just going through the motions, buildings increasingly inadequate, a role increasingly unclear. Yet there was great potential, for local church elementary schools were turning out well educated children and the town itself, now with the start of new industries, trades and a railway link was on the verge of rapid growth. For all their love of local independence Nuneaton now needed a nudge from the centre to fulfil its promise for high quality secondary education but that nudge was only accepted for boys. The impact of the changes in this crucial period are still with us today.

1. The First Signs Of Change – Green's Visit And His Recommendations
By the mid-1860s changes were afoot nationally that would change Nuneaton Grammar School for ever. In 1864 complaints about the state of English Endowed Grammar Schools had reached such a pitch that Lord Palmerston's Government instituted a Commission of Enquiry, headed by Lord Taunton.[1] In 1868, its recommendations exposed shortcomings in Grammar School education, advocating radical reforms. Many of the 942 schools were inadequate; Masters were lacking in initiative, numbers were low, the curriculum limited and old fashioned, the organisation poor. Buildings were too small, the endowments insufficient, and girls never catered for. Much of this criticism applied to Nuneaton Grammar School.

In September 1865 the School was visited by Thomas Hill (T.H.) Green, Fellow of Balliol, and on his way to become an eminent philosopher before his premature death in 1882. Representing the Commission, Green had a *long conversation* with Governors in September 1865[2] but was not impressed with Nuneaton Grammar School in general or Mr. Bucknill in particular. His visit came at a low point in King Edward's fortunes as Bucknill's age was starting to tell, the unsuccessful Undermaster Shufflebotham had recently left and new assistant Master, George Eustace, was only just starting to pick up the pieces. Green found much in need of improvement. His report, completed in 1866, entered the public domain with all the other Commissioners' Reports in 1868/9.[3] His main recommendations for Ashby Grammar School were very similar[4] to those for Nuneaton, confirming he came with an agenda for change. In Nuneaton's case the agenda seemed appropriate and he proved a highly perceptive observer. He found:

A. There was an urgent need for a larger school building which could accommodate boarders, and a decent playground.
The Nuneaton school building was criticised. It was divided by a partition into two rooms with the Master using a *recess,* not a proper room, holding just six persons. Many desks were arranged around the wall while some faced each other. This standard would be *considered inadequate* in a national school. The lack of any *educational appliances* save a blackboard was noted. It lacked what the Taunton Commission found satisfactory in only a quarter of the school buildings inspected; a good and well ventilated schoolroom with at least one other classroom, decent offices, a good Master's House, a grass playground and a healthy and accessible site. Teaching in separate classrooms was still comparatively rare and the Commission correctly predicted many schools would need to move.

B. The Upper/Lower School distinction needed to be removed.
Green noted Nuneaton's sharp distinction between the upper and lower schools – almost amounting to two separate institutions. The attempt to develop classics teaching throughout the school had only made limited progress. The aim was a common curriculum for all pupils.

C. Fees should be charged between £4-£6 yearly.
This was also in accordance with the prevailing agenda. Reference was made to clergymen and farmers in the area. The target group for the school, Green argued, should be the middle class in the locality and at this stage it was not for the sons (let alone daughters) of miners. This narrow vision was gradually to broaden over the next

100 years. But at this stage the school was expected to be predominantly for boys from middle class families.

However, because it was expected that some poorer boys would attend:

D. There should be Exhibitions for those whose families could not afford fees.
These financial grants should be up for competion by pupils from the local National Schools as well as Smith's Charity School. Also boys from nearby villages should have the opportunity to *be able to distinguish themselves.* The idea was to mitigate the effect of fees for sons of poorer families.

E. The School Master would have to be supportive of reform.
Green commented that The Master would have to *cordially throw himself into it,* [the reforms] a hint that he felt Bucknill was unlikely to do so. Though this recommendation could be more specifically applied to Nuneaton than some schools, it was not an uncommon one.

F. King Edward's endowment could be combined with that of Smith's Charity for one large important Grammar School.
Looking at the larger picture, Green inquired what the rationale was behind Smith's school now that good national schools had been up and running in the town for almost twenty years. He had a point but Smith's was to last another thirty.

2. Implications Of Green's Report

With the acute clear-sighted analysis of the intelligent outsider, Green foresaw that Nuneaton, despite recent population stagnation, was on the verge of growth. Industries such as brick making were developing and the railway brought potential growth. Nuneaton's depression was only temporary. Coal was a growing industry *and collieries will always imply the existence of a certain number of managers of the class for which a middle school [5] is suitable.* Yet despite all these possibilities *the school at present languishes.* Green felt this was partly accounted for by Bucknill's lack of leadership. However, the town as a whole bore some responsibility as there had been a lack of educational initiative. The report noted Green's anxiety to undertake reform: *I could not ascertain that there was much definite demand in the place for such an education as a good Grammar School ought to give* but if the school was reformed and improved *the supply would create the demand.* This related to his recommendations; you needed an *attractive* school with *good buildings and playground* and an *active master*. As to the present state of the school *It is not now nor has been for many years of much use to Nuneaton itself or of any use at all to the neighbourhood.*

As with most reports of this kind it, understandably, analysed the present position of the town. The mining and manufacturing transformation Green correctly predicted in the next 30 years meant a rapid development of schooling was essential and reform of the Grammar School came only just in time to adjust to this. Where small places declined to change such as Appleby Magna,[6] Grammar Schools were in danger of disappearing.

While Apprenticing pupils had ended, there had been little other change in Nuneaton Grammar School in recent years. The school was still divided into two parts and Latin not taught to the lower school despite the opinion of the report that *as far as can be inferred from their look and manner* they were *on a level socially* with the boys in the upper school. Wider social distinctions were more likely when boys were imported from elsewhere as boarders. Boys were capable of more than was being offered and there was a waste of talent with *only six boys in the Upper Department* and one boy each in the two highest classes. The Headmaster should take more interest in the lower school, especially as many *came from uneducated homes.* They were not encouraged to enter the upper school. With a guaranteed salary there was insufficient incentive for the Master to do more.

There had been little desire to reform the situation except for Canon Savage who had shown great initiative and commitment to education in the town. However, his lack of impact on the Grammar school was a good example of how entrenched its privileges were in this period. Change required state intervention on a scale hitherto thought both unacceptable and impractical. As a Governor, Savage had taken up the matter of Grammar School reform but as Green's Report remarked *a Trustee is powerless without the co-operation of the Master.* The school did not attract the children of men like Savage which is what it was supposed to do;[7] in Green's opinion it fell between the two stools of an academic Latin based education for the local middle class children and a good elementary school for large numbers of the town's children pushing the brightest ones up to a higher level. *The clergy and professional men of the neighbourhood …very seldom use it, he complained.*[8] There was only one at the time of the report and only one boy travelled more than one and a half miles. Overall, Green's report had been very critical.

3. Local Reaction

Similar reports from all over the country led to the Endowed Schools Act of 1869 which enforced changes in the statutes of many endowed schools. Green's report had noted the lack of previous interest in the town in the state of the Grammar School. However, with locals becoming aware of his comments, the developing middle class in Nuneaton had become concerned about the local quality of secondary education; they argued this must now be designed to help their children get on in life in the more competitive era that was coming. A letter to the Endowed Schools Commissioner stated that within Nuneaton there was *considerable disturbance prevailing with reference to the Commission*.[9] Thomas Lester, put his finger on the problem that had been a national scandal for many years, well illustrated in Nuneaton: *Six boys are costing 10-12 shillings a week to 'scratch' an education where no English Grammar is taught in a school expressly declared to be a 'free' grammar school for the benefit of the poor of Nuneaton.* [10] He was referring here to those few boys learning Latin under Bucknill's charge. Lester exaggerated the lack of English taught in the school but his comments concerning the poor use of the endowment struck a chord. They heralded a lively period of discussion in the town involving Commissioners, the Master, Governors, parents and the local community.

In 1869 local Solicitor Mr. John Estlin wrote to the Charity Commissioners and their reply later in the year confirmed what he had suspected, that no accounts had been produced for the Grammar School since 1866 (or Smith's Charity School with similar Governors since 1862). *The Trustees will cause omissions to be supplied without any unnecessary delay* they replied but Estlin clearly suspected inefficiency and nearly five months passed, and many letters, before the accounts were produced. Even then it was only the Grammar School's accounts and not Smith's.[11]

The Commissioners recommended Nuneaton had a new Charter for the endowed school that would be less restricting in the range of educational opportunities, offer a wider range of subjects, a different way of financing the operation with the possibility of school fees, and an altered role for the Head, whose staff would grow. The Education Act of 1870, in establishing the opportunity for all children over five to have an elementary education, would soon lead to increased numbers at Grammar Schools. Changes to Secondary education had to be agreed by the Commissioners and the Governors who were not averse to change. Canon Robert Savage died in the middle of the discussions in the autumn of 1871 but some of the others including new Governors continued to back new developments. Savage's successor as vicar of Nuneaton, Henry Walford Bellairs, also replaced him on the Governing body. He had been a Schools Inspector (see above p.125) and immediately rose to prominence in the discussions.

4. Commissioner Stanton's Visit

Nuneaton's plan of reform was drawn up by Lord Lyttelton, one of three Chief Commissioners appointed to administer the Endowed Schools Act. King Edward's would have to produce a revised scheme for its endowment, to be approved by the Privy Council and both Houses of Parliament. Lyttelton had also taken more than a passing interest

> **Atherstone Grammar School leads the way.**
>
> Rev. Edward Sanderson, formerly Undermaster at Sherbourne school, achieved great success at Atherstone in the 1860s including a boarding house (8 in 1861 17 in 1871 just after he left) and two students entering Cambridge at the end of the decade. His approach was in sharp contrast to Nuneaton at the same time. His successor Rev. Smith Churchill was also successful. There was High praise of the efficient state of the school. (Chronicle 8.7.1871)   In 1881, as Nuneaton's new Headmaster struggled to get new boarders Atherstone had 27, though boarders –with more competition from King Edward's – declined to six in 1891; however, Atherstone still had nine in 1901, comparable to Nuneaton.

in the Nuneaton scheme and had corresponded with new vicar Bellairs in such a manner as to suggest they knew each other socially.[12] In 1872 Assistant Commissioner Charles Stanton came to Nuneaton to see if there had been any significant changes since Green's report. However, as Bellairs reported to Lyttelton: *It is a probability that the school is in the same state as described by Green in 1866.*[13]

Stanton's aim was to obtain a mutual agreement on endowment reform. He saw Bucknill as the main stumbling block to reform and suggested a *liberal arrangement* [14] to pension him off. Bucknill admitted to Stanton that he *did not object to give up the school but did not wish to give up his house in which he said he had grown old.*[15] Stanton compared the school with the rejuvenated Atherstone Grammar School (see side bar). King Edward's did not come out well. Atherstone's endowment was smaller but the school had made excellent use of it. Stanton was as critical as Green about Nuneaton's Grammar School and his recommendations were similar.

- A new school with accommodation for boarders and a playground; the trustees commented that they had *something of this sort in contemplation.*
- Removal of the *two departments* distinction and *the reconstruction of the education in the school.*

- A fee of £4 or £6 a year for day boys.
- A *thorough entrance examination* open to those at the National School and Smith's school and the neighbouring villages. One or two could be admitted free.
- The Master's co-operation was needed. A *Liberal arrangement* with him would be the practical solution. He teaches *conscientiously* and imparts Latin and Ancient History *very well* but he *does not pretend any interest in the school* and does not want to have more pupils or extend his range of subjects.[16]

Barely 15 years later all these changes – with the help of a new Master – had been achieved.

As the report acknowledged the main stumbling block was Bucknill. In December 1872 Lyttelton enquired of Stanton whether the Headmaster had resigned yet.[17] Bucknill had indicated when coveting his house (see above) that he would if necessary *bow to*

Canon Henry Bellairs vicar of Nuneaton and Chairman of the School Governors 1872-1892. His casting vote ensured the building of the new Grammar School

authority but there was no sign of this, until his death in Feb 1873 resolved the problem. Bellairs in a matter of fact way reported the news to the Commissioners : *poor Bucknill died this morning.* But in the very same letter he coolly revealed the opportunities that this presented: *Can we have a notion of the kind of scheme you propose?* [18] The way was now clear for change but Bellairs revealed the lack of constructive ideas and positive thoughts concerning change in the town. *We need something substantial* [from the Commissioners] *or we shall probably drift.* [19] Bellairs, who had been in Nuneaton just over a year, had spotted the local tendency towards inertia.

The issues discussed were:
1. A new Charter
2. A new Building
3. A revised Governing body
4. The charging of fees
5. The combining of the King Edward and Smith's school endowments
6. A Change to mixed education
1-4 all came about in some form within the next few years though not without controversy and number five was to follow before the end of the century.

5. A Girls' School?

Regarding point six Commissioners were keen to encourage girls' secondary schooling. Society was starting to accept the need for more advanced female education but Commissioners had been dismayed to find only a total of 13 endowed schools for girls in the whole country. A girls' school was a possibility in Nuneaton. In writing to Lyttelton, Bellairs saw that the issues of a double endowment and girls' education were linked. He remarked *We are I think prepared to start a girls' Grammar school if we can clear off the present teachers at Smith's.* [20] [and presumably use Smith's endowment money to set up the School.] He personally favoured girls' secondary education and had been instrumental in assisting Dorothea Beale to found Cheltenham Ladies College;[21] his remarks suggested cautious optimism. However, girls' secondary education was not to come to Nuneaton until 1910.

6. The Question Of Smith's Charity

On the combining of the endowments Bellairs was aware of the difficulties. Remarking that the 1870 Education Act (see above) *has produced a greater demand for places* he realised that *Smith's helps meet that demand.* [22] Bellairs, like most other churchmen, did not want undenominational Board Schools being set up in the town. As well as their remit to give preference to *such persons who are least capable of paying for the schooling of their children*, Smith's retained the Anglican ethos of its founders retaining the provisions to *instruct the children under their care in the principles of the Christian religion* and teach *the catechism of the Church of England*.[23] The view prevailed that Smith's should remain independent. The question of the survival of Smith's was financial as well as religious. Bellairs, writing to Lyttelton, confessed that combining the King Edward endowment with Smith's charity would be opposed. The problem was that *Newdegate and the ratepayers won't like it* as *Smith's relieves the rates*.[24] Charles Newdegate had led the opposition with a petition against interfering with Smith's Charity; fear of expense encouraged maintaining the status quo. The Governors did discuss the double endowment suggestion but as Bellairs predicted it came to nothing – at least for the time being.[25] (see below for 1896 developments and the end of Smith's.)

Nationally it was felt that the middle classes, for whom these kinds of schools were largely intended, should pay something towards the expenses of a school likely to undergo the upheaval of expansion. However, the idea of a capitation (entry) fee for anyone attending the school was treated with some suspicion – some believed it the end of free secondary education in endowed schools. Lester again expressed a view; that £10 initially would be much too high for a capitation fee as *very few* parents could manage it; and he also argued that there should be no religious test before attending.[26]. The Governors wanted the high fee but the Commissioners opposed it. The ladder of opportunity for the poor was in place, but it was a narrow and insecure one.

7. Proposals For A Revised Scheme; Further Give And Take

Further opposition to educational reform focused on the new wide representation proposed for the Governing body. While the Governors originally contemplated traditional figures like the Lord Lieutenant of the County and one of the County M.P.s on the governing body,[27] it was clear that Commissioners would insist on a wider range of representation. The Governors' idea that their peers should be resident and possess £500 of real or personal wealth suggests a path as socially exclusive as it was traditional[28]. The Commissioners insisted that the forces of authority must be represented by Magistrates and more locally elected representatives must be chosen by Ratepayers. This caused those in authority locally some alarm. In his Report based on his visit to the town on 4th November, Stanton referred to the *unconcealed dismay* he had encountered at the idea of a Ratepayer election for school governors.[29] Bellairs' view was that even a £10 Ratepayer limit would *introduce a rotten element*. Stanton had been told there were *very few professional men in Nuneaton* and he agreed there was *truth in this*. Feelings of bitterness abounded. Bellairs warned him that if four particular people were elected, others would resign.[30] The sitting of Magistrates on the Governing Body also caused difficulty. No Magistrate that operated in the petty session held at Nuneaton lived in the town and so opponents of the scheme argued that a rigid application of this rule to Nuneaton would be inappropriate. This emphasised the desire of the Nuneaton people to run their own affairs as far as possible without interference from even the near outside.

The death of Bucknill in Feb. 1873 and Bellairs' subsequent request to Stanton for advice soon got things moving. In March and April 1873 Bellairs twice reported to Lyttelton *that we are working away at our scheme*.[31] The idea of combining the endowment with Smith's Charity was dropped. As Bellairs – not a universally popular figure in the town – remarked, *I doubt the wisdom of a vicar suggesting confiscation*.[32] Stanton felt *Nuneaton is not an attractive place per se* and Boarders would be a *hazardous experiment*. He suggested a wider range of subjects, English Grammar and Composition, English Literature and History, Physical Science, Algebra and Geometry, Latin and one Modern Language, Drawing, Drilling and Vocal Music.[33] This was accepted and broadly remained the curriculum followed in the early days of the new school. The Governors were forced to accept the threefold division of Governors into co-opted, representative and magisterial.

Governors won a few concessions. They *decline to entertain the question* of giving up their charity dole money (such as Willoughby's and Orton's) to add to the overall endowment for the school. These continued to be administered separately by the Trustees.[34] The Commissioners also agreed to allow the current Governors to serve for life, as had been the custom since 1553, rather than the fixed times under the new scheme for those elected in the future . Governors also refused to countenance the possibility of women Governors. The town's conservatism on this issue makes one wonder how feasible was Bellairs' idea for a girls' secondary school. The Governors also got their way on the taking of boarders.

On the last day of 1874 the Governors formally accepted the scheme that, with major modifications, would ensure the survival and guide the direction of the Grammar School in Nuneaton for 100 years. It was noted that *certain inhabitants continued to object* especially Estlin who was sent a letter *regretting his continued opposition.*[35] Many locals disliked the idea of opening up the Grammar School to those outside that *ancient parish* of the town.

Boys at John o'Groats or Land's End would be placed on precisely the same footing as Nuneaton which is a state of things quite at variance with the original Charter.[36]

Estlin demanded a local Inquiry which he claimed could be held under the terms of the Act of 1869. Others supported him. They included a much wider social range of people than involved hitherto; they argued that Governors should be resident and in possession of £500 real or personal wealth. Only £20 ratepayers should vote and church control should remain strong: the Bishop's jurisdiction should remain and be transferred to Worcester. Tuition fees should be limited to between £3 and £5 per annum.[37]

This was a plea against any degree of central direction, a jealous guarding of parochial independence in opposition to the religious liberalism of the Commissioners and a resistance to the democratic element in the choosing of Governors. But the protest was too late: the previous lack of interest in local initiatives to reform the school (despite the efforts of Canon Savage), ironically resulted in what many of the middle classes in the town opposed; greater central control and direction of education. This control would gradually tighten its grip in the 20th Century as national policy looked towards the creation of wider educational opportunities for all girls and boys of whatever creed and social class. Some objections related to points on which the Commissioners were determined to stand firm. Lyttelton would not re-consider their case and no public enquiry was held.

Here, the strange configuration of Nuneaton parish went against those trying to hold on to what they saw as local independence. There were, for example, streets that straddled two parishes and boys living in parts of Coton parish (historically always distinct) lived barely a quarter of a mile from the school, whereas boys from the farthest corner of Stockingford parish (but part of the ancient historic parish of Nuneaton) were several miles away. Stanton argued that *the interests of the school and the town itself will best be served by throwing open the benefits of the school as widely as possible.* [38] He felt the need to prevent a clique of what he saw as like-minded, narrow-minded, businessmen.

So the proposed Scheme of Government was sent for Parliamentary Ratification. Two months after the final signatures in 1876 the Governors accepted the new proposals. (See Appendix Ten) They represented a typical reform of the country's Grammar Schools with local touches pertaining to the situation in Nuneaton. It was a profound change representing as it did a modification of the King Edward foundations from the 16th Century and arguably the most significant change for 325 years. The original Trustees would continue to administer the Endowment and the Governors were now entrusted with the management of the school but the permission of the Charity Commissioners would be needed for the new buildings. The demarcation between the Governors and Head was similar to many schools. [39]

8. A New Building?

Only a new building would provide the opportunity to implement the recommended changes, expand the school and start to develop different classrooms for specialist teaching.

In July 1877 Governors formally agreed to erect a new school. A possible candidate for architect Clapton Rolfe, [40] was finishing the building of a new Church in Nuneaton on the Old Priory site in the fast growing Manor Court district of the town. Henry Bellairs, vicar of Nuneaton, (out of which parish the new St Mary's parish was being carved) Chairman of the Grammar School Governors, wanted Rolfe to design the school.

Bellairs' views carried great weight not only because of his position in the town but also his educational background. Rolfe's work at the *Abbey*[41] Church had not met with universal approval, but at the end of August 1877 he was invited to prepare plans.[42] His brief was a school to accommodate 100 boys including 30 boarders. Its cost should not exceed £3000. Two months later his initial proposals exceeded the £3000 estimate but Bellairs and the Building Committee predicted that an increased outlay *would probably not be objected to* – they were wrong. Six old and four new Governors met in September and October when Bellairs claimed to *being taken by surprise* by opposition at a lively meeting in October when twelve Governors – seven old and four new – were split on whether to continue with Rolfe's scheme. The scheme went ahead on the casting vote of Chairman Bellairs, who had thought, naively, that once Rolfe had been appointed, controversy would be at an end. [43]

The argument continued to develop in the Governors meetings. At the turn of the years 1877 and 1878 there had been a *very animated* discussion amongst them. Vicar of

Attleborough John Thomas led the opposition to Bellairs' idea of accepting Rolfe's plans. The Abbey Church *does not give general satisfaction*, argued Thomas, criticising the architect for spending too much on the new church. The personal animosity between Bellairs and Thomas was apparent. The latter accused Bellairs of pursuing his *friend's* plan. If the Governors were to *expend so great a part of a comparatively poor endowment* they should *use the utmost care* to give satisfaction in the selection of their plans. Thomas argued further that the Charity Commissioners had only accepted that the building plans fell within their general regulations about school design; this did not mean they were appropriate in this instance.[44]

9. Opposition Continues

The dispute moved up a gear at the start of 1878. Bellairs took exception to Thomas' letter to the local paper at the end of 1877 publicly setting out his misgivings concerning the plans, feeling that Governor confidentiality had been breached.[45] Was a theological argument lurking beneath the surface? Commissioner Stanton felt personal squabbles were largely unrelated to the real issues under discussion, that is the question of the amount of payment and whether alternatives to Rolfe were needed. The matter *has become to a great extent a personal one instead of being considered on its merits. My efforts were directed as much to keep down exhibitions of ill temper and angry words as to endeavour to bring some compromise between the contending parties.*[46] Contemporaries were aware of the problems. In July 1876 when requesting private voting papers rather than a public meeting for election of new Governors, the reason given was that such meetings were *almost always attended with a display of party feeling and sometimes of great bitterness of spirit also.*[47]

Despite Rolfe's plans being accepted on a Chairman's casting vote discussion and argument continued. A similar opposition was now being drummed up to Rolfe's detailed plans just as it had been concerning the details of the new Charter; the same people were involved.

The town, increasingly interested in the future of the Grammar School, joined in the debate. At a public meeting in March 1878 the scheme was criticised as being too expensive. Ezekiel Haddon asserted there was a *widespread feeling* of concern regarding the Governors' expenditure of the school's funds since some investments needed to be realised.[48] but Bellairs was determined to push the scheme through and just got his way at the Governors' meetings.[49]

The opponents of the more elaborate versions of the new building fought hard: they

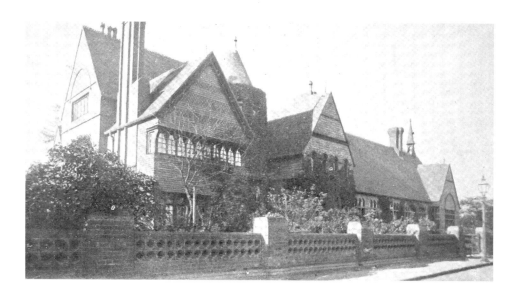

The Headmaster's House (left) and the new school building of 1880 (right) taken before the extensions of 1904

argued that there should be competition for the design and only £3,000 should be spent on it.[50] The Nuneaton scheme was seen as a *dangerous speculation* It was *Most improbable* that the number of 100 pupils would be realised and even if this were so, extra Masters would be required. The forecast that the school would soon contain 100 students, more than double the existing number, was seen as too optimistic. This was not entirely untrue in the short run – the 100 number was not reached until 1909. (see below p.187) However, in retrospect, some of the opposition seems narrow-minded and penny pinching. Because of the national depression of the late 1870s one Governor argued that it was not a good time to sell the Stivichall lands at Coventry, between the new railway and the Kenilworth Road, to help pay for the project. They were likely to fetch a much better price later. In fact great demand for housing in Coventry ensured a good price.[51]

Stanton was unimpressed with the opposition's arguments. The planned sale of the Stivichall land, which was expected to raise at least £4000, meant more than £3000 could be spent on the new building if necessary. The additional expense was seen as a statement of pride in the educational heritage of the town. Stanton commented that the design was *not unsuitable for the chief school in a town of 8,000 inhabitants. Within reasonable limits a handsome building is the best advertisement of a new school.* [52]

One other objection was that national systems were being imposed on the area. Typical here were the views of local M.P. Charles Newdegate when he later presided at the annual meeting of the Nuneaton Institute, objecting to:-

• The cost
• What he termed *Delocalisation of benefits* (presumably that non-Nuneatonians could benefit from the new educational opportunities.)
• The alteration of the school's constitution. Under Eustace he argued, the school is *a foundation that cannot be improved.* This clearly became a mistaken view in retrospect. In truth his objections were more ideological – the way that changes were being effected. He said *I do not believe in providing for the nation as a lump.*[53]

There was also concern regarding the social exclusivity of the school and its catchment area. Boarders might take precedence over local boys and fees (even allowing for scholarships) would lead to the exclusion of able boys from poorer families. However, the view of Stanton and the Commissioners was that, given the general acceptance of the three classes in society, it was reasonable that a school primarily intended for the middle classes, should ask this class – who could afford it – to pay towards the education of their sons. To a modern mind this begs two questions – would a few scholarships really be enough to include able boys from the poorer classes –there must have been a huge wastage of talent here – and why should these opportunities be denied to girls? These matters would be raised more effectively by later generations. A majority of Governors, now accepted Rolfe's design and Stanley and Ward proposed that no more than £3,500 be spent but this was defeated eleven votes to two. Opposition, though still vigorous, appeared impotent.[54]

The site adjacent to Peacock Lane (later King Edward Road) was seen as the only feasible one once the idea of building on the land acquired on the other side of Church Street had been rejected. Stanton noted that while the plans for the new building did not *completely interface* with the old site, they had the advantage of being *central and convenient.* The two lime trees would be kept. The *Slightly rising land* had good drainage. There was a visible incline on the west side, down towards the meadow and a stream. It was a *circumscribed area,* a point which caused difficulties later.[55] This Stanton saw as the main shortcoming but, in a crucial judgement, he argued that the site was acceptable if no other suitable one could be found. The Governors were to assure him this was so once the possibility of glebe land in the Hinckley Road had been turned down. A local smell was seen as a disadvantage: Bellairs referred to occasional *offensive effluvia* but the Governors eventually accepted the new scheme on the 18th June 1878. The dispute had not been so much about the need for a new school or even its siting, but about its size, design and expense. These were related: the mock Tudor design with Gothic trimmings that was accepted would be more expensive. Argument had gone on for 18 months, but the final Governor vote of nine votes to six represented a victory for Bellairs and his supporters.[56] The elaborate design of the new school would emphasise its growing status in the town.

10. The Old Headmaster's House

Details from Clapton Rolfe's design: 'Motifs of the Street and Butterfield schools (Pevsner)'

Discussion also centred on the fate of the old Headmaster's House. In the years after Bucknill first arrived in 1842 repairs were carried out regularly. However, by 1861 Dr Edward Nason (senior) reported to the Charity Commissioners that *the school, and the Head's House are old and badly out of repair. The Trustees contemplate in a few years time building on the piece of land lately purchased a new school and house for both Masters.* The

Commissioners agreed with the Governors that it was *not worthwhile to make any serious expense or repair to the Master's House if another is contemplated.* [57] Stanton was told of its poor condition. It was *visibly in bad repair.* The walls were only 9 inches thick and stuccoed to keep out damp. [58] Floors were rotten, there was only one staircase and rooms were low and small. On average, £57 had been spent annually on it in the last five years. Those opposed to change did not feel the House was beyond repair; it should remain and then a more modest new building could be constructed without the addition of the Head's house.

Those opposed to the new school also opposed a new Head's house. At the public meeting of March 1878 (see above) Ezekiel Haddon had argued that *the old House occupied by the Schoolmaster should remain.* [59] The fees lately charged for Eustace's boarders had helped finances and there was now a net income of £143 per annum. Haddon argued that a good building could eventually be produced but it was better to wait until the income had built up. Also he argued the old house should not be sold at a time of depression. [60] But the demolishers won the argument. In July 1880 when the new building was completed the days of the old Head's House were numbered: it was in a *very dilapidated condition.* The newly appointed Head was reported as being *very anxious that the building should be removed and the out offices of the school disinfected before he enters into residence.* The new Headmaster and his family entered a new Head's House whose design was carefully integrated with the design of the school. [61]

11. How Was The New Building Financed?

Commissioners agreed that, given the future income likely from fees, a portion of endowment land should be sold to raise capital, despite some local opposition. The surveyor employed by the school, Jeremiah Matthews, recommended the property at Stivichall as the one to sell for £4000 which would raise the capital required. [62] The school planned by the Governors was to be of a *substantial and permanent character suitable for the professional and commercial classes.* At least ten private boarders were to be accommodated with a maximum of 30. The existing number of 28 day boys was predicted to rise to 70 and probably 100 with boarders. [63] The annual turnover was around the thousand pound mark with revenue from the boys' fees now supplying two thirds of the income and the unsold land endowment one third so a fundamental change in income source had been effected. About £115 a year in investment income had been lost but the change in the balance of the accounting was more to do with the £730 estimated annual income from fees. No longer could a free grammar school education be had. Between 1880 and 1944 the school was run on the basis of an institution for boys of better off parents with limited –though gradually increasing – opportunities for those from humbler backgrounds by way of the exhibitions and scholarships available.

The degree of change can be exaggerated. Those going to the Grammar School in the earlier part of the century had tended to be from the better off classes in the town and Stanton had remarked earlier (see page**) that those in the English School were not significantly of a lower class from those in the Latin one. The Head's annual salary would now be £150. Tuition fees were £5 16/10d a year. Greek could be taught at £3 extra. 10% would be exempt from fees and 20% could pay part fees.[64]

12 Meanwhile…

Amidst this frenzy of activity in the mid to late 1870s the ordinary life of the school carried on. Once Eustace was promoted to fill Bucknill's place after February 1873 he was willing to move with the times and embrace reform. Boys were now entered for the increasingly popular Cambridge local exams, Ernest Driver passing the exam with honours in 1877.[65] This began a connection with Cambridge examination entries that was to last almost exclusively for over 100 years. By 1882 the school was regularly entering candidates for exams, winning 20 prizes in that year. French and now German were on offer but at an additional payment of £2 and £4 respectively.[66]

Eustace also introduced an annual sports day held in July with prizes supplied by townsfolk. Town/gown links were also emphasised in March 1878 when a concert for establishing a Library at King Edward's was held at the Vicarage Street Schoolrooms and was reported as *literally crowded with the elite of Nuneaton*. Mr. Bates, vicar choral of Lichfield, soon to join the staff on a formal basis, conducted the Grammar School choir.[67] A mixture of social, sporting and academic events now developed and continued for another century. Thus King Edward's was developing various occasions, as did many other schools at about the same time, *when the school was on public display*.[68] The first recorded use of the school Latin seal, Segillum Schola Etone, was in 1876. Unofficial sports for reckless schoolboys, however, remained traditional. In December 1879, when skating and sliding on the reservoir near the wool factory, one boy, Leslie Oldham, ventured into the river and sank in. He received a thorough ducking.[69] Numbers grew and Eustace used the agreement to take boarders which, apart from anything else, supplemented his income. According to Nason[70] it was the expectation of these boarders that resulted in the development of the sort of more organised sports that had established themselves in the better known public schools, not least nearby Rugby.

School Seal: first known use, 1876

The ingredients of success of the ever-growing public or independent schools was a broad liberal education with classics still important as a training for the mind but with a wider range of subjects, such as science, being included in the curriculum. Sport and religious habits were encouraged. A strong sense of community was emphasised, especially if there was a boarding element, with responsibilities given to senior boys. But there was still room for the individual school to develop its own particular identity, with a strong lead from the top – a Headmaster in charge of a growing number of both staff and pupils. Many of these features were part of Nuneaton Grammar School's development. Apart from the boarding element which faded by 1910, the following description of how the school ethos developed would not be inappropriate for the next 100 years up to the end of the Grammar School in 1974. Eustace took in boarders, encouraged sports, looked to widen the curriculum and maintained religious observance. His comment at the sports day in 1878 accurately reflected an increasingly popular mode of thinking about the value of more organised sport: *When a boy can run well in a race it is a proof he has endurance and that he will probably run well in the race of life.* [71]

Another clergyman, James Ridgeway Hakewill, graduate of Exeter College Oxford was appointed to assist Eustace in 1873 but left at the end of the following year. However, by 1879 Eustace had acquired two assistants rather than one.[72] Administration costs increased and instead of the two acting Governors writing any necessary letters, Henry Dewes of the legal firm Dewes and Roberts was employed – a transition to the employment of a clerk to the Governors, a post that would last throughout the 20th Century. [73]

Finances for 1879 [74]			
A simple profit and loss summary before the greater complexity after 1880. With no role for the state as yet in secondary education the largest single source of income is still the endowment but fees first collected under the new charter of 1875 are already making a major contribution.			
Balance	£163-16/5d	Salaries	£539-14/2d
Rents and Interest	£405- 7/6d	Stationary	£40-18/-
Capitation/Entrance Fees	£305-10/-	Chemicals	£3- 13/2d
Stock Dividend	£ 10-11/4d	Coal/Cleaning	£11 -4/9d
		Repairs	£5 -4/6d
		Rates/Insurance	£17-8/-
		Printing/Advertising	£4-17/-
		Incidentals	£2-0/9d
		Clerk's salary	£3-3/-
(1879)	£865-7/3d		£853-7/3d

On the eve of the building of the new school it was inspected again by Reverend R. Potter. Eustace had now had time to implant his own style on the whole school. Potter noted a *Great improvement since a few years ago* [and it was an] *efficient school.* Potter's final remarks that *the subjects taught and the system of education adopted are well adapted to the town of Nuneaton and its neighbourhood* might have suggested the school could rest on its laurels but in an indirect way also hinted at change.[75] Professional classes in the now rapidly growing town began to take more interest in the school and to see it as a possible institution for their sons. Now it was a matter of time before a new school was built. Eustace's work ensured that a new school ethos pre-dated the new building of 1880.

In February 1880 the Nuneaton Chronicle reported two apparently separate pieces of news in successive weeks. Eustace was resigning as Master and the new building was nearing completion. A new Master –the term *Head*master could now be used more accurately – was soon in post: On Monday 12th April the Governors appointed the Reverend Samuel George Waters, Foundation scholar of Trinity Hall Cambridge and 32nd Wrangler out of 120 in Mathematics, to be Headmaster, out of 46 candidates.[76] Waters was to preside over the new building and to all intents and purposes, a new school. In the same month it opened, September 1880, the death of long standing Governor Joseph Taverner was reported. A Hartshill farmer aged 87, he was described as being from *a family of English yeomen*. The last of a long line of Governors from this background had died at the same moment as the old school.[77]

CHAPTER NINE

A New School For Nuneaton: The Headship Of Samuel Waters 1880-1908

Some people only looked up to education as a means of fitting their children for any particular trade, but education should be regarded in its proper light as a means of developing the mind.
Headmaster Samuel Waters 1896

During this period the Nuneaton Grammar school changed direction and established a more favourable reputation. Before coming to Nuneaton, Samuel Waters had taught for nearly nine years at Oswestry and Macclesfield Grammar Schools.[1] His impact on the school was immense: but there were three other significant factors influencing its future direction: the new buildings, the rapid growth of Nuneaton and, after 1902, the start of state funding of secondary education.

1. Early Days Of The New School Building

Samuel Waters: Headmaster 1880-1908: The worth of the school was not what it did for the genius but for the ordinary boy

Waters was faced with a difficult initial term. Eustace took eight boarders with him to Bulkington vicarage, so just 36 boys were at the school in September 1880.[2] There was also a brief rival. A proprietory (private) school teaching Latin, Euclidean Maths, French and elementary Science was set up in Dugdale Street by the 23 year old William Westwood and charging somewhat less than King Edward's, though this new institution did not last long.[3] The average age of the King Edward pupils in 1880/1 was only a little over 11 with just one boarder.[4] This barely seems like a secondary school in our modern understanding of the term. However, many of these boys, bearing in mind the success of the National schools in Nuneaton, may well have attended the Grammar School as their second school. The average age of the first application now steadily increased.[5]

There was now freedom to run a secondary school on modern lines. What did *freedom* and *modern* mean in 1880? Being an endowed school Nuneaton Grammar was free from any school board control, financially dependent on the King Edward endowment to pay their staff. There was a major change: a free education (in the sense of no payment) would now only be provided for a few boys. Apart from the endowment, two other sources of income – bringing an opportunity to expand the school – were charging fees for a majority of the pupils and taking in boarders. The school could now earn grants to develop new subjects from organisations like the Science and Art Department, though at some loss to their independence.

There was, as yet, no sense of an organised secondary sector of education but increasing educational demands from elementary schoolchildren would help to develop this in the next few years. Though it would be inspected, the school could develop its own character. Even with the growth of different kinds of schools and an increasing emphasis on Technical Education, traditional endowed Grammar Schools were still highly regarded. Moreover, it was commonly held that any new developments must not *entail comparative neglect of studies which are of less obvious and immediate utility though not of less moment for the formation of mind and character.*[6]

The school attempted to maintain a balance between vocational studies and a more liberal education. Subjects offered expanded from Classics and English Grammar to more Mathematics (Trigonometry, Algebra and Mechanics) but also included a broader approach to Divinity, History and Geography as well as Science, Modern Languages, (French and German) as well as Art, Music and Drill taught by peripatetic teachers. At first, opportunities for radical change were limited. The comparative grandness of Clapton Rolfe's design should not hide the fact that classroom space was not extensive. Only part of the frontage in King Edward Road existed for teaching. On one side was the Headmaster's House with its accommodation for boarders, and on the other the vicarage garden, before another new building went up in 1903/4 (see below). The Hall was a traditional large schoolroom 41 foot by 20 foot with two cloakrooms 13 foot by 16-18 foot each opening off to the hall at one end.[7] At the other end were two more classrooms. The old concept of a Headmaster in charge keeping an eye on two or three other teachers was still prevalent. In this respect, not everything had changed in 1880. If the plan was to have 100 pupils (see above p.151) then, without further physical expansion, the traditional teaching of large numbers in a large Hall in a mechanistic fashion, with just two or three staff in control, would probably continue. In 1892 an Inspector described the building as *artistic but not commodious* though at that stage with 60 pupils in school it *suffice*[d] *for the present number of boys*.[8] Four forms had now emerged doing different levels of work, divided by the standard attained rather than by age.

The Headmaster's House c.1900

2. Expansion Of The Staff

The distinctive nature of the Grammar School was not to be merely its architecture. There were two important functions. One was to provide a route to the Universities, no longer just Oxford and Cambridge; the other, to round off the education of the growing number of scholars destined for employment in commerce and the minor professions. This combination meant the continuation of a central role for classics, but no longer its predominance. A Headmaster appointed who was a Mathematics Wrangler and noted for his teaching of geology[9] was a clear statement of intent to follow a more diverse path. One tactic, common at this time to other endowed Grammar schools, was to put increasing emphasis on science, distinguishing King Edward's from elementary schools.

A larger staff with some degree of specialisation developed. This was linked to a wider range of subjects and full use of the two classrooms adjacent to the larger room. In 1881 Waters had six assistants but only two of them were full time.[10] Modern Languages were developed as the appointment of French teacher Monsieur Stephany showed. There was greater emphasis on physical activity. The Grammar School had become used to games in Eustace's day but now appointed a drilling Master, Sergeant Cooper, imported a Music teacher, John Bates (a Lichfield Cathedral Choral Scholar) and a drawing Master J.J. Trego. The greater maturity of many of the staff was apparent – in 1881 Cooper was 51, Trego 43, Bates 30 and Waters himself 31. This may have been significant in distancing the school from the kind of private school that tended – apart from the Head – to have very young teachers. Only Ernest B.S. Escott (23)[11] and his replacement after one year, Ernest Robinson, (20) from Cavendish College were more in the tradition of the very young men of the past. In a local cricket match Robinson's *fine hitting was much admired* [12] the first but definitely not the last example of sporting prowess among the staff that would be a feature of the rest of the history of the school.

It was difficult to find the income to finance drill and music from either endowment income or fees and Waters arranged drill privately at his own expense from 1882-1890 before it ceased for a time. A Drill Sergeant had returned by 1899 when the calling up of troops for the Boer War, including 52 from Nuneaton, revealed an alarming state of unfitness among young British men, something which it was hoped schools could rectify. At the start of 1902, with the war still unfinished, a letter from the Imperial War Office about drilling was discussed by Governors. They agreed to the proposal if the cost was no more than £15. The letter suggested the use of live ammunition. Governors noted that the Drill Sergeant would deal with the question of the number of guns. The boys would pay for the ammunition.[13]

Staff turnover was high in the early days of the new building. Of the original Masters of 1880 only Waters and Trego were still present in 1884. Arthur Samman had a background reminiscent of earlier teachers. On the staff between 1890-96 and a Graduate of Peterhouse, Cambridge he doubled as curate at St Nicolas Church before moving on to a career in the parochial Ministry. When he left the boys presented him with a silver pocket communion service and a silver Baptisimal shell, the first concrete evidence of pupils' gifts to a departing member of staff. [14] The classical heritage of the school was still present. Latin Grammar was the first lesson of the day in Form IV, the most senior, but also frequent in the other three classes. At an additional £1 a term Greek was an optional extra and would be taken with a view to Oxbridge entry.[15] Numbers for Greek were in single figures and stopped altogether after 1897. Oxbridge entry now became a rarity until after the First World War when these Universities dropped the Greek requirement. In fact few boys stayed on beyond 15 years of age except those bound for University such as Ward and Cawthorne in 1887 to Cambridge and London respectively. Albert Basset Holman, who joined the staff in 1897 to teach Classics, did not teach Greek but concentrated on Latin and Ancient History as well as French and English. He soon became Waters' right hand man.

The Inspectors' Report of 1892 noted how hard and efficiently Waters worked. The school would have been *undermanned but for the energy and excellent organising powers of the HM*. But, added the Inspector, how could it support an increase in staff with its present income? *Masters are not overpaid.*[16] With four classes and only three full time teachers what happened to the fourth class? If not combined with one of the others, it must have been taught by the part timers such as art master Trego or a pupil teacher; the trainee present in 1892 had not passed any public examination. In 1900, with some increase in pupils, a fourth full time teacher was appointed.[17] The new building, different Governors, the leadership of Waters and, later, Holman, the rapid growth of the town and the swiftly changing educational priorities in the country as a whole were all to play their part in further expansion. When Waters retired at the end of 1908 there were still only five full time teachers and three part time (shorthand, music and drill) but within a few years numbers of full-time staff rose to eight.

3 Social Background Of The Pupils: Fees And Finances

The main educational opportunities that King Edward's was now providing was for the social class the Endowed Commissioners had intended to reap the benefits. The early names show that the manufacturing as well as the professional middle classes now saw it as a desirable place for their sons. This was emphasised by the rapid growth of the town's industries between 1880 and 1900, especially textiles, coal and brick, underpinned by railway growth. Those with a coal mining background were less prominent though William B.Cocks, future solicitor and Chairman of the School Governors was the son of a colliery agent (see Appendix11 for more detail). The Grammar school was attempting to provide educational opportunities for the social class that the Endowed schools Commissioners (and public opinion generally in the late 19th Century) intended: the middle class. The manufacturing as well as the professional middle classes now saw the school as a desirable place for their son in a way that had not always been the case with their, admittedly, less numerous predecessors. (see above p.141).

The new features of the school – apart from the buildings – soon began to stand out. In 1883 fees were raised to £3 a term for the under 14s and £3 6/8d a term for the older pupils. Apart from a reduction for under 11s in 1891 to just £7 and 10 shillings a year, these financial arrangements remained until the changes of 1904/5 when the increased numbers arrived, assisted by the pupil teachers.[18](see below) Waters also had discretion on what he charged boarders. The intention of the reformers of the Endowed Schools was that these institutions were largely for the middle classes because of the education given. It was believed that these parents could afford the moderate fees the school was charging. However, there was also a belief that boys (in some areas girls as well but not in Nuneaton yet) of exceptional ability from the working classes should not be denied the opportunities for the social advance that an education at the Grammar School might make possible. These boys were seen as exceptional in a double sense: both in academic ability and working class origin. This analysis reveals the social assumptions of the time. Scholarships or bursaries from the school endowment were offered to poor families, financed from the yearly endowment income, £350 per annum. But the take up of Scholarships proved problematical. In 1892 the Governors requested lowering the age at which they could be awarded from 12 to 10. The reason given was that *The boys who go to the elementary schools are not taught the same subjects as at the Grammar School* so the Head wanted them two years earlier. If boys arrived at 12 without having studied Latin for instance, they would be at a disadvantage. The evolution of a more varied curriculum gradually removed this problem. [19]

Canon John Deed Vicar of Nuneaton and Chairman of the Governors 1893-1923.
He arranged an exchange of church glebe land for the Old Grammar school to
facilitate school expansion, 1903

In 1895 Governors Sir Edward Newdegate and Nuneaton vicar Canon John Deed commented on the lack of financial assistance boys received. Newdegate argued townspeople should stump up money for scholarships in a process which Deed said might attract *boys from outside* – presumably more boarders.[20] Meanwhile, five endowment places were on offer – in 1896 thirteen candidates competed for them. Those successful generally had skilled working class backgrounds. [21] Educational opportunities were gradually moving down the social scale as society became more prosperous and staying on rates at school increased. Yet Scholarships did not bring equality of opportunity; the book fee and money for uniforms would still inhibit the poorest. For those attending King Edward's there was still a sense of their good fortune in being at the school and getting better than average opportunities. Without any system of student grants, scholarships were the only chance for even the moderately well-off to have the opportunity of attaining qualifications that might make degree study possible. William C. Kaye received a leaving grant of £50 to attend Birmingham University in 1905 but Governors would not be able to afford this generosity on more than an individual basis.[22] New Universities blossomed but the buds of local authority financial assistance were barely visible. As a result, students from more modest backgrounds, while they might receive assistance to stay on at school, would lack the means to go higher on the educational ladder. A scholarship winner of 1895, George Alcock, whose father was a platelayer at the Stanley brickworks, later worked as a coal loader in Hinckley, a job described by George Orwell in his essay *Down the Mine* as *dreadful… half-naked kneeling men, one to every four or five yards, driving their shovels under the fallen coal and flinging it over their left shoulders.* So, school growth remained slow but by 1900 an extra class, form five, appeared. There were just five scholars in it in 1906 preparing for more advanced courses.[23] From now on staying on until at least 17 became more common and leaving early to continue studying at another school less so.

4. A Boarding Phase

The bias towards the better off was emphasised by the taking of boarders. The accommodation in the Headmaster's House was two dormitories, one for 15 pupils and one for five or six. The Boarders Dining Room (day pupils were not to have one for some time) was described in 1892 as *sufficient at present but small in the event of increased numbers.*[24] Boarders ages ranged from 11-14.

They were from both near and far, reflecting different rates of charging for weekly boarders and permanent ones. In 1881 there had been a single boarder, Herbert W. Ellis aged eleven from Market Harborough. Waters built up the numbers – 16 by 1892 – and the traditional professional classes were starting to trust him. With boarders, Waters used the Anglican Church catechism as part of his teaching, something he did not impose on the day boys because of their more varied denominational backgrounds.[25] However, by 1901 there were just seven boarders left, from five families, coming from various parts of the country.[26] During the first decade of the 20th Century King Edward's moved in the direction of a day school with state assistance, a prudent decision given the tenor of the times. With town expansion the number of local boys attending increased, especially with the financial help from local authorities. Moreover, the proximity of Rugby, an outstandingly successful boarding school, suggested the foolishness of an attempt to match them in social exclusivity. In 1901 an application for recognition as a day secondary school was raised at a Governors meeting[27] and by 1906 the world of boarders was replaced for the moment by the world of pupil teachers, the school becoming more closely connected to the growing industrial town which it was now starting to serve more widely. A significant change of direction had occurred. From 1905-1908 the occupation of the parents was noted in the applications, and boys of working class origin started to attend in greater numbers.

5. Curriculum Changes – The Growing Role Of Science

A Schoolboy's work is never done: (Source: 1892 Inspection) Timetable for Form IV: Older boys

	9.00-9.30	9.30-10.30	10.30-11.30	11.30-12.30	2.00-3.00	3.00-4.00
Mon	Latin Grammar	Divinity	Latin Translation	Algebra	Euclid	French
Tues	Latin Grammar	Latin Translation	French	Euclid	Drawing	German
Wed	Latin Grammar	English History	Latin	Arithmetic	No School	No School
Thurs	Latin Grammar	English Lit.	Latin Translation	Euclid	Latin Unseen	Mathematics
Fri	German	Algebra	Geography	French	Chemistry	Chemistry
Sat	English History (9-10)	Latin Grammar (10-11)	Arithmetic or Trigonometry (11-12)	Divinity (12-1.00)	No School	No School

Homework: Mon – Latin, French, Euclid.
                  Tues – Latin, History, Arithmetic.
                  Wed – Shakespeare, Latin, Euclid.
                  Thurs – Algebra, Geog, French.
                  Friday – History, Latin, Algebra.
                  Sat – Divinity, Latin, Algebra.

One boy studied Greek while others learnt German.

Back in the 1870s, discussion had raged in Nuneaton over the characteristics of a new school. The Royal Commission on Scientific Instruction 1871-75, the Devonshire Commission, had reported on the need for a place for science in every grade of education. After the Local Government Act of 1888 which established County Councils, these new authorities set up Technical Instruction Committees: the Technical Instruction Acts of 1889 and 1891 permitted raising Rates for science provision. Between 1895 and 1918, the bulk of English engineers were trained at municipal institutions on full or part time courses for those over 16 though some studied in Germany. King Edward's played its part in changing this situation. The school was influenced by the demands of *Woolwich and the Civil Service Commissioners* for science and modern language teaching and it sent a successful student to Woolwich[28] (see above section three).

A distinctive role for Science teaching began. In 1882 Electricity was on the curriculum and Herbert Ellis, that lone boarder of 1881, went on to become an electrical engineer.[29] Rolfe's design for the building, frankly soon outdated, had not considered laboratories but in 1887 the Old Grammar school was kitted out as a science lab.[30] John Hogg, a Cambridge graduate, was appointed in 1891. He was qualified as a South Kensington teacher in Science, but only stayed two years [31] though donating two new prizes for the pupils' best Natural History Collections. There was a rapid turnover of science teachers: the subject was in increasing demand but without sufficient numbers both ably qualified and wishing to teach it at school level. Still, from 1891, the annual Inspection of the school had a separate science report with papers sat in Inorganic Chemistry and Physics and in 1896 seven boys were examined in Practical Chemistry.[32] Attitudes had been transformed since the classically dominated days of Liptrott, Hughes and Bucknill and there had been great progress since the first suggestion to teach *natural philosophy* in the 1850s (see above p.123) Science was now seen as a valuable part of a traditional liberal education but also of great practical value. Geoffrey, one of the de Havilland brothers, was at the school in the 1890s and went on to a very distinguished career as an aeronautical designer.

The engineering profession was now growing more quickly than church, law or medicine.[33] When in 1898 Geometrical Drawing was added to the curriculum it had to be at an extra £6 per annum fee. However, external funding was becoming available. From 1895 the Technical Education Committee had granted £50 to assist in paying for a Science teacher [34] but the relatively limited facilities were hardly conducive to a prolonged stay unless there were prospects for a new building with more sophisticated laboratory equipment. So promising young scientists came – and went. Austin Kirby, graduate of St John's Cambridge left after two years in 1903 to be a science lecturer in Antigua and follow a distinguished colonial career as a director of Agriculture, receiving the OBE in 1926.[35] A school memoir claims that his over-exuberant behaviour at the Nuneaton Conservative Club, celebrating the news of the end of the Boer War in May 1902, may have led to his premature departure. Anyway, his final lesson was a memorable one – with explosions galore.

The Board of Education at South Kensington gave awards in theoretical chemistry to J.R.F. Ding and A.W.R. Moreton in 1902.[36] Moreton went on to teach in Jersey. Opportunities for more widespread success in practically based science would soon appear. Kirby's replacement, 28 year old William Walpole Day, brought stability to the role of science teacher and he also had the advantage of the first purpose built premises for his subject. (see below) Over the next thirty years Day played a leading part in developing the reputation of the school for sound instruction in science, his name perpetuated in a school science prize. He later became Second Master and stayed until his death, aged 58, in 1932.

Other subjects in the advanced class were Latin, Mathematics, History, Geography, English Literature, French and German. In the lower two forms there was more emphasis on basic English – spelling, dictation, parsing – though class two was taught 14 different subjects in a 32 period week. The remark that *In few schools, is History so well and carefully studied* contrasted with a comment just two years earlier that geographical knowledge was *undigested. A boy who can tell all about the Trading ports of China but sets down the Euphrates in India has not taken his geography as a whole.* Maths and Natural Science, though still less than properly equipped, *seem to be above average for this grade of school* (1889) a revealing comment on other schools. Despite some criticisms, it was noted that boys were often taught to think. In 1891 pupils were praised for their knowledge and understanding of Shakespeare: they possessed *Good familiarity with the text, not just with the Commentary, as so often happens.*[37]

Homework was set every night, usually three subjects with *only one to one and a half hours* for the lower class. There was a full range of books available from *Vere Foster's Copybook* (a most successful volume on penmanship, in print from the 1860s to the 1960s) to Argett's *Electricity and Magnetism*. Classes were not rigidly defined by age but by aptitude.[38]

6. Governors

By 1900 the Governors came from a different background and performed a different role from 19th Century ones. They now represented the leading figures in the town:

Industrialists	Businessmen	Professionals	Landed	Traders
Johnson: Textiles	Swinnerton: Timber	Oakey, Brock-Harris: Law	Newgate: (Vice-Chairman)	Haddon: Grocer
Melly: Coal	Slingsby: Ribbon regalia	Hunt, Browning, Deed: Church (Deed Chairman)		
Knox: Brick	Thomas Smith: Building	Nason: Medical		

It remained an unwritten rule that the vicar of Nuneaton chaired the Governors. In 1893 in the interregnum between the retirement of Bellairs and the appointment of the new vicar John George Deed, Dr Edward Nason senior took the chair temporarily but the new vicar was soon appointed to the post.[39] These men showed more involvement and greater drive than in earlier generations and they developed ambitious plans for the School. A representative from Birmingham University joined the Governing body

–indicating a desire to make contact with the growingly important non-Oxbridge University world. The school had set its sights on high achievement for its top pupils. The everyday running of the school was left to the Headmaster. The Governors' main task was to look after the investments and property of the endowment with specific regard to maintenance and their role would increase at a time of new building as in 1902-4. (see below) But they may not have anticipated a new challenge: negotiation and discussion with the local authorities who – given their increasingly important role of financial assistance – were taking a closer interest in the size and purpose of the school, its curriculum, staffing, endowment and general financing. Vice-Chairman Robert Swinnnerton performed an active role in the property and building business using his own experience as a timber merchant to good effect.[40] *The matter was left to Mr. Swinnerton* appears frequently in Governors' Minutes especially in dealing with the numerous local tenants of school property.

The matter was left to Mr. Swinnerton: Robert Swinnerton 1848-1939 Long serving Governor for over forty years and generous benefactor of the school

7. Aspects Of School Life
Like a good number of other traditional Grammar Schools at the time, the school was developing its own character and ethos. It was conscious of developing a community, widening the pupils' range of opportunity, maintaining a broadly Christian ethos and

looking to the public schools, not only in trying to raise academic standards but also in development of games, drill, a wider range of activities, uniform and boarders. Head Boys were appointed (though not yet Prefects) and Waters' first one shows how the new Headmaster was starting from scratch. In 1881 he chose a promising youngster, Joseph Francis Ward, son of 500 acre farmer George, a School Governor. Untypically, Ward remained in post until he left in 1886: during the next seventeen years five boys did a two year stint in the post and one William Bond Cocks (later a solicitor and Chairman of the Governors) three years 1896-8.[41]

School development involved professional commitment from the staff and more work and preparation outside the classroom for the pupils. For instance staff had to form a rota for homework duty for the boarders. As Headmaster, Waters met the challenges of rapid change effectively and ran a tight ship. W.B. Cocks later recalled Waters as *small in Stature mighty in discipline! He was the type of Master more appreciated after a boy left than when he was at school. The boy who was capable of profiting by his teaching,* [largely in Mathematics] *was capable of making great headway.* [42] The image of the school in the town had grown favourably since the 1870s and Waters had impressed; in a retrospect of the year 1903 the Nuneaton Chronicle found *general satisfaction with the progress of Higher Education in our midst … Under the extremely able direction* [of Waters] *… the reputation of the Grammar Schools* [is] *being fully sustained* with *considerable distinction* for the pupils.[43] Back in 1889 Inspectors felt that *the education afforded is thoroughly sound and well calculated to advance a boy's interests to either Classics or in the professions.* [44]

The school was conscious of its growing success, Waters collecting records in a volume of memorabilia. Junior Cambridge local examinatios were entered but there was no sign of senior entry until 1885 and only intermittent success at this level until the mid 1890s. Frederick Cawthorne was one of the first to distinguish himself academically in the Cambridge Junior Matriculation examination and went on to achieve a high flying English degree at London.[45] The school also looked to aid education in the wider community. In 1891 when a Nuneaton Technical Education Committee was founded the Grammar School Masters offered their assistance with evening classes in Languages, Commerce, Science, Maths and Land Surveying. This was all taking advantage of town growth. In 1892 the Nuneaton Chronicle commented on the *rapid rise of building operations* [in Nuneaton]. *The erstwhile sleepy old town which for 20 years remained at a standstill but for the last half decade has leapt forward by leaps and bounds.* [46]

Star Pupil: Frederick Cawthorne aged eighteen in c. 1889

The Inspector of 1889 had noted that although it was a *compact little school doing good work and quite sufficient for the wants of the place* [it was] *lacking leaving scholarships of any kind.* [47] Some of the more academically successful boys left at 13 to go to a public school, as the larger independent schools were termed. In 1884 Robert Baxter Disney aged 12 (son of the vicar of Hinckley) won a £40 scholarship to Rossall, (Lancashire) going on to Worcester College Oxford.[48] More followed. Waters did not buck this trend personally since his own son Kenneth went from King Edward's to Warwick school on a scholarship in 1903. Waters himself expressed surprise that the school had managed to nurture Head Boy Ward to his outstanding achievements at Cambridge where he finished in the top four of his year. The only other Cambridge entrant in this period was Vincent Illing who, after studying at the school from 1903-1909 won a scholarship to Sidney Sussex, Cambridge and went on to do outstanding work as a petroleum geologist, making full use of his early studies of rock formations in the Nuneaton/Hartshill area.[49]

The Sports Day event first developed by Eustace in the 1870s matured under Waters. In 1906, as numbers started to expand, a good number of events were held including throwing the Cricket Ball, running and jumping events, a 3 legged obstacle race, a sack race, a tug of war and a consolation race. A separate swimming sports was also held. The use of Latin tags to describe winners, *Victor Ludorum*, or runners up who had been close to victory, *Proxime Acessit*, [50] was another example of public school practice. Three acres of the field bought in 1860 were used for exercise and there was a small uncovered 80 foot by 130 foot playground.[51] By 1892 a pavilion had been built, provided for by subscription. But the condition of the field was rough; moreover, the crowded timetable seems to have precluded the large scale development of football, rugby or cricket. At the turn of the century most of the rugby union played was by the school's Old Boys. [52]

Prizes were given for academic work as well as sporting prowess and there was now a formal prize day. As early as 1881 the Chronicle reported an *event* where desks and stool gave way to a stage. T. Disney (baritone) sang contemporary songs *Old Timbertoes* and *Blue Alsatian Mountains*; three pupils and four adults enacted dramatic scenes.[53] Over time these events would grow in frequency and sophistication. The school song was sung for the first time at the Annual Prize Day celebration in 1895[54] but many other school traditions did not develop until the 20th Century.

8. Growth Of The School: Numbers And Finance

Overall school numbers rose only slowly. The population of the town – stagnant or even falling slightly in mid century[55] was now rising rapidly. How many parents in Nuneaton wanted the Grammar school style of education and how many could afford the fees? Only occasionally was a non-payment or remission of fees recorded.

Waters was conscious of the limited growth of the school. In 1896 when numbers went down by seven boys he wondered whether there was sufficient desire for secondary education in the town.[56] A previous generation of prominent Nuneatonians had been the first to be educated at the successful elementary National Schools, often not moving on to the Grammar School. They may have felt that this level of education was sufficient for their children too. Waters reminded them that the Grammar School had wider aims: after a strong defence of a liberal as opposed to a utilitarian education Waters concluded, *the worth of the school was not what it did for the genius but, for the ordinary boy.*[57] Waters was as good as his word. Boarders declined and more examples of the ordinary boy were seen in the school. Waters' personal concern with education extended to his own staff in the Headmaster's House. In the 1880s a teenage maid was helped to realise her educational potential with support from Waters who assisted her in her reading.[58]

The changing face of King Edward's

The Leeke Chapel – an enlargement of a medieval Lady Chapel c. 1510.

Beam of 1596

The Old Grammar School 1696

The New Grammar School 1880 [Modern pic]

The Heads House 1880 [Modern pic]

Memorial Inscription embedded in the building of 1880. The foundation date was still erroneously believed to be 1553.

New buildings of 1904 [Modern pic]

New buildings of 1962

Higher Education Institutions associated with King Edward's

Birmingham University: always represented on the Board of Governors in the 20th Century and destination of numerous students.

Saltley College of Education: destination for many budding early 20th Century teachers

Emmanuel College: A special 18th Century relationship.

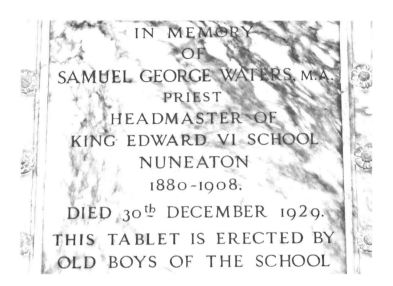

IN MEMORY
OF
SAMUEL GEORGE WATERS, M.A.
PRIEST
HEADMASTER OF
KING EDWARD VI SCHOOL
NUNEATON
1880-1908.
DIED 30th DECEMBER 1929.
THIS TABLET IS ERECTED BY
OLD BOYS OF THE SCHOOL

Reverend Samuel Waters' memorial tablet, St Nicolas Church

While numbers in the school remained around 70-75 the buildings might still be seen as large enough. However, as early as 1897 the Governors developed plans for expansion of the buildings including proper science laboratories. The old style central hall with classrooms leading off was now insufficient. Windows were needed on both sides as well as a widespread placing of classrooms to provide autonomy for the individual teacher. Land could be sold off to raise capital for science laboratories while still maintaining investment income at a reasonable level. Two other factors aided this possibility. One was financial aid from the Science and Art Department at South Kensington; the other was the closure of Smith's Charity School in 1896 which resulted in the combination of its endowment with the Grammar School and increased capital possibilities. Endowment amalgamation had first been aired in the 1870s. After National legislation moving to completely free elementary education in 1891, the need for Smith's was declining. The Grammar School Scheme of 1876 was amended and the endowments of the schools were consolidated. The Smith's town centre property was sold and a new Elementary school built on the proceeds; but the Smith's investments went to the Grammar School. As part of the deal King Edward's Governors were to pass on £20 a year to the National Schools in the town. [59]

The fortunes of the Endowment were still central to the fortunes of the school. Bolstered by Smith's income and the prospect of increasing grants from local government, land was sold and resulting capital invested in the stock market. Back in the 16th and 17th Centuries when the King Edward endowment developed, the investment had to be in property but these restrictions no longer applied. Selling property proved a sound decision as demand for building land in expanding Coventry was still considerable. In contrast, in March 1884 agricultural prices were reported as falling:[60] In 1892 the school's land at Dadlington *will probably not be let for as much as at present and the income of the school thereby insufficient.* [61]

This was typical of the increasing difficulty in re-leasing school property and a growing temptation to sell for building land, at £225 an acre in one case.

Date	Property Sold [62]	Price	Comment
1893	Orton Charity Land	£450	5 Acres and a cottage
1897	Part of Smith's Charity land, Ansley	£1000	Sold to coal magnate Sir Alfred Hickman after much dispute with him
1899	Jeffrey Woods Cross, Coventry	£437	Delayed by defaulting purchaser
1899	Land at Hartshill	£450	

But amidst shrewd financial transaction, one vital aspect of the educational future was missed. The ability to fund a separate girls' secondary school was now apparent and becoming a reality in other parts of the country. Women were now a major part of the teaching profession and the Board of Education wanted them to receive a Secondary Education.[63] Yet in 1884 an Inspector remarked of Nuneaton that *Nothing is being done for the Higher Education of Girls which is left to the chance supply of two or three adventure schools* [and] *daughters of traders were sent elsewhere to Boarding Schools.* [64]

In the Scheme approved by Charity Commissioners there was an amendment – a clause empowering the Governors to maintain, if income was sufficient, three Exhibitions for girls from public elementary schools.[65] Presumably these would be at another school: there is no evidence they were ever provided. Bellairs who retired as vicar and Chairman of the School Governors in 1892 seemed to have lost his enthusiasm for girls' secondary education or at least his powers of persuasion. The conservatism that also produced sentiment for Smith's Charity School, even when its rationale had disappeared, also meant a long delay in securing girls' Secondary Education in the town. By 1910, 20% of British university students were women[66] (though not all were awarded degrees) but in Nuneaton the first girls' secondary school was only just opening.

9. Another New Building?

Despite the sale in 1880 to help finance the building of the new school, investments and property ownership were still an important means of finance. But a new building would involve further sale and more moves towards a reliance on fees and /or state assistance. With those agricultural prices dropping, the endowment income would increasingly come from financial investments. Even just after the Smith's amalgamation, Canon Deed described the school's position as *not financially flourishing* [67] with an overdraft at the bank. Staff salary costs were increasing. Assistance with funding was needed. In 1892 there was some correspondence between Governors and Commissioners as the school made a request for funding for a carpentry shop and covered playground which *have been needed for some time.*[68] Then followed a series of letters where the Commissioners suggested the school look to the County Council for financial assistance and the school insisting that the County Council did not fund Grammar Schools. While the situation was soon to change, the school view was correct at the time. At Bablake School in Coventry science facilities were seen as more advanced. In 1897 Nuneaton Governors were *most desirous of increasing the Masters' salaries and reducing fees to prevent our boys going to Bablake … as they do now.* This was a new problem: back in 1889 an Inspector reported that with the exception of the few going on to public schools – and even these *started* their secondary schooling at the Grammar School – *Nuneaton boys rarely go elsewhere.*[69]

Charity Commissioners insisted that any capital expenditure should have the outlay replaced within a few years, so initial building plans were put on hold. The Charity Commissioners confirmed their reputation for caution. They wanted any capital expenditure re-accumulated within a few years.[70]As a result, work on buildings was confined to routine maintenance such as £128 for conversion of the Wash House to a Laundry and the painting of the outside of the school.[71]However, the property sales of the late 1890s, (see above) had suggested Governors were persistent in their desire to raise capital for a more ambitious venture. In 1900 they announced that they *require a Chemical/Physical laboratory to be fitted with all necessary apparatus.* Present conditions were unsatisfactory; using the Old Grammar School for science was *not in accordance with the regulations of the Science and Art Department at South Kensington.*[72]

In March 1900 at a Governors' meeting, with the Technical Education Committee in attendance, there was talk of raising £2,000 for a new building. £650 from the County Council had already been applied for and a further £350 would be forthcoming if the Governors could raise an equivalent sum. Then in Jan 1901 Mining Engineer Governor Edward Melly formally proposed the erection of a lab/science school. [73] Though the word school is used loosely here, there was in the initial proposal a hint of separation reminiscent of the English /Latin school division of the mid 19th Century.

The school's restricted site. In the background the school buildings of 1880 before the extension of 1904. The edge of the Vicarage garden can be seen. In the foreground on the other side of King Edward road the new house for the Cawthorne family is being constructed

Detailed planning began. In March 1902 a Building sub-Committee of the Governors was established. The first problem was the restricted site. This had been a disadvantage noted by Stanton back in the late 1870s when it was only accepted in the absence of anything more suitable elsewhere. (see above p.152) Fortunately a solution was to hand. Canon Deed offered to pass over some of his vicarage garden adjoining the Grammar School in exchange for £200 and the Old Grammar School, which would no longer be needed for Science teaching now a new science building was planned. The school could expand along the side of Peacock Lane (King Edward Road) contiguous with the existing building.[74]

There was a positive response to this scheme, which had been floated back in 1897 when expansion was first considered. As Deed put it he was willing to do business *it being so obviously to the advantage of the town and school that the Technical Classrooms should be as close as possible to the present buildings.* H.Y. Quick, a Coventry architect, was asked to submit a design for a school room accommodating 40 students and two labs each holding 25. In December the plans were approved and sent to the Education Department set up by the 1902 Education Act. [75] In June 1903 the Building Committee, with Deed deliberately absent, sealed the deal. By the end of the year Deed was undertaking his own alterations to the Old Grammar School.[76]

The new school building of 1904

During the period between the Governors' first thoughts about an extension to the buildings in 1897 and their implementation over five years later, the national educational scene had changed considerably. At the turn of the century, the centre of financial gravity shifted from Charity Commissioners to County Councils. In 1899 the Science and Art Department, particularly encouraging of the development of the teaching of science in endowed and other 'secondary' schools, was replaced by a national Board of Education planning to co-ordinate what was becoming known as secondary schooling, including endowed Grammar Schools. The Education Act of 1902 transferred many educational responsibilities from School Boards to Local Authorities, who took responsibility for both elementary and more advanced schooling. Hopes of financial assistance for the new building now increased.

10. New Buildings Planned

The questions of the new building's name and what was to be taught in it were connected. The Governors decreed that the name *Science and Art Rooms* was to be used for the new building and not *Technical School*. No cookery or handicraft was to be taught. On October 8th 1903 it was still referred to as *the new Technical school* but the concept was an extension of the Grammar School.[77] Started in late 1903, the building was completed by the summer of 1904. A substantial edifice, it fitted in well with the existing buildings in scale and materials without attempting to match it in terms of elaborate decor. The details of the interior were, unlike 1880, now the subject of greater interest than the exterior. Although Governor Joseph Fielding Johnson's proposal for a connecting door between the buildings was rejected, a Science school separate from a Classical school never developed and the school remained unified.

As part of the negotiated deal, Warwickshire County Council gave £1000 to assist with the construction.[78] In June 1904 the Governors discussed who should open this new Science and Art School. Their first four choices were all unable to do so[79] and the lot fell to vice-Chairman of the Governors, Sir Francis Newdegate, who had replaced his recently deceased cousin Sir Edward Newdegate on the governing body. Governor Slingsby presented a silver gilt key to Newdegate to open the building formally. Changes were rounded off in 1906 with ten new single desks and alterations to the dining rooms and bedrooms at School House as boarding ceased. With the additional places now available more working-class boys began to appear. In 1904 Richard Follows, whose father was a coal miner from Ansley, won a scholarship.[80]

11. Immediate Impact Of The New Buildings

The capital commitment for the new building stimulated the trend away from reliance on land endowments towards a mixture of investments, fees and local authority assistance. The sale of King's Fields in Coventry for £8,500 in 1904 produced more than the necessary capital. So, with the Smith's Charity land at Ansley also sold the following year, £6,508 was now invested in Consols and £3,315 in India 3% stock.[81] More money was now available in the way of grants from official bodies but it would come, as what many at the time saw, at a price – a limitation on the independence of the school. In 1905 Warwickshire County Council offered £150 providing £40 went to leaving Exhibitions.[82]

With the anticipated expansion of numbers, the Governors were now (1904) under pressure to reduce termly fees. *The feeling in the district ... [was] whether something could not be done to reduce the fees of the school which at present are very high – so as to enable poor boys from the elementary school to avail themselves of the higher tuition available at the Grammar School ... [This would] add to the popularity of the Grammar School.* [83] These were the comments of Mr. Horton and Mr. Bates from the Nuneaton Urban District Council who met with Governors in September 1904. They wanted fees reduced from £10 to £8-10 shillings a year for over 14s and from £9 to £7-10 for under 14s. The Governors were defensive: Robert Swinnerton argued that the powers of the Governors were limited as they had to fulfil the conditions laid down by the scheme of the Foundation. This familiar argument had a familiar retort; did Leeke not intend his money to be used for the benefit of the poor? After further negotiations with the Education Board fees were reduced to £9 for the over 14s and £7-10/- for the under 14s, but this would include all books and stationary, reducing the hidden extras.[84] A typical Governor/ local business deal resulted in Cawthorne's supplying all books and stationary.

Perhaps because of these concerns, from 1905-1908 the occupation of the parents is noted in the applications and a picture emerges of the boys' social background; predominantly middle class with around 40 in mainly trade and manufacturing including four shopkeepers, two schoolmasters and seven farmers. But the working class, especially at the skilled end, was starting to grow in number with around 14 including four clerks, a fitter, wood turner, carpenter and hatter. [85] In 1907 there were further changes. Secondary schools who wished to receive the full capitation from the local authority and the Treasury had to reserve 25% of their intake for non-fee paying pupils from the elementary schools who would attend on bursaries. This reflected the national trend, to be less rigid about the set position of social classes and see educational fluidity as desirable. It widened the social mix of King Edward's and sounded the death knell for the continuation of boarders. Town scholars now appeared in greater numbers. A quarter of pupils were on some kind of scholarship bursary or pupil-teacher scheme. This emphasised the upward trend in average age of school pupils. Often an attainment test was taken and eleven was increasingly seen as a suitable – if not the only – age for this.[86] However, the increase in numbers was also apparent in the fee paying scholars. While in 1882 44 fee payers had produced an annual income for the school of £316, by 1907 seventy fee payers netted £619. Boys now stayed an average of four years. The buildings, financing, numbers of both pupils and staff, type of intake, and whole character of the school was now changing rapidly.[87]

12. Pupil Teachers

The changes since 1900 provided another opportunity for expansion. In 1905 the school became a centre for a pupil teacher scheme and overall numbers immediately rose to 90 with 16 new students and five pupil teachers. 33 more new boys arrived in 1906. [88] The idea came nationally from Robert Morant who wished *to substitute a liberal secondary education for at least some of the period spent as a pupil teacher.* [89] In May 1906 a meeting with Director of Education Bolton King began moves for the school to be a Pupil Teacher Centre, especially in helping to meet the need for more science teachers.[90] Nationally under the policy of Morant, from 1905, pupil teachers had to be 16 and were to have two years preparatory education, preferably in a secondary school like King Edward's. The fee for taking these teachers was £8 per head. The scheme only operated for a few years but started the process of widening once more the social backgrounds from which pupils came to the Grammar School (see Appendix10). It ended in 1911 with the start of post graduate teacher training which soon developed all over the country in the next 20 years and the parallel advance of the specialist Teacher Training Colleges. Warwickshire County Council grants were no longer confined to helping the school cope with pupil teachers: £100 for 5 free places on the County Major Scholarship exam was paid annually, increasing to £200 by 1912.[91]

13. Curriculum Changes

It was not just science that benefited from the new building. An undated *abridged prospectus*, probably 1906, records English, Latin, Maths, French, German, Natural Science, Drawing, Vocal Music, Shorthand, Drilling and Manual Work. Geography and Divinity were also taught and Woodwork was soon to join them. Here the authority's involvement was crucial, for the Grammar School could not be recognised as a secondary school without *Manual Instruction*. [92] Prize Days were a regular annual feature with local worthies presiding and a regular annual private Inspection was held. Charity Commissioner Inspectors took over this task in the 1890s but with the start of greater state aid in the 20th Century came visits from County Council Inspectors after 1904. The Inspectors of 1906, examining the way the new buildings were working, seemed impressed: *The new classrooms have now been brought into use and a manual workshop has been opened, so that the school now possesses excellent buildings. The staff is a strong one and good work has been done in the past sessions.* The Drawing and Woodwork classes that had recently been developed were *very satisfactory* and there was *good discipline* in the drilling. The only criticism related to a recently taken decision: the Inspectors noted that the school was supplying books and materials but felt this *deprived them of the interest which the sense of possession gives pupils.* Nonetheless they were sufficiently enthusiastic about the experience of the pupils at the school to express the wish that boys should *enter earlier and stay longer.*[93] This presaged a further increase in school numbers which accelerated under new Head Albert 'Bass' Holman from 1909.

The school in 1906 (1) Abridged prospectus

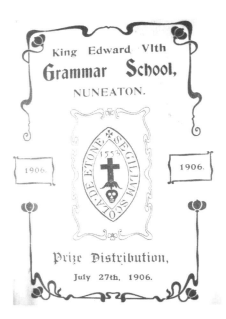

The school in 1906 (2) Prize distribution

All these rapid changes produced tension. In October 1906 the Bishop of Worcester came to present the school prizes. Conscious of speaking at a time of educational ferment he made a plea for tradition: he praised the school for still using Euclid in Mathematics, a questionable emphasis since geometry now provided a more comprehensive approach. But the Bishop argued that Euclid *taught them to get rid of sentiment in argument and allowed them that they could only establish principles which were taken from point to point*. Latin, also under attack, should continue said the Bishop though arguments justifying this had changed. Now it was seen as important because *the value of the pen and public speech would become more important and Latin gave the best style*. On religion, the Bishop confirmed the direction of the school – still definitely Christian, and still with a clerical headmaster for another 18 months, but no longer so definitely Anglican. Not all Bishops in 1906 would have asserted that the differences with Nonconformists (as Dissenters were now known) were *only minor*. [94] Not only traditionalists were worried about the pace of change. Sir Robert Morant was concerned to ensure in 1904 that literary subjects would not be totally set aside by the growth of science.[95] It seems that some school traditions developed just at the moment when the modern 20th Century world was starting to have a major impact.

The school in 1906 (3) Athletic sports

By 1908, in the midst of educational ferment, Waters decided to retire from teaching, envisaging a quiet country benefice. This he obtained in the rural location of Grandborough, near Rugby.[96] He received a pension of £120 a year after considerable consultation with the Board of Education. In leaving a little before he was sixty he avoided the long and increasingly inglorious reigns of Trevis, Liptrott, Hughes and Bucknill under all of whom the school deteriorated to varying extents in their later years. Twenty years later his successor also decided to leave while his powers were still fully intact; hence, early 20th Century attention to pensions was of great benefit to the school. Holman applied to succeed Waters. There were 141 other applicants and the short list of nine included an existing Headmaster.[97] As the professionalization of school teaching developed the idea that only a clergyman could be Head of a Grammar School had gone. But in the early 20th Century it was still not uncommon to appoint them, especially in public schools. Clearly the Governors had an open mind; Holman was able to take full advantage of their liberality on this point and obtained the post. The minds of the Governors may have already been made up that Holman be appointed. Other schools by this date were interviewing off a short list. However, the Governors decided to make the appointment immediately, a proposal to interview three men being lost by just one vote. Holman accepted the Governors' right to remove him *if according to the constitution of the said school.* His position was secure but unlike Bucknill and those before him, not untouchable. Under him, the school's transformation would continue.

CHAPTER TEN

Scholars, Staff and State: Thirty years of growth, 1909-39

A growing demand for Secondary Education … resulted in an increase of over 80% in the numbers of pupils attending Secondary Schools.
Olive Banks: *Parity and Prestige in English Secondary Education* (referring to 1914-1924)

By 1909 the future of Nuneaton Grammar School was becoming clear as a day Grammar School teaching mainly academic subjects to increasing numbers of boys from the local area, many pupils paying fees but some with free places. In this period King Edward's grew from under 100 pupils to 274. The extent of the curriculum, the number of staff, sport and extra-curricular activities, the age range and catchment area of the pupils, the role of the state and the way of financing the school were all transformed. Yet this was achieved with very limited expansion of the buildings.

1. THE NEW HEAD AND RAPID GROWTH

Albert Bassett Holman (1871-1959) played a major role in moulding the character of Nuneaton's 20th Century Grammar School. He attended Eastbourne College and then the King's School Ely and St Catharine's College Cambridge, graduating in 1893. After a time as Assistant Master at Overslade School, Rugby (now the Harris C. of E. School) he went to Osnabruck, Germany, before joining King Edward's in 1897 to teach classics. He was to stay over 30 years, retiring to Ashtead, Surrey, in 1929. Twenty years later he was still attending annual dinners.[1]

Holman, who earned £200 a year as Assistant Master, was highly regarded, not least by Waters. From 1902 the additional bureaucracy imposed upon the school by the ever-closer connections with the local authority was not something to which Waters would have been accustomed. The Headmaster pointed out that Holman *had helped him considerably in the work of the school* such as working on forms and timetables required by the Board of Education and *done out of school hours.*[2] The Nuneaton Chronicle reported that he stayed at the school *preferring to remain in Nuneaton rather than accept the more important posts which, from time to time have been offered him.*[3] The major changes of 1904-8 in both building and state funding saw their effect in Holman's time as Head. On taking up his new position, school numbers passed three figures for the first time. With boys staying longer, numbers reached 113 by 1914.[4] The school followed the national trend for by that year 60% of children in England and Wales were at school until at least fourteen[5].

Some argued that King Edward's had not grown fast enough. Just before Waters' departure, Inspector Stephens noted school numbers were *small compared to the number of inhabitants.*[6] At the stage of Nuneaton's most rapid population increase, 48% in the first decade of the 20th Century,[7] its growth outstripped the school's. The area's coal mining, engineering and manufacturing development continued to expand, hotels, banks and retail outlets all developing to provide employment. Nuneaton had become a substantial industrial and mining town. From about 1910, aided by local authority grants, the school responded and began to grow proportionally quicker than the town.[8] The next few years saw even greater expansion. By 1923 there were 254 boys, a remarkable growth. A school that, twenty years previously, might have developed as a socially narrow boarding school evolved into a mainstream state-assisted Grammar School serving the local area.

The town grows faster first, followed by the school a decade later.

	Approximate Pop. of Nuneaton	No. of Boys	No. Of staff (full time equivalent)
1901	25,000	75	4
1911	37,000	100	8
1921	42,000	213 (half fee paying)	11
1931	46,500	280	13
1938	(estimated) 50,000	274	15

Sources: GMB 20th, GMB 1923-54, Edwardian, Census material.

The trend to stay on at school longer was only temporarily halted by the outbreak of war in 1914. At first, boys under fighting age left a little earlier, being in demand in banks, offices and local government. A number of Nuneaton pupils were withdrawn by their parents because of the death of an older sibling in the forces when the younger son was required for business at home.[9]

The drive and vision of the Governors was not as apparent as when they had previously helped to lead the way around 1902-4. Their response to Inspector Stephens'enquiry made back in 1908 (why had there been a slower growth of the school than the town) was that the large majority of boys in the town were working class. This fatalistic response may have been sociologically correct but it was hardly an answer to the question and implied that little could be done. It was redolent of the days of the 1860s and 1870s when only a small number of working class boys were expected to take advantage of Grammar School education: but the overall educational vision was transformed by 1908. Governors had retained an old-fashioned attitude to social mobility through educational opportunity.

2. Why Did The Growth In Numbers Occur?

National points were probably the most significant. The war had a major indirect effect; it developed a more positive view of formal education. The first generation of people educated *en masse* in elementary schools had been seen not only as performing heroically during the fighting but also used their expertise to contribute to the war effort in many different ways. Few now doubted the value of this education and all over the country expectations for children's secondary education had risen. Pupils wished to stay longer at school, wanting more than an elementary education.

Moreover, the importance of higher qualifications in the post war world was all too apparent. Horizons were widened by the extension of the school leaving age to 14 in 1918. But could families afford extended education? The higher wages paid during the war gave some of them greater opportunity to pay for their children's secondary schooling. Here also the growing state found another role. Politicians of all political persuasions now recognised the importance of extensive education for all. The high Tory Lord Cranborne (the future Marquess of Salisbury) remarked in a House of Lords debate on the very day war ended in 1918: *Education is to be far more important than it used to be. It is a demand – a very legitimate demand – by the working classes of this country which Parliament has seen fit to meet.*[10]

These developments were re-enforced by longer term pre-war factors. In the first 40 years of the new King Edward's school, 1880-1920, the role of the state in education had grown dramatically. There was now a policy aiming to encourage children (boys *and* girls) of all social classes to take advantage of expanding educational opportunities. To reduce social class discrimination, exhibitions and scholarships were to be made more freely available. The proportion of free place scholars at the school rose to one third by 1912. The King Edward's endowment, though not insignificant, could still only provide a few free places, so the main increase was due to a greater number of scholarships provided by local authorities. Around 1910/11 there had been 39 out of 119 boys with scholarships and six student teachers a year continued to attend often until 17 or 18 years old. Nationally, by 1913 20% of grammar school boys were working class. The wider social range of pupils and the greater number staying on past 14 was reflected in Nuneaton. Taking 1910 as an example, of the 74 boys still present whose admission dates were given, 30 had been at the school at least three years – a higher proportion than hitherto.[11]

Local developments were also significant. After the 1902 Education Act local authorities took control of elementary education from school boards. New local elementary schools provided more boys for the Grammar School. There were four new Council elementary schools founded between 1905 and 1910 and by 1922 87% of boys coming to King Edward's had attended these schools.[12] In 1910 a Revised Scheme of Government reflected the wider influences on the school. Nine of the sixteen Governors represented County and Borough Councils. With a representative from Birmingham University and a parent Governor there were now only five co-opted, plus Joseph Fielding Johnson, the lone survivor from before 1876.

The personal factor in the school's growth was also crucial. Holman and his Deputy Walpole Day maintained and developed a well run and innovative school particularly strong in Mathematics and Science teaching, community spirit and administration. In 1913, the first major inspection for five years paid *high tribute to the efficiency of the school*. The appointment of Mr. Holman had been *fully justified*.[13]

The school's success did not encourage direct competition; until 1928 it remained the only Boys' Grammar in the town. In that year Manor Park Mixed Grammar was launched and in 1929 there was a tiny – and temporary – decrease in King Edward numbers, the first for over 25 years. But the overall upward trend then resumed despite the construction of three more secondary schools, Swinnerton in 1932 and Arbury and Higham Lane in 1939.[14] Moreover, Nuneaton's population still progressed, though the rate of increase slowed down. In the 1930s Grammar School intake varied between 47 and 64 each year until 1940. [15] The increase in size – and pressure on buildings – came from the longer stay of pupils now coming around 11 and remaining three to five years. As a result, by Easter 1938, there were 274 pupils, at Christmas 1942, 295, and by 1945, 318.[16] The efficiency and rapid growth of the school, by putting pressure on existing buildings, meant that, since Manor Park provided the alternative of a mixed Grammar School, King Edwards's was likely to remain single-sex.

3 Old Edwardians

They shall grow not old: School War Memorial 1914-18

The period of rapid school growth also affected the Old Boys' Association, the Old Edwardians. The first glimmering of an interest of Old Boys in the school activities had come at Sports Days in the late 19th Century when an Old Boys' race was held. Eustace had encouraged this development and was clearly influenced by public school thinking when saying *it stimulates in the present the desire to excel.* Support was patchy: in 1877 only two Old Boys turned up to race and in 1896 only Oliver Iliffe (who joined the school in 1888) wished to enter.[17] Two others started the race and dropped out so that he could claim to be the victor. Proper Old Boys activities would have to wait some years. By the 1890s, however, Old Edwardians had formed a Rugby team though with no formal organisation until 1910. By 1912 the Old Eds. annual rugby dinner featured in Nuneaton's social calendar, Holman attending as President and with recitations and traditional songs at the Black Horse Inn, Wheat St. [18]

The first concrete evidence of an Old Boys organisation (as opposed to just Rugby) came in 1914 when ex-pupils formed a Gymnasium club and requested evening use of the gym.[19] Whether this would have led to a wider and more formal body anyway is a matter for conjecture but the 1914-18 war undoubtedly saw closer bonds between those who survived. At the start of 1915 the Chronicle reported there were some 80 Old Boys in the forces on the day it also reported the death of the Governors' Chairman's son. Further reports added to the gloom but also the sense of shared experience. All told 31 old boys gave their lives, including Waters' son Kenneth in 1917. In November 1918 Holman reported 23 had been wounded and four made prisoners of war. On the 22nd March 1918 Cecil Knox won the VC for outstanding bravery in the face of enemy fire in carrying out the demolition of a bridge at Tugny, France. His brother James, killed in September 1918, had previously won the DSO.

<table>
<tr><td colspan="2">Ranks</td><td colspan="2">Decorations</td></tr>
</table>

Ranks		Decorations	
Private	13	VC	1
Pioneer (sapper)	4	DSO	1 with bar
Lance-Corporal	4	MC	4 (1 with bar)
Corporal	1	Belgian Croix de Guerre	1
2nd Lieutenant	7	DCM	2
Lance-Sergeant	1	MM	6
Lieutenant	1		
Lieutenant Captain	1		
Captain	1		

Source: Memorials project. This has a list of the fallen Old Boys with excellent details on their backgrounds, military careers and death. See also Chronicle 18.1.1915. 8.11.1918

After abortive attempts in the early 1920s there was an Old Eds. re-formation in 1928 and in the 1930s the Association made great strides. In March 1932 it had 58 members, growing to 128 by March 1934: a cricket section had begun in December 1930.[20] In the 1930s an evangelistic feeling developed with regard to recruitment. In December 1935 the School Magazine on the recent Speech Day reported the Main Speaker E.T.England (Head of King Edward's School, Birmingham) urging membership: *No school was really strong unless it had an active body of all boys.* In his history of the school published in 1936 Dr. Nason pronounced that *every boy who has had the privilege of being educated at the school ought to become a member of this Association when he leaves.* The *true custodian* [of] *School traditions* he added, should be *a strong and active Old Boys Association.* [21]

An extensive part of the school Magazine was now devoted to an Old Edwardians' section where the successes and interesting and varied careers of Old Boys were highlighted to inspire the current generation of school students. Further losses in the 1939-45 war also emphasised this feeling. Also, by the 1930s and 1940s –compared to the late 19th Century – there were far more Old Boys with a greater sense of what the school had done for them. Membership, however, was for Old Boys only. In 1933 one ticket for an Old Edwardians Dinner was sold to a non Old Boy: this caused a debate and the idea of an open club was rejected as being *Incompatible with the spirit and object of the occasion.* [22]

4. Staying On Until Sixteen

Despite the school's rapid growth, King Edward's was criticised because pupils did not stay on long enough.[23] In 1922 the Board of Education expressed national concern regarding the 74% of boys in the country who left by 15, t*he age at which the distinctive nature of the Secondary School* [curriculum] *takes full effect on the pupil.*[24] The King Edward Governors agreed on the desirability of all boys staying to 16 but at first they argued that they could only advise parents and not force them to give a pledge that their boys did stay on this long (something of throwback to the Liptrott dispute in the mid 18th Century see pages 95/96). Governors did agree to insert a clause in the prospectus advising 16 as the best minimum leaving age but added pessimistically that given *the nature of the population and approach of parents* [it is] *impossible ever to achieve.*[25] A good percentage stayed on to 15 and left somewhere between their 15th and 16th birthday. However, in 1924, Governors, under pressure from the local authority, changed policy and insisted parents give a signed undertaking that their son would not leave until the age of 16. That year two boys left early but no action was taken.[26] The seepage of under 16 loss gradually increased through the 1930s and the legal position with regard to enforcing the undertaking was not clear. More often than not nothing happened.[27]

The boys who left early would have been disproportionately from the poorer end of society and by the 1930s there was greater realisation of a link between poverty and academic under-achievement. Concerns that the poorer classes' diet had improved less than the rest of the population had led to extensive research.[28] In 1935 the school introduced free milk, nine years before national legislation on the subject. But it had acted much earlier than this for back in 1909, when he became Headmaster, Holman had been concerned about the overall fitness of the pupils and bought a height and weight testing machine to monitor their progress. In 1916 Nuneaton Governors noted that there had been *More illness in school than usual* and Medical Inspections were instituted in 1925. However, in early November 1918 at the annual prize evening Holman referred to a full attendance *in spite of the ravages of 'flu.*[29]

5. Where Did The Boys Come From? The School Atmosphere

By 1918 the School catchment area now included the neighbouring parishes of Coton to the south and Weddington and Caldecote to the north as well as –to the west – Arley and Ansley and to the south and south east Bedworth, Bulkington and Wolvey. Holman pointed out that 30 came from outside the borough of Nuneaton. Like their Masters, many boys arrived by bicycle. Those from Bedworth generally arrived by train – the buses were few and far between to some areas and seen as mechanically unreliable. At the start of his Headship in 1929 A.S. Pratt estimated that 76% of boys came from Nuneaton but most of the other 24% came from nearby.[30] But this wide catchment area and pressures of space meant that only a small proportion of all teenage boys from Nuneaton were able to attend the Grammar School. For those better off who could afford the fees there could be early entry at the age of ten and then an attempt at a scholarship at twelve or continue to pay. For a free place you had to shine in the entrance examination. At the start of 1924 40% were not fee paying.[31] So, bearing in mind the industrial nature of Nuneaton, the school's growth resulted in a growing social mix though still with some bias to the still relatively small middle class. One Old Boy attending in the mid 1930s was aware that the better off families still formed the majority of boys in the school. It was an advantage if you could afford the fees. Boys who failed the entrance exam for a free place could then be paid for by his parents at the standard rate of 3/9d a term: one who followed this route went on to achieve great academic success and an extremely distinguished career. If you were a late developer it was a good idea to arrange for well-off parents. There were still expenses to meet; up to 1939 when the policy was changed, boys had borne the cost of any travel to sports fixtures.

Tony Collett reckoned that in 1939 from Queen's Road school in the centre of Nuneaton about six out of forty boys (15%) got to King Edward's or *the Grammar School* as it was still normally known, the acronym KEGS being discouraged at this time. In the period 1929-32 five boys left Vicarage Street School bound for King Edward's on a County Minor Scholarship, rather like an eleven plus pass. These were the ones successful in the scholarship examination and the proportion though not large was above the national average.[32] There were expenses even for scholarship pupils: shoes, equipment, uniform, two sports shirts (one white, one red and white) – all from Riley's in the town. No cooked dinners were provided until re-heated ones after the war.

Some pupils found their studies hard going. School certificate required a pass in five or

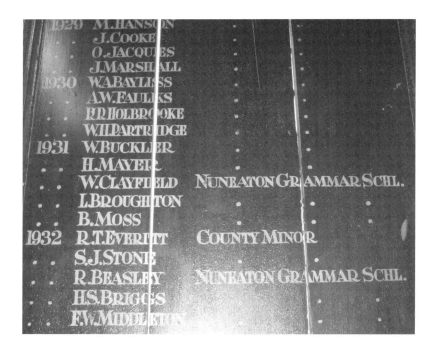

Inter-war scholarships from Vicarage Street School

more subjects including at least one from each of three groups: English subjects (what we might now label humanities), Languages and Maths/Science. Not all succeeded. Tony Collett who joined the school at the end of the 1930s thinks at that time about only 10% both stayed on into the sixth form and were successful at the Higher School Certificate level. Others persevered, taking their Highers two or three times in order to get to University, since you had to pass everything at one sitting, a process reminiscent – if somewhat tougher – of re-takes to get a higher mark at AS and A Level in the early 21st Century.

In the 1930s the School had a reputation for strict discipline. One pupil from the time found this produced a *tense* atmosphere though two others from a similar period while agreeing on the strictness, did not sense the tenseness. The school cap had to be worn in the centre of the town –including off duty at a weekend; even back in the late 1930s this raised eyebrows. J.E. Cope Vice-Chairman of the Old Edwardians' Association and Chairman of the Buildings Appeals Committee around 1960 recalled tension when he was at school – the Grammar School boys were often looked on as *prigs* and were *often set upon by boys from Vicarage Street*.[33] The school he asserted dramatically *still had enemies*.

6. The Expanding Staff

In the early years of Holman there was some rapid staff turnover. Indeed the caretaker was summarily dismissed within weeks of Holman taking the reins, a decision was backed by the Governors after *hearing the* [unnamed] *circumstances*.[34] In the two years 1909-1911 six teaching staff were appointed, several leaving within a very short space of time with only Walpole Day as Head of Science providing stability. In the two years before the outbreak of war things became steadier and, initially, the hostilities produced little impact on staffing apart from the Drill Instructor being called up to his regiment in October 1914. Anthony Day, a Hinckley Instructor, came instead at 4/- per hour plus expenses.[35] National conscription was not introduced for another 18 months and in any case teaching was initially seen as too valuable a profession to succumb to war demands. However, the situation had changed by January 1916 when single men were conscripted. Two staff immediately inquired – what happened to their pay if they enlisted under Lord Derby's scheme to raise enlistment numbers before formal conscription?[36] After *considerable discussion* Governors agreed that any gap in pay between forces and school would be compensated.

Despite requests for postponement Messrs Hurst, Goodall and N.M.Smith were all called up (Smith as a Naval Schoolmaster) in April and May 1916.[37]. The result was the recruitment of three female teachers to the school for the first time. The first woman to be appointed was Miss MacAlley, an M.A. from Edinburgh shortly followed by two similarly qualified, Miss E. Brown and –from Liverpool – Miss D.M.Vaughan. But mere replacements were not enough. With the rapid increase in numbers another teacher was needed and Miss J.M. Deardon (Higher Grade Certificate) was appointed at the lower salary of £100. Another female teacher Miss Twigg was appointed in 1917[38] as the long standing Mr. Needham was leaving for *work of national importance*.[39]

The war also highlighted the issue of teachers' pay. A rapidly growing profession led to demands for a common set of nationwide salaries. In Nuneaton before the war the most common reason for granting an increase was acceding to a request from an individual member of staff. As so often the war exacerbated a trend already present. War bonuses were being paid although as late as 1917 a teacher's request for a pay increase could be turned down. At the same time a 35/- war bonus was paid to the Assistant Mistresses though the school reflected the national policy of paying female teachers less than male ones for the same work[40]. By July 1918, after many other schools had already done the same, King Edward's adopted the policy of a standard salary scale based on a combination of qualifications and length of service. It was soon replaced after the war by a national scheme under the terms of the 1918 Education Act – later called the Burnham Scale, after the report of the Burnham Committee in 1919. Teachers at the school may not have considered themselves well paid but some Nuneaton townsfolk's perception was different. One Stockingford resident recalled a childhood memory of poverty in wartime: *you can tell how times were: even a schoolteacher from King Edward Grammar lived in a Council House* [41]

All the Assistant Mistresses were due to leave in the summer of 1919 but Miss Vaughan actually stayed on until the end of 1920. There were now eight Assistant Staff plus the Headmaster. So the result of the war was the temporary influx of female teachers but the more or less permanent loss of the pre-war staff. Mr. Smith did return but was gone by 1920. Headmaster Holman now had a rapidly changing educational world; a much bigger school, a new staff and increasing Local Authority and state funding.[42] The numbers of the staff continued to increase: by 1921 there were 11 including a full time music teacher: some went on to promotion elsewhere.

While subject specialisation was growing, especially at Head of Department level, more junior teachers were still expected to teach a number of subjects such as A.C. Gibson (Pembroke, Oxford) who arrived in 1926 to teach Latin, Maths, French and English. Sidney Reed Brett joined in 1921 and wrote numerous History textbooks for the School Certificate. One pupil described being taught by Brett as being quite inhibiting as he knew his own book so well you could not pretend to have read it if you had not. Brett argued that *there is no more common failing than that a casual acquaintance with any branch of knowledge is all that is required to produce an elementary textbook on the subject.*[43] He spoke from experience. Sixty years later two old Boys testified independently in almost identical words that Brett had given them a lasting interest in History setting out an organised system of working, making notes and writing essays.[44]

7. The Cramped Site

New school buildings between 1904 and 1961 were very limited

The growth of the school had implications for the buildings. The brief halcyon period of the immediate pre-war years, when the numbers in the school could be comfortably accommodated, was over. Cramped conditions – effectively if belatedly relieved in 1880 and then in 1904 –returned after 1918. *Study had been carried out at the school under great difficulties and the accommodation had not been as good as it should have been* remarked Governor Robert Swinnerton at the Swimming Gala prize distribution in 1920. In the same year three huts for Junior Boys were erected across King Edward Road and two rooms built over the lecture theatre. Two rooms to take 50 boys were constructed on land on the other side of King Edward Road with the idea of providing space for a Metal Workshop. The Old Grammar School was again hired to help with classroom space.[45]

The question of overcrowding had been temporarily alleviated but was still problematical. Could church glebe land also come to the rescue again? Deed again commented on *the value of keeping the school in its present place.* But Deed died at the start of 1923 and the new vicar Canon White, though co-opted on to the Governors and enjoying good relations with them, was wary about negotiating another land swop as soon as he arrived. The Governors offered £1800 for more glebe land but this was turned down and leasing or renting arrangements were discussed but never finalised. White's opinion prevailed: there should be *no disturbance of the current arrangements* for the time being. [46]

The quality of some of the accommodation was not high. One old boy recalled not only *badly-heated prefabs* but also *smoky stuffy little classrooms, originally bedrooms,* a reference to the old boarding accommodation in the Head's House now helping to deal with the overcrowding. The lack of a proper library or a room set aside for the growing number of sixth formers was noted.[47] By the end of the 1920s Governors considered it was the growth of the town which would *involve an increase in the means of accommodation.* Yet town growth had slowed[48] and so it was the greater take-up of Secondary education which was actually more pressing. While it was still possible to stay at one elementary school until leaving at 13 (14 after 1918) more and more families had ambitions for their children to transfer schools and attend secondary education classes.

When A.S. Pratt took over as Headmaster from A.B.Holman in 1929 he soon made the lack of space a theme of his headship remarking that *Even at present accommodation was not perfectly adequate.* [The art room and science lecture room were being] *used for subjects other than those for which these rooms were originally intended.* By Christmas 1931 Pratt was referring to *urgently needed extensions* being postponed *owing to the economising tendency.* In the economic slump of 1931 £70million had to be saved in public spending and teachers' salaries suffered disproportionately losing 15%. The following Christmas – 1932 – extensions were hoped for *when the financial situation made it possible.*[49] But despite the emergence of other secondary schools in the area (see above) the pressure on space continued.

One new building in the 1930s was a new pavilion. Prior to 1934 the old one had been a *shaky wooden structure at the edge of the Spinney* providing only elementary shelter. Sports teams would change in the school where they would return for any refreshment. In 1931 there were high hopes of a proper pavilion being constructed by the local authority but this idea was a victim of the public expenditure cuts of that year. Three years later Alderman Swinnerton's generous gift made one possible. Partly designed by Art Teacher D.R.Hill its opening was marked with a special cricket match but it became a war victim a few years later. *Its pleasing appearance with balcony and reed thatched roof gave a greatly improved appearance to the school field.* But this advance did not address the main question of overcrowding.[50]

Opening of the New Pavillion 1934
Left: Mayor Councillor W.T. Smith; Centre: E.F.Melly; A.S. Pratt;
Centre Background: R.W. Swinnerton; Right: Head Boy C.T.Bloxham

In 1935 the matter of a *site for a proposed extension* was discussed by the Governors. The Warwickshire Director of Education promised *an early opportunity of conferring with the Chairman* [of the Grammar School Governors] *on* [the question of] *accommodation*. [51] Once again church land was looked to as a possible solution to over-crowding. At the end of 1936 it was suggested a contract be entered into for the purchase of the piece of church (glebe) land at a price of £1,100. The vicar was invited to sell the relevant strip but nothing came of this suggestion. Despite further discussion *at some length* in 1938 the issue was still unresolved when war came. Alderman Melly argued that the whole of the Church's glebe land on the railway side of King Edward Road should be purchased for an expanded site, but this idea failed to find a seconder. [52] Norman Painting, who joined the school at this time from Leamington College, described it as *cramped and overcrowded*.[53] The temporary post First World War huts continued to be used. They were known as *the cowsheds* and bombed in the Second World War but it was a name which stuck for many years until the 1970s because of their prefabricated successors. Reed Brett in his centenary history describes them as rooms where boys *shivered in winter and roasted in summer*. Yet, despite the obvious problems, the Council argued in 1938 that they were *not disposed to purchase a new site* and had *no definite plans* for a new building. Indeed the following year it was reported to the Governors that there was *no likelihood of any new building being erected at present*. [54]

8. Property And Investment: The Local Authority

Despite the lack of assistance in finding a new site the relationship with the local authority became increasingly close – and dependent –both financially and educationally. A large independent capital venture on new premises was not realistic, but the endowment, now cushioned by the charging of fees and local authority grants, was in good shape. The trend continued to be sell land and invest the resultant capital. The Governors still could not actively seek to sell land or even name a price but were *open to offers* of which there were plenty. In 1911 Coventry Corporation suggested £25 per acre for some of the land owned at Coundon. Initially refused on the grounds it was below market price, the matter went to arbitration before being sold in 1913 and the money invested in 3% India Stock.[55] The war of 1914-18 stimulated investments. £400 was put into in 4 % war stock and £300 left on deposit. Consuls were converted to war loan resulting in a £33 increase in annual dividend. No wonder that in 1917 the financial position of the Foundation was described by the Governors as *very satisfactory*. [56]

Sales of land continued.

Date	Property	Price	Comment
1918	College Street land	£300	
1919	Dadlington land	£250	Nuneaton Wool Co. gave up rights to the school playing field in the same year
1920	Ansley	£112	Another farm at Ansley sold in 1923
1927	Hartshill Property	£2,300	Farm
1935	Coundon property	£8,400	Governors arranged a mortgage for £5,600 at 5%

Apart from areas adjacent to the school and fields, this only left the remainder of the Coundon land (taken into the possession of the War Office for a time after1917). This changed hands in 1935, sold for £8,400 though the Governors organised a mortgage for £5,600 at 5%.[57]

The proportions of the School's differing income had shifted considerably. In 1920 it was:

Total Income	£9,245
Land	£1,180
Tuition fees	£2,220
LEA Grants	£5,815
Evening classes	£30

This was a far cry from the 18th Century when the only major outlays were the Master's yearly salary and Apprenticeship fees. The endowment income was now only about 11-12% of total expenditure and even with fees and evening class income the Governors could only cover non staff expenses and a small fraction of the staff salaries.[58] By 1939, only one third of school money was from the endowment and fees. The reliance on state grants was gradually increasing, preparing for a very different post-war period. One additional property that was acquired was the Drachenfels. This house, adjacent to the school playing field, was bought for £2,600 in 1926 and let at £80 a year. In the war it was taken over by the War Office and afterwards converted for £900 into two flats and used as accommodation for newly arrived members of the teaching staff as a convenient home.[59]

Increasing dependence on local authority finance continued. When Holman became Headmaster at the start of 1909 the L.E.A. grant was just £100 a year. This increased, especially after Herbert Fisher's Education Act of 1918 when 60% of teachers salaries now became payable by central rather then local government. By 1921 it was Warwickshire County Council who gave approval to the school's employment of an additional assistant teacher (the tenth member of staff). From 1923 books and stationary were only to be obtained from County Stores. In 1926 Schools, not directly under the LEAs but receiving grants, were given the choice of continued Local Authority grants or a grant direct from central government. All but 250 opted for the former including Nuneaton.[60] Sometimes there was School/Local Authority tension. Ever since those new forms filled in out of school hours by Holman back in 1907, the weight of bureaucratic demand had edged ever upward. After 1911 Audits required a Chartered Accountant, G.C.Clay was the first. Inspectors complained about the variation in tuition fees as *an obstacle to the continuance at school*.[61]Perhaps they saw it as a throwback to the 19th Century days of a senior (Latin) and Junior (English) school. After the Burnham scale for teachers brought uniformity of pay, the authority pointed out that four teachers were receiving wages too high in relation to the new national scales; their salary must be reduced. At the start of 1924 the LEA ruled that no additional Masters could be employed for the time being. Teachers could be faced with larger classes (around thirty) as well as cramped buildings.[62]

9. A Change Of Leadership

Headmaster Holman, who had been seriously ill in 1924 resigned in 1929 *for personal reasons*. He was much praised. Many gave tribute at a special presentation in July 1929. *Bass* as they knew him had not only been popular with the boys *as few Heads … could ever have been* but had also received *the admiration of his fellow citizens*. In his retirement he could enjoy a gold cigarette case and a gold-mounted walking stick. He had as his object *to give every boy in the school a chance to develop his talents* [and] *as much liberty as is compatible with good discipline*. He had shown *untiring devotion to the welfare of those committed to his charge*. He shook hands with all the boys in the school as he left, a reflection on the intimate nature of the institution and Holman's personal concern for

The old and the new: Albert Holman

The old and the new: Arthur Pratt

the welfare of all those in it. Having arrived in 1897 Holman noted in his farewell speech that, of the 1,386 boys who had passed through the Grammar School since the new Charter of 1876, he had known the vast majority. [63]

Holman had become Headmaster after a period when he was effectively, if not officially, Second Master or Deputy Head. Would this pattern be repeated with Walpole Day replacing Holman? Governors were split. The criteria for a suitable candidate for Headship initially included no one over 45 years of age being considered, thus excluding the 55 year old Day. This produced a Governors' revolt and a comparatively rare and almost even split in their voting. By seven votes to six at a specially convened meeting just three days after the previous one they reversed the age restriction and Day was interviewed along with five other candidates. He was not successful. Arthur Simpson Pratt, just 31 years old, was appointed.[64]

Pratt had been Senior Mathematical Master at Whitgift Grammar School, Croydon. Out of over 100 individual submissions he was the only practising classroom teacher offering evidence for one of the important Hadow Reports on Education, the one of 1928. In 1931 he published his *Higher Certificate Applied Mathematics Test Papers*. He had been a Wrangler in Maths, and had an MSc. Tall, imposing with a round face and sandy hair, he stamped his own character on the school during the 1930s. A pupil who arrived on the eve of war described Pratt as *capable and competent*. At Nuneaton, his timetable was more limited than previous Heads but he taught some boys using football pools to illustrate some of his points. While Day possessed many supporters for the Headship, others favoured a young candidate to introduce change. Pratt obliged: the electric light that was now installed in the Head's house for the first time was not to be the only new light shed. At the end of 1929 it was reported that the school was *running smoothly on Pratt Spirit*. [65] In 1930 Pratt made the first major alterations to the main school hall – as the main school classroom of 1880 had now become. It was known unimaginatively, but not uncommonly in schools of this type (such as Henry VIII Coventry) as Big School. Two rooms in the Head's House were converted into an office and – for the first time – a room for a Secretary. The Head would walk from his study into Big School for assembly whereas Holman had previously walked out of his front door. The development of the authority of sixth form Prefects meant they could ensure boys were quiet before Pratt and the other staff walked in.[66]

Pratt's attitude to his staff was revealing. On the departure of Mr. N. Taylor to Leeds Grammar School in 1933 he remarked *I have realised for some time that we could not retain so excellent a Master.* This raises questions regarding his view of the status of the school, the reputation of the town and how he regarded long serving and highly respected Masters such as Day, Branston and Brett. Soon after Pratt's arrival in 1929 it was remarked that *many people in the County had the effrontery to remark on Nuneaton in a somewhat contemptuous tone.* [67] This stung the young Headmaster and his subsequent emphasis on the achievements of the school and its traditional form of organisation were a way of dealing with this prejudice. As a result Pratt was keen to emphasise old school traditions and develop new ones. As the school grew –there were 14 Assistant staff by 1936 [68]– a focus on common institutions and heritage would also be seen, like the House system (see below) to aid a sense of belonging. The replacement of the traditional service at Church on Remembrance Day by a Founders Day service on May 11th (see below) was a good example of his style of innovation. Pratt encouraged increasing staff commitment to extra-curricular activities, both sporting and non-sporting. This role was crucial for maintaining the feeling of a community with school numbers growing so quickly. In 1930 Mr. W.H.Branston joined the staff and distinguished himself in all fields teaching geography and history and with a heavy involvement in all forms of sports. He proved an immensely popular teacher, guide and friend. There was camaraderie among the staff – an Old Boy recalled that many belonged to gentlemen's clubs in the town and one or two enjoyed some lunchtime conviviality; many travelled to school by bike.

Sidney Reed Brett: joined Staff 1921: Deputy Head 1933-1954: Acting Head 1944-45

The death of Walpole Day in October 1933 – at just fifty eight –was both an immediate shock and a long term blow. Day had been pre-eminent in developing the Science side of the school recruiting excellent teachers and achieving great success with very limited facilities. He had been Commanding Officer of the Cadet Corps and was acting Head during Holman's illness [69] As Second Master, he was replaced by Reed Brett who became the second in a line of four capable deputies (see below p.245) which gave the school a reputation for both stability and administrative competence. Between them they served in this crucial post until the end of the Grammar School.

10. Curriculum And Academic Achievement

Just as the financing of the school was partly in external hands, so too national examination policies increased their influence on the subjects taught, playing a major influence in how the school's curriculum developed. In 1917 the Secondary Schools Examination Council established the School Certificate examination for 16 year olds followed by an advanced certificate at 18. This regularised the structure of exams ensuring the school followed a standard academic curriculum of Maths, English Language and Literature, History, Geography, Physics, Biology, Chemistry, Latin and French but with some Art, Music, Religious Knowledge, Woodwork and Physical Training as opposed to Drilling in the past or Physical Education in the future. It was hoped that exams would follow the curriculum rather than determine it. But often this did not happen. Still, there was a demand for a wider range of subjects which could lead to part time or evening class teachers. For example, Frank Herbert Raison, who retired in 1932 aged 65 after many years service as Head of Vicarage Street School, had taught shorthand at the Grammar School for 28 years.[70] The varying demands of a wide range of subjects meant for the first time a questioning of the need for all boys to learn Latin, a matter discussed by the Governors in 1925:[71] but for the moment all continued to delight in its treasures.

The development of the Higher School Certificate (HSC) meant two years more study at school after the age of 16, a larger *sixth* form – though still only a minority stayed on – and the introduction of Prefects with disciplinary authority over younger boys. In 1933, 15 students took the HSC, 13 of them passing with nine distinctions. Results continued to improve lower down with 28 passes at the ordinary level of the School Certificate in 1933 rising to 41 (out of 52 candidates) in 1935.[72] This statistic contained both good and bad news: a clear minority either failed the school certificate or left early without taking it; neither had anything formal to show for their educational efforts. However, at the top end of academic achievement the school was doing well for its size. Two subjects (three after 1931) were studied for the HSC. In July 1935 German was introduced. Since two languages could now be taken as part of the ordinary certificate this may have been a tactical move. Another reason was the growing importance of Germany in world affairs.

Science remained central to the King Edward curriculum and in 1925 a Lab. Assistant was appointed for the first time on a permanent basis.[73] The subject also determined some of the administrative arrangements for the classes. To be put into form *V Science* meant a boy was deemed likely to achieve School Certificate standard in two science subjects. In contrast, to be placed in *V General* meant success was seen as more likely in just one. Senior elementary and modern schools in the inter-war years provided a challenge to the Grammar School, offering as they did a vocationally oriented curriculum to children of secondary school age. As a result, Grammar Schools like Nuneaton tended to assert their traditional functions. Despite the school's particular reputation for Science, Tony Collett thought all subjects achieved success and most were well taught. Latin was still imparted to all, until the war took the teacher away; however, one old boy arriving at the school in 1935 recalls that he learnt only a *smattering*.

There was academic success under the new system. Entries to Oxford and Cambridge Universities, rare since the 1760s and the Oxbridge tradition of the Liptrott era, began to resume after 1918. This was often with two or three each year and a growing number at the expanding Redbrick Universities. Training for school teaching at Saltley College Birmingham, a Church of England Training College, proved a popular option.[74] Awards were no longer just to avoid school fees but to help at the next educational stage. County Scholarships (three in 1933 for instance) meant that boys could aspire to an academic success that would help them financially at University. *Pour encourager les autres* University letters from old boys describing their undergraduate days in Cambridge, London or Liverpool were regularly sent and published, a practice that continued for the next 50 years into the early days of the Sixth Form College. However, as in former times, many boys still did not stay on beyond 14 or 15, though the changing economic climate in the 1930s may have encouraged them to remain a little longer. Not all achieved the financial backing they deserved. In 1928 one student won the offer of a studentship at St Catharine's College Cambridge, a College which was becoming a popular destination for Nuneaton boys, but there was no other money for him.[75] Sometimes endowment and state money could combine to make a scholarship possible but there was a growing awareness of the wastage of talent.

There was always the possibility that the best boys would leave the town but it was clearly expected that others would become prominent people in the Borough in years ahead. *The time is not far distant when the offices in the town will be in the hands of the present pupils.* [They had a] *duty to cultivate as much as possible the corporate spirit* said one Prize Day speaker.[76] This had happened in the previous generation: the Clay brothers of The Grange, Leicester Road all came to the Grammar School between about 1875 and 1895 . Most stayed in Nuneaton, subsequently playing a variety of roles in the town; Richard was a local miller, Frederick the first Town Clerk of Nuneaton, Arthur a prominent Bank Manager (Barclays) and George a Chartered Accountant forming the firm Clay/Russell.[77] Expectations for the next generation of pupils was therefore high: as the boys were told, *the eyes of the town are upon you at all times.*

11. The Ethos Of The School: The House System

Rapid growth and a multiplicity of examinations had a marked effect on the school: yet it was clear that King Edward's was not all about examinations – it was a community to which you belonged, in which you studied formally but also learnt about life; how to develop individual interests, ambition and discipline, but also how to co-operate in community. During the 1914-18 war, pupils refused prizes for a certificate, the money saved going to *patriotic objects*. They also formed a Cadet force.[78] In 1921, resources now permitted launching a magazine, which contained literary contributions, news of special events, games reports, club and society activities and reports from the four different school houses. Some of the wider educational aims were also achieved through this House System, an attempt to maintain a friendly atmosphere and a sense of belonging in a rapidly expanding school. In 1926 old boy Vincent Illing, (see p.173) now Professor Illing of Imperial College London, presented a House Shield which encouraged further inter-house competition such as Junior Cricket. The names of Houses went through more than one change. They were originally related to local districts and were named Coton, Stockingford, County and Nuneaton. Three staff were assigned to each House. But in 1929 on the arrival of new Headmaster Pratt, the system was immediately changed and the Houses given the names of staff in charge of them: Day, Hill, Gale and Sheffield. The names were changed again in 1935 (after the death of Day) to the names of those believed to be the first four Heads as researched by Dr. Nason, Grene's, Ellyot's, Walton's and Sadler's, another factor reflecting the growth in historical consciousness of those early nineteen thirties. Annual Prize Days continued usually held in the local St George's Hall and the magazine published the reports of each House's progress in the year. More generally, the early editions of the magazine reflect the optimistic post war feel of the 1920s – of an improving world in general and a much better state of education in Nuneaton in particular. Articles in the Edwardian looked back, but hardly to the good old days. *It is hard to believe that the large and efficient school of today could ever have developed from the small and I must add inefficient educational unit which had its home in the building which still stands in the SW corner of the Churchyard* recalled Dr. Edward Noel Nason in 1928.[79]

12. The Ethos Of The School: Games

Nuneaton reflected the general emphasis throughout the country on the importance of team games: with the school growing quickly a first XI cricket team or a first XV rugby football team could now aspire to a higher quality. Which winter sport should predominate? The question was first raised before 1914 and the growing numbers after the First World War resulted in a successful demand in 1921 that Rugby Football replace Association. Success under the new code was rapid. In 1925 the Rugby team was unbeaten: transport improvements led to a widening fixture list. Both the external image of the school in general and the internal reputation of individual school boys in particular was now seen to depend to some extent on prowess on the sporting field. Nor was it an insignificant factor in the selection of staff. The extension of the playing fields in 1927 mirrored the growing importance of sport in the life of the school. At the start of the first term of 1933 hockey was introduced and rugby confined to the autumn term. This was described as a controversial move and the poor weather affected fixtures, but the following year was more successful. Nevertheless, Rugby was permanently established as the major winter sport where success was seen to raise the school's reputation.[80] Games were increasingly central to school life and in 1934 a new Games Committee was set up, formally minuted, with Brett as Chairman. In 1935 a Groundsman was employed for three pounds a week and in 1937 boxing –at eight weights – was included in the House competition and granted financial support, which was also given to the Scout Troop. In providing many great sporting opportunities for boys the school jealously guarded these privileges. In 1938 it was asserted that *no boy should be allowed to play for any outside club during term time without the permission of the Games Master*. This had to be obtained each time and would be given only in exceptional circumstances. Up to 1939 boys had borne the cost of the travel to Sports fixtures but this system was on the point of change as war intervened.[81]

The two major games: the Cricket team of 1932
Back Row from left: N. Taylor Esq., S.J. Hall, A.J. Savage, H. Allen, F. Burrows, C.F. Hawkes, E.J. Orme, A.V. Barnett.
Front Row: B. Whitehead, F. Gouge, C.T. Bloxham (Captain), A.C. Draycott, F.M. Frankland.

The Rugby team of 1932
Back Row from left: G.L. Ismay, J.F. Archer, M.A. Tulloch Esq., J.L. Kenworthy, F. Foreshaw, F.H. Shilton, A.C. Draycott.
Seated: L.F. Bennett, N.V. White, W.C. Shade, C.T. Bloxham (Captain), F.O. Burrows, J.W. Davies, H. Tatton
In the front: S.J. Hall, F. Gouge

13. The Ethos Of The School: Activities

Increasing numbers of pupils also led to the formation of new clubs and societies like debating, photography, literary, rifle, drama, meccano, stamp and cycling. A little later came the scientific and photographic society restricted initially to the science sixth. Each individual activity only affected a minority of students but all indicated a real desire to become truly educated –that is learn about, try to understand, reflect on and be influenced by events and developments outside one's own immediate experience. Debaters, for instance, had wide horizons. Even when the subject was of more parochial interest the question could still be one with national relevance: for example, *The school curriculum is too restrictive in that it does not include sufficient practical education* (Passed 23-8). The dominance of the academic curriculum is seen here but it was being questioned. It was also reflected –consciously or unconsciously – in a school debate in which staff took part in early 1933 at a time when the Oxford Union was making waves by passing a motion about not fighting for King and Country: *The study of dead languages has no place in modern life.* Unsurprisingly, classics teacher Mr. Chambers was among the opposition but the motion was carried 18-11.[82] On the literary front, the library lists in the Magazines of the 1920s bear witness in that age of reading which was pre-television (let alone internet). Radio was but in its infancy; it was an age that teachers of literary subjects today, especially in their more unrealistic moments, yearn to re-create. Only the cinema seduced. In April 1928, 51 boys (20% of the total) were recorded as using the lending library directed by Reed Brett. Books were steadily added between the wars.

The old Fives Court survived until the re-building of 1961-3

The school provided some of Nuneaton's cultural entertainment. For instance in 1926 it staged *the first amateur dramatic performance in Nuneaton since the Shakesperian Society became defunct* . The cultural opportunities of a liberal education were clearly apparent. H. Knight wrote a contribution in the Magazine on *unappreciated Beethoven* [remarking that] *very few have heard of his string quartets and trios* but making an eloquent plea to try to listen to and appreciate the great composer. Sometimes there was just such an opportunity as when in 1928 not Beethoven's but Mendelssohn's trio in D minor was played by two members of staff and a lady teacher from the Girls' High School. Inter-school debates with the Girls in the 1930s were an early sign of co-operation that was to take an unexpected turn in the early 1940s.[83]

14. The Sixth Form

Pratt aimed to develop the sixth form. The *tone* and *efficiency* of a school, he argued, depended *to a very large extent* on its calibre. He was keen to build on the work of Holman who had *given a greater amount of freedom to the sixth form than was given in many schools*. Pratt enhanced the role of prefects, getting them to organise Assembly for morning prayers and giving them distinctive caps.[84] House Colours, with *distinctive silk ties*, were awarded for the increasingly important rugby, cricket and athletics. The precise style, shape and colouring of your blazer or tie gave you a particular status which assumed great significance, at the time at least. Some of the school *traditions* were only just getting under way.

The introduction of the School Certificate in 1917 inevitably imposed curriculum restraint on grammar schools. The school was formalising its relationships with the Universities and – recruiting staff from the Universities – they did not always have the teachers to initiate a major re-direction of work towards vocational and practical subjects. In Nuneaton a typical Grammar School academic curriculum continued to be followed. Study did not consist entirely of conventional lessons, however. Visits formed part of the widening of the educational scene. They took place to Cadbury Bournville and the Motor Show at Olympia, a holiday in Edinburgh (August 1932) while the Scouts viewed a local colliery (Haunchwood) and camped at a then peaceful Drayton Manor. There were also visits to Paris.[85]

15. Links With The Church

The growing historical consciousness within the school in the 1930s has been noted. Appropriately, relations with the Church were maintained or even strengthened. Like his predecessor at Nuneaton parish church, Canon Deed, Canon John White, Vicar 1923-40 was a Governor; he became vice-chairman and, briefly Chairman in 1940 after the death of the long serving Robert Swinnerton. After 1918 the School had attended in force for the annual Remembrance service where Holman – a regular attender at the Church – read one of the lessons.

With the arrival of Pratt the procedure changed with the introduction of a Founders' Day service. This would recall the 11th May 1552 (actually believed to be 1553 until 1932), *O God our Help in Ages Past* would be sung, an exhortation would be read (in the first year this was done by Alderman Melly) with a specific mention of King Edward VI, John Leeke and the parishioners of Nuneaton. This annual service continued for about 50 years throughout the time of the Grammar school and into the early years of the Sixth Form College.[86] Guest preachers' hold on historical events varied. Perhaps it was their unhistorical speculations that encouraged Dr Edward Noel Nason old boy (briefly), Governor, locally highly respected doctor from a highly respected family to perform detailed and heroic researches into the school's history saving many documents. Nason may also have been stimulated in 1932 by a visit from Canon Edwin Savage, Dean of Lichfield, reviving memories of his Father who was the former Vicar of Nuneaton and active Grammar School Governor, Canon Robert Savage. [87]

The Rugby team of 1934/5
Back Row from left: J. Wilson, J.A.T. Bourne, S.E. Adkins, W.H. Robinson, W.H.M
Branston Esq., A.F. Jacques, S. Gregory, R. Parr, W.H. Partridge
Seated: B.N.Ward, L.F.Bennett, F.Gouge (Captain), W.F. Cummins, L.C. Allton.
In front: J. Startin, S.R.Moore

King Edward's had changed greatly in the past generation. In the Founders Day Service of 1934 Canon Stuart Blofeld, an old boy from the 1880s, referred to the better relations with the Governors and the Church than hitherto and, as others had done, remarked on major improvements. *Education with all its difficulties* (financial cuts) *was a finer and better thing than ever it was* in his own boyhood: narrowness had given way to breadth.[88] By the end of the 1930s the tall and imposing Arthur Pratt was clearly in command of a growing and successful school but then its most challenging period arrived. The strains of war were to take their toll on the school – and its Headmaster.

CHAPTER 11

Damage, Recovery, Delay: War and Postwar 1940-1952:

The nature of a child's education should be based on his capacity and promise, not by the circumstances of his parents.
(1944 Education Act)

King Edward's was badly damaged by bombing in May 1941. Thanks to help from the girls' High School and not a little improvisation, the boys' school survived and recovered. Education still flourished but not at this stage in decent buildings. Post-war brought back free education with some vestiges of independence. The year 1952 involved looking back, with the aid of 400th birthday celebrations, and forward with new Articles of Government and Voluntary Aided status.

1. The Start Of The War

The new school academic year, commencing in September 1939, was just about to start when war was declared. As a result the start of term was held up. While the delay for the 5th and 6th formers was only a few days, it wasn't until the end of the month that the junior boys were able to re-start.[1] Staff were soon called up for military service and temporary replacements included ladies. Teachers came from St Bride's Helensburgh (Maths and Science) and Wolverhampton Girls High School (English). Tony Collett recalls that two of the ladies who came were quite young and given a rough ride by the boys.[2] One clear difference was the frequent and obviously disruptive air raid warnings. Probably for the first time in the school's 400 year history there was, for a while at least, no one to teach Latin. While the effects of war initially seemed reminiscent of 1914-18 they were to become more dramatic.

Hours were altered; the day began at 8.30 and ended early at 3 p.m. There was concern about the dark hours but at their meeting at the end of September 1939 the Governors were informed that *No provision had yet been made for protection in the case of air raids.*[3] This approach was soon to change. The first effect on the school of the tense international situation had actually occurred some months before the war broke out.

Founded nationally in 1938, an Air Defence Cadet Corps (ADCC) branch was formed at the school in May 1939, 121 squadron. Cadets were paid 3d per week and the Air Ministry promised a capitation fee of 3s 6d for each proficient cadet. They were sent to undertake vital work on RAF stations, handling aircraft, moving equipment, filling sandbags, loading ammunition belts or carrying messages. Numbers grew and in February 1941 the Squadron was absorbed into the newly founded Air Training Corps (ATC) and a second unit 411 (Borough of Nuneaton) was formed. These provided valuable initial training for prospective pilots and also support crew. A Cadet camp was attended in August 1943 with some flights and also instruction in Musketry. K.C.Kendall – an Old Boy discharged from the RAF – became the Warrant Officer.[4]

There was considerable enthusiasm for this venture and a number of schools wrote to the Air League asking permission to wear their own uniform. The King Edward VI Nuneaton correspondence took a peculiar turn. Who would command the school squadron? Headmaster Pratt wanted to but only if he could wear his own Observer Corps wings. The Governors wrote to the Air League outlining the request and that Pratt would otherwise refuse to command.[5] We have no record of the reply but permission was apparently refused since Schoolmaster Harry Branston and not Pratt became the Flight Lieutenant Officer Commanding.[6]

Both the importance of the work of the Air Cadet Corps and the wicked waste of war was tragically brought home in 1940. Leslie Allton, Head Boy 1937, a successful pupil and outstanding athlete – captain of four different sports – was killed in September, within two weeks of being posted to 92 Squadron at Biggin Hill, Kent. Flying near Maidstone, Allton, suffering oxygen starvation, crashed with fatal results. A cup for the best all round school sportsman was instituted in his memory.[7]

War Service was undertaken by 276 Old Boys in the forces – 33 died and 10 were wounded. Several members of staff gave distinguished service. Among them were:

Major E.G.Bennett	Intelligence Corps	Mentioned in Dispatches
Commander L.Draycott	Royal Marines	Mentioned in Dispatches
Major I. Dawson	King's Regiment	Instr. Lieutenant
Lt. Col. J.W.Dunnill	The Green Howards	D.S.O.
Captain E.E.McCarthy	Royal Artillery	
Lieutenant A.N.Willee	R.N.V.R.	

Draycott and McCarthy both returned to the staff after the conflict.[8]

These distinctions were matched by old boys with several receiving the DFC.

They shall grow not old: School War memorial 1939-1945

2. The School Is Bombed

Nuneaton survived relatively unscathed at the time of the serious and prolonged bombing of Coventry in November 1940 but its time came on the night of Friday 17th May 1941. The bombs fell on the town centre and Church Street killing long-serving Governor Edward Melly (aged 83) and his wife Harriet. In Nuneaton on that night 100 died and 170 were injured.[9] The blitz was at its most intense on the Friday night and well into Saturday morning damaging or destroying six schools two hospitals and two churches.

The Grammar School was badly affected: most roof tiles were blasted and windows shattered, the *cowsheds* on the other side of King Edward road were almost completely destroyed and the Science Block and Gymnasium seriously damaged. The Woodwork room, the Library and the Tuck Shop were no more. Only one classroom was unaffected, Room 2, which was to survive until the re-building of 1961-3.[10] Many parts of the Head Master's house were less seriously damaged – a chance event that was to affect the way the school buildings developed.

Pupils were forced to grow up before their time. Even before that dreadful night, the older boys had assisted a rota of staff on firewatch duty, now they helped issue tarpaulins to people whose roofs had been damaged.[11] In June 1942 incendiary bombs fell and did further damage. Under fifteens wanted to fire watch too and initially this was allowed with parental permission until it was stopped by the Fire Guard Officer.[12] Teacher Harry Branston recalled that an unexploded bomb from the raid was found in King Edward Road in the garden of Assistant Caretaker, Mr. Mills, but the heavy rains for something like a week meant it could not be removed. Much rain fell during the next three weeks causing further damage to the bombed building. As Branston remembered: *During the whole of this time, the scattered textbooks, desks and equipment at the roofless and windowless school were exposed to the rain.* The Edwardian later reported that *in room five snow fell on unprotected desks.* The recently constructed pavilion was severely damaged in the air raids and the broken windows and wrenched-off doors remained for many years after the conflict had ended. The Weddington Road Sports Ground had also been lost through enemy action. It was disastrous for many, but at the time *bomb damage was so much part of our experience that we did not find the situation strange or unpleasant* reminisced one old boy. He continued: *the dilapidated condition of the usable classrooms encouraged the more confident boys, between lessons, to throw handfuls of mud around, write on walls and even carve initials into the wall-plaster.*[13]

War damage of Friday 17th May 1941: the roofless cowsheds

War damage: the main building

War damage: the pavilion

Headmaster Pratt and his family moved to a substantial property in Old Hinckley Road and his house was now used as temporary classrooms for the younger boys, where four rooms (two small bedrooms and a partitioned dormitory from boarding days) were heated by open fires with Victorian grates.

While pupil numbers did not show the dramatic increase of the First War they remained steady at just over 300 causing acute accommodation problems. A month after the bombing eight of the Governors met in the office of the Clerk in Newdegate Place and discussed the contingency plans which were already underway. The Girls' High School Headmistress Miss Grant had swiftly and generously offered room for part of the curriculum to be continued on her premises.[14] At the High School while girls and senior boys would meet at prayers and shared the Library, they were often kept apart. At this time only boys used the Chemistry Lab. They also frequented an annexe full of asbestos sheeting. To get to this Annexe the King Edward boys went past the Primary room where the mixed class of Preparatory pupils sat – this caused great excitement. King Edward pupils were banned from the High School field or from running about. If they arrived after lunch from the boys' site they were not allowed into the school grounds until the exact time of their lesson, so they formed a long queue outside the school. However, the exigencies of the time produced some unforeseen developments. For example Reed Brett taught a small mixed Higher Certificate History class since there were two girls studying the subject at this level. Appropriately this was in a room between the boys' annexe and the mixed kindergarten, the nearest thing to neutral territory between the boys' and girls' areas. Senior Boys and Girls would take part in mixed Assemblies.[15]

Arrangements were now set in train to effect repairs to the school so that with the use of the Girls' school for older pupils, the St Nicolas Parish Hall for first year boys, six rooms in the Head's House for the second year, some use of the Mining School and repairs to areas less badly damaged, a rough and ready timetable could be supplied for all boys by the start of the new school year in September. Given the circumstances it was a rapid recovery. Although the offer from Nuneaton Girls' High clearly played a major role and was much appreciated, Deputy Head Reed Brett believed that it was essentially the strong school community spirit built up in previous years, which allowed King Edward's to recover as it did. The psychological scars healed quicker than the physical ones.[16] Don Jacques recalls that discipline suffered as boys' classes at the Girls High School had to wait for 15-20 minutes between classes as staff travelled from King Edward Road: this provided a convenient slot for nefarious activity.[17] In 1942 a 'Dalton system'[18] operated – at certain times some of the boys were not required to attend; instead, work was set to do at home, and brought back later, hardly an ideal situation.

Some ordinary school life persisted. Boys continued to travel from some distance into the town, Don Jacques recalls one arriving on the *fish train* from Shilton and a good number still came from Bedworth until Nicholas Chamberlaine School opened in the early 1950s. The proud or nervous wartime new boy in his *brand-new cap black barathea blazer with school badge and grey shorts* could doubtless also have been seen immediately before 1939 and just after 1945.[19] Sport suffered though cricket matches continued against local opposition such as Hinckley Grammar School.[20] Clubs and societies soldiered on; the school Music Society kept going and the progress of the war gave the debaters a new topic: *A direct assault on Hitler's West Wall should be made this year.* It was passed by 6 votes to 5. The number attending the debate– presumably 11 – was described as *disappointing*.[21]

But war turned some principles upside down. In 1943 a defiant poem was published by a pupil on the subject of Hitler ending with the line *And now we will kill you.*[22] At any other time in the history of the school such a written remark about an individual would have undoubtedly been censored. But out and out war changed matters. This had an unattractive side. Governors were now eager to discriminate against any expression of pacifist opinion. In January 1941 one Governor proposed that conscientious objectors should not be appointed as masters in the event of vacancies occurring and this was agreed. The wider nature of this discrimination soon became apparent. In November 1944 acting Headmaster Reed Brett asked Governors if he was allowed to consider an application from a member of the Society of Friends (Quakers) to fill a vacancy for teaching religious knowledge. In a rare interference with the Head's conventional right (including an Acting Head's) to appoint junior staff without formal reference to the Governors as a whole body, the reply was that *the appointment should not be made at present but the matter could be considered later if necessary*.[23] This seems odd. Would *later* not be too late for an appointment? Would the end of war mean the end of discrimination against Quakers and their pacifist beliefs? It was not made clear.

3. School Life Goes On

By 1943 repairs to the main hall meant that it was back in commission but disruption was common. The following year the bomb-damaged gym was demolished by a pull on a tug-of-war rope by members of the Rugby team. It *collapsed with a readiness that was alarming in view of the fact that it had been the custom for Masters and the School Captain to take boys into it when they were to be caned.* The Edwardian for Summer 1944 reported the last term of the boys at the Girls' High School and by Christmas the Science Block was *back in commission.* This generation of pupils lived a life unlike any others at the school before or since. The usual strict rules on uniform were inevitably relaxed. [24] The same could also be said for the teachers with the wartime Staff Room also acting as a centre for the Fire Guards and as a base for the ATC. Masters were still coming and going in addition to the changes imposed by wartime. At Christmas 1943 Mr. C. Brown (Chemistry) 1938-43, who had achieved exceptional success, went to Hull Grammar School. At half term at the end of October 1944 Headmaster Pratt suddenly left to go to take up an ordinary teaching post at Repton School and Reed Brett, his deputy, temporarily took over as Acting Head.[25]

School activities continue: the cricket team of 1943
Back Row from left: R.C. Walker, D.R. Silver, H. Fitton, F. Bazeley, J.H. Moore, F. Ellis (Scorer)
Seated: E. Taylor, R. Jones, G. Mason (Captain), J.L Glazier, D.F. Jacques
In front: D.L. Jackson, R.R. Arnold

Wartime provided testing conditions which could bring out the best or worst. One of the great heroes of King Edward's in the 20th Century was George Attwood who was first involved with caretaking as a young man as early as 1902. Returning in 1916 on a part-time basis and becoming full time in 1922, he was an outstanding caretaker and his heroic and uncomplaining work for many years greatly assisted the running of the school, especially in wartime and in some difficult winter weather, notably that of 1947. Described as a *friend to all*[26] he finally retired to much praise in September 1949.

Academic work continued throughout all the disturbances and – against all odds – outstanding results were achieved. In 1942 four of the fourteen available Warwickshire County Scholarships went to King Edward's pupils, to read Medicine, German, Mathematics and Science. The following year, of the 13 boys that sat the HSC, 11 obtained Certificate awards and one a State Scholarship. 35 boys were awarded the ordinary School Certificate. 21 had at least one *very good* award. In 1944 reference was made to *so many scientific successes in the past* but that now, County Major Scholarships were also awarded in English and History. In 1945 the number entering the HSC exam had risen to 18.[27]. Successes included Ewen Broadbent the son of a Baptist Minister and his Scottish wife. Head Boy and Cricket captain in 1942, Broadbent went on to St John's Cambridge to read Modern Languages. The war interrupted his studies there but after leaving Cambridge in 1947 he took the home Civil Service and the Foreign Office examinations. He was in the top three of both and went on to a distinguished career.[28] One of his obituaries described this phase of his later life as *a way of giving back something to a society in which he felt fortune had favoured him.*

A comparable and almost contemporary (born two years later) wartime success was Philip Randle, son of a Queens Road baker and one of the world's foremost researchers into mammalian metabolism. He read Natural Sciences at Sidney Sussex College, Cambridge, gaining a First in Part II Biochemistry, and then Medicine at University College Hospital before returning to Cambridge to carry out its first research studies on

---

War disruption fails to stop pupil progress

Sir Ewen Broadbent
Broadbent joined the Air Ministry as an assistant principal in 1949. He rapidly made his mark and after being private secretary to two official members of the Air Council he was private secretary to three successive secretaries of state for air, from 1955 to 1959. His upbringing and schooling had left him with a strong social conscience and after his retirement was involved with the Look Ahead Housing Association dealing with the homeless of London.

Sir Philip Randle
Many of Randle's findings were concerned with insulin's role in metabolism and with the control of secretion of the hormone from the pancreatic islets of langerhans beta-cells. The ideas generated by his investigations laid the foundations for countless subsequent other studies and have a direct bearing on the understanding of diabetes. He was awarded his PhD in 1955 for a thesis entitled Studies on the Metabolic Action of Insulin and was immediately appointed Lecturer in Biochemistry at Cambridge University.

Charles Henry Plumb (Lord Plumb of Coleshill)
While forced to leave the school suddenly in 1940, to join his father's farm, he later achieved great success in public life as President of the National Farmers Union and later, as a member of the European Parliament of which body he is the only British person to have been President.

insulin.[29] Broadbent and Randle were simply two of many who showed that academic success could emerge out of the most testing physical conditions and a school atmosphere which also influenced the direction and principles of their whole life. For one pupil, however, his enforced leaving of the school at the age of 15 did him little harm. To aid his Father on his Coleshill farm in the wartime food production drive, Henry Plumb was suddenly withdrawn from school right in the middle of Harry Branston's Geography lesson at the age of 15. Agriculture would be Henry Plumb's life and lead to a distinguished career.[30]

4. Wartime Activities

One product of wartime was the formation of a Parents' Association in December 1942 to *Foster and support the welfare of the school*.[31] In different circumstances after the war it performed a valuable role, not least in money raising. The weekly fire watch continued involving four pupils a night and duties including Christmas Day. Boys also helped with the Warwickshire harvest in the summer. In 1943, available for duty throughout the county, they were sent to Wormleighton in the far south of the county, 80 boys staying there for a fortnight. Staff would visit every so often. One ex-student who had moved on to Birmingham University was much praised for joining them. He *sacrificed his whole vacation to camp work* acting in the multifarious roles of Quartermaster, Entertainer, Organ mender and Assistant Cook: his name was Norman Painting. Another pupil recalled a similar camp at Claverdon *where we slept in army bell tents by the side of a large, well equipped Scout hut.* Initially the boys were paid a mere 4d an hour but Headmaster Pratt cycled around the farms and successfully negotiated sixpence an hour with all of the farmers but one, *who thought that we would work for nothing!* [32] The harvest camps continued for at least two years after the war.

Founders Day, commemorated as usual in May 1941 just days before the bombing, was marked each succeeding war year in St. Nicolas Church; apart from shattered glass and minor damage in the Chancel this had luckily escaped the severe damage of the school next door. In the service of 1942 the Reverend Bains from Rugby poured scorn on Nazi ideology and asserted that one purpose of the service was to attack *Nazi blasphemy*. In 1944 the atmosphere was more relaxed and more parochial. An address from Nuneaton vicar Marcus Knight referred to School History as *connected to that of the parish church.* He argued that *Libera* meant freedom to pursue all knowledge and Grammatica should not be interpreted too narrowly. [33]

5. Background To The 1944 Education Act

In the late 1930s before the war an elderly Dr Edward Noel Nason had looked back 60 years to his 1870s schooldays and reflected on enormous social change. The rigid three class educational thinking of the earlier time had been diffused by the decline of the landed interest, the ascendency of the middle classes, political democracy, world war, economic transformation, the increasing role of central government, the growth of socialism, developments in religious thinking, the emancipation of women and the changing status of Great Britain as a world power. It was now accepted that all available educational potential should be unlocked regardless of background.

National events with regard to education were moving apace and the war did not act as a block on reform for long. The result was an increase in state influence over the fortunes of the school that takes us back four centuries to Elizabethan times. Since the Hadow Report of 1926 secondary education was seen as the aim for all. There would be a two stage education with a break at eleven when pupils could attend non-selective central schools – known as Modern Schools. The fee paying Grammar Schools such as Nuneaton fitted into this and it did not lead to any great change in their aims. These were to *provide a route to the Universities*[34] for some and for others to top off the education of the growing number destined for employment in commerce and the minor professions. Nuneaton Grammar School would, however, revert to its original idea of offering a free education. Plans to remove the fee paying element in state Grammar Schools developed so that all children regardless of their parents' financial status could be educated to a higher level. The trend had been in this direction for some time: the number of free place Grammar School children doubled between 1920 and 1932 when 209,000 free place children were nearly half the total[35] and the proportion had steadily increased in Nuneaton. But at central level there was a desire to see greater uniformity in this area. Local conditions, the attitude of local Education Authorities, school tradition and endowment variations (where they existed) meant that educational opportunity depended in part on where you lived.

While the rigid three class educational thinking – so prominent in 1880 – had gone, a tripartite way of approaching education was nonetheless coming into its own. This was to have a direct impact on King Edward's. The economic problems of 1931, followed by public spending cuts and the subsequent depression, had delayed change. However, by 1938 the publication of the Spens Report produced more specific suggestions as to how a re-organisation of Secondary education might take place. It argued that, aided by the School Certificate exams for which public and endowed Grammar Schools had entered the majority of students, *the ancient Grammar School was adopted too exclusively as the model for the Secondary School.* [36] It also asserted that the secondary curriculum must cater for different needs. Emphasis on the importance of Technical Education meant that overall, three types of secondary school could be developed: Grammar, Technical and Modern and its influence on the 1944 Education Act can be seen. Spens however, had also considered a multi-lateral school where, streamed by ability, all pupils could attend the same institution. This suggested what we would now call a comprehensive system of education.

However, Spens acknowledged the dangers of both too large an institution and the possibility of the purely academic side to a school being unduly diluted. Moreover, there was a growing faith in the ability of intelligence quotient testing to pick out accurately the abilities of pupils at the age when the Secondary transfer was to take place. These factors made it more likely that the reform of schools would encourage development of the tripartite system that did emerge after 1945. The War did not delay change as much as might have been imagined. Indeed, Churchill, preoccupied with international affairs, gave his President of the Board of Education Richard (Rab) Butler licence to pursue his chosen path and he produced a major Education Act in 1944. Free secondary schooling for all was a central feature of the proposals coupled with a raising of the school leaving age to 15 and eventually 16. Mere elementary schooling was no more, education for all would follow a primary, secondary and – possibly – a Further Education route. There would now also be a Minister of Education.

6. Voluntary Aided Status For The School:

How would all this affect Nuneaton? The Grammar school would remain, as would the Girls High school. As long as some pupils had continued to pay fees, admission to the school had never completely been on the basis of perceived intellectual ability. Once an assessment was introduced, the 11 plus, this was no longer – theoretically – the case. However, the confidence of 1944 in the ability to select accurately at eleven through testing, diminished considerably in subsequent years. Given the numbers in the town likely to be deemed as suitable for the Grammar/Technical end of the spectrum, Manor Park School would become a mixed Grammar/Technical[37] while other Secondary Schools built in the 1930s – such as Arbury and Higham Lane could become part of the Secondary Modern provision. The main change for King Edward's was its future status, given that fee paying was to end.

Endowed Grammar Schools were travelling in several different directions. Some had become independent, others had already sold off most of their endowments and would now become completely controlled by the local authority. The option for King Edward's without an excessively large endowment[38] was Voluntary Aided status. Under this the state would aid the Foundation by paying the everyday running costs but the school would retain its governing body with its mix of two thirds Foundation and Representative Governors and one third local authority representatives. They were allowed to determine the *character* of the *voluntary* school and ensure any wishes of the founder that were still practical were observed. The Governors collectively were responsible in respect of the capital and income of the school endowments. Building decisions were made by the Governors who would have to raise a half of any expenditure on any construction while the local authority provided the other half. All pupils would attend free.

To opt for aided status required both the will and the means. There would need to be a reason for wishing to retain a degree of independence from the state, to maintain a particular school ethos. Secondly, there had to be a sufficient endowment and/or fund raising ability in the local area to make this wish a practical one. Many of the schools opting for Aided Status were Church schools but about 100, including King Edward's, were not.[39] There was not really a specific ethos, peculiar to Nuneaton Grammar School that the Governors of King Edward's, as one of these 100, wished to perpetuate. Admittedly the overall atmosphere of the school was Christian in a general sense and a string of early to mid 20th Century Heads (Holman, Whimster, Sumner, Usherwood) were active members of the local parish church.[40] However, Nuneaton Grammar had been an interdenominational school since the middle of the 19th Century. The motive for its new status was more a general desire to maintain an overall approach to education that had evolved, particularly since 1880, with a long tradition of suspicion of outside interference. The endowment, producing an income of over £1,000 a year from the investments in 1939/40 but declining in the war, was clearly insufficient for the school to go it alone;[41] but a desire to maintain a very limited degree of independence by becoming a Voluntary Aided Grammar School was a practical possibility. The Governors also felt, correctly as events were to prove, that the reputation of the school in the town was sufficiently high and the inhabitants sufficiently well-disposed towards it, that there would be a generous response to any appeal for money. This argument would be re-enforced in another way; in reducing the local authority costs on the school, overall rate levels could be kept down. This was something of considerable historical significance in Nuneaton. From 1870 to 1902 the creation of a school board at the elementary level of education had been rendered unnecessary because of the comprehensive provision of the elementary church schools set up in the late 1840s by Canon Savage and by the relatively stagnant population of Nuneaton until the 1880s. However, the maintenance of this position until 1902 was seen as quite an achievement. This independence was clearly something of which the inhabitants had been intensely proud and many wished to maintain it in some form.[42]

7. Post-War Delays

The delay in getting the new building meant the old Science Labs continued in use until the early 1960s

It would take a few years after 1945 to organise the new Voluntary Aided status. The physical recovery of the buildings, however, took much longer. In 1948 War damage alone was estimated at £14,507.[43] The original claim of £9,500 in June 1941 had risen because *costs of building and engineering works have increased to a considerable extent.* [44] Urgent requirements were:

- New clear glass.
- A new Chimney stack for the Hall.
- Replacement for damaged stone transomes and mullions.
- New ceilings/roof/partitions for art room.

However, despite this, King Edward's was at the end of a long queue.

- 5,000 schools had been damaged or destroyed by air raids and there was a serious shortage of labour and materials.
- Moreover, it was the ones completely destroyed that would get the earlier resources. Circular 245, issued as late as 1952, stated the Ministry was *unable to include in building programmes any work to design or replace unsatisfactory premises of existing schools.*
- In addition priority was in the primary sector. This was because of the challenge of the rising younger school population. In 1945 there were 796,000 births increasing to 1 million in 1947 and further rises were anticipated.[45]
- When increased attention was finally paid to the secondary sector of education it was the new Secondary Modern sector that got priority. The remark made by the Ministry of Education with regard to another location in 1947 could equally well have applied to Nuneaton: *The Ministry of Education would not sanction a new grammar school building until the Secondary Modern provision in the area was improved.*[46]
- Yet other national factors were adding to the pressure of numbers. The school leaving age was raised to 15 so there would be no early leavers. Somehow, well over 300 boys had to be accommodated.

Thus began a long wait. After he was appointed Chairman of the Governors in 1942, in the aftermath of the school's bomb damage, Harry Cleaver was convinced a new site was necessary for a school already cramped before 1939 and now in a desperate state.[47] Yet despite his best efforts – and they were immense – it was not until 1963 that the school finally managed to acquire the complete set of new buildings it so badly needed: and these were on the existing site, somewhat extended.

8. A New Site For The School? Interminable Delays 1945-52

In the immediate post-war years the re-location of the school was anticipated. The search had begun as early as July 1945 when Harry Cleaver investigated a possible site on the north side of Hinckley Road where North Warwickshire and Hinckley College later stood.[48] By the end of the following year this 16 acre area was seen as the best option[49] and it was large enough to accommodate the playing field urgently needed: at that time use of playing fields was dependent on the goodwill of Nuneaton Rugby Football Club. The Education Committee agreed to a sub-committee to discuss matters with the Governors but detailed ideas had to wait for the County Education plan of 1947. This document, the *Development Plan for the Administrative County of Warwick WCC Education Committee Report,* included the excepted districts[50] of Nuneaton and Solihull because the population of these towns was over 50,000. The Report commented in general that *necessary improvements to a school can often only be secured by re-building it entirely on a new site.* As a result the plan for King Edward's was to buy a new site for £5,000 in the 1947/8 year and then spend over £200,000 over the subsequent four years. The aim was that the post war birth bulge could then be accommodated in a school which would change from a two to a three-form entry.[51]

It never happened. The broad reason was the post-war administrative complexity of purchasing school property in the context of a Voluntary Aided institution. As a result King Edward's lived hand to mouth on its buildings for nearly 20 years. The specific stumbling block was the plan to make the school a three form entry one. While Governors did not oppose this in principle, the local authority made it clear that this change would be classed as building a new school. This would require Governors' commitment to the cost of its construction. The problem was that under the new Voluntary Aided code being negotiated at that time, Governors would have to meet half the cost of a new school which they regarded as beyond their means. This partly helps to explain the delay in publication both of the school's new Articles of Government and the confirmation of the Voluntary Aided Status until 1952. In December 1947 the Governors wrote expressing reservations regarding the Warwickshire Development Plan but also formally applying for Voluntary Aided Status. In January 1948 the LEA replied, requesting *further information regarding the financial status of the Foundation.*[52] The Governors' specific concern was the question of a two or three form entry school and how the burden of expense would be shared. Charity Commission approval for the proposed new status would have to be obtained. The Governors wished for a meeting with L.E.A. representatives but the Ministry felt this unnecessary and insisted that neither the Voluntary Aided status application, nor a proposed conference with the Ministry, could go ahead until the school's financial hand was revealed. In May 1948 the Governors were asked for more detailed justification of their estimates regarding future income from real and personal property.[53] The Ministry was also keen for the Governors to ascertain whether the War Damage Commission could assist with some of the expenses of re-building. Governors saw the Ministry as uncooperative; the Ministry saw the Governors as less than candid about their financial position.

There were also differences of opinion as to the nature of the new institution to be constructed. By 1948 the LEA and the Further Education Council wanted a new all-embracing Technical College. This would include not only a School of Art but, initially, King Edward's as well. In a proposal prefiguring a radical but aborted scheme at the start of the 21st Century, all three institutions would take a large area adjacent to Hinckley Road, but the Governors opposed this three-in-one plan. A site almost opposite on the south side of Hinckley Road was now investigated for the new Boys Grammar School but this idea also

> **The Development of Nuneaton's Technical College.**
>
> The County Mining and Technical school, started before 1900, had inadequate premises in Coton Road with an annexe in Norman Avenue. The Art School met in Nuneaton's Art Gallery. There had been plans for a new site as early 1935 but – as with King Edward's – economic stringency and then the war had prevented the desired change.[54] The Technical College eventually re-located to Hinckley Road in 1958, some years later than envisaged by the original development plan. From the original colliery management and engineering courses it had widened its curriculum to include a variety of technical and vocational training.

floundered. It was Church glebe land and –at that stage – there was the possibility of constructing a new church there, so a deal was not feasible.[55] Negotiations with local authorities remained tense. In 1949 the Council asserted that if the Governors were willing to sell the school field to them it would *expedite the purchase of the new site* at Hinckley Road. Governors cautiously agreed to give a first refusal on any sale of land to the Local Education Authority but remained sceptical about the direction of future developments.[56] In that year the Grammar School was removed from the 1951-54 building programme. Headmaster Whimster described the decision as *monstrous*. [57]

Further delays occurred immediately after 1950. According to Birmingham politician Leonard Cleaver (son of Governor Chairman Harry) these were caused not only by the problems of location and the legal complications concerning Voluntary Aided Status and the new Instrument of Government, but also by the credit squeeze and stop-go economic policy of the early 1950s. These resulted in temporary cutbacks in educational expenditure and the continuing emphasis on accommodation for younger pupils with building priorities still lying elsewhere.[58] The belief that a new site would eventually be found delayed other projects, for instance the need for a new Gym. It would not be built while there was the prospect of a move. In 1949 climbing frame apparatus was to be supplied rather than a new Gym since it could be removed to a new site.[59] Optimism faded but remained in muted form until 1952. In his Centenary history published that year just in time for the festivities Reed Brett referred to *when the school is erected on a new site.*[60] A last moment of hope was reported by Harry Cleaver at the 400th Anniversary celebrations. He asserted that Nuneaton was at the top of the list for new Grammar Schools in Warwickshire but after this expectations faded.[61]

9. Recovery Of Routines: School Life In The Late 1940s

The cricket team of 1946
Back Row from left: Mr J.B. Bennett, S.Ghent, J. Gilbert, T.R. Bates, R. Hayward,
G.A. Heath (Scorer).
Seated: L. Brownson, R.A. Siddons (Vice-Captain), P.H. Cook (Captain), J.R.M
Branston (Hon. Sec.), A.A. Horne.
In front: J. Lucas, J.W. Wykes

All the delays meant the physical difficulties encountered by King Edward's were prolonged. The school's post war conditions were harsh and affected the way teaching was conducted in circumstances far from ideal. There was no replacement for the Gymnasium and P.T. classes had to take place in the inadequately sized School Hall with portable apparatus, no changing rooms, showers or storage lockers. The kit was kept in pupils' desks. While the field was convenient for Physical Training use of it was dependent on good weather. Biology was taught in one of the *new* classrooms across the road. Science labs lacked a supply of low-voltage electricity to the benches and it was difficult to darken two of the rooms. Missing doors and cupboard drawers remained unreplaced after war damage.[62] The Hall was too small for either full Assembly or PT and the Library had to be used as a form room. The school field was another problem. In 1943 its poor state as a result of wartime damage resulted in a letter to the Borough Solicitor but by the start of 1944 no action had been taken: Governors were told that labour shortages made immediate action to improve its condition unlikely;[63] so the boys themselves undertook some remedial action, removing war debris to make it possible to play a game of Rugby.[64] But there was still no room for a cricket square between the Rugby pitches.

The school's approach was business as usual as far as possible and horizons had been widened. It signed up to the International Schools Fund – twinned with two schools, one in Sandane, Norway. In late 1945 a charity collection for Jewish Refugee children raised £3 5/9d. School trips, which had developed considerably in the 1930s, were resumed. These tended to be industrial and practical rather than scenic and recreational with a visit to Coventry's gasworks, the Atomic Train Exhibition and the local telephone exchange.[65]

With a free education now available the social range of boys increased further: one old boy recalled the occupations of classmates' parents where he knew them. Though a small, random and possibly unrepresentative sample it is still revealing of the position just after 1945.

- Coal-miner (3)
- Schoolmaster (2)
- Bookmaker
- Carpenter
- Fireman
- Golf Professional
- Stationmaster
- Owner of a small bus company
- Political Party Agent (Labour)
- Postman
- Solicitor
- Tailor
- Town Clerk

This was a good social mix by any standards. Reginald Hollis, attending in both the war and post-war periods, was the son of a Bedworth collier: he later became the Anglican Archbishop of Montreal. [66]

In place just as the war was ending was a new Head, Donald Cameron Whimster (1905-1991). From a Scottish background, as well as Westminster School and Trinity Cambridge, he was appointed in February 1945 and took up his position in April, soon making an impression: *how great a relief it was to know that in our new HM they had a man prepared to stick to the task of little by little overcoming the obstacles and circumstances created by recent difficulties* said the Chairman of the Governors at the Speech Day in late 1945. When Whimster left in 1951 the compliments continued: it was virtually admitted that he had picked up the pieces, and not only literally with regard to the buildings: *the late HM [Pratt] had left unexpectedly and the whole organisation of the school the Governors knew not to be satisfactory.*[67] Uniform rules were now re-enforced with vigour with caps now compulsory for the senior school. There was a basic blue blazer with a maroon one for the sixth formers with braid and silver piping for sports colours and prefectorial authority [68] and all pupils now attended a weekly Wednesday Assembly at the parish church.[69] The school was conscious of retaining its (often quite recent) traditions and was still creating new ones: under new music teacher, C. R. George, a choir developed and Mr. George played an organ voluntary to the school each Wednesday in Church.

> **Headmasters move on**
>
> Whimster became Head of Weston Super Mare GS the first of four consecutive Nuneaton Grammar School Heads that used King Edward's, their first Headship, as a stepping stone to lead other Grammar Schools. Sumner went to Archbishop's Tenison's Grammar School Kennington in 1960, South London, Usherwood to Lewes Grammar School, Sussex, in 1967 and Rowland Brown to High Wycombe Royal Grammar School, Buckinghamshire, in 1975.

As well as having oversight of the post war recovery of the school, and campaigning for school re-building, Whimster also organised the formal application for Voluntary Aided Status that the school made in 1946.[70] Bureaucratic delays (see above) meant the new forms of Instrument and Articles of Government were not received by Governors until March 1949. Only in November 1951 were Governors told the articles would finally be published early the following year, the centenary year when, symbolically, the old School Charters were repaired and displayed.[71]

While news of a new site was awaited, a temporary recovery was the order of the day. By the spring of 1948 the Library had been re-established in the former Head's House and a war memorial commemorating the dead of the 1939-45 conflict, designed by H.R.Jephson, had been put in place on a platform in the Old School Room. With pupil numbers at 333, twenty more than in 1944-6, space was again at a premium.

The St. Nicolas Church Parish Hall was being used for exams. But school life was getting back to normal. In 1947 the school orchestra was reported as *beginning to find its feet.*[72] The essay prizes donated by the Vicar of Nuneaton and W.H.Cope were both flourishing again and the winning efforts duly printed. War added to the prizes: in the summer of 1947 the Lesley Allton Cup for athletics was awarded for the first time.[73]

Dramatic Productions: the Merchant of Venice 1946. With English teacher **J.B. Bennett** *as Shylock. Cast:*
Top row left to right: Gaoler: **H. Barden**, *Salarino:* **J.P.Bland**, *Salanio:* **G.E.B Stubbington**, *Prince of Morocco:* **D.G.Rist**, *Launcelot Gobbo:* **D.T.Jacques**, *Old Gobbo:* **E.W.Leonard**, *Tubal:* **H.C. Jones**, *Clerk of the Court:* **T. Browning**.
Seated left to right: Lorenzo: **K.Dyas**, *Jessica:* **K. Dolby**, *Bassanio:* **C.L.Paul**, *Portia:* **C.B.Hill**, *Shylock:* **J.B.Bennett**, *Antonio:* **J.M.Cope**, *Nerissa:* **G. Brown**, *Graziano:* **H.F. Ferguson**, *Duke of Venice:* **F.H.Latham**.
In front: Balthazar : **J.M. Sharrod**, *Page:* **T.A. Bailey**, *Stephano:* **J.R.M.Branston**.

School debating resumed meetings frequently joining with the Girls' High School. Subjects included, *Gambling is a Major Evil and should be prevented by law* and *Women should have equal pay for equal work.* This latter motion was passed by 21 votes to seven with the girls outnumbering the boys and, according to the less than impartial editors of the Edwardian, the girls, all voting one way, *just followed like a flock.* House competitions had been revived. Societies were active: aeronautical, meteorological, electrical, chess, as well as school plays. Easter 1946 had *seen Farewell to the last of the ladies ... who have undauntedly entered an all male establishment and grappled courageously with unfamiliar circumstances.* Not all staff returned after war service; for instance E.G.Bennett was appointed Assistant Director of Education for West Suffolk. He had come in 1934 from Derby to teach languages and had been on distinguished war service.[74]

After the trials and tribulations of war, the freezing conditions of the winter of 1947 were less taxing than a later generation might have found them. At the end of the school year the Head looked back and, after praising the wonderful efforts of caretaker George Attwood reported that *just one morning's school was lost in the bad winter ... by Spartan fortitude and British extemporisation.* Many boys and staff would have been able to walk to school though it must have been difficult for those struggling in from Ansley, Arley and the like.[75]

Typically for the time, speakers at formal events urged the boys on to great deeds when they left. At the end of 1947 the Prize Day speech came from Charles Morris, Head of King Edward VI, Birmingham, and shortly to be Vice-Chancellor of Leeds University. He recalled the character of 19th Century Grammar Schools with *Indomitable spirit, character, lofty ambition, great enterprise, capable of holding their own and keeping their heads in the most novel and surprising of circumstances – out resolutely to the four corners of the world establishing business and trading posts prospecting and exploring and ever unselfconsciously maintaining their high English standard. Unless British youth stormed the world in the same indomitable spirit we had little future.*[76] Spartan fortitude was clearly to be followed by Imperial enterprise.

> **The winter of 1947**
>
> Between 23rd January and 27th February 344 tons of chippings and grit were put down by Nuneaton Borough Council. Correspondents complained that the footpaths are a disgrace. Apparently Hinckley's were much better, they used salt. Two coal pits closed due to weather as 30-40% of miners could not get in. Output was 16% down over the winter. Because of power cuts London papers failed to arrive for the first time in living memory. Given all this the school did very well to keep going normally.
> *Nuneaton Observer*
> *28.2.1947 and 7.3.1947.*

Academic achievement ignored the theoretical handicap of poor buildings. It continued with four County Awards in 1947 and two open Scholarships to Pembroke College,

Cambridge. Sporting successes too resumed: J.S.Deeming was selected as Captain of the English Schools Rugby team versus Wales. The Old Eds organisation revived even though there was no cricket ground available for them. Their membership increased from 22 at the end of the war to 71 a couple of years later.[77]

Two post- war Heads: Donald Whimster. 1945-1952

Two post- war Heads: Thomas Sumner 1952-1960

10. A Change Of Leadership

By 1950 the worst was over but the next decade was to prove one of frustration, waiting for a new building. In 1951 Whimster left to take a Headship at Weston-Super-Mare and the appointment of his successor Thomas C. Sumner was made from 240 applications. Sumner was born in Goole, attended Harwich High School and was Penge scholar in Physics at London University. He was an RAF signals officer in the War after which he taught at King Henry VIII School, 1945/6 and then Hull Grammar School, before coming to Nuneaton.[78]

The new Head had – for someone in his position *an unusually full teaching timetable.* His role resembled his immediate predecessors (and his immediate successors) both in taking a full part in the life of the town, in his case in the Rotary Club and the George Eliot Fellowship and he was keen on maintaining the broad Christian ethos of the school. Also in common with many other Heads he was scathing about Government spending priorities: *the country can find £9 million for a Battleship, obsolete before it is cancelled but cannot find £200,000 for Universities to teach them what will never be obsolete.*[79] Here, alive and well, was the view of University as a liberal education of lasting value as opposed to specific vocational knowledge that might rapidly become outdated.

Sumner was reported as having *Independent and outspoken views on modern education.* These were trenchantly expressed from time to time. He strongly believed that *Grammar Schools had been neglected since the war in favour of Secondary Moderns.* However, he saw University as very much for the minority. In the same speech he asserted that University entry should be more selective – it was *too easy* to get in.[80] Sumner provided vigorous leadership: his early time as Head saw the final completion of the new Articles of Association and Instrument of Government as well as the Quarter Centenary celebrations in 1952. In that year he would have been amazed if he had been told that, even though he would remain in post for a further eight years he would not, despite every effort, see the promised new buildings for the school.

11. New Articles Of Government 1952

The Instrument and Articles of Government were documents equivalent to what would have been a new Charter in past times. The Instrument dealt with the election, organisation, tasks and procedures of the Governing body. The Articles referred to the conduct of the school, finance, equipment and premises, appointment and dismissal of staff curriculum, times and admissions.

They reflected the changed state of the school as a result of the 1944 Education Act and the Voluntary Aided Status obtained by the school as a result. They changed the official name of the institution from King Edward VI Grammar School to King Edward VI School; though boarders had not been seen for nearly 50 years, they were still officially an option. The Governors had to provide regular financial estimates on the cost of maintaining the school to the local authority and keep them up to date with the need for any repair of the school premises; this was a particularly apposite point considering the continuing sub-standard post-war condition of the buildings. In return, the bulk of the expense of running the school was in the hands of the Local Education Authority (LEA). The choice of books, stationary, furniture and apparatus was left in the hands of the Governors.

The number on the Governing body was raised to 18 with a majority of Foundation Governors.

Governors	Foundation Governors	Representative Governors
Total number 18	Total Number 12 Six picked by existing ones plus: Two Magistrates, Two Parents, One Edwardian, One representative of Birmingham University	Total Number 6 County Council Four Borough Council Two

Voluntary Aided status had other implications: the Governors still retained the absolute right to select the Headmaster. Two members of the LEA had to be present and could speak but, crucially, not vote on the appointment. The LEA could however, prevent the Head's dismissal by the Governors if they so wished. Assistant Masters would also be appointed by the Governors though their terms and conditions were to be determined by the LEA. The same applied to non-teaching staff and the Clerk to the Governors. The *general direction of the conduct and curriculum of the school* was in the hands of the Governors but *subject to the provisions of the Development Plan for the area by the Minister [of Education]*.[81]

12. Quarter Centenary Celebrations

The modern relationship with the local authority did not preclude a strong consciousness of a more independent past. The year 1952 – 400 years since the Edwardian Foundation – presented an opportunity to emphasise the ancient nature of the Foundation. One form of celebration was the commissioning of a work of school history, something of an update of Dr Nason's work from 1936 with extensive quotations from it.[82] Reed Brett co-ordinated the compilation. Events were staged concentrating on reflecting important areas of the school's life in more recent years. There was an Old Edwardian's dinner, a cricket match against first-class players and a major dramatic production. In escaping from post-war austerity it did locally for the school what the Festival of Britain had done for the country in the previous year.

In some ways it was the life of the school over the last 80 rather than 400 years that was being celebrated. However, some events were more conscious of the full span. This was achieved theatrically with the special production of three plays, *Abraham and Isaac* (thought to be the kind of play performed in the Foundation year 1552) *The Critic* (Sheridan's 18th Century drama) and a 20th Century Review. They were connected by three prologues. There was *spectacular* lighting and sound recording and *nothing like this has been seen or heard in Nuneaton before*.[83] A.E.Jebbutt of the Old Eds Dramatic Society assisted English teacher S.R.Gibbs with the production. So it became, literally, an eloquent testimony to School and Old Boys co-operation. Frank (Tut) Moore, an indefatigable worker for the Old Edwardians, had founded the drama branch of the organisation (with Jebbutt) after the war when he also played a major role in resurrecting the Old Eds.

A speech from the Earl of Warwick referred to the importance of the King Edward tradition. The Nuneaton Chronicle reminded its readers that the week of celebrations *serve[s] to remind us of the debt which the town owes to this ancient institution* [with its] *long history of distinguished figures*.[84] Whilst this debt is hard to quantify, the use to which leading citizens of the town put their locally based education into serving their community had clearly been considerable in the more recent history of the school since 1880.

When preaching at the special Founders' Day 400th Anniversary service in May 1952, former Chairman of Governors and ex-vicar of St. Nicolas Nuneaton, Canon John White, referred to 1552 as the start of a new era for learning, based on Reformation religion, the Classics and morality. Now, in a time of post-war recovery with a new Head, new Articles of Government, Voluntary Aided status and hopes for a new school building, he sensed a similarly new period of development for the school. It proved to be the final era for the Grammar School as such, though not the end for the King Edward's educational foundation.[85]

CHAPTER TWELVE

The Last Years of the Grammar School: 1952-74

If patience be a virtue we can console ourselves that we have a very virtuous community.
Headmaster Sumner 1957

The delays in obtaining new buildings stretched right across the decade of the 1950s. However, with the backing of the local community, improvements were finally achieved. The school continued its sixth form growth, academic success and range of sporting and extra-curricular activities, with slowly increasing numbers of staff. By 1970 very different challenges and opportunities were on the horizon.

1. The Start Of The Sumner Era

In the 1950s the school's sixth form continued to grow and this helped sport, clubs and societies to flourish. However, the Autumn 1955 edition of the Edwardian criticised the boys who *set their own interests before the school* [and] *merely for pocket money take part-time work instead of turning up for a school team.*

For the previous generation of pupils the school had – outside their home and family – essentially been their life, in a way unknown to scholars in previous centuries, or subsequently. By 1954 the Edwardian had noted a worrying element of *pre-meditated violence in juvenile crime,* the main cause being *the period of violence in which we live.* Certainly local cultural life had often centred on the school. The Edwardian of Summer 1955 described the town as *dull streets of struggling suburbs spreading into the countryside like an ugly weed.* There was *no permanent theatre* and *few concerts.* The character of the town had developed at *a period when dignity and beauty were sacrificed to grim necessity.*[1] In the 1950s the school saw itself as a local oasis for the Arts.

The treatment of new boys was gentler than earlier ages – caps trampled in the mud rather than the 19th Century pelting of top hats with handkerchiefs under which stones were concealed. Though the school remained boys only, King Edward's accepted a small number of female pupils for advanced level science in the late 1940s and early 1950s, a reflection of greater male liberality and higher female aspiration but also the indifferent Science facilities at the Girls' High School. Some girls came for science lessons as late as 1967 because of timetable clashes at the High School.[2] Another sign of change was the acceptance of a female Governor, Amy Moreton in 1953.[3] This contrasted with the determined opposition on this point by her grandparents' contemporaries at the end of the previous century. Non-wartime female members of staff however, would have to wait until the early 1970s when mixed education at King Edward's was being anticipated.

2. Pupils: Intake And Curriculum

Parents of King Edward boys were conscious of being in a privileged minority. Lack of agreement with the local authority had ensured limitation to a two stream school. In 1952 there were 365 boys with 40 of them in the sixth form. The yearly intakes could be as high as 70 making for classes well over 30 until the development of Nicholas Chamberlaine School as a comprehensive for Bedworth in the mid 1950s eased the pressure. Around half a dozen boys were transferred in from Secondary Moderns and a similar number went the other way at 13. The leaving of boys before 16 – legally allowed until 1972 – had never been completely stopped.[4]

After a common first year with no distinctions made, boys were now streamed into Latin (L) and Modern (M) streams, with Latin scholars spending less time on French, PE and Maths. However, only a small number went on to study Latin at O Level. Though still essential for some University courses the alternative of two foreign languages, French and Spanish, was increasingly being taken up. By later – though not contemporary – standards the options for sixth formers were limited. The Science Sixth was generally larger than the Arts Sixth; around 25 in the two classes generally took Chemistry, Physics and either Biology or Maths while in the Arts Sixth English, History, French and Spanish were commonly studied. Sometimes tricky subject choices had to be made, such as Art or History.[5]

The 1950s were not a time when much consideration was given to taking students with disabilities into mainstream education but King Edward's had one notable exception, Richard Hodges. He was born with type two spinal muscular atrophy: this adversely affected the nerves in the spinal cord leading to a breakdown between the brain and the muscles and he was confined to a wheelchair. His acceptance in 1953 was a close run thing: initially, the King Edward's Governors declined his application on the grounds that the premises were unsuitable but on appeal this decision was reversed and ground floor classes were arranged. Hodges went on to have a distinguished school career and was joint winner of the school History prize in 1956. Because of his disability he was less successful at being accepted at London University and had to take an external degree. He went on to be Nuneaton and Bedworth Borough Solicitor and was also a prominent figure on local health bodies.[6]

3. Pupils: Achievement

Considering the limited size of the school there was considerable academic success: in the 1950s there were nine Open Scholarships, eleven State Scholarships and 140 County Awards, a decent number for a two stream Grammar School. More and more were taking and succeeding at O Level. At Speech Day in 1956 Governors' Chairman Harry Cleaver contrasted the *bad condition of the school buildings* [with the] *continued success of the pupils*. Yet high academic achievement was not for everyone and at this time less than half the original intake stayed on to A Level. Horizons were lower: in 1956 there were over 50 boys in the sixth form for the first time, a result Sumner regarded as *excellent* but was still under 50% of the intake.[7] In the 1960s this low proportion staying on into the sixth came in for criticism but until this time, to have most pupils staying to 16 was seen as an advance and sixth form entry a definite bonus. Now the numbers post-sixteen grew rapidly. Further examination successes in the 1960s reflected national trends in the linked areas of increasing numbers of O Level passes and increasing sixth form participation. Moreover, the concept of a liberal education still held as an Edwardian editorial pointed out; *the school does not only teach boys to pass GCE exams, it educates them*. Prefects assumed greater responsibilities. In 1955 Governors discussed the possibility of an honorarium for the Prefect acting as Head Librarian but rejected the idea as *any boy should feel proud of being chosen to do this in a voluntary capacity.* [8]

4. Deputy Heads And Other Staff

With the school's growth the position of Deputy Head or Second Master was increasingly significant. This post had begun to evolve soon after 1900 when Holman had assisted Waters in the additional administration required by the greater local government involvement in financing and the increasing numbers (See Chapter Nine). Further developed by Holman's Successor Walpole Day, the idea of a senior and long serving Member of staff assisting with the everyday running of the school was now well established and continued with Day's successors. In 1954 Deputy Head Reed Brett retired after 21 years in the post; he was replaced by Harry Branston for the next twelve years. Although Brett and Branston were very different people (Branston the more extrovert, lively and overtly inspirational, Brett patient and unflustered) there were similarities. Both men spent most of their professional life at King Edward's, both teaching History and both, successively, Deputy Heads. They took a professional view of their responsibilities, never counting the hours worked despite moderate pay, saw a liberal education as central to the ethos of the school, ensured its smooth running on a day to day basis and inspired many boys in different ways, Branston in a wide variety of sports and in the Air Cadets, Brett in the Library and numerous societies such as history and debating. Both were keen supporters of the House system and extra-curricular activities. Nor were they alone on the staff in adopting this approach typical of many secondary schools of all types in this era. Brett spent 33 years at the school 1921-1954 and Branston 36 years 1930-1966.[9] They provided a stability to the overall character of the school. Between 1966 and 1974 Deputy Head Harold Fisher more than capably continued this tradition.

Deputy Heads: the heart of a school: Harry Branston: Joined Staff 1930 Deputy Head 1954-1966

Harold Fisher: Joined staff 1950   Deputy Head 1966-1974

The disruption caused by the war until 1945 did not entirely disappear for a number of years. Staff turnover remained high between 1949 and the start of 1952 during which time there had been ten changes – over half the teaching staff.[10] The state of the buildings may have discouraged longevity, but there remained a solid minority who stayed and helped maintain stability; as the physical environment improved the majority of staff began to stay a little longer. As at other times in the school's history it was not always easy to find adequately qualified teachers, even more so with the variety of subjects now taught. However, they were praised by Inspectors *especially the younger masters* for the *vigorous* life of clubs and societies in the Inspection of February 1952.[11] In little more than half a century the professional commitment of teachers had made giant strides.

5. Extra-Curricular And Sport

Ventures out of classroom and school now developed such as the one to Paris in 1951 with 49 boys. Contacts with the French town Roanne also developed during this decade. House competitions thrived in sport, drama and other activities. Occasionally, new organisations developed. For instance, in a burst of historical consciousness a John Leeke Society was formed in 1959. The Fives court was still in use throughout the fifties. The school was involved with Squadron 13 with its Headquarters at the Pingles. It included proficiency flying exams and an annual camp. There was a revival of interest in Air Cadet activities and 20 boys formed a Junior organisation known as *Flight*.[12]

There were some ambitious stage productions in the 1950s such as Richard II in 1954. This followed *extensive alterations* to the stage which made it a possible venue to stage larger enterprises there instead of having to resort to St George's Hall in the town. With their lighting and sound arrangements and stage construction these events showed off the scientific as well as artistic capabilities of the boys. In 1955 a performance of George Bernard Shaw's *The Devil's Disciple* drew praise from the reviewer who pointed out that one Kenneth Loach, later an eminent film-maker, was *rapidly acquiring many of the arts of the actor*. There was outstanding achievement in chess in 1954 when the entire school team was selected for Warwickshire.[13]

Rugby and cricket had become the major seasonal sports in which if you had a modicum of talent you were expected to play. There was a revival of a debate last staged in the 1920s – should Soccer or Rugby be the football code in the school? Soccer was attempting a comeback. The Edwardian of Autumn 1955 reported that there was *a fair amount of argument between members of the lower school this term on the subject*.[14]

Some argued that the switch from soccer to rugby on arriving at the Grammar School was a difficult transition for many boys – even off-putting. Refereeing soccer was easier and there were fewer injuries. But all these points were vigorously disputed. Rugby was seen as a game full of skill, speed and excitement: it stayed. It was unlikely while the Grammar School survived that numbers would be sufficient to allow teams in both codes without a thinning of talent to the detriment of the overall standard of each sport; this was deemed unacceptable. Soccer would have its revival later under the aegis of the Sixth Form College.

As with academic life, sports facilities were far from ideal. Complaints about the condition of the playing field had been made ever since the war and as late as 1954 it was described as *a veritable pocket handkerchief of a field* which was frequently waterlogged. But the following year there were extensive drainage operations and the part formerly used for agricultural purposes was levelled. By the autumn of 1957 the field was, finally, fully in commission again. A new Pavilion was also to mark the quarter centenary with something literally more concrete.[15] The one of 1934 had never properly recovered from the damage of 1941. £800 had been raised for a new one to go with a new school by 1951 but – when it was apparent that the new school was not going to materialise – plans were put on hold. In another community effort, over £2,000 was raised. Wally Green, the Handicrafts teacher, and a volunteer sixth former, offered their services free for some of the interior carpentry work. They were largely responsible for the roof and the flooring. It was stories such as this that continued to maintain and re-mould the fiercely independent attitude to educational expenditure that continued in the town for many years. But at the time this attitude was not unusual, nor new; indeed in straightened economic times it was encouraged by those at the centre, especially at a time of economic squeeze. Referring to the plans for a new pavilion back in 1931 the Board of Education had commented that it was a *very general practice* to meet *substantial amenities* from private sources.[16] In the climate of post-war austerity this view still held. The local authority was not prepared to countenance a full time Groundsman.

Parents v. School cricket match May 1953: but the Parents Association role was not merely sporting and social

6. Parents Association And Old Edwardians

Two other organisations also gave valuable support to the school. In the early 1950s the Old Edwardians membership grew from 329 members to 507. Membership showed the wide variety of careers followed by Old Boys, [17] Sadler's Wells, RAF, Teaching, Accountancy, Technical Manager, Sports Coach. Fund-raising remained an important element in their make up conscious of the school's Voluntary Aided Status and its desire at this time to conserve capital for the long delayed building project.

The Parents Association had become a strong organisation with both social and money raising functions. At the peak of frustration with regard to a new building, the mid 1950s, the role of the Association evolved from merely offering moral support to becoming a pressure group. Noting the *callous neglect* of the school's case for re-building by the Ministry and its *continued ignoring of Nuneaton's need* it organised a petition of protest to both the Ministry of Education and Warwickshire County Council. The fight for improved buildings had stimulated membership. The Association membership in 1957 included 315 out of 347 sets of parents, about 90% of those eligible.[18]

7. Expansion Of Existing Buildings? Interminable Delays Continue. 1952-61

The Parents' petition showed that there were wider building concerns in the 1950s than the Pavilion. The Centenary celebrations of 1952 had been the last time there was any hope of a new site for the school. The cost of a new building could certainly not be met from private sources. In 1953 it became apparent that *the land in Hinckley Road had not been acquired and apparently will not be for a long time.* 1954 was an especially low point when Governor Chairman Harry Cleaver bewailed that *there did not seem to be any prospect of a new school for generations.* The Edwardian complained about the appalling state of the buildings: with *prefabricated and rusting* classrooms, as well as *Victorian bedrooms* (a reference to the use of the Headmaster's House) *the school is not getting a good deal.* Those less directly involved with the current school felt the same way. Old boy Professor Illing, addressing the school in 1952, had been *aghast at the conditions in which teaching was carried on in the present building.*[19]

The Parents petition had not pulled its punches: there was still no gym to replace the one bombed 15 years before. P.T. classes were held in the Assembly Hall, with no changing/washing facilities. In the whole school there were only six wash basins —on Ministry standards there should have been 30. There was no interval shelter for bad weather and only three classrooms were up to ministry standard. Storage arrangements were *pitiable.* Only the first year cloakroom had heating —drying facilities were lacking. Physics and Chemistry Laboratories, even if combined, would not meet Ministry standards. The Handicraft room needed to be almost twice as big and the Assembly

Hall, at 50 foot by 20 foot was insufficient for 360 boys. There was no sick bay. Heating was *primitive* – coal fires and stoves. *The education of two generations of boys has suffered.* The frustration of Headmaster Sumner showed through when, describing examination results as *not all bad* he argued that they could be raised by *improvements in our wretched accommodation.*[20]

Yet those improvements were further delayed. In October 1954 the Governors were told that there was *no chance of getting a new school for a very long time*; changing policy, they now looked to improve and slightly expand the existing site with new classrooms, a science wing, dining room, assembly hall, and re-built gym. [21] In March 1955 it was generally accepted that *the school is now probably to remain on its present site*. But attempting to develop a town centre position was a tricky manoeuvre. Back in the 1870s Endowed Schools Commissioner for Nuneaton, Mr Stanton, had shrewdly predicted difficulties: he had pointed out that the building of the new school almost adjacent to the previous one, though possible, was probably not the ideal solution because it was a restricted site (see Chapter Eight). Delays now came from all sides: by November 1956, possibly in response to the parents' petition, Nuneaton MP Stan Bowles optimistically reported that a scheme to expand the existing premises would finally go through: Yet even then it was reported that *the County Architect is being very difficult.*[22]

The Slow Progress Of Plans For The New Buildings

1953-4	The school would not be re-locating to a new site
1954-6	Expansion of existing site blocked in all directions
1956 (Nov.)	Nuneaton's M.P. is confident plans will finally go through
1957	Opposition to school expanding on to Church glebe land
1958 (May)	Compulsory purchase order for glebe land
1959	Grant assistance limited to 50%
1960	Work agreed in principle but precise timetable not fixed until Nov.
1961 (Jan.)	Work begins: public appeal starts
1961 (May)	£34,000 raised
1962 (Autumn)	Buildings nearly complete
1963 (Jan/Feb.)	Completion delayed by harsh winter conditions
1963 (Summer)	Work largely completed

8. Practical Problems Of School Expansion

Practical problems still loomed large. It was uncertain on which side of the school expansion would take place. On one side the Council opposed a Churchyard site but on the other it was becoming doubtful if the parish church be willing to part with the vicar's glebe land. Canon Herbert, vicar and Governor, faced a conflict of interests similar in reverse to Hugh Hughes 150 years earlier (see Chapter Six) and initially seemed co-operative. At an Extraordinary Meeting of Governors Herbert expressed no objection to Grammar school expansion in principle although any scheme required Parochial Church Council and Diocesan approval: the permission of bereaved relatives was required for any encroachment on the churchyard.[23] These provisos proved a stumbling block. Eventually the agreed option by Governors and local Council was an expansion into church glebe land. But this was not agreed by the church. Moreover, the property boundary disputes were not settled as constructively as in the time of the more autocratic Canon Deed who could simply make his own decisions. Representative democracy had now come to the Church of England and the St. Nicolas Parochial Church Council was unwilling to give authorisation to sell the glebe land. Compulsory purchase was now seen as the only way forward: this led to legal wrangling unpleasantly reminiscent of earlier times in the school's history.[24]

All this added to the school's feelings of frustration and despair. The Governors complained that the school was so much below standard and inadequate for the proper education of the boys of Nuneaton especially in its science provision, and the extension was an *urgent necessity*. Chairman of the Governors Harry Cleaver felt that in 1957 the legal difficulties in acquiring the desired land were *practically insurmountable*. The vicar, Canon Herbert, caught awkwardly between a rock and a hard place, resigned from the Governing body.[25] Because of the compulsory purchase order a public inquiry had to be held, leading to further delays.

The pupils had also been all too aware of the difficulties. The Edwardian Magazine complained that *we at KEGS should have got a new school long ago.* [26] Staff impatience, too, reached its peak. Tired of working in sub-standard accommodation, the news that the public inquiry regarding the compulsory purchase order had to wait until June 1958 proved the breaking point. A staff deputation of protest demanded the Inquiry be brought forward and went to the relevant Governor sub-committee.[27] The tactic worked: the Inquiry was held a month earlier on 3rd May and the order was approved in July.

9. Political Attitudes And Financial Strains

Other difficulties remained. There were complaints that the local (Labour) Council was less than totally supportive of the plans. Leonard Cleaver, now a Conservative M.P., smelt a political conspiracy. In September 1960 he reported that *interminable delays* were being exploited *to acquire control of the school* with some Council members hoping that these delays would result in a lack of cash and a subsequent loss of aided status.[28] The Inquiry in June 1958 had revealed the Borough Council was not in favour of the Voluntary Aided Status of the School.[29] If the school became Controlled rather than Aided, argued Cleaver, the LEA might adapt the existing building plans to avoid further delays but this was not guaranteed and, by many, not desired. Cleaver went further: he claimed there were *extreme socialists* in Nuneaton who would *do away with Grammar Schools altogether*. In fact the principle of all schools being comprehensive was passed by the Labour Party Conference back in 1951 and became mainstream Labour Party policy within two or three years. Cleaver assured his correspondent that *we are going to fight to maintain our status and want all the official help we can get.* [The socialists] *want to reduce its status as an Aided School. My father has been working since 1942 to get the school modernized. The socialists must not win this school – there is £50,000 extra to find.*[30]

In terms of the Governors' financial contribution to the new buildings, difficulties had overtaken the project: building costs were up but investments had depreciated. The original regulation for a Voluntary Aided School had been that 50% of the money for a new development had to be found from the school's own resources. It was somewhat galling for Nuneaton to discover that, while new national legislation promised voluntary aided schools 75% assistance from 1959, the fact that the Nuneaton Grammar School scheme had, in principle, been agreed earlier meant that the 50% rule still applied to them. This further lowered morale. The school's contribution to the total costs might exceed £60,000, roughly half the total sum.[31] The foundation income was the second highest in the County but the Governors would not sell all the investments and any loan charges would be considerable. The new gym that was also desired would have to be costed separately: this resulted in a further £14,000 over and above other additional work planned which included a bungalow for the caretaker at £2,500. A loan was obtained from the Buttle Trust of £5,000, interest free for seven years.[32]

10. Work Starts – And Finishes: 1961-63

The new decade brought a new Headmaster and, coincidentally, new hopes: in the summer of 1960 Thomas Sumner left to be Head of Archbishop Tenison's school at

Kennnington and was replaced by Derek. W. Usherwood, cast in traditional Headmaster mould as a Cambridge graduate who had been Senior Classics Master at Warwick School. He soon received good news. In September 1960 David Eccles, the Minister of Education had a significant meeting with Harry Cleaver which was reported to *have gone far* towards resolving remaining financial problems. Harry Cleaver had used his son's political connections to good effect. Finally at the Speech Day in Nov.1960 it was announced that *Work will begin in Jan 1961* and would last 18 months. The cost of the new buildings was expected to be £105,753 with the school contribution being £52,000. The overall cost to the Grammar School included £13,000 for the new Gymnasium meaning £65,000 had to be found. [33]

A Public appeal was launched by Harry Cleaver to meet the shortfall. Harking back eighty years to the new building of 1880 he anticipated that the new buildings would be sufficient to *educate boys for another 80 years.* [He did not think] *the school would need enlarging* [34] for a long time owing to the growing demand for *technical* [rather than academic?] education in Nuneaton. He did not anticipate the arrival of girls, a Sixth Form College and extensive new buildings just fifteen years later. As on previous occasions educational trends had proved impossible to predict. Cleaver's initial feeling was that the sum could be met without recourse to a public appeal. This soon proved too optimistic.

In January 1962 when the buildings were *growing quickly* a Modernisation Fund was launched with £3,000 donated by Cleaver himself. The aim was to fulfil the school's obligation to maintain Voluntary Aided status by finding the 50% of the cost required and separate funding for the gym. A successful campaign centred on calls to 600 parents for fund raising with 21 team leaders spread over the town organising visits. Within a month of the launch there was noticeable progress: after the start of the appeal Harry Cleaver wrote to Warwickshire Chief Education Officer Yorke-Lodge that *our appeal is going very well and it looks as if we shall be able to order the gym before the builders leave*, clearly an advantageous timetable. By the following month he reported *the building is going on rapidly* and by May the total raised had reached £34,000.[35] Building work finally got underway and by Spring 1961 the Edwardian was reporting that *gone are the screen of trees between vicarage and school, the cycle sheds and the churchyard levelled to a lawned garden.* [36]

The changeover to meals cooked in the school's own kitchens in the new block began at the end of January 1962 and the new Dining Room was finished in March and the Hall by September. The design of the new Science Laboratories evoked praise from eminent architectural historian Nikolaus Pevsner, not a man particularly complimentary about Nuneaton and Bedworth generally. He referred to the *successfully placed crescent, concave towards the church and vertically weather boarded all along the first floor.*[37]

By Autumn 1962 the buildings were *nearly complete* and the gym *taking shape*. Some old parts disappeared such as the music room book store, as did the necessity for classes in the Parish Hall and Vicarage Street school. The Appeal ended triumphantly in July with £35,400 obtained and Voluntary Aided status was maintained. The community had rallied round and the links between school and town had never been stronger.[38] At Speech Day the Chairman of the Appeals Association (and Vice-Chairman of the Old Edwardians) W.H. Cope praised Cleaver, describing him as a man of *optimism* who *had put everything into the future welfare of the school.*[39] The £34,000 may have saved a greater sum in rates but one suspects that it was the pride in maintaining some form of limited independence as a Voluntary Aided School that gave the greatest pleasure. The severe winter of 1962/3 provided one last frustration but the buildings were largely complete by 1963.

Harry Cleaver and his wife admire the new gymnasium with Headmaster Derek Usherwood: 1962

11. School Life In The 1960s And Early 1970s

The Grammar School now entered its final phase. Games provision widened and tennis became an official school sport in 1960 though not for another two years did it really get into its stride. The school's atmosphere was still Christian but things were changing: in 1962 a branch of the Student Christian Movement (SCM) was formed just before Easter: *We welcome the agnostic, the atheist and the curious*[40] In 1970 the speaker at the annual Founder's Day service bewailed the lack of Christian commitment among the young. A survey among the King Edward sixth formers established that 90% no longer attended any church service on a Sunday. [41] Conventional Christian belief was no longer the majority position among the boys.

Sixth form teaching was by no means didactic. Classes would have been quite small – occupying a fair amount of staff time and life was very different. Eight was about the average sixth form class size taking up considerable staff time. In the Edwardian in 1962 there was a reflection by an arts student on life in the sixth form. He found it very different from life in the lower forms. *We are taught comparatively little. The knowledge which we gain is taught gradually by discussion rather than by actual formal teaching by a Master … the Masters contribute on almost equal terms.* Such were the opportunities of small classes. The difference was in attitude as well as method and atmosphere: *fewer traditional views are now imposed on us. The teaching is less dogmatic. There is very rarely one correct way of doing anything.* [42] One wonders whether the science students would have made similar comments. The writer had been positive about his experience and did not long for spoon feeding. His major criticism seems to be the suddenness of the change; being treated as schoolchildren one day and young adults the next meant a substantial jump to maturity was expected overnight.

The sixth form was likely to grow further. It was increasingly losing its image as a specially privileged place for a few lucky students, and senior students were expected to set an example to younger boys. It was also seen as a gateway to University. Higher Education horizons were widening nationally and the opportunity of a degree loomed for children of parents who had never had the opportunity: it was a complete reversal of Headmaster Sumner's opinion in 1953 that to get to University was too easy. This was brought home by the very different attitude of his successor Usherwood who argued in 1964, in a speech to mark Prize Day at the Co-op Hall,[43] that *Major change* was needed in national policy with regard to University places; he meant rapid expansion. The end was followed by the means: by 1962 local authority maintenance grants became available for all who achieved places at University. By the 1970s the concept of educational equality related to races as well as classes. However, the development of a substantial ethnic minority in the Edward Street area of the town in the 1960s came too late to have much impact on Grammar School numbers: a small number of boys from the Indian sub-continent did join the school between 1970 and 1974.

The school was not unaffected by other aspects of the educational ferment of the late 1960s. As well as comprehensive plans, (see below) the idea of pupils having a say in the running of the school developed. The Edwardian reported that the first meeting of the School Council had taken place on 19th Nov. 1968. This was *a forum for discussion and airing of opinions pertaining to the everyday running of the school*. However, Student militancy in the late '60s was largely confined to the Universities. A motion to change Saturday games matches from the morning to the afternoon was hardly revolutionary and in any case was rejected by 16 votes to 14. But regular balloting for Prefects had developed and the Council endured into the days of the sixth form college. The School provided students for the Youth Parliament that developed in Nuneaton in 1969. In the Edwardian of Autumn 1969 with the Vietnam war raging, and the protests against it, Rhyss Burris wrote an impassioned article under the title *Make Love not War* arguing that we should *turn to sanity as an international policy*.[44]

12. Teachers And The Curriculum

King Edward's in the 1960s could be described as a traditional Grammar School. Curriculum-wise subjects remained academic and, in the lower school at least some were taught in much the same way as twenty years before. However, the school was not immune to new thinking. Different approaches to the teaching of Science and Maths developed in the 1960s, the New Mathematics and Nuffield Science, focussing on the idea of child-centred learning and change of emphasis from the didactic method to self-discovery. School trips became more ambitious and by the late 60s participation in educational cruises was being planned. The first took place in 1969 on the SS Uganda steamship visiting the Mediterranean and North African ports. Rugby tours could now venture abroad such as to France at Easter 1969. Music continued to be active with performances at special occasions as in the past – speech day, carol service and annual concerts but also with a madrigal group and peripatetic instrument teaching. In the Spring of 1964 an electronic organ was purchased for use in the new Assembly Hall.[45]

Modern Foreign languages were holding their own. After 1945 Spanish had developed

Dramatic productions: House plays provided another chance for competition and a chance for boys of all ages. This is from 1963

as well as French but Latin numbers suffered a national decline reflected in Nuneaton. In the Edwardian of 1971 Latin Master T.J.Tracey set out the case for Latin,[46] which in previous generations had been the staple fare for the older, more academic boy. He argued pragmatically that it was needed for many University courses and a qualification in just Latin might be easier to acquire than its alternative –two modern foreign languages. However his argument also echoed earlier times: that a proficiency in Latin gave a sound grammatical base to one's knowledge in general and a grasp of etymology in particular. Classical studies were of great historical value, he argued, and many of the ideas of that time still needed to be understood since they formed the basis of much of western civilisation. His lament that there were now only two teachers of Latin in the town[47] shows the higher educational expectations of the 20th century compared to previous eras. Up to the mid 19th Century there had never been more than one.

Despite the Voluntary Aided status, the influence of the local authority over school affairs was ever-growing. They now provided the bulk of the financing and the actual money spent by the school itself over a year was comparatively small. Administrative staff were employed by the local authority: Laboratory assistants, a School Secretary and

Assistant, plus a caretaker and – for a while – a groundsman, were the only non-teaching staff. In the Autumn of 1972 the first female teacher appointed in peacetime – Marjorie Riley – arrived to take Mathematics and the following year, with the prospective sixth form College in mind Margaret Reynolds (replacing Tracy as the Latin teacher) and Yvonne Collins (Modern Languages) also joined the hitherto all male staff. But these appointments were made with the knowledge that the boys Grammar School was to become a mixed Sixth Form College.[48]

13. Comprehensive?

Back in 1944 it was not inevitable that King Edward's would continue as a selective Grammar School. The Education Act of that year did not set up a compulsory tripartite system, Grammar, Technical, Modern: it left the system open to local authorities to decide. The Warwickshire authority, like numerous others, considered the arguments for and against a multi-lateral school (similar if not identical to the later termed comprehensive) and a new all ability school was planned for Bedworth: Nicholas Chamberlaine School opened in 1952. But the general opinion expressed in the document was that *it would be dangerous to tamper with the existing Grammar Schools*. While Nuneaton was an excepted district and policy could therefore be different, these districts were expected to consult with the main County Council before they produced any plan. In the late 1940s this was not likely to spell the end of the two Grammar Schools in Nuneaton. Indeed their number was added to as Manor Park had been converted into a Secondary Grammar/Technical School. More radical change took place nearby with Nuneaton appearing to be surrounded by educational innovation. Headmaster Sumner explained the position with a hint of scepticism in 1957. The Grammar School was *between the upper millstone of Coventry's comprehensiveness and the nether millstone of the Leicestershire experiment.* In a speech to the Rotary Club five years earlier he had referred to the drawback of large schools and the danger of the Head not knowing all his pupils; more than 500-600 in a school, he argued, was too large; there was *over-administration.* Equality of opportunity, he asserted, should not mean identical schools but, rather, a variety of them. In the Autumn of 1955 the Edwardian ran an editorial on comprehensive schools. It argued in favour of selection: assessment of potential would be needed at eleven, (which some thought too early) but was felt necessary to give time to cover the curriculum range by the time of 'O' Level.[49] On the basis of this argument examinations seemed to be determining not only the curriculum but also the structure of schooling.

Critics of selection at 11 years old multiplied in the 1950s and early 1960s. Transfers from Secondary Moderns did occur (see above) but were very limited. Picking up new work and ways of study – as well as a different set of classmates – was daunting. The hoped for flexibility in the system had not occurred. Moreover, the tripartite system of Grammar, Technical and Modern had become bi-partite in many places. Many areas merely paid lip service to the Technical side of schooling: in having Manor Park school described as a proper Grammar-Technical school Nuneaton was hardly typical. The increasingly rigid division at eleven was attacked and powerful questions raised. Could children at any age be rigidly defined as academic, practical or nothing in particular? And could this diagnosis be made for all children at the same age on the basis of a common examination? Comprehensive proponents argued that fewer children would leave school *untouched* by all the education offered. Would some of those assigned to an academic education at eleven have benefitted from a less traditional curriculum? Could other late developers and those good at literary or mathematical subjects, but not both, have thrived in the competitive learning environment of the Grammar School?

In October 1964 the new Labour Government was committed to a policy of spreading

Derek Usherwood, Head: 1960-1967

Rowland Brown, Head: 1967-1975

comprehensive education. Early in 1965 the Circular 10/65 required Local Authorities to draw up appropriate local plans. Governors wanted the King Edward foundation to remain an academic institution and came to believe that the best way to achieve this within a comprehensive framework was for the Grammar School to become a Sixth Form College. They emphasised the rights of parents to choose an Aided school for their offspring. A new Head faced the challenge of re-organisation. Derek Usherwood left in 1967 to become Head of Lewes Grammar School, Sussex. His successor was Rowland Brown, (1933-2010) brought up in Hampshire and a Modern Languages graduate of Worcester College Oxford. A barrister as well as a teacher, he was well qualified to deal with the legal, financial and administration challenges ahead. [50] (In 1993 he was to receive the OBE for services to education.)

In a special open meeting in the Spring of 1968 the Chief Education Officer for Warwickshire described the provisional plans for Nuneaton's 12-16 schools and a 6th Form College based on King Edward's, as *a step into the unknown*. He asserted that every twenty years or so in 1902, 1918, 1944 (and now 1965) major change was always likely in the educational system. He argued for a sixth form College as the earlier maturation of the teenager made a more adult community feasible at 16-18, and there was a need to focus on the growing post 16 provision in a more concentrated fashion. Opposing this, the retired Harry Branston, attending the meeting, expressed his concern that with *highly qualified staff concentrated in Colleges* there was the danger of *dilution of standards in the main schools*. Nevertheless, the majority of Governors, Parents and Old Boys wanted the school to remain an academic institution. They took the pragmatic view that *if change there must be* the sixth form College option was the most acceptable. This was reminiscent of their Nuneaton predecessors 430 years previously. Back in 1540, anticipating the imposition of future reform, they decided to fly with the prevailing wind, abolish the Leeke Chantry and set up a place of learning instead.[51]

King Edward's had to raise a proportion of the funds for re-organisation as a result of their Voluntary Aided Status, with estimates varying between £30,000 and £50,000. So far the Governors had agreed in principle to go along with the scheme; if the money could not be found to maintain the school's Voluntary Aided position Governors' Chairman Stan Drakeley replied *they could go their own way*[52] and the state connection could be ended. However, if the Governors could not find their share of the money for re-organisation, how could they be financially healthy enough to go independent? On the other hand the feeling regarding the maintenance of at least a small degree of independence by retaining the Voluntary Aided status was very strong. This meant the support of a Voluntary Aided Sixth Form College in a comprehensive scheme was always the most likely solution and thus, the Grammar School as in the traditional meaning of the phrase would end.

14. Working Party

A working Party to plan this 16-19 education first met on 24th November 1970.[53] By the following year plans had sufficiently matured towards the idea of developing a Junior College to cover all 16-19 education in the Borough though this was *an abstract term intending to combine the two Constituent colleges*. These Colleges would be King Edward's and the North Warwickshire College of Technology and Art (NWCTA). Which institution taught which course was clearly a sensitive issue. An undated memorandum from NWCTA stated that *we should be free to offer GCE A Level examinations in whichever subjects are taken as part of another course or might be taken as part of a course*. Councillor Derek Forwood was not convinced that the proposed scheme was truly comprehensive. Forwood did not wish the 6th Form College to be *restricted to GCE work*. Rowland Brown's view was that it was *expensive and wasteful to duplicate courses*. It was, he argued, *logical to develop the respective excellence of the two Colleges*. So Forwood's suggestion of Business Studies at King Edward's was rejected (for the moment). Forwood was worried about an *elite College* (King Edward's) with NWCTA then seen a *poor relation.* [54]

The term Junior College was accepted after some hesitation. There would be a Joint Advisory Board to give advice to all pupils and parents and a Joint Board of Studies to co-ordinate the planning of courses. Plans were made in the spirit of educational optimism and an expectation that student staying on rates might increase. However, the degree of change in this respect was not appreciated at the time. By 1980, with an expected 1,200 in the age cohort, it was predicted that only 25% would be continuing their education beyond 16. So the Junior College was expected to have full time 700-800 students with about 300 at King Edward College. This proved quite an under-estimate and again emphasises the difficulty of predicting educational trends. Initial building designs were estimated to cost £40,000 plus £15,000 for conversions and modifications. *A full and Comprehensive range of education facilities for students over 16* was planned including 24 different subjects for King Edward's, which was becoming less educationally isolated. Those in charge steered the negotiations regarding the Junior College to a successful conclusion negotiating difficult matters such as catchment areas. The result was a 47 form entry base for the Junior College and 12 form entry base for the Bedworth school, Nicholas Chamberlaine.[55]

So, little more than ten years after the new buildings of the early sixties further expansion was required at King Edward's : space would be planned for Mathematics rooms, a Music Room, Student Common Room, Lecture Theatre and a Medical Room.[56] Some of this was obtained. With a purpose-built administrative block on the ground floor the Mathematics Department acquired their specialist room teaching units upstairs as well as a Head of Department room. These opened in 1975. Music did not get a new room as such but gained the large area which had started as the main school room in 1880, was then known as Big School after 1904 and since 1961 had been the Library: a new staff room was located next to the Maths Department and the old one was divided into several music practice rooms. Building plans went ahead and once again a request was made for *the Glebe land* of the Church to be defined, as school expansion would make another foray into this area.[57] However, here the circumstances were about to change. With the retirement of Canon Herbert in 1973 the old Vicarage and surrounding garden were to be sold making land more easily available for expansion. Once again sufficient room had been squeezed out of the old site. All Rowland Brown's legal and administrative skills were required to negotiate for what he considered adequate resources. For instance he requested four lab technicians, using the precedents of other 6th form colleges elsewhere, as well as a full time Librarian. These developments were at the cutting edge of educational development for, as Brown pointed out, in this area *we are entering upon fresh ground.*[58] The role of a Headmaster (now increasingly known as a Head Teacher) had changed. Concern with building and budgets loomed ever larger. Numbers had steadily increased and the annual turnover likewise.

There was much greater optimism about the future of modern European languages at a time when Britain was on the point of entering the Common Market. Russian was originally on a list of prospective languages to study while an undated discussion paper (probably 1972) asserted that *it is unlikely that more than 20 students per year group would opt to study Italian.* As to a member of staff teaching another subject for the rest of the timetable, it was pointed out that *the absorption of small fractions of teaching time is much more difficult within a College catering solely for students of this narrow age band than it is in an all-through school.*[59] The Grammar School in the early 20th Century had employed Masters to teach a diverse range of subjects but at least one would have been taught at a more elementary level.

The transition was effected reasonably smoothly and quickly. In September 1972 the last 11 plus intake arrived in the Grammar Schools. The following year 11 year olds stayed at their middle schools for an additional year and probably for the first time since the days of William Trevis (but for very different reasons) no boys entered the Grammar school that year. In 1974, again with no new intake, the existing third and fourth years were moved to join their female equivalents in a residual Mixed Grammar School set up at the Girls High School, now called Etone. This left a Fifth year group of Grammar School boys who continued at King Edward's. But the rest of the students – no longer called pupils – were sixth formers. The Upper Sixth were those boys who had progressed through the Boys Grammar School from 1968 whereas the lower sixth consisted of a mixed intake from not only the Boys Grammar School but also from the Girls High School and the Mixed Grammar School Manor Park. In addition there were a number of entries from other schools, some of them local Secondary Moderns such as Higham Lane School. Arbury School was now shut down and replaced by Roman Catholic 12-16 school, St Thomas More.

By July 1975 the last remnants of the Grammar School pupils, the Upper sixth and Fifth years had, respectively, left the school or been absorbed in the second year intake of the Sixth Form College. From being a normal Grammar School in the academic year 1973-4 – except for the absence of a first year, King Edward's was completely transformed by September 1975. Now there were two large mixed years of students of both sexes and varied educational backgrounds. In that transitional year the maroon blazers had continued to be defiantly worn by the upper sixth pupils even though uniform had officially been abolished in September 1974. The College officially distinguished between dress for work (ie normal lessons) and dress for play – such as activities and games on Wednesday afternoons – though this distinction was not to last. Uniform had disappeared for good; more significantly the Grammar School had become a Sixth Form College. The Headmaster of King Edward VI School was now the Principal of King Edward VI College.

15. Conclusion

The history of Nuneaton's first school is a long, well documented, fascinating one. John Leeke may not have been aware of the form his legacy eventually took, but it was substantial, significant and long-lasting. In the same way many of the wealthy Guildsmen of Coventry would be surprised to have learnt of the use to which the wealth of their lands was put after the Reformation. The Grammar School very rarely educated girls or even the majority of Nuneaton's boys, but its role in the town's history was clear, significant and influential. Outside the ranks of a small elite at one end and the very poorest at the other it had frequently (if not always) taken a wide social range of pupils. Its achievement in the past was less its uniform excellence than its longevity – it survived in times of difficulty and adapted in times of opportunity. In opening its doors to more boys in the town the English *school* of Benjamin Rayner of the early 19th Century meant it continued to give a free education to many boys up to 1880. After this the quality of education given improved considerably: as the town grew the school was in a position to provide both a liberal and scientific education, effective despite all the difficulties of a cramped and then bomb-damaged building. It had adapted again – at the cost of losing some of its much revered independence – to play a much more significant role in the life of the town in the twentieth Century, gradually widening its social intake, especially when returning to a free education after 1944. Among its staff in this later period were some impressive, thoughtful and influential Headmasters and Assistant Masters. The positive influence on their charges may not always be measureable in a precise sense but their value was none the less real for all that. Their effects are still with us.

End Notes

Chapter One

1. Shakespeare Centre Library/archive Deeds/Papers DR 10/506 5th May 1502 DR10 506 (Shakespeare Centre) Accessed on line: www.nationalarchives.gov.uk Access to Archives. (A to A)

2. *A Descriptive Catalogue of Ancient Deeds* ed. H.G. Maxwell Lyle Vol 1 1890 (Descriptive Catalogue) B925 British History Online: *Confirmation of the grant... by Richard Werall... to Richard Hondford, prior of Erdebury, ... and John Leeke, of Nuneton, ... of lands and tenements... in Chelverscoton...* 11 Edward IV.

3. Descriptive Catalogue Vol 2 1894 p.298ff B. 2408. *Grant by John Baker of Nuneton, to Richard Cok', vicar of the parish church of Nuneton, John Leeke and Richard Astell of the same, of a tenement and curtilage in le Bondynd in Nuneton,* 15 Edward IV.

4. *Calendar of Fine Rolls* 4Henry VII p.103: *Appointed of tax in Warwick*

5. Will of John Leke 2.7.92 PROB 11/9 Records of the prerogative Court of Canterbury. A to A.

6. *Victoria County History of Warwickshire* Volume 2 p. 347 (VCH2). See also Warwick County Record Office (WCRO) CR2730/22 1492

7. Shakespeare Centre

8. *Warwickshire Feet of Fines* Vol 3 1505/6 p. 221 Ref 2803 (Nuneaton Library): Abstracted from the P.R.O. originals by Lucy Drucker

9. *Rental and Survey of Sir Marmaduke Constable's rental and estate in Nuneaton, Horston, Attleborough, Stockingford, Burton Hastings and Stretton Baskerville 10th October 1543 and 13th February 1544.* f4 p.7 p.34 f27v p.63, f31 p.71 Nuneaton Library. (Constable Rental) This rent roll is a description of the location and occupation of all Sir Marmaduke Constable's lands obtained by him on the dissolution of Nuneaton Priory in 1539. For Sir Marmaduke see p.14-15, 25-6

10. *Victoria County History of Warwickshire* (Volume 6) p.120/1 (VCH6) The Leeke/Astell share of the property was bought by Henry Smythe who died in 1514.

11. Wills of Richard and William Astell; David Paterson and Ian Rowney: *A Short History Of the Parish Church of St. Nicolas Nuneaton* [Second edition 2007] pp.12-13 (Paterson and Rowney)

12. Will of John Leeke Junior 10.7.1508 PROB 11/16 (Leeke Will) Records of the Prerogative Court of Canterbury. (A to A) See also Will of John Leeke [Senior] 2.7.1492 PROB 11/9 Records of the prerogative Court of Canterbury. (A to A)

13. After death, few people were believed to be immediately ready to come face to face with God. In purgatory they could complete their penance and the prayers of the living could aid their passage, shortening the time and the degree of suffering. The Virgin Mary and the Saints could be prayed to, interceding for the person's soul with the hope of salvation on judgement day.

14. For instance, the Chantry priest at Tamworth was also *morrow mass priest* providing an early morning mass for travellers and workmen before schooling his youthful charges who, presumably, were not up as early. (A.F. Leach *English Schools at the Reformation* (1968) p. 14). (Leach)

15. For an example of a larger legacy see Appendix One, p. 313

16. Leeke Will 1508. See also VCH2 p. 342

17. Mortmain: Literally *dead hand*: a kind of impersonal ownership after death endorsed only by the Monarch and secure in that it was recorded on Patent Rolls or Close Rolls. Leeke Will 1508. See also VCH2 pp342/3

18. Obits were an inexpensive way of praying for the souls of the dead suited to a small legacy such as Leeke's. On two consecutive days, one being the anniversary of the Founder's death, the bells would be tolled and services held (vespers, matins, lauds) completed with a Requiem Mass. (Alan Kreider: *English Chantries: The Road to Dissolution* (1979) p.8 (Kreider)

19. Leeke Will 1508. This is the translation of Edward Nason *A History of Nuneaton Grammar School* pp1-2 (Nason *History*)

20. Compared to most other foundations, Leeke's wording was general. See Appendix One.

21. Kreider p.83. See Appendix One. I have benefited in this section from assistance by Dr. Steven Gunn of Merton College Oxford.

22. Nicholas Orme *Medieval Schools From Roman Britain to Tudor England* (2006) p.294 (Orme)

23. Orme pp 295-6 and 312

24. VCH 2 p. 28 Though under no legal obligation to help, some Chantry priests would assist an incumbent rather like a later curate.

25. Orme p.32

26. For St. Nicolas see Paterson and Rowney p.40

27. E.A Veasey *Nuneaton: A History* 2002 (Veasey) His estimate on pp.38-9 is based on a calculation from a careful analysis of the Constable Rent Roll.

28. Arbury Priory, a smaller institution, was a victim of the first wave of dissolutions in 1536.

29. Orme p. 238

30. Where endowments were larger, Orme (p.295) records that, in the 1530s, Chantry trustees were asking priests to perform other tasks such as teaching children but Nuneaton's money had simply not been enough for both. By the 1540s the Chantry element was no longer much in demand.

31. By 1543, apart from the chantry lands, the Leeke family owned little property in Nuneaton and did not live in the town. The yearly 'obits' at Arbury Priory would have stopped with its dissolution in 1536. (see footnote nine above)

32. Paterson and Rowney pp.21 and 12

33. Orme (p.314) cites over 20 examples in just three counties, Essex Sussex and Somerset

34. Diarmid McCullough *The Later Reformation in England* (1990) pp17-18

35. Joan Simon *Education and Society in Tudor England* (1967) p.216 (Simon)

36. Simon p. 224

37. Chantries Act 1547 Quoted in Ethan Shagan: *Popular Politics and the English Reformation* (2003) p. 236 (Shagan)

38. Protector Somerset: Edward Seymour, Duke of Somerset, became Lord Protector of England in March 1547 two months after the accession of the boy King Edward VI. Both religious conviction and financial pressure pushed his Government towards a complete dissolution of the Chantries.

39. Kreider p.1

40. There were now over 2000 (Shagan p. 238) and nearly a quarter of all English parishes had one.

41. Simon p.224

42. Nason *History* p.2 and S. Reed Brett *King Edward VI School Nuneaton* (1952) pp 11-12 (Reed Brett)

43. Sir Walter Mildmay and Robert Kelway were appointed in August 1548 as Special Commissioners overseeing Chantry Dissolution and deciding whether any institutions should be allowed to continue. Mildmay was genuinely interested in education, helping to re-constitute Chelmsford Grammar School as King Edward VI Grammar School Chelmsford in 1551. In the 1580s he founded Emmanuel College Cambridge, from proceeds he had gained from a suppressed Dominican Friary. A.G. Dickens *The English Reformation* (1967 edition) p.286. See also the Dictionary of National Biography article on Mildmay by L.L.Ford. Online edition 2004 (DNB)

44. VCH 2 p.342

45 Shagan p. 244/5. In 1544 Richmond borough (Yorkshire) took control of the endowments for six chantries and the priests were pensioned off to continue their praying.

46. Simon pp224-5

47. For example St Alphage, Solihull. *Clergy of the Church Of England Database* Online (CCEd)

48. Including Chelmscote (near Brailes) in Warwickshire. See Appendix One for further details.

49. Occasionally a Chantry priest might run a school on barely £5 a year (eg Ledbury, Herefordshire Simon p.234) but fees might well then be charged.

50. For Chantries shut for more selfish reasons see Appendix One.

51. Quoted in VCH 6 p. 32 and Shagan p.296

52. Simon p.192. Warwick school was re-founded in 1545 due to such a sale. VCH 2 p.304

53. This is a major theme of Shagan's book. e.g. p.296. He argues that the people of Nuneaton showed loyalty not merely to the King but to the religious policies of the day, referring to the Injunctions of 1547 against idolatry.

54. Pilgrimage of Grace 1536. A Yorkshire-based rebellion led by Robert Aske protesting against the first wave of Monastic dissolutions.

55. *Constable Rental* Volume 2 f36 p.66

56. Veasey pp.38-9

57. Simon p.225

58. VCH2 p.342. For Coventry's resistance see Simon p.223

59. A comparable but less favourable arrangement would be Grimsby where a Chantry worth £4 5/- 6d was closed and the money transferred (without addition?) to fund a school Orme p. 395. Fn 38

60. £10 was not particularly high: a common settlement figure was £13 6/-8d (or 20 marks).

61. *Letters patent of King Edward VI School Nuneaton Warwick County Record Office* (WCRO) H001/22 undated translation believed to be early 18th Century (Letters Patent). The original document was lost many years ago.

62. Simon p.294

63. Except where noted otherwise the source for the information on Governors land is the Constable Rental.

64. Virgate: The amount of land that a team of two oxen could plough in a single annual season, thirty acres.

65. A Copyholder held a copy of the medieval court Roll granting his family right of occupation of a property. It is thus a form of landholding distinguished from freehold, leasehold or tenancy. Constable Rental f33v p.72

66. See also Veasey p.40
67. VCH2 p.220
68. Nason *History* p.3
69. John Lawson & Harold Silver *A social history of education in England* (1973) p.100 (Lawson and Silver)
70. VCH2 p.343

Chapter Two

1. WCRO 2730/22 *Conveyance by William Bywarke of Noneton, bellman to John Leke … of a messuage in le chircheyarde lying between a tenement of the Prioress to the north, and a tenement of the Hospital of St John to the south and extending in length from the King's Highway to the millpond there.*
2. Nuneaton historian Ted Veasey thought the mill ponds were about where the George Eliot Gardens are now. See his map in Veasey p.39.
3. Malcolm Seabourne *The English School: its Architecture and Organisation:* Vol I to 1870 (1971) p.17 (Seabourne Vol. 1)
4. WCRO H1/24 Accounts of the School Bailiffs 1560-1588 (Bailiffs Accounts)
5. Quoted in J.H. Brown *Elizabethan Schooldays* (1933) p.20. (Brown)
6. Bailiffs Accounts
7. Dr Nason's transcripts from early Governors Account books Undated: believed to be the 1930s. WCRO H1/52 p.12 (Transcripts)
8. Veasey pp 38-9
9. Transcripts p.19, p.23 and pp. 34/5
10. Transcripts pp. 57 and 59
11. Seabourne Vol 1 p.14
12. Bailiffs Accounts
13. For Rugby School See W.H.D. Rouse *Rugby School* (1898)
14. Transcripts p. 21
15. Transcripts pp 34-5 and p.66
16. Drawn up from information in Transcripts pp17-35
17. *Victoria County History of Warwickshire* Volume Eight (VCH8) p.402. See also VCH2 p.344
18. Transcripts p.22
19. Constable Rental: f56 p121/2. See also Veasey p.40
20. Transcripts pp 26/30 Though Leach in VCH Vol 2 p.34 says it was later producing £3 a year.

21. WCRO H1/39 Papers relating to the school lands and rents (Lands and Rents)

22.VCH4 p.172

23. Transcripts

24. Transcripts

25. Transcripts

26. Richard Willoughby: this is his first appearance and (with John Suffolk) one of the first Governors not appearing in the Constable Rent Roll of 1543. He was wealthy as the beneficence in his will of 1587 was to show. For his relative at the school see p.39 below.
Robert Lee: he was a Freeholder in 1543 with a messuage *in the church* held by the Hospital of St. John in Coventry. Constable Rent Roll f3v p.6

27. Transcripts p.67

28. This included some familiar names in connection with Grammar School history in the 16th and early 17th Centuries, Butterton, Willoughby, Vynsent, Suffolk, Wright, Chaplyn, Cleyton, Stratford. Most governors took £2 parcels, Thomas Bayles and John Suffolk junior taking £4 but John Lawrence merely 10/-. At this stage funds totalled over £100 (£102 1/-4d). Transcripts.

29. Transcripts. Unpaginated section at the back of earlier financial records.

30. There are very few records of this kind after1588 until much later.

31 Transcripts p.14

32 Transcripts p.65

33. Transcripts pp. 66-68

34. *Memorials of Cambridge* (Greatly enlarged from the work of J. Le Keux By Charles Henry Cooper, FSA. 1901) on www.archive.org.
 See also www.redfirst.com Sir Marmaduke Constable of Flanborough Author RHB 1887

35. Transcripts p.11

36. For more details of the Constable family lands see www.tudorplace.com.ar

37. VCH4 p.166. In 1564 Sir Ambrose Cave, Chancellor of the Exchequer, bought the remaining Constable lands in Nuneaton but he died four years later and the property was later sold twice more and split between the Paget and Aston families. For the Aston family, see Chapter Four.

38. A Resolution that, if requested by the bailiffs to come to the school to discuss its business, they must not refuse without good cause or forfeit one shilling (5p)

39. Transcripts p.18

40. Transcripts

41. Transcripts Unpaginated section at the back of earlier financial records.

42. In Olney, Lincolnshire, as late as 1614, a presentment (formal statement for legal

consideration) was made to the Archdeacon of York urging the erection of a school by twenty freeholders, seven of whom could only make their mark. (Seabourne Vol1 p.36)

43 Transcripts H1/ 52

44. Constable Rental f43v. p.93. Tenants at Will held their land at the will of the landlord. This meant they had no security of tenure and could be given notice to quit at any time, even if all conditions of occupation, such as payment of rent, have been met.

45. National Archives Kew. Court of Chancery Records 1556-8 C 1/1477/14 (A to A)

46.Transcripts p.18

47. National Archives Court of Chancery Six Clerks office C1/1314 (A to A)

48.Veasey p.42

49. Copies of *The orders for the Free Schools of Nun-Eaton* 1609 WCRO H1/36 (School Orders)

50. Rosemary O'Day *Education and Society 1500-1800* (1982) p.74 (O'Day)

51. School Orders

52. Nason *History*. Introduction p.X Leach p.112

53. W.A.L. Vincent *The Grammar Schools 1660-1714: Their Continuing Tradition*. p.52 (Vincent 1660-1714) John Lawson *A Town Grammar School through Six Centuries: a History of Hull Grammar School against its Local Background* (1963) p.75 (Lawson)

54. William Harrison *Description of England 1577* p.41 quoted in www.bartleby.com

55. School Orders

56. Simon p.180.

57. Vincent (1660-1714) p.46 gives the example of Madeley Staffordshire 1645 (in the unsettling time of the Civil War). Later, Nuneaton was very slow in getting a Girls Secondary school off the ground – this had to wait until the 20th Century. (see below)

58. Bailiffs Accounts: list of books bought for poor children.

59. Simon p.15

60. Helen Jewell *Early Modern Education in England* (1998) p.5. (Jewell)

61. Quoted in Foster Watson *The English Grammar Schools* to 1660: their Curriculum and Practice (1968 Edition) pp. 41/2 (FW 1660)

62. Injunctions of Queen Elizabeth 1559 Quoted in Brown pp 49-51 and A.F. Leach *Educational Charters and Documents* p.494 ebooksread.com

63. It was the same feeling for the need to control from the centre that eventually lead to the authorisation of one fresh translation of the Bible, the King James (Authorised) version, though this had to wait until the beginning of the 17th Century. In the meantime the Bishops' Bible and the Geneva Bible (both Testaments widely available by 1576) would be those most commonly used in the school.

64. School Orders 1609

65. FW 1660 pp 41-2

66. O'Day p.135. Between 1561 and 1579, Thomas Bentham, Bishop of Lichfield and Coventry, though a conscientious man, had many difficulties in his large diocese and tended to focus on the Staffordshire part, leaving Thomas Lever as to look after Warwickshire. Though Lever was keen on schooling other priorities took up his time.

67. Elizabethan pronouncements of 1571 by the Province of Canterbury (FW 1660 p.18) leave one in no doubt. *No one should be admitted to teach youth…in schools unless he has been approved by the ordinary* [the Diocesan Bishop].

68. Seabourne Vol1 p.49

69. Levi Fox *A Country Grammar School* (Ashby de la Zouch) 1967 pp.40/1. (Fox Ashby) Fox argues that only the largest schools would have provided the income for this. Even at a prestigious school such as Winchester a fire was lacking since *in winter the sun keeps well to the south and gives our chilled frames all its warmth.* (Quoted in: Seabourne Vol.1 p. 56)

70. School Orders

71. Enticing good behaviour by reward rather than punishment was a possibility. The Puritan school master John Brinsley, appointed in 1599 at Ashby, suggested in his book, *Ludus Literatus,* rewarding pupils for good work with the possibility of some *little boke or money* which the Governors at King Edward's would certainly have been able to afford. But there is no sign of this in Nuneaton until a much later period.

72. Brown p.22. Levi Fox *Early History of King Edward VI School Stratford.* (1984) p.12

 73. School Orders

74. School Orders

75. Jewell points out (p.61) that the investigations in 1575 of the then Archbishop Of York (about to be translated to Canterbury) Edmund Grindal found 54/138 clergy in the Yorkshire area deficient in Latin.

76. Accounts. See also VCH Vol2 P.343. Simon p.321 says that in 1583 only one third of incumbents were graduates.

77. VCH 2 p.343.

78. VCH 2 p.343.

79. VCH 2 p.38

80. Paterson and Rowney p.9

81. Nason *History* p.6

82. Paterson and Rowney pp 21-2

83. Whittington had taught at Henry VIII's Court before being given a succession of Crown livings by the King including Nuneaton and Mancetter. In his text book he controversially

advocated using Latin from a very early stage in the learning process so that English was never written down (except for Latin to English translation) and rarely spoken.

Cartwright had debated with religious radicals and conservatives on a national level personally supporting the Protestant Radical Peter Martyr Vermigli in debates in Oxford in 1549. He then *abjured* (renounced his faith on oath) and supported Queen Mary again debating in Latin – this time on the other side – against Nicholas Ridley a leading Protestant. See Paterson and Rowney pp.21-2

84. Transcripts pp. 30

85. Transcripts pp34-5 Mr. Burton (1581) Mr. Yates (1584) and Mr. Heath (1586) all received £13-6/-8d.[92]This was 20 marks, a standard figure fixed for Cathedral schools in 1547 (Orme 317) In 1563 Cleyton had received £4 6/-8d for just a quarter's wages – a larger sum (Transcripts p.7). In the early 1570s the normal figure was £12 though in 1575 the Master was only given £8-19/-2d.

86. Transcripts pp. 30-31

87. CCEd

88. W.E.Tate: Sources for the study of English Grammar Schools, *British Journal of Education studies Vol 2 No 1 Nov 1953 p.74.* (Tate) Kenneth Charlton The teaching Profession in 16th and 17th Century England p.35 in Paul Nash (ed.) *History and Education* (New York 1970)

89. Transcripts pp 66-68

90. See Appendix Twelve for list of Masters and Ushers/Undermasters

91. Transcripts pp 31-35

92. e.g. Leicester 1574 and Hull 1579. Simon pp. 377/8.

93. Transcripts p.14 Ambrose may be the son of Richard Vynsent: he was next of kin when Vynsent died in 1582 and obligated to repay the £20 bond his father(?) had taken. Robert Chaplyn was probably related to the Governor and one-time bailiff of the same name (unless the Governor himself was the Usher).

94. Francis Clement *The Petty School (1587)* Quoted In Jewell p.80

95. Foster Watson The Beginning of Modern Subjects in England (1971 reprint) p.138

96. VCH Vol 2 p.345. Launder was applying to be Usher again.

97. Venn's *Alumni Cantabrigiensis. Alumni of the University of Cambridge from earliest times to 1900* Online version (Venn). A pensioner did not possess a scholarship but paid for his own keep.

98. www.tudor place.com.ar Elizabethan peerage (Willoughby of Eresby)

99 DNB article on William Burton by Richard Cust (Cust)

100. Cust. Though more associated with work on Leicestershire (e.g. *Description of*

Leicestershire 1622) Burton remained linked to the North Warwickshire area by marriage, since his bride in 1607 was Jane, daughter of Humphrey Adderley of Weddington. His son, Cassibelan, was born there but the DNB says *we don't know of his education* – was it at the Grammar school?

101. There is evidence from elsewhere of the high quality of Latin fluency that could be achieved by the young. For instance Stratford Grammar school not only produced Shakespeare's learning but one of its historians records that Richard Quinney wrote in *astonishingly mature* Latin to his father in London when just 11. Leslie Watkins *The Story of Stratford School* (1953) p.3

102. DNB article on Robert Burton by J.M.Bamborough

103. Robert Burton *The Anatomy of Melancholy* p.219 (Authorised copy 1651 published by Harvard University 1914 Google books)

104. Oliver Elton *Michael Drayton: a critical study with a Bibliography* (1905) p.12 ebooksread.com

Chapter Three

1. WCRO H1/25 Accounts for building the new school (New School Accounts)

2. According to Seabourne Vol.1 pp. 42 and 44 (Fn 29), Kington, Herefordshire in 1625 is the earliest school building recorded where a specific architect is named, John Abel.

3. New School Accounts

4. Transcripts. Robert Vynsent senior owed £6 and was ordered to repay by the 1st Jan 1596. Likewise Marmaduke Lee had to find his £4 by Jan 10th.

5. Transcripts. It is especially recorded on the back of the last page of accounts and dated 1595 : this is fortunate, since the other accounts for the 1590s have not survived.

6. Transcripts p.19 and p.24

7. All the items listed are referred to in H1/24 Accounts

8. T.W. Baldwin *Small Latine and lesse Greeke* (1944) pp. 609-10 www.durer.press.illinois.edu

Martin Luther, as quoted in his *Works* (Philadelphia: Fortress Press, 1967), 54:210–211:

9. VCH Vol.2 p. 344. In *Ludus Literatus* (1612) John Brinsley – schoolmaster at Ashby de la Zouch stages a conversation between two Masters where one complains that Grammar Schools should not be *troubled with teaching ABC* but his colleague, though agreeing in theory, argues for realism and then discusses how best to teach simple English. Clearly this was the actual position in Nuneaton and in many other grammar schools by this time.

10 D. Cressy *Education in Tudor and Stuart England* (Cressy) p.31

11. Letters Patent WCRO H1/22

12. H0001/36 Free school orders (1609 Orders) These are also printed in Nason (pp. 20-26) in their original proposed format before the amendments of the Bishop.

13 For a full development of these ideas see Craig Muldrew: *The Economy of Obligation: the culture of credit and social relations in early Modern England* (1998). Muldrew's survey of urban court records shows that the rate of civil litigation expanded in the late 16th century to reach the highest level ever experienced in English history.

14. Vincent (1660-1714) p.173

15. J.P.Anglin: Frustrated Ideals: the case of Elizabethan Grammar School Foundations: in *History of Education Vol.11 No4 (1982)* p.270.

16. Anglin pp276-78

17. See end of Appendix Three for examples of financial mismanagement in other schools

18. Marchamont Nedham *A Discourse concerning schools and School-masters* (1663) p.4 Quoted in Vincent (*1660-1714*) p.174.

19. Nason *History* p.13 Nason refers to *a certain Mr. Gurrey* and Leach in VCH Vol2. p.344 to a *Mr. Harvey* , but it is clear from later references that the person referred to is the Vicar of St. Nicolas, Nuneaton, William Gurie.

20. VCH Vol.2 p.344 Nason *History* p.14

21. Nason *History* p.8 Reed Brett gives the date Inge started as 1594 and there is some doubt here. The revealing comments (see Appendix 10) made by ex Usher Edward Launder to the Master Mr. Crawford relate to the 1590s but this is the only reference to Crawford that we have. VCH (Vol.2) p. 345.

22. Disputes between the Governors and Richard Inge and between Inge and Richard Farmer, schoolmaster: some undated and some 1611-12 WCRO H1/32 (Governors against Inge). These documents are difficult to decipher and in many places I have relied on Dr. Nason's invaluable *Transcripts* of them in WCRO H1/52

23. Governors against Inge

24. Transcripts. In 1610 Inge claimed his right to receive the full salary and, after accepting the reduced figure of £5 for his first half year payment, he then rcfused the £2.50 offered for the subsequent quarter.

25. Venn.

26. Venn. Farmer later became vicar of Daventry, from where he seems to have originated, and where he also died in 1648.

27. Governors against Inge/Transcripts. See Appendix Three

28. Transcripts

29. Transcripts

30. WCRO H1/34 Richard Chamberlayne and Anthony Reay, schoolmaster, against

Richard Ford, John Wright, John Stratford and others of the Governors in the Court Of Chancery 1617-18 (Reay against Governors). As with the Richard Inge case the illegibility of this archive again means heavy reliance on Dr Nason's Transcripts H1/52.

31. Reay against Governors/Transcripts. The Governors had made the same allegation about a fall in numbers against Inge just a few years before (see above). For Cock Fighting see Vincent 1660-1714 p.42

32. Reay against Governors/Transcripts

33. Reay against Governors/Transcripts

34. Reay against Governors WCRO H1/34/16. One adjacent record is dated 1617.

35. CCEd

36. A sizar was a Cambridge Undergraduate who received an allowance for his study. He was excused his *sizes* (tasks) performed by College servants.

37. CCEd

38. Joseph Foster: *Alumni Oxoniensis The Members Of The University Of Oxford*, Online version (Foster)

39. On the subject of the professionalization of teaching see Patrick Orpen Schoolmastering as a profession in the seventeenth century: the career patterns of the grammar schoolmaster. *History of Education* 1977 Vol 6 No 3 p. 185 (Orphen). Orphen's analysis of Warwickshire and Worcestershire Masters 1601-1640 shows about 60% were what he describes as *temporary professional*, that is performing the role of teacher prior to an incumbency. Teaching was much less well paid – with an average annual salary of £17-18 in 1640, (though considerably more in Nuneaton) contrasting with an average of £42 for a vicar and £78 for a rector.

40. In this year his license as schoolmaster at Nuneaton was confirmed. CCEd

41. For example, Thomas Dugard was 15 years a teacher in Warwick and then 35 as Rector of Barford. Orpen 187. This is exceptionally long but there was often a ten year wait.

42. Foster. The two were William Boswell in 1634 and David Everett at the very end of Packwood's time in 1640. Either they were and the school was omitted from the record which did happen or, more likely, they were privately educated, suggesting the wealthier classes of the area did not use the school at this stage.

43. Lawson p.7

44. See also the quotation in Jewell p.5 *Every man strains his fortunes to keep his children at school* (James Howell – letter to the Earl of Dorset 1652). See also Lawson p. 267.

45. CCEd

46. *Journals of Sir Richard Newdigate* WCR0 CR 136A/14 p.284 and CR136 A/7 p.45. For Packwood see also Darren Oldridge *Protestant concepts of the Devil in Early Stuart*

England. History April 2000 pp 235-238 who quotes from the Newdigate papers.
47. Foster

Chapter Four

1. WCRO H1/35 The Governors against William Trevis, schoolmaster in the Court of Chancery including briefs against him and witnesses called against Trevis … about ill-treatment of pupils. WCRO H1/35 (Governors against Trevis).

2. In 1648 Edward Stratford obtained the Manor of Horestone, originally granted as part of his Nuneaton lands to Sir Marmaduke Constable but soon passing out of his ownership and going through numerous hands in the intervening period. VCH Vol.4 p.166-7. See also Ann Hughes *Politics Society and Civil War in Warwickshire* (London 1987) p.11

3. Venn and Foster

4. Born in 1640 Sir Willoughby was already a baronet, his father having been killed in the Civil War in 1646.

5. Venn

6. Sir Willougby was fortunate. The Restoration of 1660 re-opened all the traditional opportunities for gentry especially those families where members had given their lives for the Royalist cause. He returned to the family lands and had two spells as High Sheriff of Cheshire.(Venn)

7. W.A.L. *Vincent: The State and School Education in England and Wales 1640-1660* (Vincent 1640-60) pp. 39-40

8. Vincent 1640-1660 p.60

9. Such as Thomas Pocock, ejected from Reading Grammar School in 1648 and Thomas Widdowes from Gloucester Grammar School though Widdowes managed to obtain another post. Vincent 1640-1660 p.71.

10. 1642 was when the Master of Trinity, Dr. Thomas Comber was imprisoned by Parliamentarians and twenty fellows (including Trevis) were dismissed. Comber remained imprisoned for 11 years until his death. This experience clearly had a great impact upon Trevis. Venn. See David Hoyle's article in DNB on Comber.

11. For instance Royalist Daniel Rawlett of Wolverhampton Grammar school retained his post. Vincent 1640-1660 p.73 .

12. Vincent 1640—1660 p.51

13. Vincent 1640-1660 pp 64 ff. Particular attention was to be paid to *common haunting of taverns or alehouses* and *drunkenness* Cressy: p. 38.

14. Ivan Roots: *The Great Rebellion* (1966) p.177

15. In 1642/3 those who refused the Puritan Solemn League and Covenant Oath at

Cambridge University (including William Trevis future Master of Nuneaton Grammar) *many betook themselves to the painfull profession.* [of teaching] *T. Fuller History of the University of Cambridge since the Conquest 1655* Section vii pp169-170. Quoted in Vincent 1640-60 p.66.

16. Vincent 1640-60 p. 100.

17. Vincent 1640-60 p.100

18. Paterson and Rowney p.7. Richard Pyke, Vicar of Nuneaton 1655 to 1677, was a known Puritan appointed in the Protectorate but conforming to the demands of the Restoration Monarchy by agreeing to take the oath subscribing to the Act of Uniformity in 1662. Trevis later regarded him as a time server and detested him and his views. The feelings of dislike were mutual.

19. Governors againstTrevis. Barford had apparently made the agreement *fearing to be put out in the late times.*

The legibility of this archive varies though a greater proportion is readable than the papers regarding Richard Inge and Anthony Reay. However, there are still times when I have had to rely on Dr. Nason's transcripts. When comparison can be clearly made these are seen to be most accurate and helpful. So, see also Transcripts H1/52 .

20. Governors against Trevis. Under oath in 1666 Trevis refers to having *continued* the agreement. Later Governors' evidence referring to the same matter, and confirming the arrangement says of Trevis, *and so he hath continued for these ten years.* The longevity of Barford, or his wife, remains uncertain. A Mrs. Barford, widow, is on the Hearth Tax Returns for Nuneaton in the 1670s but we don't know if the Barfords stayed in the area after 1656.

See Margaret Walker (ed.)*Warwickshire Hearth Tax Returns* (Introduction by Philip Styles) Vol.1 (1957) p.148. For a more recent analysis of Hearth Tax in Warwickshire see Tom Arkell (ed.) *Warwickshire Hearth Tax Returns, Michaelmas 1670* (2010)

21. Lawson p.86

22. Lawson p.109. See Appendix Three part A

23. An information of severall particulars of the late tumult in Nunn-eaton in the County of Warwick, 1665 *(Tumult in Nuneaton).* This is a lengthy deposition by Trevis and almost entirely an account of the troubles in 1665, but with a very brief reference to the more minor difficulties of 1662. In his account of the events of Thursday November 30th 1665, Trevis records that in 1662 Ralph Wright *animated scholars … to … a wicked enterprise.* Information sworn by William Trevis before the Commissioner of Oaths, Richard Hopkins, on 25th April 1666.

24. Tumult in Nuneaton: Wednesday 29th November 1665

25. Tumult in Nuneaton Thursday 30th November

26. Tumult in Nuneaton Friday December 1st. Trevis recounts that when he bought a scholar to be examined before the Justices he was *accosted by Mr. Sadler, a mercer, (and professed Anabaptist) and 4/5 other rude fellows who used opprobrious language.* After Newdigate arrived they complained to Trevis that his actions had brought Justices to the town. A good number of townsfolk had been involved in the protest.

27. Tumult in Nuneaton. Friday December 8th.

28. Existing Governors John Stratford, Ralph Wright, Job Muston, Muston senior, Jonas Caldecott and Gervase Buswell were joined by new ones William Dudley, Robert Nutt, Richard Orton, Robert Shiers, Mr Alcott and John Judkin. According to Trevis – hardly an impartial witness – they were elected unanimously and had been selected by Trevis' great enemy Gervase Buswell. None were sympathetic to Trevis. They granted ten shillings of their charity money to Luke Mortimer, who had been arrested after the disturbances. *Tumult in Nuneaton* Tuesday December 12th.

29. Governors against Trevis H1/35/12 . Of £33 (a very good wage for six months) £29 and nine shillings was tendered to Trevis and the remaining £3 and eleven shillings was withheld. Though possibly likely a simple warning regarding his behaviour the approach was confrontational and probably designed to engineer a crisis. It succeeded.

30. Governors against Trevis H1/35/34

31. Governors against Trevis but also relying for clarification on Nason Transcripts H1/52. Trevis duly petitioned the Bishop on 20th April 1666 who ordered the Governors to pay the full salary. The Bishop backed Trevis: *His Lordship requires the Governors ... to pay him his salary as formerly without any abatement* (H1 35/1) The attitude of the Governors was criticized. But the Governors were determined to force the issue and now wanted Trevis dismissed. They still refused to pay Trevis and took the matter to Court of Chancery who straightway on May 7th 1666 ordered the immediate payment of the reduced salary of £29 9/-. On 14th July they referred the matter back to the Bishop. (H1 35/15)

32. Governors against Trevis

33. CCEd. Trevis was formally appointed schoolmaster on 24th April 1662, though in reality he had been in the post over six years. This meant that a few months later on the 16th August he could subscribe to the Act of Uniformity more straightforwardly as *a person already in office.* This detail seemed to confirm the legitimacy of his appointment.

34. Transcripts H1/52 pp41ff. One document stated that Trevis was *Elected placed and put into position of the said school* by John Stratford, James Caldecote Job Muston *and all the other Governors.* Trevis also claimed to have honoured his agreement to pay Barford the £10 annually which he said he continued to do. Not all the original legal judgement is now

legible (H1/35 *Trevis*) and again we have to thank Dr. Nason for transcribing some of the information. However, the evidence concerning Packwood and the nine Governors is based on a short piece written in a different hand at the foot of one of the original documents, so it was clearly a factor in the judgement. This part is clear in the original documents.

35. Transcripts

36. Governors against Trevis H1/35/21 (see also H1 35/ 7) has a torn and dated section again quoting the Orders of 1609 *That the Schoolmaster be careful and diligent.*

37. Transcripts

38. It is clear that the Anthony Reay ruling was seen as a crucial precedent. In a legible part of H1 35/4 it quotes from previous judgements: *The Governors shall pay forthwith to the said Anthony Reay twenty pounds towards his wages.*

39. WCRO 136 B5127 Newdigate Papers Quoted in Eileen Gooder *The Squire of Arbury* (Coventry 1990) p. 61 (Gooder)

40. VCH2, Nason Chapters Nine and Ten. Leach in the VCH acknowledges that Trevis' staunch royalism may have played a part but inclines to the view that the charges against Trevis were regarded as *frivolous.* Seldom has frivolity gone to so much trouble.

41. Vincent 1660-1714 p.64

42. Charles Hoole *A new Discovery of the old art of teaching schoole*: John Brinsley *Ludus Literarius* Both Quoted in Cressy p. 91

43. For instance, between 1673 and 1718 the long-time incumbent at Basingstoke Grammar School, John James, was charged with *unreasonable correction and whipping* which led indirectly to the illness and death of more than one boy. Causing illness or permanent injury was unacceptable even then. While the general consensus was that the rod on the hand or the backside was acceptable – even if administered severely and frequently –striking a boy around his head or face and pulling his hair nose or ears was not: Vincent 1660-1714 p.61. Nonetheless James survived in post for many years before eventually resigning when a major Court Case was instigated against him.

44. *The Spectator* August 1711 Quoted in Vincent 1660-1714 p.65

45. But it was ineffective and in 1698 a second appeal demanded an Act to remedy the foul abuse of children at schools, especially in the great schools of the nation. C.B Freeman: The Children's petition of 1669 and its sequel: *British Journal of Educational Studies* 1966 Volume 14 p.216

46. Gooder p.61. Gooder assumes that discussion concerning an Usher to assist Trevis meant that one took office at that time but there is no evidence of an actual appointment until the 1690s.

47. Trevis often insisted on collecting rents in person. It was said that he would stand in the doorway with his rod and receive the school rents. (Edwardian April 1923)

48. There were only 4/5 scholars left *and for the last two months not one. Trevis* H1 35/22 See also Nason *History* p.47

49. Nason Transcripts

50. Salaries of Schoolmasters in the 1670s compiled from the Wase manuscripts C.C.C. Oxon 390/1-3 in the Bodleian Library. Quoted in Vincent Grammar Schools p.171: not all schools gave returns – Warwick School for instance is missing. Vincent's appendix is compiled from Wase. Christopher Wase undertook a major survey of English Grammar Schools in the early 1670s. In October 1676 the Master's annual salary at King Edward's Birmingham was raised from £40 to nearly £69. Anthony Trott *No Place for Fop or Idler, The Story of King Edward's Birmingham* (1992) p.25 (Trott)

51. Orphen p.191. Orphen's comment that in this period Nuneaton Grammar School enjoyed *stability* raises eyebrows.

52. Richard Dunmore: *This Noble Foundation. A History of the Sir John Moore School at Appleby Magna in Leicestershire.* (1992) p. 24 (Dunmore) See also Appendix Three part B.

53. Governors against *Trevis* H0001/35/2 This is torn and faded and for some of the material we again have partly to rely on Nason Transcripts especially p.47 but there is also a long quotation in Leach VCH p.346. In face of this defiance the Bishop did nothing. Thomas Wood, Bishop of Lichfield and Coventry1671-92, rarely visited his diocese and was suspended for laxity by Archbishop Sancroft in 1684. (Smith, Endowed Schools p.8.)

54. Governors against Trevis H1/35/23

55. WCRO H1 43/3. Petition of the Inhabitants of Nuneaton to the bishop for licence for John Holmes of Chilvers Coton to teach in a petty school.

56. VCH Vol 2p.346 Non-Jurors were those clergy and schoolmasters who refused to take any oaths of loyalty to new Monarchs William and Mary after the deposition of Roman Catholic King James II in 1688.

57. The following details are from the Will written in February 1694 and proved on 4th June 1695. The first reference to Liptrott is his licensing on 10th April 1695. CCEd

58. Gooder p.62 records Sir Richard Newdigate visiting the dying Mrs. Trevis in 1682.

59. Charter of 1694 H1/23. Translation of the school letters patent of William and Mary (See next chapter.)

Chapter Five

1. WCRO H1/23 Translation of the school letters patent of William and Mary (Charter of 1694)

2. Charter of 1694

3. Dudley Ryder's son John Ryder became a young vicar of Nuneaton in 1721 and later an Archbishop in the Church of Ireland.

4. There is evidence of a William Liptrott, thought to have been born in Lancashire around 1620, as Master of the Kings School at Chester after 1657 and then of his own school at Weston, near Runcorn in Cheshire till his death in 1688. He appears to have been ejected from his Chester post after 1660. James Liptrott was almost certainly his son (www.genforum.genealogy.com/liptrott). See also King's School Chester website. (www.kingschester.co.uk)

5. Smith Endowed schools p. 14. See also Appendix Five part C

6. Tate Vol2 no I p.69

7. For the change of ownership of the *Old Grammar School* as it became known after 1880 see Chapter Nine

8. WCRO Miscellaneous Papers 1841-1973 DR 962/4/3 (1954) Letter H.N. Jepson to Canon Herbert. Page 3. 18.2.1954

9. Locke: *Some thoughts concerning Education* (1692). He felt the tasks required such as preparing orations in Latin were excessively hard and the result for the boys was to *bid them make bricks who have not yet any of the materials.* Latin composition for most was *Making bad verses of his own in a language that is not his own.* Moreover, time should be spent on other important subjects such as arithmetic, geometry, history and geography. Quoted in Stanley J.Curtis and Myrtle E.A.Boultwood *A Short History of Educational Ideas* (5th Edition 1977) p.247

10. WCRO H1 45/85 King Edward VI School. About 200 receipts and Vouchers for work done on the school. 1636-1810 (Receipts and Vouchers)

11. Frank was the youngest son by the Baronet's first marriage. Sir Richard was to re-marry and the son of his second marriage, Roger, was to inherit Arbury Hall. However, it was Frank's relatives that eventually inherited through Francis Parker Newdegate in 1806. By May 1702 Frank had been accepted at Trinity College, Cambridge and in 1705 took a Commission to be Lieutenant of Foot.

12. The main source of information about scholars at this early date was if they matriculated at Oxford and Cambridge but we know little about those who did not.

13. Receipts and vouchers (No. 100) 6.5.1699

James Liptrott received £30 for sixth months salary See also Receipts and Vouchers (No.99) 15.05.1708 where Liptrott was paid the same amount. (This set of documents is muddled and incomplete)The lack of increase in this salary in the 18th Century, while he saw money he felt was frittered away on poor apprenticeship arrangements, was another cause of friction between Governors and the third Liptrott, Thomas. See pp. 96-7

14. Venn and CCEd

15. Seabourne Vol. 1 p.121.

16. Nason *History* p.55

17. Paterson and Rowney p.25

18. Venn

19. Paterson and Rowney p.19 and CCEd

20. Venn and CCEd

21. Joseph Cardale went up to Trinity College Oxford but then changed to St John's Cambridge in 1732, and brother George followed to St John's in 1735. After Cardale moved to Hinckley in 1735 he, sent his youngest son William to Eton in 1740: was he better off now he was the recipient of two livings? The Cardale Liptrott connection might account for other boys coming from Leicestershire to Nuneaton Grammar School in the 1740s and achieving considerable academic success. (Venn, CCEd)

22. Joan Simon, Town Estates and Schools in the 16th and 17th Century p.25 in Brian Simon (ed.) *Education in Leicestershire 1540-1940* (1968)

23. Only Oakham school (18) (with a special Johnson scholarship) Bury St Edmunds (18) and Eton (16) had more. Harrow sent just 4, Repton 6 and Uppingham 2. E.S. Shuckburgh History of Emmanuel College (1904) www.archive.org/stream/emmanuelcollege and Venn

24. Venn/CCEd

25. Vincent 1660-1714 p.78. Milton felt there was too much formal grammar and an excessive concentration the literature of Greece and Rome to the exclusion of other valuable writings.

26. Paterson and Rowney p.44

27. Venn

28. *Francis Trotman for £281 and five shillings assigns to Peter Whyley her* [sic] *interest in the advowson and rectory of Witherley.* 23.4.1735. (Deed endorsed in Chancery 9th October 1752). Witherley Estate Records DE 322/1/8 Leicestershire, Leicester and Rutland Record Office. (A to A). CCEd.

29. CCEd: Chambers remained Rector (and his own patron) until his death in 1788 at the age of 51. Three years later the advowson passed to the next incumbent, John Fisher, and remained with the Fishers until 1967 by which time Geoffrey Fisher of the fourth generation of the family had retired from his own ecclesiastical post – Archbishop of Canterbury.

30. Richard S. Tompson *Classics or Charity : the dilemma of the 18th Century School* (1971) (Tompson) p.32

31. The forty pupils would probably be spread over 8 years in chronological age from 8/9 to 16/17. So if there were 40 boys in those 8 years this is about 5 boys per year. Oxbridge entries would be a very select group.

32. Account and Order Book of the Trustees of the Charity of Richard Smith (Smith's Charity) WCRO 2730/21 p. 28

33. Veasey p.81

34. Smith's Charity p.28.

35. As argued by John Lawson. *Generally speaking* [for the labouring poor] *a University education was out of the question.* Lawson p.131

36. Smith's Charity p.3

37. Veasey p.62. The courage of John Liptrott, Nuneaton curate and nephew of School Master Thomas Liptrott was reported by his brave actions to have reduced the tension over the rioting. Paterson and Rowney p.25

38. Tompson p.2

39. Nuneaton's population more than doubled between the estimate of 1670 when there were 415 households and a population calculated as 1,867 (Veasey pp.53/4) to that of the first national census taken in 1801when households had increased to 1,121 and the population to 4,535. Veasey p.77

40. Sanderson, J.M. The Grammar School and the Education of the Poor, *British Journal of Educational Studies Vol 11 p.39* (1962). On the figures researched by Tompson, Nuneaton was one of 152 Grammar Schools not converting to paying subjects. This was the most common option. 21 simply did not change at all and 115 added paying non-classical subjects while continuing free classical teaching . [Did 46 charge for all?] Tompson p.77.

41. Fox Ashby p.59

42. WCRO DR 925/71/1 Case of the Nuneaton Charter with Lord Mansfield's opinion (Mansfield Judgement) 28.2.1756

43. Lawson and Silver p.238.

44. Lands and Rents.

45. Lands and Rents. This is an isolated but significant piece of evidence that the Apprenticeship scheme was operating, though to what extent remains unclear.

46. Nason *History* p.56

47. Receipts and Vouchers No.182

48. Receipts and Vouchers

49. Transcripts

50. Transcripts

51. Foster Watson 1660 p.128. John Locke *Some Thoughts concerning Education* Quoted in Stanley Curtis and Myrtle Boultwood *A Short History of Educational Ideas.*p.246

52. Quoted in Tompson p.48

53. See Appendix Eight Section A

54. Transcripts. *An information on the relation of some inhabitants of Nuneaton* [at the instigation of Liptrott] *against Governors … for a discovery and account of the surplus profits of school revenues about £600 and to have such surpluses applied for the benefit of the Master in advance of this salary in repair of School House, the Master's House and in placing out poor boys taught in school* 1744.

55. Mansfield Judgement. Material is also found in H1/42 – Eighteen papers relating to the Appointments and Resignations of Governors. (Appointments and Resignations) This includes *Nuneaton School Charter with Lord Mansfield's opinion thereon* (H1/42/16).

56. H1/48 *Copy of an order of the Governors of 1788 concerning applications for Apprenticeship, 1806 and 62 Apprenticeship indentures 1806-51* (Apprenticeships)

57. Apprenticeships. H1/48/1 After 1806 Apprenticeships were carefully monitored in the way the Order required. This lasted nearly 50 years until the last Apprenticeship in 1852 after which the Governors decided to stop the scheme.

58.www.webspinners.org.uk/weddingtoncastle

59.CCEd

60. Appointments and Resignations

61. WCRO H1 40/38. 39 Papers relating to financial matters (Financial Papers)

62. Financial Papers (No. 11)

63. Financial Papers see 27.7.73 for Joseph Warden

64. For the wider ramifications of the legal squabbles over curriculum in Grammar Schools see Appendix Eight Section A.

Chapter Six

1. CCEd

2. Property in Church Street, Nuneaton, 1785-1874 WCRO 715/112-13 and 122-5 (A to A)

3. WCRO H1 40 Thirty Nine Papers relating to Financial matters 15.7.86.

4. WCRO H1 42/17 Eighteen Papers relating to the appointment and resignation of Governors. (Appointments and Resignations) 13.07.1788

5. WCRO H1 37 Opinion of Counsel concerning the additional powers of the Governors. 28.9.1830 (Opinion of Counsel)

6. Opinion of Counsel. See also WCRO 715/188-192 for Beet's land transactions in

undated (between 1762 and 1844) documents relating to Nuneaton properties. (A to A)

7. Opinion of Counsel 28/9/30

8. Liptrott bought four copies of the work and Trusswell wrote lyrics for some of Key's carols: in the first book he also contributed (over the initials T.T.) a poetic dedication to his musical friend under the heading *To Mr Joseph Key on his Eight Anthems and Te Deum*. www.immanuelsground.com (Warwickshire Composers of Church Ground) Quoting the Midlands Counties Tribune of 28th October 1855

9. Nason *History* p.64

10. Smith's Charity 17th January 1797 p.28

11. CCEd

12. Venn

13. DNB entry on Cobbold by H.G.C.Matthew

14. Venn

15. DNB entry on Cobbold by H.G.C.Matthew

16. Venn

17. Paterson and Rowney p.25

18. CCEd

19. CCEd

20. Receipts and Vouchers H1 45/193

21. John Roach *A History of Secondary Education in England 1800-1870* (1987) p.7 (Roach)

22. Roach p.11 quoting the External examiner of Warrington Grammar School 1853.

23. Population figures based on Veasey estimates p. 53 and the 1801 census.

24. Receipts and Vouchers. H1/45/193 This figure is mentioned in a section containing miscellaneous accounts but no breakdown of the figures is given.

25. Receipts and Vouchers

26. Appointments and Resignations H1/42/14

27. Appointments and Resignations H1/42/14

28. See David Paterson: George Eliot as Historian: in *George Eliot Review* 2010. (Paterson, Eliot)

29. Receipts and Vouchers

30. I have argued for the historical accuracy of Eliot's portrait in Paterson, Eliot:

31. Parliament held final authority as the supreme law-maker. See Appendix Eight.

32. See Appendix Eight.

33. Receipts and Vouchers: evidence from 1809.

34. Receipts and Vouchers. To Mr. Rayner 11.4.1805 Five copy books to enter boys names, 2/6d. See for instance HI 45/70 and H1 45/37 where Rayner, not Hughes, signs for over £3 worth of books and equipment.

35. Rayner's will shows that he owned property in Eccleshall, Staffs including the Blue Bell public house as well as property in Stockingford, over four acres, including the White Lion pub. In Nuneaton he had property in Church Street and the Rose and Crown pub in Abbey Street.

36. Receipts and Vouchers

37. Receipts and Vouchers H1 45/37, Bowditch's Navigation included weather, volcanoes, tides, metaphysics, jurisprudence and the civil law as well as definitions of medicine, anatomy, surgery, pharmacy, chemistry and botany. Mathematics was valuable as giving us a *just habit of reasoning*. Significant emphasis was placed on science.

38. Tompson, R.S. The English Grammar School Curriculum in the 18th Century: A Reappraisal. *British Journal of Educational Studies* 1971 Vol.19 p.39

39. Nicholas Carlisle *A Concise Description of the Endowed Grammar Schools in England and Wales* (1818) (Carlisle)

40. Joan Simon Town Estates and Schools in the 16th and 17th Century in Brian Simon (ed.) *Education in Leicestershire*. See especially pp131-141.

41. Carlisle. The Eton Grammar, first published in 1758, was the standard Latin textbook until replaced in 1867 by the Public Schools Latin Primer. Stanley J. Curtis – *History of Education in GB* (5th edition 1963) p.86 (Curtis).

42. Paterson, Eliot pp.78-9

43. For examples at Birmingham and Coventry see Appendix Eight

44. Nuneaton Chronicle (Chronicle) 7.1.1871 quoting old documents.

45. WCRO H1/41/4 Forty papers relating to investments, 1803-1874 King Edward VI School

46. WCRO H1/26/9 Account Book and Ledger Receipts. Hughes rent on the Master's House was a nominal 5 shillings a year.

47. WCRO H1/30 Governors' Minute Book 1846-72 (GMB 19th)

48. WCRO H1/48 Apprentice Indentures 1806-51. (Indentures)

49. See E.P.Thompson *Making of the English Working Class* (Penguin edition 1968) pp303/4 for unfavourable legal rulings as early as 1759. There was a *catastrophic slump* in Coventry in the years between 1828 and 1832 which would also have affected Nuneaton. See Peter Searby *Coventry In Crisis* (Coventry Historical Association Pamphlet 1977) p.1. The Statute of Artificers or Apprentices of 1563, almost as old as the school, was more honoured in the breach than the observance well before its formal repeal in a series of Acts of Parliament in 1813 and 1814.

50. Charity Commissioners Report 1834

51. From 1821-59 adverse legal advice prevented the building of a new schoolroom at

Warrington Grammar School (Roach p.20). Wolverhampton Grammar School had similar difficulties. (Roach p.71)

52. In 1795 Lord Justice Kenyon alluding to Grammar schools described *empty walls without scholars and everything neglected.* H.C. Barnard *A History of English Education since 1760* (1969 edition) p.16

F. Marvin *Century of Hope* (1919) p.204 commented: *It has been estimated that the condition of our public or higher schools was worse between 1750 and 1840 than at any time since King Alfred.* (Quoted in Barnard p.71) Tompson's valiant efforts to show some schools were in much better shape has modified but not destroyed this picture.

53. Roach p.212

54. Charity Commissioners Report 1834

55. Penny Cyclopaedia for the Society for the Diffusion of Useful Knowledge (1833) www.archive .org (Internet archive digital library of free books).

56. GMB 19th 16.11.1830. (Attached document)

57. Attached to the back of the Charity Commissioners files on King Edward VI Nuneaton (National Archives ED 5045 dealing with the 1870s) are these conditions of service (copy) when Thomas Docker was appointed in 1830. This includes the Bond. (Articles of Agreement 21.12.30)

58. Opinion of Counsel 28.9.1830

59. Venn (earning about £50 a year [cf Nuneaton school]

60. By 1845 Docker was Rector of Elstead, Surrey and died there in 1849 aged just 46, probably of cholera which hit the village in that year. [Venn.] See also Elstead village history website (www.elstead.org.uk)

For the Robert Evans connection see note 62 below.

61. Fletcher Report. The Fletcher Report (Relating to North Warwickshire) was part of a Royal Commission survey on the state of the Handloom Ribbon weaving industry in Britain. It gave valuable information on the social make up of the relevant towns. Fletcher was an Assistant Commissioner.

62. For instance George Eliot's brother, Isaac Evans, attended the dame school just across the road from their home at Griff House run by a Mrs. Moore. He was later privately tutored by Docker in Coleshill and continued private Latin lessons with him when Docker took up his position in Nuneaton in 1830. (see *Diary Of Robert Evans* Vol 1 1830-32 Nuneaton Library) Robert Evans was clearly satisfied with Docker's tuition and would have known a number of Grammar School Governors. I have benefitted in making these points from a useful dialogue with Professor Kathryn Hughes on Docker, Robert Evans and Isaac Evans.

63. £304 according to the Fletcher Report of 1840.

64. Chronicle 7.1.1871 quoting the Charity Commissioners Report of 1835.

65. Chronicle 7.1.1871

66. Very tricky Greek grammar, in particular the complexities involved in conjugating its verbs, was known to put off many students.

67. See footnote 62 above re. Docker tutoring Isaac Evans.

68. And later at Guy's Hospital. Chronicle 8.10.1896

69. Fletcher Report

70. See Veasey pp. 59-60

71. Test and Corporation Acts – originally passed in 1661 and 1673 respectively, in the Restoration period of Schoolmaster Trevis, they required evidence of attendance at the Church of England, seen as a religious test, before taking many civil and military offices either nationally or on local Corporations. Many Dissenters/Nonconfromists got round the Act by attending their parish church occasionally such as for Easter Communion. The repeal of the Acts thus regularised a largely existing position though their removal was symbolically significant.

72. For Southampton see Roach p. 109. For Chelmsford see Anthony Tuckwell 'That honourable and gentlemanlike House' A History of King Edward VI Grammar School, Chelmsford quoted on the website summary www.kegs.org.uk (Chelmsford website)

73. Chelmsford website

74. WCRO H1 26/7/8 Account Book and Ledger of the Governors 1780-1870 Sept 29 1842

75. Rugby Annual School Register Vols 1 and 2 1675-1874 (London 1880) It is just possible Bucknill attended Nuneaton Grammar School briefly before going to Rugby.

76. Venn

77 George Eliot Scenes of Clerical Life (2007 Wordsworth edition) p.47

78. Census of 1851

79. David Paterson Xhosa Youths in England 1859-64. Bulletin of the Scottish Institute of Missionary Studies New series 6-7 1990-91

Chapter Seven

1. Quoted in David Allsobrook Schools for the Shires (1986) p.106 (Allsobrook).

2. See WCRO H1/49/1 p.562 which contains a printed copy of An Act for improving the condition and extending the benefits of Grammar Schools 3 and 4 Vict. Cap.LXXX. VII (1840).

3. WCRO H1/49 Fair copy of Charity Commission scheme for the school 1846. (Charity Commission) This new scheme related not just to the Act of 1840 but also to an Act of

1812 concerning *a summary remedy in the cases of abuses of Trusts created for charitable purposes.*

4. Charity Commission 14.12.1846

5. Charity Commission 14.12.1846

6. Stockingford 1846, Abbey Green 1847, Vicarage Street School (originally known as Church Lane School) and Attleborough 1848. Veasey p. 84

7. Nason *History* p.65

8. The giving of prizes was recommended in the first report by Wiliam Drake in 1849: see GMB 19th 21.12.1849

9. WCRO H1/30 Governors' Minute Book   1846-1871 (GMB 19th) 21.12.1849. The school introduced an order of merit and in 1853 the examiner could not separate the top two students, Estlin and Iliffe.

10. GMB 19th 21.2.1853

11. GMB 19th 21.12.1855 and 12.6.1847

12. GMB 19th 24.9.1853

13. GMB 19th 21.12.1859

14. GMB 19th 23.6.1860

15. The Report was the one issued by Endowed Schools' Commissioner T.H.Green (mentioned in detail later in the Chapter). It is summarised in National Archives Charity Commissioners Secondary Education Endowment Files ED 27 (ED27) Nuneaton, King Edward VI Grammar School 5045 28.3.1872 (Green) It is also summarised in the Nuneaton Chronicle of 14.5.70 quoting the Blue Book, Schools Enquiry Commission published in 1869.

Delectus –Elementary books for studying Latin and Greek. Eutropius: A standard History of Rome.

16. Charity Commission H1/49/2 15.4.1846

17.GMB 19th 3.7.1856 Charity Commissioners: correspondence with the Governors. ED 27 5040 Form of Enquiry 25.7.1861

18. ED 27 5040 14.6.1861

19. ED 27 5040 24.7.1861

20. Nason *History* p.65. The Undermaster received a considerable though not entirely fixed amount. The Governors seemed anxious to reduce the differential – especially as they were now coming to envisage a wider spread of the classical tradition throughout the school.

21. GMB 19th 12.4.1847. 29.9.1847 30.12.1847.

22. GMB 19th 24.6.1850 and 12.3.1851

23. GMB 19th 9.9.1851 and 8.10.1851

24. GMB 19th 9.9.1851 8.10.1851.

25. Venn. In Pizey' case his ambition was clearly to run a school of his own which he did shortly afterwards in Great Crosby , Liverpool. Thomas Ainsworth who succeeded Pizey had been a teacher in Preston from a young age. (Census Material 1841,1851,1861).

26. GMB 19th 19.1.1852

27. GMB 19th 21.12.1857

28. For Testimonials see Testimonials on behalf of J.B. Bryant Schoolmaster, WCROH1/44

29.GMB 19th 17.2.1863

30.GMB 19th 14.2.1865 and 11.3.1866

31. Reverend Bryant had been successful with French and later on Shufflebotham may well have taken the subject since – when he left – enquiries were resumed for another teacher: it seems that Assistant Master Eustace took it up when he arrived in 1865.

32. David Paterson: The Gentle Savage in *Warwickshire History* Summer 1989. Drake's Reports are in GMB 19th 21.12.1853 and 21.12.1854. Census of 1851

33. Charity Commission

34. GMB 19th 11.3.1865

35. GMB 19th 21.6.1846 GMB 19th 21.12.1849

36. Eustace, however, did unofficially revive it. Canon Savage's youngest son, Edwin, recalled his individual early morning (6.30 a.m.) Greek lessons with Eustace in 1866-7 in Eustace's house *overlooking the vicarage orchard*. Apparently the 6.30 a.m. start was at Eustace's suggestion. Probably no other pupil was studying it in the normal school day by this time. WCRO DR0925/77/1 Letter from H.E.Savage 25.7.1932

37 GMB 19th 21.12.1849 Drake's Report

38. GMB 19th 21.12.1849

39. GMB 19th 21.12.1849

40. GMB 19th 21.12.1849

41. GMB 19th 21.9.1868

42. Census figures

43. GMB 19th 21.12.1854 and 21.12.1855

44. Edwardian Dec 1928.

45. GMB 19th 25.4.1853

46. GMB 19th 25.4.1853

47. GMB 19th 9.9.1851

48. Edwardian Dec. 1928

49. George Read to go on into Latin school, agreed in February 1849, was a typical example. GMB 19th 7.2.1849

50. GMB 19th 24.6.1870 and 21.12.1870

51. GMB 19th 1846-1871 passim. Census returns for 1851 1861 and 1871

52. GMB 19th 21.12.1854. 14.7.1855. 3.7.1856. 20.12.1861. 12.6.1860.

53. GMB 19th 9.1.1852. 2.6.1857.

54. ED27 5039 27.3.1860

55. See for instance minor repairs in GMB 19th 23.6.1866 and 24.6.1870

56. ED 27 5040 6.7.1861

57. Edwardian Dec 1928

58. ED 27 5041 Purchase of the Almshouses 22.7.1861 and 1.8.1862

59. ED 27 5041 Purchase of the Almshouses 22.7.1861 and 19.5.1862

60. Such as the payments by the Nuneaton Wool Company who paid over £15 annually in the 1870s. H1/31 Copies of letters 1874-82 12.4.1878

61. GMB 29.9.1865 24.9.1866 14.2.1867

62. WCRO H1/30/9 Ledger Receipts

63. For examples see GMB 19th 23.10.1848 24.6.1858 25.9.1858 23.6.1860

64. GMB 19th 15.4.1864.

65. GMB 19th 29.9.1868 and 22.6.1869.

66. GMB 19th 14.12.1846

67. Census 1871

68. GMB 19th 13.11.1870

69. Allsobrook p.134

Chapter Eight

1. Grammar schools were frequently *subject only to the autocratic control of the Master, the whim of the Trustees and theoretically the jurisdiction of Equity Courts* (Allsobrook pp.3/4). The 19th Century economist Nassau Senior said that the middle classes would question the spending of taxes on education if their children's needs were not being met. (Allsobrook p.144) This may have stimulated the petitioning of Palmerston's Government to set up a Commission into the Endowed Schools in 1864 .

2. GMB 19th 3.11.1865

3. Green's conclusions: ED 5045 28.3.1872 See also a summary in Nuneaton Chronicle 14.5.1870

4. Fox Ashby pp. 76-7

5. Middle school here means middle in terms of the social class anticipated to be attending (i.e. between upper and working).

6. Appleby Magna ceased to be a Secondary Grammar school after 1904. (Dunmore pp.83-5)

7. In 1857 Charles and Alfred Savage, born in 1845 and 1847 respectively, joined King

Edward's but their father was clearly dissatisfied and younger sons Ernest (b.1849) and Edwin (b. 1854) attended Atherstone Grammar School in the early 1860s, before moving to the new public school, Haileybury. Chronicle 7.12.1878 and Haileybury School Registers in the National Archives Library.

8. Our researches suggest that this underestimates the representation of professionals' sons at the school but Green was visiting at a very low point.

9. ED 27 5045 18.8.1869.

10. Nuneaton Chronicle 28.5.1870 (Chronicle)

11. ED27 5044 Estlin first wrote on 2.7.69 and after he had written six more letters the King Edward accounts were eventually announced as ready in a letter of 27.11.69

12. See ED27 5045 17.5.1872.

13. ED 27 5045 5.12.1872

14. ED 27 5045 28.3.1872

15. ED 27 5045 11.12.1871

16. ED 27 5045 28.3.1872

17. ED 27 5045 5.12.1872

18. ED 27 5045 7.2.1873

19. ED 27 5045 7.2.1873

20. ED27 5045 17.5.1872

21. Elizabeth H. Shillito *Dorothea Beale Principal of Cheltenham Ladies College 1858-1906* 1920 e book University of California www.archive .org Page 27

22. ED 27 5045 17.5.1872

23. Smith's Charity CR 2730/21

24. ED 27 5045 7.2.1873

25. ED 275045 3.4.1872

26. ED 27 5045 17.7.1872

27. ED 27 5045 1.3.1873

28. ED 27 5045 11.12.1871

29. ED 27 5045 11.12.1871

30. ED 2750 45 1.3.1873 and 2.4.1873 A £10 Ratepayer limit would effectively exclude the poorer classes.

31. ED 27 2.4.1873 and 8.5.1873

32. ED 27 5045 12.5.1873

33. ED 27 5045 8.5.1873 and 12.5.1873

34. ED 27 5045 12.5.1874. The separate administration of the charities lasted for the remainder of the life of the Grammar School. In 1959 the Clerk of the Governors sent three

Trustees a *ten shilling ticket to be given to some old inhabitant of Nuneaton.* Correspondence of G.H. Twist, Clerk to the Governors WCRO 2730/14 21.1.1959.

35. ED 27 5047 31.12.1874

36. ED 27 5045 24.12.1874

37. ED27 5047 5.8.1874

38. ED27 5045 4.11.1874 and 20.11.1874

39. DR 0925/71/4 New Scheme of Government for Nuneaton Grammar School

40. Clapton Rolfe (1845-1907): An architect based at Reading and then Oxford, considerably influenced by the Gothic revival style, especially in his earlier years. See www.oahs *Three Oxford Architects*

41. Right from the start the newly constructed church on the site of the Priory ruins was mysteriously known as the Abbey church not the Priory church.

42. Chronicle 16.3.1878

43. Chronicle 21.10.1877 24.9.1877 3.10.1877

44. Chronicle 29.12.1877

45. Chronicle 5.1.1878

46. ED 27 5054 24.6.1878

47. ED27 5051 29.7.1876

48. Chronicle 16.3.1878

49. Chronicle 27.5.1878 A Resolution disapproving of the selling of the endowment lands was defeated by two votes. That the School House be repaired and not pulled down was lost by four votes. To keep the costs to £3000 as nearly as possible was lost by two votes.

50. Opponents of the scheme argued that other new schools had cost less. One for 312 pupils at Birmingham cost £1,700 with 10 square feet per pupil seen as sufficient. At Bulkington a school for a similar number had cost just £1,800. (ED 27 5054 7.6.1878)

51. ED 27 5054 24.6.1878

52. ED27 5054 24.6.1878

53. Chronicle 31.10.1879

54. ED 27 5054 24.6.1878

55. ED 27 5054 24.6.1878

56. Chronicle 22.6.1878

57. ED 27 5040 6.7.1861

58. ED 275054 26.4.1878

59. ED 27 5054 26.4.1878

60. ED 27 5054 26.4.1878

61. ED27 5057 17.7.1880

62. ED 27 5053 17.1.1877

63. ED27 5054 2.1.1878

64. ED 27 5047 28.4.1876

65. Chronicle 10.3.1877

66. ED 27 5051 18.9.1876

67. Chronicle 28.7.1877 See also 3.8.1878 when George Taylor, coal merchant, supplied the marquee for the sports.

68. Trevor James: *The contribution Of Schools and Universities to the Development of organized Sport up to 1900.* (Phd Thesis 1977) Chapter Four p.49. http://hdl.handle.net/2381/4224

69. Chronicle 28.2.1876 Observer 12.12.1879

70. Nason *History* p. 70

71. Chronicle 3.8.1878

72. WCRO H1/31 Copies of letters sent out by Governors 1874-82 18.11.1874 (Governors' letters)

73. Governors' letters 10.2.1876

74. Chronicle 16.04.1880

75. Chronicle 20.12.79 Nuneaton Miscellany No 12 p.6 Nuneaton Library (Miscellany)

76. Governors' letters Chronicle 16.4.1880

77. Observer 24.9.1880

Chapter Nine

1. ED27 5051

2. WCRO 2730/3 Register of pupils and fees paid 1880-1935 (Admissions)

3. Chronicle 23.10.1880

4. Admissions and 1881 Census

5. WCRO 4232/3/1 Register of applications 1876-2003 (Applications)

6. Bryce Committee Report 1895 p.48 quoted in Barnard p.207

7. ED 27 5051 Inspection of 1892 (1892 Inspection)

8. 1892 Inspection

9. Venn. Chronicle 16.4.1880 and 30.7.1880

10. Reed Brett p.36 (but this does not say full-time or part-time) WCRO 4232 /7/2 Staff Registers 1880-1945 (Staff Registers)

11. Census of 1881. Ernest Escott, later Ernest Bickham Sweet-Escott, was a Classics graduate of Balliol and later a distinguished Colonial Governor. He came as the new school began, leaving a year later for his first colonial post in Mauritius. Teaching was still seen as a rite of passage to more ambitious posts elsewhere.

Cavendish College, a short lived institution from 1873 to 1892, was a County College, based in Cambridge, offering inexpensive degree courses to entrants below the normal age and also training teachers. Roach p.171

12. Chronicle 1.7.1881

13. CR 2730/3 Governors Minute Book 1897-1923 20.1.1902 (GMB 20th).

Volunteer and cadet corps started in schools in the 1860s but were not very prominent until the South African War of 1899-1902. John Roach *Secondary Education in England After 1870* p.132.

14. Venn and Chronicle 17.4.1896

15. Admissions and1892 Inspection

16. 1892 Inspection

17. Staff Registers 5.1.1900

18. Governors' letters 16.3.1880 and King Edward VI School *Memorabilia,* Chilvers Coton Heritage Centre (*Memorabilia)*

19. ED 27 5058 12.5.1892

20. Chronicle 2.8.1895

21. 1895 Scholarship winners: fathers were a platelayer at brickworks, two carpenters and a drapers assistant. One was deceased. (Admissions)

22. Kaye received two more grants of £40 as his course proceeded. Governors Minute Book GMB 20th 21.8.1908

23. *Memorabilia*

24. 1892 Inspection

25. 1881 Census and 1892 Inspection

26. 1901 Census

27. GMB 20th 9.9.1901

28. Woolwich Academy, founded 1741 for the training of engineers. Brian Simon *Studies in the History of Education* (1960) p.118

29. Census of 1891/1901

30. ED 27 5065 19.5.1897 and 1.6.1897

31. Chronicle 16.1.1891. Not on the staff in the Inspection Report of 1894 (ED 27 5051), Hogg went to Darlington Grammar School after which he taught at Technical Colleges in London.

32. Chronicle 31.7.1896

33. P.W. Musgrave *Society and Education in England Since 1800* (1968) p.58 (Musgrave)

34. GMB 20th 17.1.1898. This grant was still being requested in 1909 GMB 20th 20.7.1909

35. Venn

36. Reed Brett p.43. *Memorabilia*

37. ED 27 5064 Examiners' Reports April 1890 to April 1902

38. In 1892 form four, the most advanced, ranged in age between 12 and 15 years old, form three 11-14, form two 9-13 and form one 8-11. All classes had 15-17 pupils except form one with ten. Some of these classes combined at times. (1892 Inspection)

39. Governors lists based on census and local newspaper material

40. GMB 20th 13.10.1908 and 18.11.1908

41. *Memorabilia.* Reed Brett p.59

42. Edwardian July 1928

43. Chronicle 1.1.1904

44. ED27 5051 Report for 1889

45. *Memorabilia.* Frederick Cawthorne went on to school teaching having his own school in Felixstowe. Conversation with Michael Cawthorne. Census of 1911

46. Chronicle 1.3.1892

47. 1889 Inspection

48. Admissions

49. *Memorabilia* and Chronicle 31.7.1891. DNB article on Illing by J.G.C.M. Fuller

50. *Memorabilia*

51. 1892 Inspection Report

52. Old Edwardians Rugby was mentioned in the Chronicle in 17.2.1897 and 3.12.1897 though the Old Edwardians Rugby Football Club was not formed officially until 1910.

53. Chronicle 30.12.1881

54. ED27 5046 28.2.1876. ED27 5064 Examiner's report for 1895

55. Veasey p.97

56. Chronicle 31.7.1896

57. Chronicle 31.7.1896

58. I am grateful to Sheila Humberstone for telling me of Waters' action.

59. The decision to close Smith's was taken before the end of 1892 and King Edward Governors agreed to the terms of the amalgamation of the endowments the following April. But a good opportunity for selling did not appear until 1894. As always the change was opposed. After much protest and a threatened petition to parliament, the necessary legislation to amalgamate the endowments was passed in 1895 and a petition of opposition withdrawn. 5060 25.11.1892 5059 24.2.1894. 5066 29.6.1895 4.3.1895

60. ED27 5062 11.6.1897 referring to a report of 7.3.1884

61. ED 27 5051 12.4.1892 Inspector's comment

62. GMB 20th 11.7.1897 13.9.1897 12.6.1899 and 10.10.1903

63. Michael Seabourne and Roy Lowe *The English school: its architecture and organization Vol.2* 1870-1970 (1977) p.100 (Seabourne and Lowe)

64. ED 27 5060 7.6.1884 Report of Mr. Lefroy who had visited the school on 9th May.

65. ED 27 5066 27.2.1894

66. Seabourne and Lowe p.117

67. ED 27 5065 8.5.1896

68. ED 27 5065 21.7.1892

69. ED 27 5051 – 1889 Report and ED 5065 29.6.1897

70. GMB 20th 21.7.1897

71. GMB 20th 14.3.1898 and 12.6.1899

72. GMB 20th 9.2.1900 and 21.7.1897

73. GMB 20th 12.3.00 and 21.1.1901

74. GMB 20th 11.5.1897. 14.6.1897 See GMB 20th 21.3.1902 for the first meeting of the Building Committee

75. GMB 20th 8.10.1903 and 18.719.02 and 12.7.1902

76. GMB 20th 21.3.1902 and 19.6.1902

77. GMB 20th 27.2.1903 and 8.10.1903. One contemporary postcard from the Veasey collection has the title *Nuneaton Grammar and Technical School*

78. GMB 20th 5.12.03 and 12.1.04

79. The four were J.L. Dugdale, The Marquis of Hertford, J.K. Bourne (Atherstone) Bolton King (new Warwickshire Director of Education) .

80. GMB 20th 12.09.1904

81. GMB 20th 18.3.1904 and 17.2.1905 and 19.6.1905

82. GMB 20th 29.7.1905 However, they adapted and later on in the year granted a retrospective scholarship to W.C. Kaye – now studying at Birmingham University 20.10.19 05 see above note 28.

83. GMB 20th 12.9.1904 See also Chronicle 16.9.1904

84. GMB 20th 12.9.1904 and11.10.1904

85. Admissions

86. Applications, Admissions. See also Lawson and Silver p.382

87. Admissions

88. Admissions. From 1898 the scheme was started when the pupils were 15. Pupil teacher centres were increasingly linked with a school. (Curtis p.291)

89. Musgrave p.86 Sir Robert Morant (1863-1920) was a leading Civil Servant and educationalist. After helping with the drawing up of Education Act of 1902 he laid down

clear regulations and objectives for the increasingly important and state funded Secondary sector of Education. Beatrice Webb remarked that *he has done more to improve English administration than any other man.* (DNB entry by Geoffrey K. Fry)

90. GMB 20th 25.5.1906

91. GMB 20th 15.4.1910 and 24.1.1911

92. *Memorabilia* and GMB 20th 20.10.1905

93. GMB 20th 25.9.1906

94. Miscellany 12 p.186 GMB 20th 23.10.1906

95. Seabourne and Lowe p.15

96. GMB 20th 22.7.19 08 and 20.7.1909

97. GMB 20th 11.12.1908 J.F.H.Berwick, Head of Gainsborough School, and four clergymen.

Chapter Ten

1. Venn, and Edwardian Spring 1949 and Spring 1959

2. GMB 20th 22.1.1907 and 20.1.1902

3. Chronicle 18.12.1908

4. Admissions

5. W.B. Stephens: *Education in Britain 1750-1914* (1999) p.103 (Stephens)

6. GMB 20th 30.10.1908

7. Veasey 111 42,000 in 1921 46,500 in 1931 and 50,000 by 1941. Nearly 20% growth.

8. Admissions. The birth rate in Nuneaton was the highest in Warwickshire in 1923 but the exceptionally rapid growth of previous years was not maintained as migration rates to the town declined.

9. For the general point see Lawson p274. An example from Nuneaton was when Mr. Cross' son Hereward was taken home after the death of his elder son Edward in the Army on 4th October. All fees were cancelled. His father required him on his Weddington farm. GMB 20th 15.10.1917.

See also p.3 of Eric Ballard, Chris Holland and Anglea Crabtree: *The Nuneaton and District Memorials Project (King Edward VI Grammar School Memorial)* (Memorials Project) See also Census returns 1911.

10. Viscount Cranborne. Schoolteachers (Superannuation) Bill November 11th 1918 Hansard 1161 Hansard online (www.hansard.millbanksystems.com)

11. Stephens p.103. Admissions

12. GMB 20th 8.6.1922

13. GMB 20th 4.6.1913

14. Veasey p.118

15. Applications

16. Edwardian Easter 1948, Christmas 1942, Summer 1945

17. Chronicle 12.2.1897

18. Chronicle 23.2.1912

19. GMB 20th 27.1.1914

20. Edwardian December 1928 Christmas 1932 Summer 1934

21. Nason *History* Introduction p.x

22. Old Edwardians Minutes WCRO 4232/5/ 2 21.3.1933

23. GMB 20th 11.6.1920

24. Quoted as a County Council Assertion in GMB 20th 11.6.1920

25.GMB 20th 11.6.1922

26. WCRO 4232 Governors' Minutes 1923-1960 (GMB 1923-60) 14.10.1924

27.Apparently the lack of action was because one boy left *a long time ago* and the other *is living too far away* [Withybrook].

28. A Nutrition Committee of the Medical Research Council was set up in 1922. After 1927 there was increasing awareness of poor health among many schoolchildren. John Boyd Orr's influential *Food Health and Income* appeared early in 1936. See Derek J. Oddy, *From Plain Fare to Fusion Food: British Diet from the 1890s to the 1990s,* pp. 116 to 125.(Google Books.co.uk). Free milk was seen to boost British farmers as well as poor children's calcium levels.

29. GMB 20th 26.1.1909 17.1.1916 GMB 1923-60 6.3.1925 Chronicle 8.11.1918 (at the height of the world wide flu pandemic)

30. Chronicle 8.11.1918. Don Jacques to David Paterson. Nuneaton Observer 25.11.1929 (Observer)

31. Applications. This was very approximately in line with national trends: the Number of free place Grammar School children doubled in England and Wales between 1920 and 1932 by which time the 209,000 free place children were over 48% of the total. (Lawson and Silver 394)

32. Honours Boards in Chilvers Coton Heritage Centre. Reminiscences of two old boys. The proportion of boys obtaining scholarships was very approximately in line with national trends: the Number of free place Grammar School children doubled in England and Wales between 1920 and 1932 by which time the 209,000 free place children were over 48% of the total. (Lawson and Silver 394) Armytage (p.207) calculated that in 1935 between 11 and 12% of children (boys *and* girls) from elementary schools attended Grammar School

33. Miscellany 12 Page 186 24.4. 61. This is a Point I have had confirmed by two ex-pupil

recalling the early 1940s. One old boy stated that some pupils were greeted with the taunt: *Grammar bugs have ugly mugs.*

34. GMB 20th 26.1.1909

35. GMB 20th 19.10.1914

36. GMB 20th 17.1.1916 Men aged 18 to 40 were told that they could continue to enlist voluntarily, or attest with an obligation to come if called up.

37. GMB 20th 17.4.1916

38. GMB 20th 17.4.1916 16.10.1916

39. GMB 20th 20.3.1917 30.4.1917

40. GMB 20th 22.1.1917 16.7.1917

41. GMB 30th 14.7.1919 and 31.1.1921 David Howe *Willingly to school? The story of 900 years of Education in Warwickshire* (2003) p. 56 (Howe)

42. GMB 20th 8.7.1918. 2.1.1919 14.7.1919 19.1.1920

43. Private conversation with the author September 2009. Edwardian July 1928

44. Evidence of two Old Boys in conversation with the author. Reed Brett published a number of history text books and an important biography of 17th Century parliamentarian John Pym.

45. GMB 20th 30.7.1920 19.1.1920 GMB 1923-60 18.10.1929

46. GMB 20th 10.5.1922 GMB 1923-64 6.4.1923 16.10.1923

47. GMB 1923-60 6.3.1925

48. The growth from 42,104 in 1921 to 46,521 in 1931 was much more modest than at the start of the century (Veasey p.111)

49. Edwardian December 1929 Christmas 1931 Christmas 1932 Observer 25.11.1929

50. GMB 1923-60 15.2.1931 and 31.5.1934

51. GMB 1923-60 29.11.1935

52. GMB 1923-60 3.11.36 and 17.3.1938

53. Howe p. 186

54. GMB 1923-60 1.7.1938. GMB 1923-60 28.3.1939

55. GMB 20th 4.5.1911 23.1.12 28.1.13

56. GMB 20th 23.7.1915 15.10.1917

57. GMB 20th 21.8.1918 31.3.19 11.6.1920 23.1.1.23 GMB 1923-60 19.2.35. In 1917 the War office took possession of the remaining fields at Coundon under DORA (Defence of the Realm Act) 15.10.17

58. GMB 1923-60 12.2.1931 GM 12.2.1931

59. GMB 1923-60 8.2.1926 and 20.5.1926 GM 2.7.1940 GM 3.3.1947

60. GMB 20th 31.1.1921 GMB 1923-64 6.4.1923

61. GMB 20th 12.9.1904

62. GMB 1923-60 16.10.1923. 24.1.1924

63. GMB 1923-60 24.6.1924 Chronicle 26.7.1929 Edwardian April 1929.

64. GMB 1923-60 21.1.1929. 24.1.1929

65. Hadow Report 1928 Books in Public Elementary Schools – www.educationengland.org.uk GMB 20th 11.10.1929. Dec. 1929 Magazine. The phrase *Pratt spirit* was based on a comment made in a speech by Pratt himself. (Observer 25th 1929 *Pratt's Motor Spirit*)

66. Reed Brett p.49

67. Magazine July 1933 and Dec 1929

68. WCRO CR 4232 2/3 Account Book 1936-50

69. GMB 1923-60 16.10.1933 Chronicle 4.8.1916 GMB 1923-60 22.3.1924

70. GMB 1923-60 5.7.1932 baldly states his contract was terminated with one month's salary in lieu of notice.

71. GMB 1923-60 6.3.1925

72. Edwardian 1935

73. GMB 1923-60 6.3.1925

74. In 1929 13/18 boys passed the Cambridge school certificate and there were two more Oxbridge Scholarships. Dec. 1925 L.W.Andrew and J.C. Larkin Open Scholarships in Science at Oriel and Downing respectively.

75. Edwardian April 1928

76. Edwardian Dec 1929

77. Census information 1881, 1891, 1901

78. Dec 1929 and private conversation with the author.

79. Edwardian *As We Were* Dec 1928

80. GMB 1923-60 1.2.1927 Edwardian March 1934

81. WCRO 4232/2/1 Games Committee Minutes. 3.12.1934 and 17.9.1937. 17.1.1938 5.6.1939. In future boys would just contribute 6d each towards the travel costs of a trip.

82. Edwardian July 1928 July 1933

83. Edwardian April 1926 April 1927 April 1928

84. Observer Nov 25 1929 For Prefects see Reed Brett p.49

85 Edwardian Christmas 1927, December 1928, Autumn 1932

86. The Founders' Day address was regularly reported in the Magazine. The summaries the boy editors made of the address/sermon delivered by a clergyman each year would have done their Tudor and Stuart predecessors proud.

87. Edwardian Christmas 1932

88. Stuart Blofeld had been Principal of that Saltley Training College so popular with Nuneaton Grammar School pupils, and Chairman of the Governors of King Edward VI School Birmingham. He attended King Edward's from 1882 to 1889. Edwardian July 1929 and Christmas 1934

Chapter Eleven

1. GMB 1923-60 29.9.1939
2. Staff Registers 1880-1950. Tony Collett memories
3. GMB 1923-60 29.9.1939 See also www.aircadets-wbw.org Warwickshire and Birmingham wing ATC
4. Edwardian Christmas 1943
5. Peter Adey: *Aerial Life: Spaces, Mobility, Affects.* (2010) p.35
6. Between Sept 1916-Jan. 1919 Pratt was in the Admiralty Royal Navy Air Squadron RNAS, the air arm of the Royal Navy merging with the Army's flying corps in 1918 to form the RAF (RNVR attached). Subsequently he was in the RAF reaching the rank of Lieutenant on demobilisation. See Chronicle 3.11.1944
7. Coventry Evening Telegraph 25.10.2006. In 2006 part of a new housing complex in Biggin Hill Kent, build on part of the aerodrome from where he had flown, was named after him as Allton Lodge.
8. Edwardian Easter 1946
9. Chronicle 6.10.1946
10. Edwardian Spring 1958.
11. Tony Collett's Memories
12. GMB 1923-60 10.12.1942 25.1.1943
13. Reed Brett pp53-4. Edwardian Easter 1942. Old boy memories.
14. GMB 20th 16.6.1941
15. Memories of Don Jacques and Sheila Humberstone
16. GMB 1923-60 16.6.1941 and 4.12.1941.
17. Memories of Don Jacques
18. Originally used in Dalton High School Massachusetts and popular in the Australian outback, this method of individualised learning was introduced in Nuneaton for pragmatic rather than ideological reasons.
In February 1945 King Edward's Governors accepted responsibility for damage by boys to the Girls' High School when they were transferred to the High School Site. GMB 20th 9.2.1945.
19. Don Jacques and other old boy memories

20. Chronicle 8.5.1942

21. Edwardian Christmas 1943

22. Edwardian Christmas 1943

23. GMB 1923-60 13.11.1944

24. Old Boy Information. Edwardian Summer 1944 and Christmas 1945

25. The Governors wrote to Mr. Brown congratulating him on the *great success* had had achieved. GMB 20th 24.1.1941 Edwardian Christmas 1943.

For Pratt's departure see Chronicle 3.11.1944 Observer 3.11.1944 and Edwardian Christmas 1944

26. See Edwardian April 1928 for their interview of Attwood. See also GMB 1923-60 16.6.1949

27. Edwardian Christmas 1942 and Christmas 1943. Summer 1944 and Christmas 1945

28. DNB article on Broadbent by Frank Cooper.

29. DNB article on Randle by Stephen J.H. Ashcroft and Richard M. Denton.

30. www.myfarminglife.org – interview with Lord Plumb of Coleshill 2009

31. Edwardian Easter 1946

32. Edwardian Christmas 1943: www.bbc.co.uk People's War

33. Chronicle 8.5.42 Edwardian Summer 1944 The school was anxious to hold on to the alternative interpretation that *free* meant freedom from state and church – an argument used when requesting money for building extensions up to the 1970s – and even beyond into the days of the Sixth Form College.

34. Seabourne and Lowe p.95

35. Lawson and Silver p.394

36. Barnard p.260

37. The Conversion of Manor Park into a full Grammar/Technical School was completed by 1954 when they had 566 pupils. The staff had risen from 16 to 27 and children were coming as far away as Coventry and Sutton Coldfield. Chronicle 8.10.1954

38. The war affected endowment income: Income from Personal Estate reduced to £986 in 1941/2 and to £790 in 1942/3. It recovered a little post-war but was still below £1000 at £977 in the financial year 1947/8 CR 4232 2/5 Account Book 1936-50 (Account Book)

39. Education Bill *House Of Lords Debates 26 January 1967 vol 279 cc708-46* (Baroness Brooke of Ystradfellte). Hansard on line.

40. Holman had a fixed seat in the parish Church, appropriately in the Leeke Chantry Chapel. (Edwardian Summer1929) Sumner was the possessor of a theological diploma and he and Usherwood were both Secretaries of the Nuneaton Parochial Church Council.

41. Account Book: on the eve of war the income from personal estate was £1115 and from

fees £1,714. But the income from state grants was £6,161.

42. In most towns the size of Nuneaton the Churches had been unable to provide an elementary school place for every child. As a result, after the Education Act of 1870, many areas set up an elected School Board to raise money via the rates for the construction of new schools and their running expenses. But in Nuneaton's case the Board schools – and the rate rise that went with them – were successfully opposed.

This attitude continued for many years. Old boy Professor Illing's remark in 1952 *we don't want to be taken into national institutions* was typical of the independent spirit of the times.

43. Correspondence of G.H. Twist, Clerk to the Governors WCRO 2730/11 (Twist): letter from County Architect 25.6.1948.

44. Twist 4.4.1949 and 15.4.1949

45. The circular commented that *the only certainty is that in the next five to six years there will be a very great increase in the number of young people entering school.* In 1955 it was 790,000 and in 1964 over 1 million. (Seabourne and Lowe p.154). It was estimated that the number of pupils reaching the age of five before 1952 would exceed the number reaching fourteen by 16,000. This resulted in a preoccupation with new primary Schools and meant relatively few secondary schools built until after 1950 (Seabourne and Lowe p.186). Primary spending was £9.1 million compared to Secondary £6.63million.

46. Lawson p.282 Seabourne and Lowe p.153

47. GMB 1923-60 7.2.1943

48. GMB 1923-60 20.3.1946 and 13.11.1948

49. Observer 20.12.1946

50. Excepted Districts: towns with a population of over 50,000 such as Nuneaton could opt out of county educational control and have their own separate education authority

51. Development Plan for the Administrative County of Warwick WCC Education Committee Report (Development Plan)

52. Voluntary Aided Schools Correspondence 20.1.48 – Ministry of Education to School Governors

53. Ministry of Education to Clerk of Governors 18.5.1948. Voluntary Aided status was finally formally implemented on 1st March 1949. (Twist)

54. Development Plan

55. GMB 1923-60 13.11.1948.

56. GMB 1923-60 16.6.1949

57. Twist, Whimster to Twist 10.10.49.

58. Correspondence of Harry Cleaver, Chairman of the Governors WCRO 2730/6 20.7.1960 (Cleaver)

59. Twist 19.5.1949

60. Reed Brett p.57

61. King Edward's 400th Anniversary Folder WCRO 4232 4/56 (Anniversary folder)

62. Inspection Report 1952.

63. GMB 1923-60 25.1.1943 and 24.1.1944

64. Don Jacques

65. Edwardian Christmas 1945 and Spring 1948. In 1947 eminent physicist Joseph Rotblat organised the Atom Train touring exhibition, two railway carriages filled with exhibits and demonstration experiments, which aimed to educate the public about nuclear energy and its risks, whether used militarily as a weapon or peacefully as a power supply.

66. Old Boy Memories

67. GMB 1923-60 28.2.1945 and Staff Registers. Edwardian Summer 1951. 68. Don Jacques. Edwardian Christmas 1945

68. Old boy memories

69. Canon Herbert, the new vicar of St. Nicolas, reported in 1946 that the school/church partnership *had been greatly strengthened during recent months by the practice of the Grammar School in coming to church every week for their service.* Chronicle 17.5.1946.

70. GMB 1923-60 19.7.1946.

71. GMB 1923-60 3.3.1949 10.319.1949. 18.919.1952. WCRO 2730/16 Instrument of Government 1952

72. Edwardian Christmas 1947

73. In memory of the outstanding student who became a Spitfire Pilot but crashed in 1940. (see p.216)

74. Edwardian Summer 1948 Christmas 1945 and Christmas 1946

75. Edwardian Christmas1947.

76. Edwardian Christmas 1947

77. Edwardian Spring 1948. Summer 1948.

78. Nuneaton Miscellany Four Page 57 1953 and Edwardian Autumn 1951.

79. Inspectors Report 1952 Miscellany 4 Page 57 1953
The battleship that cost about £9,000,000, was Britain's last battleship built for war service, HMS Vanguard, completed in 1945. Too late for the war, she took Royalty to South Africa and was then used as a training ship before she was scrapped.

80. Miscellany Vol.4 p. 57 1953

81. New Articles of Government 1952.

82. Apart from updating the story to 1952 there was just one major addition to Nason's material. Since the good doctor had written his account in the 1930s, papers had come to

light in the Newdigate collection which vividly described the anti-Trevis rioting of the mid 1660s.

83. Anniversary Folder.   Chronicle 9.5.1952

84. Anniversary Folder.

85. Anniversary Folder. A few years later there was further evidence of a renewed awareness of the longer perspective. In reference to the search for Charters with regard to School History in 1960 the Edwardian commented: *If the ghost of Mr. Trevis still walks it must have perceived that times had indeed changed.* Edwardian Summer 1960.

Chapter 12

1. Edwardian Autumn 1955 Summer 1954 Summer 1955

2. GMB 1923-60 4.10.1951. Private conversation with author.

3. GMB 1923-60 29.2.1953

4. GMB 1923-60. Records from the 1950s

5. Old Boy reminiscences

6. Evening Tribune Obituary July 3rd 2008. GMB 1923-60 30.4.53 and 25.5.53. Edwardian Autumn 1956

7. Edwardian Summer 1960, Spring 1956, Autumn 1956

8. Edwardian Spring 1962. Governors Minutes 1954-60 WCRO 4232 1/1 (GMB 1954-60)

9. Staff Registers

10. Staff Registers

11. Inspection Report 1952

12. Edwardian Spring 1952 Autumn 1959 Spring 1958

13. Edwardian Spring 1954 Summer 1955

14. Edwardian Autumn 1955

15. Edwardian Autumn 1955 Autumn 1957 GMB 1954-60 18.11.1955

16. WCRO 4232/2/6 Photos –Premises A short account of the opening of the pavilion is included amongst the photos. GMB 20th 8.5.31

17. Edwardian Spring 1963

18. Edwardian Spring 1956 and Autumn 1958

19. WCRO 4232/1/2 Governors' Minutes 1954-60 (GMB 1954-60) 13.10.54. Edwardian Autumn 1954 Chronicle 16.5.1952. See also Chronicle 5.11.1954 Illing remarked that *he would never forget Sammy Waters who taught him the beauty of learning, that desire to arrive at the truth, a desire given to them by God, which had been the lodestar of his life.* He also praised Holman and Day.

20. Chronicle 9.12.1955 25.5.56 Edwardian Autumn 1956.

21. GMB 1954-60. 30.10.54 Twist WCRO2730/12 17.3.1955

22. Cleaver: Stan Bowles M.P. to Harry Cleaver 8.11.1956

23. GMB 1954-60. 12.1.1955 27.1.1955

24. GMB 1954-60. 10.10.1957

25. GMB 1954-60. 4.12.1956 Cleaver: Cleaver to Lord Hailsham, Minister of Education 21.3.1957. GMB 1954-60 10.10.1957

26. Edwardian Spring 1959

27. GMB 1954-60. 27.3.1958

28. Cleaver: Leonard Cleaver to Geoffrey Lloyd M.P. 12.9.1960

29. GMB 1954-60. 28.6.1958 and 25.7.58

30. Cleaver: Leonard Cleaver to Geoffrey Lloyd M.P. 20.7.1960

31. Cleaver 13.5.1960.

32. Cleaver 12.7.60 13.1. 61 and 15.5.62 See also GMB 1954-60 10.3.60. The Frank Buttle Trust is a charity set up in 1953 and includes educational grants for the benefit of children.

33. Edwardian. Summer 1960 Cleaver Correspondence 28.9.1960 Cleaver to Todhunter 15.5.1962. The actual total cost was £130,000, £67,000 from the school including the Gym. The Ministry contributed £63,000. Nuneaton Observer 26.1.63

34. Cleaver 15.11.63

35. Cleaver 15.1.62 14.2.62 20.2.62 15.5.62

36. Edwardian Spring 1961

37. Nikolaus Pevsner and Alexandra Wedgwood *The Buildings of England: Warwickshire* (1966) p365

38. Edwardian Spring 1962

39. Edwardian Autumn 1958

40 Edwardian Autumn 1962. Later in the decade a Christian Union was formed.

41. Edwardian Autumn 1970

42. A.P. Arnold Edwardian Spring 1962 entitled *Six months in the sixth*.

43 Nuneaton Miscellany 4 p.282 See also Edwardian Spring 1964

44. Edwardian Spring 1969 Autumn 1969

45. Edwardian Spring, Autumn, September 1969

46. Edwardian Spring 1971

47. The other was at the Girls' High School.

48. Edwardian Autumn 1972

49. Edwardian Autumn 1957 Chronicle 8.9.1952 Edwardian Autumn 1955

50. Edwardian Spring 1967

51. Edwardian Spring 1970

52. Borough of Nuneaton Circular 3.12.1970 reporting on the meeting of the working party on 16-19 Education (Working Party) 24.11.70

53.Working Party 3.12.1970

54. Working Party 4.5.71

55. Working party 22.6.71 PJ Rogers to M.L Ridger Borough Education Officer to County Education officer undated letter but certainly after July 1971

56. Headmaster King Edward VI School to P.J.Rogers 14.3.1972

57. Borough Education Officer to Rowland Brown 3.2.1972

58. Headmaster King Edward VI School to County Inspector 8.11.1972

59. Undated discussion paper on Language teaching at the Junior College.

Appendices

References are to the authors found in the Bibliography

APPENDIX 1

The Leeke Chantry And The Foundation Of The School
A) Granting Of The Licence

Alan Kreider in *English Chantries* criticises the traditional idea that the ravages of the Black Death in 1349 resulted in a dramatic increase in Chantry foundations by showing that the period of most rapid growth in the counties he studied (including Warwickshire) was in the first half of the 14th Century. (Kreider p.86) Kreider's analysis further shows that the number of licences in mortmain granted declined dramatically after 1450. In Warwickshire before this date, one licence had been granted about every three years. But then Kreider says there were only five between 1450 and 1499 and only one – presumably Leeke's – after 1500 (Calendar of Patent Rolls and Letters and Papers of Henry VII, I-VII). However, it seems there were at least two: *William Porter Clerk in Chancery to John Mascall deputy of the Hanaper…of a warrant directive delivered to be approved letters patent authorise Henry Smythe and John Leeke to alienate lands for the founding of perpetual chantries in Coventry and Nuneaton respectively* (14th March 1508 Calendar of Close Rolls Henry VII Vol2). Leeke's legacy was relatively small and this may have aided the granting of the licence. It can be contrasted with that of Richard Bexwyck a wool merchant who, in the same year as Leeke, 1508, was able to leave sufficient money for two priests for his Chantry one of which was to *teach in a fre schole.* (Graham and Phythian p.7)

I am very grateful to Dr. Steven Gunn of Merton College Oxford for pointing out to me the difficulty of obtaining mortmain licenses at this time.

B)Wording Of The Licence

Leeke worded his Will in a particular way, with a conditional clause making alternative provision for his legacy if the mortmain licence was refused. This has traditionally caused a degree of puzzlement. It seems unlikely that many could have anticipated that

Chantries would be dissolved a generation later. While the number being founded was declining they still played a significant role in society. In 1508 with Henry VII still on the throne and the country more stable than it had been for many years, Chantries seemed secure. Leeke may have been aware of strong Lollard beliefs in Coventry, critical of church abuses, though rarely, specifically, Chantries. John Blomstone from Coventry attacked purgatory directly and was brought before the Bishop in March 1485: *Prayer and almes auayle* [avail] *not the dead; for incontinent after death, he goeth either to heauen or hell: whereupon he concludeth there is no purgatory.* (Quoted in Foxe's Book of Martyrs Book 6 Page 777 www.ccel.org)

There were also critical murmurings that Chantries allowed wealthy people a better chance of salvation; but systematic attacks on the concept of purgatory developed later with Martin Luther's objection to Indulgences in 1516. Only in the 1530s was it clear that they were a matter of much dispute in England. In 1534 Archbishop Thomas Cranmer banned preaching on certain controversial subjects to try to keep the religious peace: purgatory was now the first subject on the list. (Shagan p.241)

Nevertheless it is true that within a year or two of Leeke's will, chantry foundations did become less common and there was a gradual move to leave money for other purposes such as setting up a school, without the chantry provisions that had commonly accompanied it in the past. What is clear is that from about the time of Leeke's will in 1508 and the reign of the new King Henry VIII from 1509, the requests to set up Chantries gradually diminished over the next 30 years. The number of educational clauses (though Leeke's was not strictly this) became a higher proportion of Chantry requests, with the idea of the priest performing two functions, praying and teaching.

However, Leeke's precise kind of insurance clause is uncommon and this has led to speculation. Did Leeke anticipate the death of Henry (who died the following year 1509) and wonder whether the new young King, Henry VIII, would change policy? No direct evidence exists. Alternatively did an increasingly tight-fisted Henry VII see in Chantry income something he could confiscate. But Henry VII strongly supported the Roman Catholic Church. However, what Henry was doing at the end of his reign was frequently refusing permission for mortmain licences, the income from which would no longer be taxable. So, it is most likely that this difficulty in obtaining these licences in the period 1505-09 explains the wording of the Will. Kreider refers to *Unprecedentedly onerous* mortmain fines from 1505.

This explanation has the advantage of tying in with the rarity of other wills with Leeke's kind of conditional clause as licences became easier after the death of Henry VII in 1509. The short-lived difficulties with obtaining the licences would not have produced many wills with this phrasing outside the 1505-09 period.[26] Once problems were overcome it would be easy to find a Chantry priest; clergy without a living were not uncommon and would welcome this opportunity for *security*.[27]

A Comparative Exercise

Most Grammar schools were founded on far more specific instructions than Leeke's for Nuneaton. For example in the same year 1507, a Chantry priest at Enfield was specifically instructed to teach pupils *to know and read their alphabet letters, to read Latin and English and understand grammar and to write their Latin according to the use and trade of Grammar Schools.*(Simon p.94) Kreider points out that *if they can obtain the King's licence* (p.84) was a phrase appearing more often in the 1505-1510 period. In 1509 we have a revealing example of a Chantry being endowed in a will with more complicated conditional clauses. A London grocer, Robert Beckingham, left money for a Chantry at St Olave's Church Southwark with the proviso that if one was not set up within two years of his death his executors could divert the money for a *free school* in Guildford. As the Chantry was not set up in Southwark the school in Guildford was indeed established in 1512. This re-enforces the idea that mortmain licenses were really difficult to obtain around 1505-09. Nuneaton and Guildford were both given King Edward re-foundations. Orme (*Medieval Schools* p.326) calls them the only schools founded by Edward VI not to have been *apparently* linked with Chantries but they were, though in an indirect way. The boys of the Guildford school were obliged to pray for Beckingham's soul, thus making the school a Chantry school and so vulnerable to closure in 1547. The nearest wording I have found to Leeke's is Henry Wormenstall at Newbury and Greenham back in 1466. After his request for a Chantry priest, he added that the feoffes (the Trustees administering the charity land) could *alter and change the same foundation from time to time as to their discretion should seem good.* (Leach p.114/5.)

C) The Dissolution Of The Chantry And The Start Of Nuneaton's First School. The Case For 1540/1.

The only basis for 1542 as the foundation year for the school was a phrase used by the Commissioners looking into the state of Chantries in 1548.[50] They would examine the source and value of the endowment and the case for provision of alternative income for any school, or other institution such as a hospital, and record their findings with a certificate. But income, if there was to be any, should come from a separate source. All Chantry money was to be confiscated even if the Chantry had been abolished within the last five years.[51] At this stage it was anything but clear if any monies would be returned for schools to continue. The phrase *vntill now* is ambiguous to our 21st Century ears here since clearly the Chantry had not existed for some time. However, despite this phrase it seems likely that *aboute* is being used in the old English sense of *outside of* meaning in effect *more than six years*.[54] The Shorter Oxford English Dictionary gives the first meaning of about as *on the outside of*. The earliest date of the second meaning, *somewhat near*, is given as 1567.

Saying the Chantry had not been in existence for *about* in the sense of almost exactly six years would not have impressed the Commissioners who had orders to seize the assets of any Chantry up to five years old (or five and a half years by the time they got round to actual inspections). The five years started on the first day of the current Parliament in 1547. To be precise *at any time within five years next before the fourth day of November last past if within five years before the first day of parliament they existed or were so applied.* (Leach p.66)

It would look conveniently co-incidental if not downright suspicious that it had been abolished just outside the confiscation deadline. More likely, the Commissioners are saying that they are satisfied that the Chantry has not been in existence for *at least* six years, using *About* in the sense of *outside of* (more) and it is therefore not within their remit to authorise the seizure of funds now being used for a useful purpose. Moreover, the fact that a school was already in existence with a small endowment satisfied them. There is an outside chance the Chantry survived altogether and escaped detection. The Constable rent roll (e.g. f36 p.66) records several pieces of land in 1543/4 as still occupied by the Chantry priest. *The Chantry priest of Etone hold freely land from the lord one tenement in the market place with garden now occupied by William Smythe.* While this might have been a historical turn of phrase for lands formerly used to finance the Chantry, and now financing a school, there is no reference to a school property.

Could it be that the Chantry still existed but was not disclosed by the inhabitants in 1548? The Chantry Commissioners in areas adjacent to Warwickshire were occasionally deceived, for instance in Gloucestershire, Oxfordshire and Staffordshire (Orme 320). Hidden Chantry properties were discovered in Yorkshire, Essex and Suffolk as late as the 1570s (Shagan p. 252). Interestingly these Chantry lands continued to be used as income, none being revived as they might have been in the time of Queen Mary after 1553. The system relied on the co-operation of local inhabitants. According to Orme the County Commissioners, whose recommendations were always accepted by Mildmay and Kelway, relied heavily on a *surveyor* a local man of standing, possibly a J.P. who used his knowledge of the area to compile an accurate report. But his *temptation to conceal information from the Crown was strong* (Orme 319) .

The continuation of the Chantry is therefore not an impossible scenario but it begs two major questions. How could both Chantry and School be funded from Leeke's small endowment? Also, it leaves uncertain what then happened eventually to the Chantry. On balance it seems likely that the Chantry was dissolved around 1540. Certainly many other Chantries were shut between the Dissolution of the Monastries in the late 1530s and the end of the Chantries in the late 1540s. Kreider refers to the *climate of uncertainty that people in all parts of the realm moved on their own initiative to dissolve intercessory institutions.* (Kreider p.157) Therefore the dissolution of the chantries *did not begin with the Chantries Acts of 1545 and 1547. Instead it began – unofficially – approximately a decade earlier with … piecemeal dissolutions* (Kreider p.154). Many of the other Chantries were shut for more selfish reasons than Nuneaton's. In Yorkshire there are examples of Chantries closing in 1537, 1539 and 1542 and three examples in Exeter in 1542. And there are other instances of early closure from Essex, Buckinghamshire and London. (Shagan pp243/4.) A few others in Warwickshire used their money for the wider benefit of the *Commonwealth*. Hampton in Arden constructed a bridge and Mancetter used the money to start a school (VCH Vol2 p.32).

D) The endowment of 1552

A.F. Leach in the Victoria County History of 1908, Nason in the School History 1936 and Reed Brett in the Centenary booklet 1952 all suggest the increased endowment for Nuneaton was due to John Dudley, Earl of Warwick (VCH2 p. 342/3, Nason *History* p.3 Reed Brett p.13). Elevated to become Duke of Northumberland in 1551 and the new Lord Protector of the boy King Edward VI, his power was clearly considerable. Nason argued that Northumberland *had been mainly instrumental in obtaining the School Charter.* However, this assertion lacks direct evidence. While it is true Northumberland held lands nearby in Worcestershire and Staffordshire, the more local lands acquired when he was made Earl of Warwick were quickly sold.

The powerful connection was more likely through Henry Grey, the Marquess of Dorset, who owned lands at nearby Astley, Weddington Castle, the dissolved priory lands at Arbury and some land in Nuneaton itself. (*Constable Rental* f10v p22a Duke of Suffolk one tenement one croft I dimidium (half) yerdland ,10/- see also further property on f27 p.63). Dorset – who became the Duke of Suffolk in 1551 – has been described as being at that time *the leading man in Warwickshire* (DNB article on *Dorset* by Robert C. Braddock) and was also the father of Lady Jane Grey who married Northumberland's son, Guildford Dudley. Northumberland was plotting to put Lady Jane on the throne after the death of Edward VI. He succeeded but she only lasted nine days. Until Dorset/Suffolk made a full recantation and renounced the Protestant faith in November 1553, his position was precarious.

APPENDIX 2

Nuneaton Grammar School Books of 1607

Title	Description
Macropedius	Georgius Macropedius was a Dutch humanist schoolteacher The book was probably his *Epistolica,* a textbook on letter writing, first published in London in 1576 and frequently reprinted, the last as late as 1649. The Stratford printer Richard Field is known to have issued some locally.
Sententiae Pueriles	Simple Latin sentences for pupils consisting of sayings of wise men in Latin first set down by Erasmus and collected in the 1540s by Leonhard Cullman, the English title page being *Sentences for Children English and Latine.* It was the first Latin book after an ABC in Latin.
Prymmers/ Psalters (3)	Henry Bynneman's work would have been used for service books and study of the Psalter, possibly to help the boys sing the services at St. Nicolas. Some early Primers contained an ABC, very elementary if it was in English but this might well have been in Latin.
Horn books	A *wooden tablet with a handle having on the wood a written or printed sheet containing the alphabet and covered by a sheet of transparent horn fastened to the Tablet.* Like many other educational materials of the time, Nuneaton's Horn Books would have been produced on license from John Wolfe (printer to the City of London) from 1587 to 1605 when his widow relinquished the claim and the monopoly was taken over by the Stationers' Company.
Five Grammars	Lily (see text)
Aesop's Fables	See Text

APPENDIX 3

Grammar Schools: Legal And Financial Difficulties Of The Early 17th Century

All sources taken from *Governors against Inge*, *Reay against Governors* and *Transcripts* unless otherwise stated.

For the Commission of Charitable Uses see the discussion in Tompson pp105-107.

A. The Governors' Dispute with Richard Inge and William Butterton

When the Governors dismissed Schoolmaster Inge, on grounds of inadequacy, the Schoolmaster fought back vigorously. He made legal counter-claims and accused the Governors of embezzlement. Given the amounts of money earned, and not spent on the school, it seems a plausible claim, but the Schoolmaster over-reached himself. Purely on grounds of inadequate salary Inge had a strong case. The profits from the endowment had continued to rise and were now nearing £100 annually, yet the Master's salary had always remained somewhere in the region of £10-£15. Had Inge focussed just on his right to a full salary he may have been more successful in taking on the Governors, as his successor, Antony Reay, was to show later.

Aided by Vicar Butterton, however, Inge went further. The arguments were complicated because of the continuing uncertainty surrounding the question of land ownership of a strip of Grammar School territory. Had the Grammar School encroached on to Church land when it expanded in 1595/6? It had apparently been settled at the time not only with the compensation to the then vicar to the tune of £5 (see main text) but also a rent of £1 a year paid to the church. But subsequent payment might be taken to imply ultimate church ownership of the land. Butterton claimed the right of ownership of the School and Inge the right to teach in it. Butterton's local origins made the Governors feel they had done him a favour in getting him the post of vicar of St. Nicolas which in view of the amount paid (c.£100 a year by this time) and its distinguished previous incumbents, was seen as a plum living. This made the dispute all the more bitter. However, it was not a unique case. The proximity of church and school lands gave rise to difficulties elsewhere. In 1651 at Repton School the occupant of an adjacent house complained about the noise under his window from 200 boys. He brought an action for trespass and then things

318

turned nasty with wall building, dumping of refuse and blows. (Vincent 1660-1714 pp139-40)

Inge's and Butterton's first legal action was their appeal locally to the Commission of Charitable Uses (Nason *History* p.15) to claim Inge's right to occupy the Schoolhouse as Master. These Commissions were appointed to hear cases by the Lord Chancellor under the Statute of Charitable Uses. Twelve jurymen from the County would investigate and issue an appropriate decree. An appeal could be made against their decision to the Lord Chancellor: these appeals became – as in the case of Nuneaton – very common. Because of the frequency of appeal the Commissions fell into disuse but this put the onus more directly on Chancery, increasing both its workload and its reputation for slowness.

The Commission found in favour of the Governors but it was clear that trust between the two sides had irretrievably broken down and there would be further legal appeals. Inge tried a second time to regain his position financially supported by townsman Richard Chamberlain. However, Sir Thomas Forster, a Justice in the Court of Common Pleas and a Warwick Judge of Assize, again found in favour of the Governors. John Suffolk junior and John Stratford were prominent in the defence of the Governors case; they were to pay for this later.

Inge's next move was to exploit his support from the Church by attacking his successor, Farmer, claiming his appointment was invalid. With Butterton's assistance, Inge persuaded the Bishop of Lichfield and Coventry to order an *Inhibition* whereby Farmer was forbidden to teach in the school. Technically all school appointments in the past should have had the Bishop's approval and Farmer's had not. In theory this form of Episcopal Licensing went on in endowed Grammar Schools until the1869 Endowed Schools Act but the regulations became more honoured in the breach than the observance. However, despite this, even in the early 17th Century it was seen as a serious enough omission to render any Governors' appointment without it invalid. As late as 1795 it was quoted in a legal case concerning appointment, *Rex v. Archbishop of York* (Barnard p.14). Legally speaking, then, the Bishop was on sound ground. However, he had not formally re-instated Inge (had **he** been approved by the Bishop when appointed?) and the Governors were hardly likely to want to let matters rest here.

If the Bishop was to be overruled, there was nothing for the Governors to do but to go to the very top, and appeal to the High Court of Chancery, which was effectively the final Court of Appeal on legal questions regarding schools of royal foundations. Here the tide turned again, for at considerable expense the Governors got something of what they wanted in 1611. The Governors obtained a similar *Inhibition* against Inge teaching as the Bishop had done against Farmer but without over turning the Bishop's ruling on Farmer. The legal case the Governors presented was wide-ranging and very involved. Statutes were cited going right back to the 9th year of the reign of Henry III (1225) concerning the rights of the individual and the early legal interpretations of Magna Carta (1215). The Nuneaton School Charter of 1552 was used to show the powers granted to the Governors to appoint and remove the Master. Governors claimed Inge's removal was valid. They also claimed that his replacement, Farmer, had been properly appointed as an M.A. *sufficiently learned in the Latin tongue* [to] *teach freely boys coming to the school.*

Now there was deadlock. No one had really benefitted from the legal battle. Neither teacher was legally employed and the Governors had spent a fortune – over £16 – on legal costs in Chancery. If they had spent a small fraction of this on increasing Inge's salary the problems might have been avoided. At this stage the Governors were having the best of the legal arguments. Between 1612 and 1614 Inge made two more attempts to regain his position: although unsuccessful, he put the Governors to further expense when they had to defend another action for legal confirmation of his claim to the schoolhouse.

Vicar Butterton continued to be a thorn in the flesh to the School Governors. There was a major clash over the choosing of Churchwardens between the pro and anti-Governor parties. Butterton was trying to impose his own choices, John Whylls and Edmund Buswell. The dispute of words became a fracas according to the Governors petition – with Whylls, Buswell and others attacking and striking the two Governors. Stratford's son was also assaulted. Butterton raided a chest located in the church but containing private school documents. The Governors expressed outrage at this, but it was no act of mindless vandalism. It enabled the Inge-Butterton anti-Governor party to acquire the legal information concerning the property investments and income of the School. The Governors petitioned the Court of Star Chamber in 1615 for the return, under oath, of the chest and its contents claiming that Butterton, Inge, nine other named people and *divers other evil disposed persons* had conspired against the Governors. They stood accused of *unlawfully and forcibly* [taking and carrying] *the said iron-bound chest...* [and] *riotously and unlawfully* forcing it open, removing the legal documents. The three locks would have three different key holders; this precaution was supposed to ensure that the opening of the chest would be with the consent of all interested parties. Such security usually worked; this time it didn't. The petition was granted, but by the time the stolen goods were returned, Vicar Butterton and his supporters had digested revealing contents and were shortly to use them to devastating effect.

B. The Governors Dispute with Anthony Reay and Richard Chamberlain

Although Reay had been offered more money than his predecessor, Inge, the study of the school accounts had convinced townsman Richard Chamberlain that Reay should demand still more salary. This may have been partly mischief-making but there was also some genuine concern that Governors had been feathering their own nest – and that of their friends – with the endowment money. As a result the Governors were *misapplying the endowment* and failing to make the most of it for the purpose for which it was supposed to be used according to the Edwardian letters patent– education of local boys in grammar.

A Bill of Complaint was made against the Governors. Financed by Chamberlain, this argued that Reay had security of tenure and his employment merely year by year was illegal: in addition, his salary should increase in proportion to the profits of the land. The only other valid use of the money was for maintenance and repair of the school. In January 1619 some ten years after the disputes had begun, the Governors, who had previously won most of the battles, now comprehensively lost the war that they were fighting for their rights. The information from the chest about the school's finances meant that the *misemployment* of the Governors was laid bare for all to see.

The ruling of the Lord Chancellor was a victory for Chamberlain and Reay's contention that all the profits of the endowment should go to the salary of the Master after any necessary maintenance and repairs *and to no other use* [and also] *that the said Governors should not misemploy the same.* This judgment was applied to future revenues but also *for such stocks of money which* **heretofore** [my emphasis] *have been raised by the Governors.* In addition, *Good orders may be made for the better government of the Schoolmaster and scholars and the disposing of the said rents and revenues for the maintenance of the said school.*

Clearly the contents of the chest had revealed misapplication of funds. Full details of the terms and conditions of all the leases had now to be given to the Chancery Court. One complaint against the Governors concerned the very low rents charged for leased property followed by a fine for the lease's renewal. Some *ancient tenants had been displaced and lands leased to others,* [sometimes] *near friends of the said defendants*, not quite jobs for the boys, but subsidised rents for their friends. This form of financing was not unusual but was clearly making inadequate use of substantial funds. Nor was the Court convinced by the Governors' excuse for this; that some of their property was Lammas Land* traditionally held as land with common rights of grazing at certain times of the year and so land for which they could not charge so much rent.

* Lammas (Loaf Mass) Land. Traditionally land from which on 1st August, Lammas Day, the first fruits of the harvest were donated to the church in the form of a loaf of bread from each parishioner – a kind of tithe – from the first crop of wheat. After 1st August for the rest of the year – and until the next sowing of wheat – tenants of Lammas land (who had rights of enclosure while their corn was grown) had to accept others grazing their animals on what had effectively reverted to *Common Land.*

On the other major question of the *security* of tenure, the judgement was equally emphatic. The Schoolmaster *shall have his place absolutely granted to him without any proviso bond or security.* This then not only ruled out a year by year contract but also outlawed dismissal by the granting of a gift to the Master before dismissing him. The judgement made it clear that the *tendering to him* [the Master] *a ring as had heretofore been used* was illegal. (We don't know with which Master or Masters this had been used). The only circumstances for removal would be for bad behaviour but even here the Bishop of Lichfield and Coventry had to approve of the sacking.

The judgement also touched on both the purpose of the school and the role of a *grammatical Usher*. An Usher could be appointed. However, *neither the master nor the Usher shall teach any scholars in that school other than Grammar scholars only.* Only those intending to stay and learn Latin would be accepted as pupils. The Master himself would decide if the *numbers warranted* an Usher.[36] Given the size and social composition of the town, it seemed unlikely that numbers for Latin would be very high. The increasing size of the school in former years had probably been caused by an increase in the *petties,* those young boys who would need more tuition in English before they could consider even elementary Latin. But the petties would frequently come – and then go – having obtained a short but free elementary education. Was this a valuable educational function that endowed schools such as Nuneaton could perform or was it against the legal stipulations of the Charter? Whether King

Edward's should provide an education for the non-Latin students was frequently to be argued over in the 17th, 18th and early19th Centuries (even when other schools developed an elementary education) until the question was eventually resolved by Latin ceasing to occupy such a dominating place in the educational curriculum of Grammar Schools.

C. And Elsewhere...

Nuneaton Governors were not unique or even unusual in misapplication of funds. In Birmingham in 1638 the Attorney-General accused the Governors of another King Edward's school of *a greedy and covetous desire to enrich themselves ... to the utter disherison [sic] and destruction of the said school*. (Trott p. 17) Problems re-surfaced later. In 1711 the Master alleged the Birmingham Governors had *lavished away great and unnecessary sums in re-building* (Vincent 1660-1714 pp 179-187). In other places too problems lasted even longer than in Nuneaton as in Bath where the mismanagement was not discovered until 1735 when the revenue was described as *notoriously mismanaged, neglected, misconverted and misapplied*. Nor were Nuneaton matters ever quite as bad as at East Retford where in 1699 it was exposed that since 1670 the annual revenue had been over £145 but the Master's salary just £29. But Nuneaton's Governors do not come out well. In contrast, the Master at Blackburn attributed his good salary to the *Faithfull* improvement of the school income by the Governors.

A grammar school still held out opportunities to children of prosperous artisans because it could at best give them a classical education on a par with that received by landed gentry. N. Hans *New Trends in Education in the C18th* (1984) suggests many of the aristocracy and not a few landed gentry were still having their sons privately educated. Few academies were developed before the Dissenting ones of the 18th Century.

Certainly the 17th Century was a time when a wide range of endowed Grammar Schools were sending pupils to Oxbridge. For instance, St John's, Gonville and Caius, Christ's and Peterhouse took boys from 857 different Grammar Schools between 1600-1660. (Vincent 1660-1714 pp208/9) At this time about a thousand boys went up each year but this was halved in the later part of the century.

Nuneaton Grammar School's finances recovered from the legal expenditure of the 1610s, but by the time of the outbreak of Civil War in 1642 there was a further strain on many school endowments. Fighting costs and poor harvests generally led to falling rents and high prices in the late 1640s. Nationally there was frequently a drop in endowment values as rental payment could be easily disrupted. The Commissioners for Charitable Uses would try to preserve school endowments from sequestration but there was no guarantee they would always be successful. However, after 1644 schools were exempted from rate assessment and, with state ownership of church lands, money to the tune of £18,000 went to support schoolmasters and preaching Ministries after 1649. Some schools remained in difficulty. Preachers may well have received the lion's share of this largesse. Unfortunately we lack Nuneaton school records for the period of Civil War fighting. A Commission of Charitable Uses was set up to investigate the situation at Rugby school in 1653 where the Master was in serious pay arrears and the buildings *in need of urgent repair* (Vincent 1640—1660 p.51).

APPENDIX 4

The Case against Trevis 1667
A. Testimonies

(All these testimonies are in *Governors against Trevis* also clarified on occasions by Nason *Transcripts*)

Joseph Copson complained about the treatment of his son.
Last February Trevis Master of the Grammar School did so beat and abuse his son about the head that the blood came out of his nose and mouth.

William Morris and his wife
do affirm that their sonne William was … abused and beaten about the head … [he] could eat nothing but liquids that were purposely made for him from Tuesday that he was soe hurt until the Friday night following.

Roger Willis, a former pupil, asserted that Trevis
Whipped me so cruelly by giving me about 20 lashes at a time that I fell down from the boys back twice… He hath several times pulled me out of the school by the hair and then threatened me so much about the head with his fists that I shall never recover myself to be free from such a cruel pain in my head which was occasioned by his misusage of me.

Thomas Hill interestingly used identical wording and added he had seen Trevis attack Roger Willis at the same time. Trevis, he claimed, had *several times come into the school full of beare and then without cause hath abused me and others.*

John Wright swore that, eighteen months previously, his son John was whipped until *as the boys said, the blood dript from his tayle to his shoes and he was soe sore that he could neither sit nor lie in his bed.* It took him a fortnight to recover.

Mr. Copson pointed out that his son
was unfit for business for some months after.

Luke Mortimer, told of Trevis being *so full of beere that he hath fallen down upon the town bridge.*

He was no friend of Trevis to be sure, but others had a similar tale. William Pigott testified that *Mr. Trevis two several nihjts together in one alehouse he sett both nyhts until clear daylight he went away…much inflamed with liquor.*

Trevis was so drunk he was unable to stand up. **John Drakeley's** evidence is almost illegible now but the word *alehouse* clearly appears in it.

Though these incidents may have been out of hours, this would not have been regarded as behaviour irrelevant to his performance as a schoolmaster. Besides, **Mr. Piggot** added that Trevis had also been *playing at bowles amidst scholars who should have been at school.*

Many found Trevis' whole manner highly offensive. **Roger Willis** asserted that some boys were not attacked for bad behaviour but for no reason (other perhaps than Trevis' inebriation). Trevis had *most shamefully abused the boys by pulling them up and down by the hair and hitting them about the head and that he hath whipped them so much that they have been fayned to pull the twigs out of their britch.*

His violent behaviour was not confined to the students. When in Wiliam Rason's house Trevis took exception to a request for money from a Mr. Sprote. As **Francis Friswell** testified: *Trevis put on his coate and cloake and came down out of the room in which he was shut the street doore and fell upon Mr. Sprote as he sat at the fire and then abused him by pulling him by the hair and fighting with him in so much that if I had not been there, there might have been manslaughter and Mrs. Rason might have been hurt because she was thrown down by them.* [32]

B. The Governors case against Trevis

Charge one asserted *that his cruel and hard usage of the Schollars hath driven almost all the scholars away insomuch that they are fallen from 100 to 20 and scarce so many.*

Charge two (part one)
 That he seldom or never comes to Church with his scholars as the order directeth [Given Trevis' bad relations with vicar Richard Pyke this is hardly surprising].

Charge two (part two) that the conduct of those boys that were left was poor *with horrible cursing and swearing…besides other rudeness, as not giving respect to their superiors.*

Charge three said *that contrary to the patents he hath demanded and actually received several pounds of money for admittance as well as fining for non-attendance.*
[The idea of a free education was still taken seriously or at the very least an infringement of the rules which could be used as a stick with which to beat Trevis.]

Charge Four stated *That he never used prayers in the school, according to the orders.*[39]

Charge five *That he hath several times debauched himself with excessive drinking so much that he hath not been able to teach and neglects his school by frequenting of Bowling alleys.*

Charge six He was also accused of refusing *to teach several men's children* and *that he speaks contemptuously of the Governors and hath denied their authority.*

APPENDIX 5

How typical were the problems of Nuneaton Grammar School 1660-1700?
A. The tradition of shutting out

This may have started with the demand for pre-Christmas jollifications. This could explain why St Andrew's Day, 30th November, was a traditional day for these festivities. It was widely accepted and revived considerably after the Restoration. But even moderate Puritan writers did not disapprove. A distinguished Master and serious writer on education such as Charles Hoole in *A New Discovery of the Old Art of Teaching School* (1660) felt this was *a custom that could safely be retained as long as the Master is warned beforehand and the boys behave themselves merrily and civilly.*

The barring out was sanctioned by statute at Witton (Norfolk) where *they bar and keep forth of the school the schoolmaster, in such sort as other scholars do in the great schools* (Brown p.122). In some parishes there was the tradition of *potation pence* where money would be used to supply the schoolmaster with drink. But this does not appear to have been necessary in Trevis' case as he seems to have had all too much access to alcohol. However, at times the privilege was abused. For example, at King Edward's Birmingham Grammar School on 26th November 1667 pupils not only barred their Master from entering but in a seemingly similar incident to Nuneaton's at a similar time *threatened him with pistols and for the space of two hours made such attempts by casting in stones and bricks, as well as breaking the wall and wainscot of the said school, as might endanger his life.* (Resolution of Birmingham School in Carlisle Vol 2 p.632 Quoted in Cressy p. 93. See also Trott p.22).

The custom continued throughout the century. In 1690 Manchester Grammar School Master William Barrow was kept out of the school for a fortnight (Vincent 1660-1714 p.66). The case bears resemblance to Nuneaton with food and ammunition – which was actually used – being passed to the boys by their supporters in the area. In 1685 Coventry Corporation ordered the dismissal of Samuel Frankland, Master of King Henry VIII School, because of continual problems with shutting out. Nonetheless Franklin survived a further six years. Later generations looked on the practice less favourably. Dr. Johnson later referred to it (1779) as *a savage licence* practiced till about 1700.

B. Grammar School decline in the Warwickshire, Leicestershire and Staffordshire area in the late 17th Century

After 1660 it became less fashionable to leave money for the benefit of endowed schools and in Nuneaton's case not surprising. Significantly, when the Governors were entrusted with money by one of their own, it was not directly for the school. In 1677 Richard Orton gave to his fellow governors of Nuneaton Grammar School some land then let at £3 per annum for the use of twelve poor men. This charity continued to be administered for the next 300 years.

Other schools suffered both financially and personally. The normally steady Ashby Grammar school went through a period of difficulty between 1655 and 1668 including an enquiry in 1657 to *redress the misemployment of lands goods and stocks of money* (Fox Ashby pp.48/9). Sometimes the Civil War had an adverse effect. At Rugby when Raphael Pearce ceased to teach shortly before his death in 1651, the school buildings were dilapidated and *the schoole house end in all his tyme was stopped with straw to keepe out rain and wind* (Vincent 1640-1660 p.40, quoting Rouse. School beams and benches were broken up to provide the master with firewood. A Commission of Charitable Uses was issued out of Chancery and an inquiry was held into the affairs of the school in 1653.(Vincent 1640-1660 p.51). Their troubles continued: between 1683 and 1686 only 3 boys entered the school, though by the 1690s it was starting to recover under Henry Holyoake, Master from 1688. (Rowse p.88)

The only schools with a decent reputation near Nuneaton were Ashby, whose fortunes under Samuel Shaw, Master from 1669 to 1696 were as great as Nuneaton's under Trevis were disastrous, and Tamworth where George Antrobus' move from Chester attracted pupils from Staffordshire, Leicestershire and Warwickshire. (Joan Simon Town Estates and Schools in the 16th and 17th Century (p.45) in Brian Simon (ed.) *Education in Leicestershire*.) Between 1660-1679 Tamworth School sent at least 13 students to just four Cambridge Colleges. (VCH Vol2 p.346.) Nuneaton sent none.

Nuneaton's weakness stimulated competition. In 1686, in the later period of Trevis' inactivity, another Grammar School was formed in North Warwickshire at Kingsbury by Thomas Coton. He wanted a conscientious teacher and specifically desired that a clerical Head spend most of his time on the task of teaching and *to exercise the Ministry but very seldom.* Some of the schools being founded at this time were focused solely on basic 3Rs for the poor but Kingsbury included Latin in their curriculum as well as *The*

Bible The Accounts Latin and a good secure hand. (A. Smith p.10.) For the foundation of Apppleby Magna School in the 1690s see main text p.73

It was not only Midland schools that encountered difficulty in the mid 17th Century. Hull Grammar School numbers declined from 100 in 1629 to 29 in 1680. (Lawson 103)

C. Why were Midland schools attractive to some northern teachers?

Moving south from Lancashire and Cheshire seems to have occurred frequently because those counties had been particularly affected by contractual arrangements whereby a Master was given a fixed salary. For example, George Antrobus, who came to Tamworth from Chester (see B above), might have known the Liptrotts and so have been aware of the situation in Nuneaton.

The fixed salary was unrelated to income from any lands owned and their salary had frequently remained very low. In 1658 William Liptrott in Lancashire was receiving £40 a year, considerably less than Trevis, and there is evidence from this year and 1678 that his salary was not always paid on time; so the security (as much as the higher income) of the Nuneaton post would have been attractive to his son. (Evidence in Chester and Cheshire archives ZA/B/2/122v-123 9th Sept., 1658 and ZA/B/2/188 7th June, 1678 A to A)

So it is likely James Liptrott was attracted by the higher salary offered in Nuneaton; for their part the Governors would see him as a completely fresh start after the disasters of the Trevis era.

APPENDIX 6

Smith's Charity School

Smith's Charity School possessed properties in Stockingford, Hartshill and Ansley as well as a house in Coton. The salaries would be a good deal less than King Edward's with £15 for the Master and £11 for the Mistress. A 21st Century audience might disapprove of the much lower salary for the elementary Schoolteachers than at the Grammar School and of the smaller wage for the same work for the Mistress as compared to the Master. Contemporaries however, would have noted different points: firstly that there was a school at all for those children outside the social milieu of the Grammar School, and secondly that it provided – for the first time – a chance for girls from the Nuneaton area to acquire an education. That Education – up to an elementary level at least – was seen by many as of benefit for all children although others felt it might give them ideas above their station. So, this education was not to aspire children to a reach high level but rather fit them for the social position they would expect to occupy in life. This assumption would limit the numbers likely to move on to the Grammar School.

The Charitable origins and social aims of the Smith's Foundation were apparent when it outlined that: *Preference shall be given* [to] *such persons who are least capable of paying for the schooling of their children especially of such who receive alms or collections of the said parish, before the children of such who are more capable of paying.*

The statutes were Anglican. Queen Anne's reign (1702-1714) had seen a great number of schools of this type founded in reaction to the setting up of Dissenting academies which had appeared in considerable numbers in the late 17th century. The Academies had taken advantage of the Toleration Act of 1689, when Nonconformists, excluded from the educational and religious establishment restored in 1660, now became free to set up their own educational institutions.

Therefore the main aims of Smith's School were inculcation of Christian principles for the poor, learning in a *Fair and legible hand the four rules of arithmetic,* addition, subtraction, multiplication and division. These Charity schools were seen as the only way in many towns to perform this function until the development of the Sunday

School movement at the end of the 18th Century which often provided a similar basic education and caused a decline in the number of charity day schools. However, Smith's continued to function through the 19th Century even surviving the establishment of four Church schools in the late 1840s and the 1870 Education Act. This was not a rival school to King Edward's but rather a complement to it serving a poorer section of the community (at a more elementary level) in an increasingly class conscious age.

APPENDIX SEVEN

The Apprenticeship System: Who Was Involved? How Did It Work?

The 25 different occupations to which the Apprentices were put out were those that maintained the traditional system:

Tailors	10
Cordwainers	9
Carpenters/Joiners	7
Butcher/Baker/Grocer	7
Blacksmiths	5
Weavers	3
Wheelwrights	3
Stonemason	2

At one or two a year this, though revealing, does not tell us about the mass of students. There were five Apprentices whose father was a labourer and for these boys the scheme opened up the possibility of acquiring a skill and advancing socially. This was only just over 10% of the total, a degree of social mobility provided by the school, though very modest and limited. The skilled working class provided 22 of the boys and small businesses ten, including four innkeepers. One Master of Smith's Charity School, Nathaniel Parnell, was successful in the Apprenticeship application for his son.

How far did the scheme take the boys away from the town? Around 22 stayed in Nuneaton or its environs, (such as Attleborough) a similar number remained in Warwickshire in what we might now term the industrial West Midlands, Birmingham (6) Coventry (4) as well as the odd one going to Walsall and Dudley. Fourteen found their way into Leicestershire including six to Hinckley but only two further afield than this one to Sheffield as an apprentice cutler soon after the restrictions on entering this trade from the outside were removed in 1814; just one went to London. Other places included Kenilworth, Keresley and Atherstone.

The total number of Apprentices in the whole of Nuneaton between 1705 and 1834 was 783 (Lane Volume 1 p.27). Joan Lane points out that the idea of Half Apprentices developed in North Warwickshire ribbon weaving towns (p.92). Grammar School Apprentices seem typical of the town as a whole. My analysis of how far the Grammar School Apprentices stayed in Nuneaton produced 22 staying out of 64, just over a third (34.4%). This is almost an identical result to Lane's analysis of all Nuneaton's Apprentices when she says *Even an area as distressed ... as Nuneaton kept over a third (34.1%) of its Apprentices.* (Lane p. 123)

Only rarely do we have a record of how well these apprentices fared: for instance there was an alleged beating of an apprentice at Hinckley in 1850, and Governors investigated. This at least shows some concern with the aftermath but the example is very late, coming at a time when the Governors were about to end the system. In 1851 one applicant to take apprentices was refused on the grounds he ran a public house: yet less than ten years earlier publican Benjamin Rayner had still been the Undermaster. The scheme was fading. At the end of 1851 the Governors declined to offer any Apprentices stating, officially, economic grounds. Yet, rather than financial stringency, it was social change, including the demise of apprenticeships offered, that had led to its demise. Just two boys applied in 1854 but then the decision was made that no more were to be placed out. It was also a case of choosing to spend the money on other things such as French teaching which started in 1853 though the aim was to make this self-financing – and prizes for pupils. In February 1853 the Minutes record £25 donated to St Nicolas for Church extensions: While this donation had the advantage of obtaining guaranteed sittings available for the Master and private boarders, it does not suggest financial penury.

APPENDIX EIGHT

A The Legal Complication In Changing The Grammar School Curriculum 1760-1840

There was no general public legislation regarding endowed Grammar Schools in the 18th Century though private acts to amend school statutes were possible if expensive. The *Visitor* in the guise of the local Bishop had the power to alter regulations but this rarely occurred by this time. The Court of Chancery was the judicial authority. The Attorney-General, the legal officer of the crown, had a general responsibility in cases concerning charities. He could initiate proceedings in Chancery if malpractice was suspected. Again this was infrequent.

Joan Simon refers to the educational trend in Grammar Schools towards two separate schools often developing a classical school under the chief schoolmaster and a lower or English school under the Usher. The later could divide into a reading and writing school while the classical school had very few pupils. She writes of the state of the Grammar schools after 1780: *In general it appears that where the schools were governed by independent Trustees* [as was Nuneaton] *the situation was one of decay and even disintegration* (Simon *Town Estates and Schools* p.131). Oundle with no pupils in 1791 had 45 the following year by introducing a mixed curriculum. Manchester Grammar School offered two kinds of courses and Burton on Trent had a wide range of courses by 1814. In Rugby numbers rose from 66 in 1778 up to 245 in 1794. While many factors were at work here it was done on a *modified classical curriculum.* (O'Day pp.200-03)

Leeds Grammar School wished to widen their curriculum which had been restricted to the classics by the wording of the Foundation. Lord Eldon's judgement indicated that any clearly expressed wishes of the Founder of an Endowment could not be overridden. While he also suggested a gradual introduction of other subjects as well as Greek and Latin was perfectly legal, it was the first part of his judgement that received the most publicity. Tompson (*Classics or Charity*) argues that Eldon's verdict was not as disastrous for change as it has been portrayed. Certainly a good number of schools such as Nuneaton were introducing a range of other subjects and, while maintaining a classical element, did not necessarily teach this to all scholars. Only after legislation in 1840 were all restrictions on what could be taught in an endowed grammar School unambiguously removed (Roach 89). Sir Eardley Wilmot's Act gave the Courts more general powers to change school statutes and to enlarge the range of subjects taught. There was local interest in new buildings and new schemes of management. Provision could be laid down for an annual examination of the school.

B The General Extent Of The Crisis In Grammar Schools In The Late Eighteenth Century.

There is some controversy over just how poor a state Grammar Schools were in at the end of the 18th Century. The much quoted Lord Chief Justice Kenyon referred in 1795 to *empty walls without scholars and everything neglected except the receipts of salaries and emoluments* (Barnard p.16.). However, more recent authorities such as Tompson dispute how universally true this was.

As to the cause Tompson attacks the older writer Leach's pre-occupation with *long scholastic reigns* which *we are to believe* says Tompson doubtfully, *presupposes an aged and … incompetent officeholder who, it is inferred, causes the school to decline with him.* (Tompson p.9) Yet in Nuneaton's case there is evidence that with Liptrott, Leach was correct. In other towns there were some great long reigns by distinguished Masters in the 19th Century but Liptrott and, later, Hughes were operating at a considerable age towards the ends of their Masterships: it was taking its toll.

Liptrott's 55 years as Master is particularly long even in an age when 40 year Masterships were not uncommon. Henry Allen at Charlbury for 53 years (1680-1733), John Graile at Guildford School 52 years (1646-1698) and Joseph Dale 49 years at Stockport (1703-1752) nearly match it (Vincent 1660-1714 pp.118/9). Only John Etcholls (Wase) at Mottram Grammar School (1608-1670) seems to be longer and this was in the previous century.

Hughes' decline in the second half of his Mastership (c. 1810-1830) has some similarity with Nuneaton's larger neighbours. Hughes' contemporary John Cooke, Head of King Edward's Birmingham (1798-1834), oversaw a flourishing boarding house decline to just one boy and discipline was so lax that local constables had to be called in on occasions. Cooke's over-zealous corporal punishment and poor health in his later years did not help his reputation and the school suffered accordingly. At Coventry (King Henry VIII) Grammar School, William Brooks was Head from 1779, the year Hughes came to Nuneaton (though not yet to the Grammar school), until 1833. After 1802 Brookes seems to have ceased teaching and all the work was done at a lower level by the Usher. (Trott pp49-51, Marson, Metcalf and Burton p.25) Where there was no Usher, as at Ashby Grammar School, the similarly ancient John Prior, Master 1763-1803 found himself in failing health with just 3 or 4 boys shortly before his death. (Fox Ashby p 63-4).

APPENDIX NINE

The Liptrott Era. How many boys attended and from what social groups?
J.F Pound (p.14) points out that the intake of a Grammar School in a rural landed area such as Bury St Edmunds in Suffolk (where only 20% were artisans and tradesmen) would be very different from one in Manchester (Manchester Grammar School). The better off in Nuneaton were frequently not landowners but modest tradesmen (see Peter Whyley moving to Birmingham in Chapter Five). The population of Nuneaton in 1750 is uncertain though 50 years later it was about 4,000 and estimating about a third under 15 and perhaps a sixth between 7 and 15 years old there could have been approaching 1000 children of these ages. These figures are very approximate but it is clear that only a small percentage of children were attending school and even fewer numbers the Grammar School. Veasey estimates 120 at Smith's and 140 at Coton in the early 19th Century and certainly less in the mid 18th when these schools had only just become established.

On this very rough calculation the percentage of children attending school in Nuneaton may have been very approximately between five and ten but possibly less in 1750. This ties in with W.B. Stephens' estimates that (p21) in c.1750 some 4% of the total population were attending school. This would mean no more than 300 children at the very most between all schools in Nuneaton and neighbouring Chilvers Coton. Moreover, all the ones we know, admittedly atypical, came from Leicestershire so how many were attending from North Warwickshire? Were there very few? Were they there but not aiming for or failing to get into Oxbridge? Was Thomas Liptrott running a school for sons of Leicestershire gentlemen including clergy with ambitions for their sons? Since Liptrott had no Usher it is unlikely that the number of non-Latin scholars was large as they would have distracted him from his more advanced teaching.

APPENDIX TEN

Nuneaton Grammar School. Revised Scheme of Government: 1876

There were fundamental alterations to the composition of the Governing body
- Two nominated by Magistrates to serve six years.
- Five co-opted members appointed by the Governors to serve eight years.
- Five Representative Governors, elected by the Ratepayers of the ancient parish of Nuneaton and two by parents of boys on the roll at least one year before the election.

Government and Finance was to be organised and open:
- **They would meet a minimum of twice a year in Nuneaton** with a quorum of four and just two were required to summon a special meeting, the Chairman having the casting vote (a fact that was soon to be significant).
- **A Minute book** and Annual accounts were to be kept with an annual abstract published in a local paper (it was, in the Nuneaton Chronicle).
- A clerk was to be appointed .
- There would be an annual inspection.

Only the emboldened points had applied before.

There would be no ambiguity regarding the position of the Headmaster
- He now had to be a graduate of *an Imperial University*.
- There would be six months notice of dismissal.
- He could take boarders at his discretion.
- He could *dwell in the residence assigned.*

The precise relationship between the Governors and the Master was now clarified. The governors would decide:
- Curriculum.
- Terms and Hours.
- Number of Assistant Masters.

The curriculum would be widened. While the Headmaster would decide the precise details it should include:
- Reading and Writing, Maths and Arithmetic.

- Geography and History.
- English Grammar, Composition and Literature.
- Latin and One Modern European Language.
- Drawing, Vocal Music and Drilling.

The school would be less definably Anglican: local objectors had been defeated on these points.
- The Headmaster did not have to be in Holy Orders.
- He did not have to be Anglican. There was to be no religious discrimination relating to staff or pupils.
- The Bishop's rights would only be exerted through the Charity Commissioners.

Fees could now be charged and a minimum Entrance Standard was to be set
- Entrance and tuition fees were fixed by the Governors at between £5-10 a year. There were to be no extras and no discrimination between pupils.
- Nonetheless it was open to all boys so some scholarships could be offered, both Exhibition scholars and Foundation scholars. With the latter no more than 10% could have all fees exempted.
- Three exhibitions were awarded for local boys aged between 12-14.

The delay until 1876 was explained by Viscount Sandon Vice-president of the Committee of the Council of Education in answer to a question from Gloucester M.P. Charles Monk. (Monk's interest may have been that he was Hugh Hughes' grandson). Sandon replied:

The scheme for the Nuneaton Grammar School was approved by the Committee of Council on Education, according to ordinary practice, on the 17th of April, 1875. It was then, under the Act, obliged to be advertized for two months, and a Petition having been presented, it was laid upon the Table of both Houses at the earliest moment—that is to say, the 24th of June, 1875. The Session closed before the two months had expired during which it had to lie on the Table of both Houses, and therefore it has again to remain on the Table of both Houses for two months during this Session, at the end of which time, unless either House should address Her Majesty against it, it will receive the Royal Assent.

Hansard: vol 228 cc701-2 House of Commons Debates 28 March 1876

APPENDIX ELEVEN

Social Background Of The Pupils At The End Of The 19th Century

Town growth had a major impact on the type of pupil attending the Grammar School. Hat Manufacturers Hall and Phillips moved from Atherstone to Abbey Mills in 1885, Lister's Mill branched out from Bradford in 1895, nine new collieries opening in the area between 1855 and 1904, coal production increasing tenfold and also rising employment in the brick and tile firms of the Stanley brothers and James Knox, and the textile factory of Fielding and Johnson. (Veasey Chapter 11) So, the children of industrialists Johnson, Clay, Slingsby, Gibberd, Stanley, Melly and Townsend, joined sons of professionals Nason and Cookson medical, Iliffe and Lester pharmaceutical, and Oakey legal (Admissions).

Those with a coal-mining background were less prominent but William B. Cocks, future solicitor and Chairman of the School Governors was the son of a colliery agent. Sons of the cloth were particularly numerous, Deed, Waters and De Havilland, as well as sons of Anglican clergy from other areas including the Fishers from Higham on the Hill. The school remained distinctively Christian with an ordained Headmaster. However, it was not exclusively Anglican. Herbert and Alfred Bunting – two of the original boys entering the new school in 1880 were sons of the Abbey Street Wesleyan Methodist Minister James Bunting. Baptist Minister's son David Asquith also attended. The school was no longer a free one for poor children as it had once – though not necessarily accurately – seen itself (Admissions and Census of 1881).

The Inspection in 1892 did an analysis of the boys fathers' occupations: exactly half of the 60 pupils came from solidly professional, manufacturing or farming homes while the remainder were *lower professional, managers and shopkeepers* . Seven boys had no father living and were probably the beneficiaries of the scholarships. The period between 1880, when fees were imposed, and 1904-7 when Scholarships increased, is likely to have been the least socially mixed period since the 18th Century. However, a few scholarships did provide opportunities for some with working class backgrounds (1892 Inspection).

One boy who attended was Arthur Stanley, the son of Jacob Stanley, a Cambridge graduate and artist living in Newdegate Square; sometimes boys came from further afield. Dudley Baxter, a solicitor from Atherstone sent his son of the same name. Farmers' sons came such as Joseph Henry Clay, son of Joseph Hood Clay. One effect of the introduction of some science lessons is shown as Clay junior became a Chemist's assistant in Birmingham. The range of possible occupations was widening at the end of the century. However, even if children were destined for the family business, a good formal education was increasingly deemed essential. Hence one pupil was William Cawthorne, (see Chapter 9) son of the eponymous Nuneaton bookseller and printer who had come from Grantham in the 1860s and established a business still running in the 21st Century. Leslie Oldham, the pupil who received a thorough ducking in 1879 (see Chapter Eight) took up farming in the Barford area of Warwickshire – as had his father. (Admissions, and Census of 1881 and 1891)

The liberal humanistic side of education was not ignored. In 1886 J.F.W. Johnson, destined for a technical education, achieved a distinction in philosophy in his Cambridge local exams. In 1890 he passed out of his training at the Royal Artillery Woolwich, the Royal Military Academy training artillery officers and engineers. He was top student with a Commission in the Royal Engineers and prizes for Fortification, Tactics, Topography, Chemistry and Physics. He was a Pollock gold medallist, a prize for the best cadet of the season. (Memorabilia)

Pupil Teachers

A good example of the widening social intake was Harry Goode. Harry was born in Handsworth, Birmingham as Harry King. He was adopted by Bulkington couple Thomas and Margaret Goode and came as a Town Scholar in September 1907 at the age of 14, nearing 15, having initially been to school in Bulkington and then Queen's Road School in Nuneaton under the pupil teacher scheme. His schooling was free; indeed he was paid £10 a year for attending and working satisfactorily, provided that afterwards he taught in a local authority school for at least a year. Some boys did just this and then took up another job as Goode did in 1912 at Alfred Herbert's tool making factory in Coventry. Where Goode was perhaps less typical was in his distinctive and distinguished First World War record as a pilot before dying in a plane crash in 1942 at the age of 49. (www.66squadron.co.uk)

Some of the pupil teacher education proved directly beneficial to the town. Ernest Randle began as a Pupil Teacher at Queen's Road before moving to King Edward's. Subsequently he taught at Fitton Street School and retired as Head of Alderman Smith school, Nuneaton in 1961. Charles Streather went as one of the first scholarship pupils in 1907. Then he became a pupil teacher at Queen's Road before going to St Mark's Coventry and eventually Saltley Training College. He also became a local Headmaster, at Higham Lane School. (Observer 9.3.1962 and Beryl Kerby)

In 1911 the school decided to abolish the 7/6d entrance fee, thus widening access to the school still further.

APPENDIX TWELVE

Masters

c.1540-1552	?? William Molysidyall, Chantry priest (pre Edwardian endowment)
1552-1558	?
1558	Henry Greene*
1559	Ellyot
1559-60	Walton
1560	Sadler
1560/1	Harmon
1561	Leven
1562	Walker
1563	Betts
1563	Nicholas Cleyton*
1565	Bowley
1567	Donner
1575	'Discharge of a Schoolmaster not thought sufficient'
1575	Downes
1579	Burton
1584	Yates
1586	Heath
1595	Richard Inge
1611	William Farmer
1614	Anthony Reay
1624	Zachary Perkins*
1625	Josiah Packwood*
1640	William Barford
1656	William Trevis^
1695	James Liptrott
1712	William Liptrott*
1732	Thomas Liptrott*
1788	Thomas Trusswell (technically remained Undermaster but ran the school single-handed for six years).
1794	John Spencer Cobbold*
1799	Hugh Hughes*

1830	Thomas Docker*
1842	William Bucknill*
1873	George Eustace*
1880	Samuel George Waters*
1909	Albert Basset Holman
1929	Arthur Simpson Pratt
1944	Sidney Reed Brett (Acting)
1945	Donald Cameron Whimster
1951	Thomas Sumner
1962	Derek Usherwood
1967	Rowland Brown

* Known for certain to be ordained ^ Ordained deacon but not priest.

Ushers/Undermasters

1567	Marmaduke Vyncent
1568	Hues
1568	Robert Chaplyn
1581	William Knight
1584	Thomas Breamer
c.1590	Edward Launder (Reference in VCH Vol 2)
c. 1595	Edward Pynne, referred to as *a schoolmaster* in Nuneaton in 1597, is mentioned in Smyth's 17th Century Berkeley Manuscripts in 1597 as *a lewd and factious knave* mixed up with Roman Catholic spies. I am grateful to Trevor Carpenter for this reference.
1597	David Wight (mentioned in CCEd but no other reference). He may have replaced the disgraced Pynne as Usher in this year.

For about 100 years from about 1600 to 1693 there is no record of an Usher being employed though there may have been some in the early seventeenth century

| 1693-5 | John Holmes |

The three Liptrotts from 1695-1788 declined to appoint an Usher, or Undermaster, as they were now called.

1788	Thomas Trusswell
1801	William Green
1802	Benjamin Rayner
1843	Suffolk

1846	George Perry
1850	Beckwith
1850	Charles Thomas Pizey*
1851	Thomas Ainsworth
1854	Ainsworth, brother of Thomas
1856	John Barker Bryant*
1861	George Perry (for a second time)
1863	Edwin Shufflebotham*
1865	George Eustace*
1873-4	James Ridgeway Hakewill*
1875-1880	Two unnamed Assistants to Eustace, now Master

Sources: Nason, Venn, Testimonial Evidence WCRO ED27 5040 6/7/61

~~~~~

After 1880 the School employed a number of Assistant Staff. The concept of a Second Master (or Deputy Head) was to develop.

Second Masters

c. 1904	Albert Basset Holman
1909	William Walpole Day
1933	Sidney Reed Brett
1954	Harry Branston
1966	Harold Fisher

Ushers' pay in the 16th Century

1567	Marmaduke Vynsent £1
1568	Mr. Hues 7/- Robert Chaplyn 10/-
1569	Robert Chaplyn £2-10/-
1571	Ambrose Vynsent 10/-
1572-3	Unnamed probably Robert Chaplyn £3
1574	The Masters salary fell £1 to £11 and the Usher's rose £1 to £4 until 1581
1581	£5 shared between Robert Chaplyn and William Knight
1582	Wiliam Knight £4- 15/-
1584	Thomas Breamer £4

Select Bibliography

Primary Sources

Warwick County Record Office (King Edward VI School Nuneaton Archive)
Mainly H1, CR 2730 and CR 4232

H1/3 Conveyance by William Bywarke of Noneton, belman, to John Leke, William Milwarde and others of a messuage in Nuneaton in *le Chircheynd*.

H1/19 Conveyance by the trustees of Nuneaton Almshouse Charity Estate to the Governors of the Grammar School of the almshouse building and site adjoining the churchyard 12 July 1862.

H1/22 Translation of the school letters patent of Edward VI. (Undated early 18th Century).

H1/24 Accounts of the school bailiffs 1560-1588.

H1/25 Accounts of the Governors for building new school 1595-1599.

H1/26 Account book and ledger of the Governors 1780-1870.

H1/30 Governors' minute book 1846-1871.

H1/32 Disputes between the Governors and Richard Inge, schoolmaster, and between Inge and Richard Farmer, schoolmaster.

H1/33 John Suffolke and others of the Governors against Humphrey Tompson and John Muston, churchwardens, William Butterton, vicar, and others, in the Star Chamber c. 1615-1617.

H1/34 Richard Chamberlayne and Anthony Reay, schoolmaster, against Richard Ford, John Wright, John Stratford and others of the Governors, in the Court of Chancery.

H1/35 The Governors against William Trevis, schoolmaster, in the Court of Chancery.

H1/36 Copy of *The Orders for the Free Schools of Nun-Eaton* 1609.

H1/37 Opinion of Counsel concerning additional powers of the Governors Case for opinion of counsel and opinion of Mr. Knight of Lincoln's Inn 1830.

H1/39 17 papers relating to the school lands and rents, 16th Century to 1815.

H1/40 39 papers relating to financial matters, 1694-1785.

H1/42 18 papers relating to the appointments and resignations of Governors.

H1/43 Petition of inhabitants of Nuneaton to the bishop for licence for John Holmes of Chilvers Coton 1693.

H1/44 Testimonials on behalf of J.B. Bryant, schoolmaster, 1856.

H1/45 About 200 receipts and vouchers for work done on the school.

H1/46-47 Valuations of school lands in Coventry and Stoke 1848 and 1859, half-yearly.

H1/48 Copy of an order of the governors of 1788 concerning applications for apprenticeship, 1806, and 62 apprenticeship indentures, 1806-1851.

H1/49 Printed copy of *An Act for improving the Condition and extending the Benefits of Grammar Schools*, 3 and 4 Vict. cap. LXX.VII (1840). Copy of Charity Commission scheme for the school, 1846.

H1/51   An Address delivered by the Rev. W.S. Bucknill, B.A., headmaster on 20th May 1853 [at] the celebration of the 300th Anniversary of the school's foundation [wrongly calculated as 1553 not 1552].

H1/52 Mr. Mason's [actually Nason's] transcripts from the early governors' account books and from 17th cent. legal papers, undated but believed to be the 1930s.

CR2730/1 and H1/1 Mary, (1553) confirming the original letters patent of Edward VI of 11 May 6 Ed. VI.

CR2730/2 and H1/2 Letters patent of Elizabeth, confirming the above 26 Jun. 1559.

CR2730/3 Governors' minute book 1897-1922.

CR2730/5 Register of pupils and of fees paid by them, term by term.

CR2730/6 Correspondence of H. Cleaver, Chairman of the Governors 1956-1969.

CR2730/7 Correspondence mainly of H. Cleaver, Chairman of the Governors, about the final accounts for the rebuilt gymnasium and other building and maintenance work, 1960-1965.

CR2730/8 Correspondence of H. Cleaver, Chairman of the Governors, with J. Todhunter of the Ministry. of Education legal branch and others, about finances, arbitration in a dispute with builders and architects, war damage to the gymnasium, etc. 1960-1965.

CR2730/11 and **CR2730/12** Correspondence of G.H. Twist, Clerk to the Governors, 1945-1949 and 1949-1955.

CR2730/15 Governors' annual statements of account of all school funds for the years 1928-41, 1944, 1947-9, 1952, 1953, 1958, 1960-64, 1966-8.

CR2730/16 Board of Education scheme for Nuneaton Grammar School, 1910; Instrument of Government made by the Ministry of Education regarding the constitution of the Governing Body, 1952; Articles of Government setting out how the Governors shall administer the school, 1952.

CR2730/17 1959-1968 Duplicated minutes of Governors' meetings.

CR2730/18 c.1950-1962 H.M.I.'s report on the school, 1952; headmaster's report to

Governors, 1957; modernisation fund campaign booklet and leaflet, 1962; photos from school play.

CR2730/21 Account and order book of the Trustees of the Charity of Richard Smith of Westminister, under his will proved 1716.

Recent CR4232 Archive

1/1 Governors Minutes 1923-54.

2/1 and 2/2 Games Committee 1934-61.

2/3 Account Book 1936-50.

2/5 Photos including war damage.

2/7 Staff Registers 1880-1945 and 2/8 1880-1950.

4/56 40th Anniversary folder 1952.

Old Edwardians 5/1 5/2/3 Minute Books.

Other WCRO files

Journals of Sir Richard Newdigate WCRO CR136.

DR962/4/3-5 1841-1973 Miscellaneous papers letters re demolition of Old Grammar School, 1954.

DR0925/71/1-4 (18th Cent copy) case of the Nuneaton School Charter with Lord Mansfield's opinion thereon. New Scheme of Government for Nuneaton Grammar School.

DR0925/77/1 Letter from H.E.Savage 25.7.1932.

~~~~~

National Archives Kew

Secondary Education Endowment Files ED 27. Charity Commissioners correspondence with the Governors. 1860-1903 (28 files)**5037** Application of income: **5039** and **5041** Advice on purchase of land: **5040** Advice concerning grant to Church; Provision of residence for master: **5045** Mr Stanton's Report: **5047** Endowed Schools Scheme: **5049** and **5053** Purchase of property near Coventry: **5051** Questions concerning appointment of Governors: **5052** Lease of mineral rights: **5054** Purchase of land and erection of new school buildings: **5057** Sale of materials of old master's house: **5058** Questions concerning Exhibitions, appointment of representative Governors, appointment of clerk . **5059** Proposed sale of old school and erection of new school buildings: **5060** Mr Lefroy's Report; Mr Mitcheson's Report: **5062** Proposed sale of land near Coventry: **5063** Approval of Co-optative Governors' Reports of School Examiners: **5064** Examiners' Reports April 1890 to April 1902: **5065** Erection of carpenter's shop and covered playground: Additions to school buildings: **5066** Endowed Schools Scheme.

Rugby Annual School Register Vols 1 and 2 1675-1874.

Haileybury School Registers from 1862.

~ ~ ~ ~ ~

William Salt Library Stafford

Calendar of Fine Rolls 4Henry VII.

Calendar of Close Rolls Henry VII Vol2.

Nuneaton Library

Nuneaton Chronicle 1868-1956 Nuneaton Observer 1877-1974.

Rental and Survey of Sir Marmaduke Constable's rental and estate in Nuneaton, Horston, Attleborough, Stockingford, Burton Hastings and Stretton Baskerville 10th October 1543 and 13th February 1544.

Diary of Robert Evans Vol 1 1830-32 Nuneaton Library.

Edwardian Magazines 1921-1974.

Warwickshire Feet of Fines. Abstracted from the P.R.O. originals by Lucy Drucker Nuneaton Miscellany Volume Four.

Chilvers Coton Heritage Centre

Memorabilia collection of material relating to King Edward VI School.

Vicarage Street School Honours' Boards.

Photographic Collection.

King Edward VI College

Warwickshire County Council Education Committee: Development Plan for the administrative County of Warwick May 1947.

Correspondence on the status of Voluntary Aided Schools 1948-1964.

Warwickshire County Council Education Committee: draft scheme for further education and plan for county colleges September 1948.

Committee and Working Parties on re-organisation 1969-73.

Financial Estimates 1972-1974.

Secondary Sources

Books

Adey, Peter. *Aerial Life: Spaces, Mobility, Affects* (2010) .

Allsobrook, David. *Schools for the shires: The reform of middle-class education in mid-Victorian England* (1986).

Archer, R.L. *Secondary education in the 19th Century* (1966).

Arkell, Tom (ed.) (with Nat Alcock). *Warwickshire Hearth Tax Returns, Michaelmas 1670* (2010).

Armytage, W. H. G. *Four Hundred Years of English Education* (1964).

Ballard, Eric, Holland, Chris, and Crabtree, Angela. *King Edward VI Grammar School Memorial* (2010).

Barnard, H.C. History of English Education from 1760 (1969 edition).

Brown, Howard J. *Elizabethan schooldays : an account of the English grammar schools in the second half of the sixteenth century* (1933).

Carlisle, Nicholas. *Concise Description of the Endowed Grammar Schools in England and Wales*, 2 vols. (1818, reprinted 1975).

Curtis, S.J. *History of Education in Great Britain* (5th edition 1963).

Curtis, S.J.and Boultwood, M.E.A. *An introductory History of English Education Since 1800* (1966).

Curtis, S.J. and Boultwood M.E.A. *A Short History of Educational Ideas* (1970).

Charlton, Kenneth. *Education in Renaissance England* (1965).

Cressy, David. *Education in Tudor and Stuart England* (1975).

Cressy, David. Literacy and the social order : Reading and Writing in Tudor and Stuart England (2006).

Dunmore, Richard. *This Noble Foundation. A History of the Sir John Moore School at Appleby Magna in Leicestershire.* (1992)

Eliot, George. *Scenes of Clerical Life.* (Wordsworth edition 2007)

Fox, Levi. *The early history of King Edward VI School Stratford-upon-Avon.* (1984)

Fox, Levi. *A Country Grammar School: A History of Ashby-de-la-Zouche Grammar School through four centuries, 1567-1967* (1967).

Gooder, Eileen. *The Squire of Arbury* (1990).

Graham, J.A. and Phythian B.A. *Manchester Grammar School 1515*-1963 (1965).

Hans, N. *New Trends in Education in the 18th Century* (1984).

Howe, David. *Willingly to school? The story of 900 years of Education in Warwickshire* (2003).

Hughes Ann. *Politics, Society and Civil War in Warwickshire, 1620–1660* (1987).

Jewell, Helen M. *Education in early modern England* (1998).

Jones, Donald K. *The making of the education system, 1851-81* (1977).

Kreider, Alan. *English chantries : the road to dissolution* (1979).

Lawson, John. *A Town Grammar School through Six Centuries: A History of Hull Grammar School against its Local Background* (1963).

Lawson, John and Silver, Harold. *A social history of education in England* (1973).

Leach, A.F. *English Schools at the Reformation* (1968).

Marson, G.L., Metcalf, F.H. and Burton, A.A.C. *King Henry VIII School* (1945).

Moran, Joann H. *Education and Learning in the City of York* (1979).

Musgrave, P.W. *Society and Education in England since 1800* (1976 edition).

Muldrew, Craig. *The Economy of Obligation: the culture of credit and social relations in early Modern England* (1998).

Nash, Paul. (ed.) *History and Education* (1970) (See particularly the essay by Kenneth Charlton on the teaching profession in 16th and 17th Century England).

Nason, E. N. *History of Nuneaton Grammar School* (1936).

O'Day, Rosemary. *Education and Society 1500-1800* : the social foundations of education in early Modern Britain (1982).

Orme, Nicholas. *Medieval schools : from Roman Britain to Renaissance England* (2006).

Orme, Nicholas. *Education and Society in medieval and Renaissance England* (1989).

Paterson, David and Rowney, Ian. *A Short History Of the Parish Church of St. Nicolas Nuneaton* (Second edition 2007).

Pevsner, Nikolaus and Wedgwood, Alexandra. *The Buildings of England: Warwickshire* (1966).

Roach, John. *A history of secondary education in England 1800-1870* (1986).

Roach, John. *Secondary Education in England 1870-1902* (1982).

Roots, Ivan. *The Great Rebellion* (1966).

Rouse, W.H.D. *Rugby School* (1898).

Seabourne, Michael. *The English school: its architecture and organization Vol.1 1370—1870* (1971).

Seabourne, Michael and Lowe, Roy. *The English school: its architecture and organization Vol.2 1870-1970* (1977).

Shagal, Ethan. *Popular Politics and the English Reformation* (2008).

Simon, Brian. (ed.) *Education in Leicestershire 1540-1940* (1968) especially Simon, Joan. *Town Estates and Schools in the 16th and 17th Century.*

Simon, Brian. *Studies in the History of Education* (1960).

Simon, Joan. *Education and Society in Tudor England* (1967).

Stephens, J.E. (Ed). *Aspects of education: 1600-1750* (1984).

Stephens, W.B. *Education in Britain 1750-1914.* (1998).

Stephens, W.B. and Unwin, R.W. *Materials for the local and regional study of schooling 1700-1900* (1987).

Thompson, E.P. *The Making of the English Working Class* (Penguin edition 1968).

Tompson, Richard S. *Classics or Charity? The dilemma of the 18th century grammar school* (1971).

Veasey, E.A. *Nuneaton: A History* 2002.

Vincent, W.A.L. *Grammar Schools: Their Continuing Tradition, 1660-1714* (1969).

Vincent, W.A.L. *The State and School Education in England and Wales 1640-1660* (1950).

Watson, Foster. *The English Grammar Schools to 1660: their curriculum and practice.* (Reprinted 1968).

Watson, Foster. *The Beginning of Modern Subjects in England* (1971 reprint).

Walker, Margaret. (ed.) *Warwickshire Hearth Tax Returns* (Introduction by Philip Styles) Vol.1 (1957).

Watkins, Leslie. *The Story of Stratford School* (1953).

Victoria County History of Warwickshire Volumes Two, Four and Six

Vol.2 (1908) ed. William Page Vol. 4 (1947) ed. L.F.Salzman Vol. 6 (1951) ed. L.F.Salzman.

Articles

Anglin, J.P. Frustrated ideals: the case of Elizabethan Grammar School foundations, *History of Education Vol 11 No 4* (1982).

Curtis, M.H. The alienated intellectuals of Early Stuart England, *Past and Present* (1962).

Freeman, C.B. The Children's petition of 1669 and its sequel, *British Journal of Educational Studies* (1966) Volume 14.

McCullogh, Gary. Education and the Middle Classes: The Case of the English Grammar Schools, 1868-1944, *History of Education* Volume 35, Issue 6 (November 2006).

Oakeshott, A.M. d'I. The Restoration and the grammar schools, *Journal of Educational Administration and History* Vol 5 No 2 (1973).

Orpen, P. Schoolmastering as a profession in the seventeenth century: the career patterns of the grammar schoolmaster, *History of Education Vol 6 No 3* (1977).

Paterson, David. The Gentle Savage, *Warwickshire History* (Summer 1989).

Paterson, David. Xhosa Youths in England 1859-64, *Bulletin of the Scottish Institute of Missionary Studies* (1990-91).

Paterson, David. George Eliot as Historian, *George Eliot Review* (2010).

Pound, J.F. The Social and Geographical Origins of the English Grammar School Pupil: Bury St Edmunds and Manchester Grammar School in the Reign of George II, *History of Education Society Bulletin* Vol 37 (1987).

Sanderson, J.M. The Grammar School and the Education of the Poor, *British Journal of Educational Studies* Vol 11 (1962).

Simon, J. The state and schooling at the Reformation and after: from pious causes to charitable uses, *History of Education* Vol 23 No 2 (1994).

Smith, A. Endowed schools in the Diocese of Lichfield and Coventry 1660-99, *History of Education* Vol 4 No 2 (1975).

Stone, L. The educational Revolution in England, *Past and Present* 28 (1964).

Tate, W.E. Sources for the study of English Grammar Schools, *British Journal of Education studies* I (1952-3), 2 (1953-4).

Tompson, Richard S. The English Grammar School Curriculum in the 18th Century: A Reappraisal, *British Journal of Educational Studies*, Vol. 19 No. 1. (1971).

Webster, C. The Curriculum of the Grammar Schools and Universities 1500-1660: a critical review of the literature, *History of Education* Vol 4 No1 (1975).

Williams, A.R. The Charity School Movement 1700-1750, *History of Education Society Bulletin Vol 9* (1972).

Phd Thesis

Lane, Joan. *Apprenticeships in Warwickshire* 1700-1834 (1977) Copy in Warwickshire County Record Office.

On Line Sources

Access to Archives

Shakespeare Centre Library

A Descriptive Catalogue of Ancient Deeds ed. H.G. Maxwell Lyle

Property in Church Street, Nuneaton, (Warwick County Record Office 715/112-13 and 122-5 1785-1874)

Wills of John Leke 1492 and 1508

Will of Benjamin Rayner 1857

Will of William Trevis 1695

Court of Chancery Records 1556-8 C 1/1477/14

Dictionary of National Biography
See articles on: Sir Walter Mildmay, William Burton, John Spencer Cobbold, Robert Morant, Ewen Broadbent, Philip Randle.

Venn Alumni Cantabrigiensis Alumni of the University of Cambridge from earliest times to 1900

Joseph Foster: Alumni Oxoniensis
A biographical register of The University Of Oxford, 1715-1886

Hansard
www.hansard.millbanksystems.com

Coventry Evening Telegraph
Nuneaton Evening Tribune

Hadow Report 1928
Books in Public Elementary Schools – www.educationengland.org.uk

Phd Thesis
James, Trevor. *The contribution Of Schools and Universities to the Development of organized Sport up to 1900.* (1977) Leicester Research Archive http://hdl.handle.net/2381/4224

Books on Line
Baldwin, T.W. *Small Latine and lesse Greeke* (Illinois 1944), the book of days.com
Burton, Robert. *The Anatomy of Melancholy* (Authorised copy 1651 published by Harvard University 1914), www.books.google.com
Cooper, Charles Henry. *Memorials of Cambridge* (Greatly enlarged from the work of J. Le Keux FSA. 1901), www.archive.org
Foxe, John. *Book of Martyrs* (Original Latin edition 1559), ed. William Byron Forbush (1963 edition), Christian Classics Ethereal Library, www.ccel.org
Leach A.F. Educational Charters and Documents, (Original edition 1911), www.ebooksread.com
Luther, Martin. *Works* (Philadelphia: Fortress Press, 1967), www.durer.press.illinois.edu

Oddy, Derek J. *From Plain Fare to Fusion Food: British Diet from the 1890s to the 1990s,* (2003) books.google.com

Penny Cyclopaedia for the Society for the Diffusion of Useful Knowledge (1833), Internet archive digital library of free books, www.archive.org

'RHB' (Author) *Sir Marmaduke Constable of Flamborough* (1887), www.redfirst.com

Saint, Andrew. *Directory of British Architects* Vol2 (2001), www.oahs.org.uk

Shillito, Elizabeth H. *Dorothea Beale Principal of Cheltenham Ladies College 1858-1906* (1920) e book University of California, www.archive.org

Shuckburgh, *E.S. History of Emmanuel College* (1904), www.archive.org/stream/emmanuelcollege

Tuckwell, Anthony. *That Honourable and Gentlemanlike House* A History of King Edward VI Grammar School, Chelmsford (2001) Text summary on the school website, www.kegs.org.uk

Individual Websites

www.66squadron.co.uk

www.aircadets-wbw.org

www.bartleby.com

www.bbc.co.uk/People's War

www.ccel.org

www.durer.press.illinois.edu

www.elstead.org.uk

www.myfarming life.org

www.genforum.genealogy.com/liptrott

www.immanuelsground.com

www.kingschester.co.uk

www.theclergydatabase.org.uk

www.tudor place.com.ar

www.webspinners.org.uk/weddingtoncastle

Census Returns

1841-1911 on www.findmypast.co.uk

GENERAL INDEX

Emboldened entry = illustration e.g. **137**

For Pupils, Governors, Teachers and other schools see separate index

Index of Pupils of King Edward's